TREATING
ADOLESCENTS

THE JOSSEY-BASS LIBRARY OF CURRENT CLINICAL TECHNIQUE

IRVIN D. YALOM, GENERAL EDITOR

NOW AVAILABLE

Treating Alcoholism
Stephanie Brown, Editor

Treating Schizophrenia
Sophia Vinogradov, Editor

Treating Women Molested in Childhood
Catherine Classen, Editor

Treating Depression
Ira D. Glick, Editor

Treating Eating Disorders
Joellen Werne, Editor

Treating Dissociative Identity Disorder
James L. Spira, Editor

Treating Couples
Hilda Kessler, Editor

Treating Adolescents
Hans Steiner, Editor

Treating the Elderly
Javaid I. Sheikh, Editor

FORTHCOMING

Treating Posttraumatic Stress Disorder
Charles R. Marmar, Editor

Treating Anxiety Disorders
Walton T. Roth, Editor

Treating Difficult Personality Disorders
Michael Rosenbluth, Editor

TREATING ADOLESCENTS

A VOLUME IN THE JOSSEY-BASS
LIBRARY OF CURRENT CLINICAL TECHNIQUE

Hans Steiner, EDITOR

Irvin D. Yalom, GENERAL EDITOR

JOSSEY-BASS
A Wiley Company
www.josseybass.com

Published by Jossey-Bass
A Wiley Imprint
989 Market Street, San Francisco, CA 94103-1741   www.josseybass.com

Jossey-Bass books and products are available through most bookstores. To contact Jossey-Bass directly call our Customer Care Department within the U.S. at (800) 956-7739, outside the U.S. at (317) 572-3986 or fax (317) 572-4002.

Jossey-Bass also publishes its books in a variety of electronic formats. Some content that appears in print may not be available in electronic books.

Library of Congress Cataloging-in-Publication Data
Treating adolescents/Hans Steiner, editor.
    p.   cm.—(A volume in the Jossey-Bass library of current clinical technique)
    Includes bibliographical references and index.
    ISBN 0-7879-0206-3 (alk. paper)
    1. Adolescent psychotherapy. 2. Adolescent psychopathology. I. Steiner, Hans, 1946–. II. Series:
    Jossey-Bass library of current clinical technique.
RJ503.T74 1996
616.89'022—dc20

95-44176
CIP

Printed in the United States of America
FIRST EDITION
PB Printing   20 19 18 17 16 15 14 13 12 11

CONTENTS

FOREWORD

At a recent meeting of clinical practitioners, a senior practitioner declared that more change had occurred in his practice of psychotherapy in the past year than in the twenty preceding years. Nodding assent, the others all agreed.

And was that a good thing for their practice? A resounding "No!" Again, unanimous concurrence—too much interference from managed care; too much bureaucracy; too much paper work; too many limits set on fees, length, and format of therapy; too much competition from new psychotherapy professions.

Were these changes a good or a bad thing for the general public? Less unanimity on this question. Some pointed to recent positive developments. Psychotherapy was becoming more mainstream, more available, and more acceptable to larger segments of the American public. It was being subjected to closer scrutiny and accountability—uncomfortable for the practitioner but, if done properly, of potential benefit to the quality and efficiency of behavioral health care delivery.

But without dissent this discussion group agreed—and every aggregate of therapists would concur—that astounding changes are looming for our profession: changes in the reasons that people request therapy; changes in the perception and practice of mental health care; changes in therapeutic theory and technique; and changes in the training, certification, and supervision of professional therapists.

From the perspective of the clientele, several important currents are apparent. A major development is the de-stigmatization of psychotherapy. No longer is psychotherapy invariably a hush-hush affair, laced with shame and conducted in offices with separate entrance and exit doors to prevent the uncomfortable possibility of patients meeting one another.

Today such shame and secrecy have been exploded. Television talk shows—Oprah, Geraldo, Donahue—have normalized psychopathology and psychotherapy by presenting a continuous public parade of dysfunctional human situations: hardly a day passes without television fare of confessions and audience interactions with deadbeat fathers, sex addicts, adult children of alcoholics, battering husbands and abused wives, drug dealers and substance abusers, food bingers and purgers, thieving children, abusing parents, victimized children suing parents.

The implications of such de-stigmatization have not been lost on professionals who no longer concentrate their efforts on the increasingly elusive analytically suitable neurotic patient. Clinics everywhere are dealing with a far broader spectrum of problem areas and must be prepared to offer help to substance abusers and their families, to patients with a wide variety of eating disorders, adult survivors of incest, victims and perpetrators of domestic abuse. No longer do trauma victims or substance abusers furtively seek counseling. Public awareness of the noxious long-term effects of trauma has been so sensitized that there is an increasing call for public counseling facilities and a growing demand, as well, for adequate treatment provisions in health care plans.

The mental health profession is changing as well. No longer is there such automatic adoration of lengthy "depth" psychotherapy where "deep" or "profound" is equated with a focus on the earliest years of the patient's life. The contemporary field is more pluralistic: many diverse approaches have proven therapeutically effective, and the therapist of today is more apt to tailor the therapy to fit the particular clinical needs of each patient.

In past years there was an unproductive emphasis on territoriality and on the maintaining of hierarchy and status—with the more prestigious professions like psychiatry and doctoral-level psychology expending considerable energy toward excluding master's level therapists. But those battles belong more to the psychotherapists of yesterday; today there is a significant shift toward a more collaborative interdisciplinary climate.

Managed care and cost containment is driving some of these changes. The role of the psychiatrist has been particularly affected as cost efficiency has decreed that psychiatrists will less frequently deliver psychotherapy personally but, instead, limit their activities to supervision and to psychopharmacological treatment.

In its efforts to contain costs, managed care has asked therapists to deliver a briefer, focused therapy. But gradually managed care is realizing that the bulk of mental health treatment cost is consumed by inpatient care and that outpatient treatment, even long-term therapy, is not only salubrious for the patient but far less costly. Another looming change is that the field is turning more frequently toward the group and family therapies. How much longer can we ignore the many comparative research studies demonstrating that the group therapy format is equally or more effective than higher cost individual therapies?

Some of these cost-driven edicts may prove to be good for the patients; but many of the changes that issue from medical model mimicry—for example, efforts at extreme brevity and overly precise treatment plans and goals that are inappropriate to the therapy endeavor and provide only the illusion of efficiency—can hamper the therapeutic work. Consequently, it is of paramount importance that therapists gain control of their field and that managed care administrators not be permitted to dictate how psychotherapy or, for that matter, any other form of health care be conducted. That is one of the goals of this series of texts: to provide mental health professionals with such a deep grounding in theory and such a clear vision of effective therapeutic technique that they will be empowered to fight confidently for the highest standards of patient care.

∽

The Jossey-Bass Library of Current Clinical Technique is directed and dedicated to the frontline therapist—to master's and doctoral-level clinicians who personally provide the great bulk of mental health care. The purpose of this entire series is to offer state-of-the-art instruction in treatment techniques for the most commonly encountered clinical conditions. Each volume offers a focused theoretical background as a foundation for practice and then dedicates itself to the practical task of what to do for the patient—how to assess, diagnose, and treat.

I have selected volume editors who are either nationally recognized experts or are rising young stars. In either case, they possess a comprehensive view of their specialty field and have selected leading therapists of a variety of persuasions to describe their therapeutic approaches.

Although all the contributors have incorporated the most recent and relevant clinical research in their chapters, the emphasis in these volumes is on the practical technique of therapy. We shall offer specific therapeutic guidelines, and augment concrete suggestions with the liberal use of clinical vignettes and detailed case histories. Our intention is not to impress or to awe the reader, and not to add footnotes to arcane academic debates. Instead, each chapter is designed to communicate guidelines of immediate pragmatic value to the practicing clinician. In fact, the general editor, the volume editors, and the chapter contributors have all accepted our assignments for that very reason: a rare opportunity to make a significant, immediate, and concrete contribution to the lives of our patients.

Irvin D. Yalom, M.D.
Professor Emeritus of Psychiatry
Stanford University School of Medicine

INTRODUCTION

Hans Steiner

You have to have chaos within you to give birth to a dancing star.

FRIEDRICH NIETZSCHE

Adolescence is a time of unparalleled threat, change, challenge, and opportunity. Nowhere else in human development do we encounter such a major transformation in such a short time in so many domains: our bodies, minds, abilities, and interpersonal relationships.

Our bodies go through rapid growth and development. Our muscle mass seems to increase overnight. Secondary sex characteristics appear and become the source of attention and concern. Our appearance, which for so many years has been quite stable, becomes altered to such an extent that we sometimes have difficulty recognizing ourselves. And yet, we cannot stop looking at ourselves in the mirror. Our minds begin their steady expansion to adult scope. When teachers demand that we perform unprecedented feats of learning, we discover to our amazement that we are indeed able to deliver, contrary to our own expectations. We note a new tone in our interactions with adults. They now sometimes treat us as equals. They even solicit and earnestly consider our opinions. And, most important, there is a new undercurrent in our social interactions, an added new dimension and new excitement that suddenly turns age-old playmates and acquaintances into objects of desire.

At any given time, we feel out of synchrony with ourselves, strangely off balance. When everything in us and around us is changing, it's hard to find our bearings and remain solidly grounded; yet this is precisely what our families and society expect us to do. As we prepare the final exit from the protective social structures of childhood, we need to convince others—and ourselves—that we are ready to take the big step. We need to rely increasingly on ourselves, or at least appear to, while taking on new and unprecedented risks.

Adolescence is also a time of great excitement, an opening to the world and a discovery of what we stand to inherit. It is a time of growth and acquisition of new instruments, skills, and emotions. We discover that we know more than our fathers—a frightening and exhilarating concept. We notice that others notice us, and this provides a new thrill and threat at the same time.

The theme of adolescence and the changes it brings has intrigued artists and writers for centuries. It is reflected in many works of art and literature. One of the earliest versions of it is the medieval epic of Parsifal by the German knight Wolfram von Eschenbach (1170–1220). This is the story of a boy who grows up at the side of his single mother, Herzeloyde (translated "heartache"). She keeps from him the knowledge that his father was a knight who fell in battle. One day, as he is wandering in the woods hunting game, he encounters several knights and is fascinated by their weapons and their armor. He mistakes them for gods and prays to them. They correct his misperception, showing him all their gear in detail, but succeed only in convincing him to become one of them. Thus begins a long and arduous journey through medieval Europe where Parsifal encounters multiple challenges; he learns about pride, love, and dignity; pity for the suffering of others; and his own strengths and weaknesses. The story of Parsifal was set to magical music by Richard Wagner. Modern-day versions are depicted in the trials and tribulations of Holden Caulfield in *The Catcher in the Rye*, and Hans Castorp in Thomas Mann's *Magic Mountain*. We invite you to explore these works as excellent interpretations of the turmoil and power of adolescence.

It is not surprising that the rates of psychopathology increase dramatically during adolescence. There are biological, psychological, and social reasons for that. New syndromes appear as never before in development, and old ones persist, assuming new shapes and forms. Many of these changes are dramatic in character but surprisingly inaccessible to the clinician, as they are present for only brief periods of time. Also, bad habits that may develop in this period have not had time to crystallize into a way of life quite yet. Thus, through timely intervention, a clinician has a unique opportunity to eliminate suffering such habits might cause, thereby preventing chronic impairment. Interventions can also have a major impact with younger children, but there is an essential difference with adolescents that soon becomes apparent: the ways and means of communication and understanding used with and by adolescents are as powerful and have as much impact as those associated with adults. This fact makes the task of addressing problems faster, easier, and sometimes more enjoyable than when working with children. It is not uncommon to find quantum leaps of change taking place in very short periods of time with these young people. Again, threat and opportunity are closely knit together.

Still, most clinicians find it difficult to engage with adolescents. The reasons for this are complex, but one usually ranks high among them: therapists often want to forget their own most difficult period of development. Most of us are happy to have escaped into an adult world, where life is stable and predictable. We have no desire to revisit the maelstrom of uncertainties that the adolescent period of development presented to all of us. For better or worse, we have forged our identities and have consciously forgotten the days when it was possible to feel like Alexander the Great in the morning and to be on the dark edge of chaos by the afternoon, when we felt that a bright future as a film star was certain as we looked at ourselves in the mirror prior to the prom date, but knew by the end of the evening that we would be spinsters for life.

We are required to take on these age-old dilemmas once again as we engage with adolescent patients. To be able to provide sustained and effective help, we have to remember the pain and exhilaration of the moment, without belittling or patronizing the patient. There is an immediacy to this work that is usually not found in working with adult patients. Consequently, it is common to get caught by surprise and rediscover unfinished business within ourselves. If you wish to be effective in making contact with this age group, you must enjoy paradox. You must also have a good sense of humor and be flexible. You must be willing to stand with one foot in your own past without being consumed by it, not be afraid to be parental when that is needed, and yet be quick enough to step back into the role of the professional when necessary. This is a tall order. No wonder most of us prefer the tranquil world of adult interaction and easily pay the price of slow change for the reassurance that the world is orderly after all.

We hope that many of you find excitement in working with this age group. As with anything in life, there are risks and rewards. All of us who have spent the better part of our lives working with adolescents and their families obviously think the latter outweigh the former. This book is meant to give you some guidance, but ultimately it is our patients who truly make experts of us all. In addition to the books mentioned above, I always recommend that our trainees see certain movies: *Fanny and Alexander* (Ingmar Bergman, director), where the dawn of adolescence is described in two very different family milieus; *My Life as a Dog* (Lasse Halstrom, director), from which we regain a precious understanding of the reactions and explorations of early adolescence; *Stand by Me* (Rob Reiner, director) where we see feats of heroism, idealism, friendship, and selfishness performed altogether in a very short span of time; and *Amarcord* (Federico Fellini, director), which so beautifully portrays the full spectrum of life's complexities through the eyes of a mid-adolescent teenager. Also, read the references given below and spend some time looking at photographs and films from your own adolescence. Listen to the music that speaks to the youth of today. Such a comprehensive approach to the subject is most helpful, we find, in allowing us to blend fact with empathy and preparing us properly to enter the world of adolescence, where time and energy are boundless, and opportunity for growth and change is the order of the day.

The mental health professional working with adolescents also needs to be prepared to be part of a team. More often than not, the treatment of adolescents requires the close collaboration of several people and without such collaboration treatment will usually stall. Parents, teachers, pediatricians, and the mental health team need to compare notes frequently so they can change course or renegotiate contracts as needed. This is not an area of medicine where "lone wolves" do particularly well as therapists. Again, the reasons for this are complex, but are mostly rooted in adolescent psychology: internal structures are unstable, as are relationships; divide and conquer is a favorite pastime of the teenager. Which of us does not remember the intricate schemes we engaged in to spend time with a friend who was off limits? Some of those same dynamics rapidly become apparent in treatment, as the patient attempts to neutralize a certain painful awareness in a conflicted domain. Some of the emergent discrepancies of the patient's situation are not brought about consciously by the teenager. Others, however, are cleverly engineered and require a full court press by everyone concerned to avert negative consequences. This immediate response is possible only if all concerned are prepared to coordinate their efforts to the fullest.

This book is organized to follow the emergence of specific syndromes in the course of development. It begins with an introductory chapter on general treatment principles that I prepared with my colleague Shirley Feldman, a developmental psychologist with special expertise in adolescent issues and the senior author of the authoritative volume *At the Threshold*. The remaining chapters address specific syndromes as they emerge in adolescents between the ages eleven and eighteen. The early adolescent syndromes—those that usually make their appearance in the first half of the developmental phase—are discussed first, followed by the late adolescent ones. These syndromes, of course, can appear out of this sequence. For instance, about one-fifth of eating disorders appear in patients before the completion of puberty, but four-fifths appear from mid-adolescence on.

The authors of the chapters are all from the Division of Child Psychiatry and Child Development at the Stanford University School of Medicine. We do not suggest by these selections that our division has a monopoly on expertise in the field, as there are many other excellent academic centers in child and adolescent psychiatry in the nation. However, our division, although small, usually ranks among the top four or five most prolific academic settings, and we thought it useful to present "the Stanford approach" to give the clinician a more cohesive picture of a kaleidoscopic and complex situation. All our authors have many years of experience treating adolescents, and each of them is a director of a subspecialty clinic in the areas they discuss. Their recommendations are based not only on their own clinical experience but also on scientific knowledge drawn from the literature and gained through their own scientific studies.

We realize that the successful blending of experience and technique is a difficult task in the mental health field because we are required to track so much information simultaneously and make sense of it by recognizing patterns. We have to integrate all the information into a broader social context. We need to keep in mind the physical limitations, the biological givens of each patient that limit potential and call for adaptation. This process in adults is quite complex, but is even more challenging in the adolescent age group because of the speed with which events develop and change occurs in these young people. Simultaneously, chords are struck within ourselves playing forgotten tunes; old demons raise their heads and need to be used as a source of information about the clinical situation. We have to perform our interventions while we appear relaxed and receptive, warm and supportive, and above all, professional.

Some experts have called the treatment of adolescents the "calculus of the mental health sciences"; I tend to agree. The treatment of patients in this age range is unlike that of any other: much more aggravating, yet much more rewarding and fun. It will take some time to acquire the necessary skill, but in our eyes, the investment is well worth the result.

We all hope that our book will give the novice a jump start in working with adolescents. We believe that additional benefits accrue to clinicians who become involved with this age group: work with children and adolescents generally leads to a deeper understanding and appreciation of the principles of development, and this knowledge in turn enriches a therapist's understanding of adult cases. Once we directly observe an individual's process of becoming a person, we are better able to help those who merely tell us about this process in retrospect. By expanding our skills to new areas, we can gain a new understanding of well-traveled paths. Everybody wins: our patients, because we will be better therapists; their parents, because they get back their children whom they think they've lost; and we ourselves, because we find new professional fulfillment.

ACKNOWLEDGMENTS

This book grew out of many years of working with disturbed youths of all levels, backgrounds, and pathologies. These young people were truly our greatest teachers and mentors. To them and their parents who helped out and worked with us so intrepidly, we all say thanks (especially E. K., N. A., T. M., and S. A.—you know who you are).

I also greatly appreciate the support of Frances and Ted Geballe and Bette Moorman who supported many of the scientific studies that led us to these complex clinical recommendations. I am always touched by the genuine interest in and love for children, adolescents, and our future that is manifest in this kind of philanthropy.

Such a book is also not possible without lots of "hands-on" help. We thank Alan Rinzler from Jossey-Bass and my secretary, Ms. Marsha Wallace, for expert editorial assistance. Their battle cry of "onward and upward" helped us through many tough spots and made the whole experience of writing this book a most pleasant journey.

NOTES

P. xiv, *One of the earliest versions of it is the medieval epic of Parsifal:* von Eschenbach, W. (1961). *Parsifal.* (Moushon, Trans.). New York: Vintage Books. (Original work published 1205).

P. xiv, *The story of Parsifal was set to magical music by Richard Wagner:* Wagner, R. *Parsifal* [Opera in three acts; compact disk]. Berlin Philharmonic. (1981). Deutsche Grammophon.

P. xiv, *Modern-day versions are depicted in the trials and tribulations of:* Salinger, J. D. (1945). *The catcher in the rye.* Boston: Little, Brown.

P. xiv, *and Hans Castorp in:* Mann, T. (1964). *The magic mountain.* Chapel Hill: University of North Carolina Press.

P. xvi, *In addition to books such as this, I always recommend that our trainees see certain movies:* Bergman, I. (Writer/Director). (1982). *Fanny and Alexander* [Film].

P. xvi, *we regain a precious understanding of the reactions and explorations of early adolescence:* Halstrom, L. (Director). (1985). *My life as a dog* [Film]. Svensk FilmIndustri.

P. xvi, *where we see feats of heroism, idealism, friendship and selfishness performed:* Gideon, R., et al. (Writers), & Reiner, R. (Director). (1986). *Stand by me* [Film].

P. xvi, *beautifully portrays the full spectrum of life's complexities through the eyes of a mid-adolescent teenager:* Fellini, F. (Writer/Director). (1973). *Amarcord* [Film].

P. xvi, *Also, read the references given below and spend some time looking at photographs and films from your own adolescence:* Schulman, T. (Writer), & Weir, P. (Director). (1989). *Dead poets society* [Film].

P. xvii, *the senior author of the authoritative volume:* Feldman, S. S., & Elliott, G. (Eds.). (1993). *At the threshold: The developing adolescent.* Cambridge, MA: Harvard University Press.

P. xviii, *Simultaneously, chords are struck within ourselves . . . a source of information about the clinical situation:* Shapiro, J. (1992, May 25). Poltergeists. *New Yorker.*

Für Anni Steiner, denn mit ihr hat alles begonnen

TREATING
ADOLESCENTS

I

GENERAL PRINCIPLES AND SPECIAL PROBLEMS

Hans Steiner and S. Shirley Feldman

In the morning I want to be dead, because I can't face the day. At noon I want to live forever, because Sarah smiled at me. In the afternoon, I want a red sports car, because this geek next door has one. And in the evening I want to be anywhere but home because you are fighting with Mom again about nothing. Are you serious when you ask me "What do you really want?"

FIFTEEN-YEAR-OLD BOY,
IN RESPONSE TO HIS FATHER'S QUESTION
IN THE FIRST MONTH OF TREATMENT

As Thales of Milet (circa 600 B.C.E.) said, "Panta rhei"
[Everything changes].

One of the great joys of psychiatry is contributing to the personal growth and development of individuals who for a variety of reasons are off course in their lives' trajectories. Nowhere is this task more gratifying than with patients in adolescence and

Note: This chapter was made possible by grants to Dr. Steiner from the Eucalyptus Foundation and to Dr. Feldman by the Stanford Center for the Study of Families, Children, and Youth.

childhood. To intervene early and in a timely fashion with teenagers can save them years of misery and can prevent perceived wrongs from becoming a dominating influence in their lives. Such interventions are uniquely rewarding because they not only relieve suffering but also prevent future pain.

This opening chapter is organized in three parts: first, we describe some general principles of development; then we address special problems that make working with the psychiatrically disturbed adolescent more challenging than working with adults and children; and finally we end by outlining a prototypical treatment plan.

The treatment of adolescents is qualitatively different from that of children, a point easily understood by clinicians. Play, the major form of communication with children, is no longer useful with teenagers. Although verbal interchanges of adolescents resemble those of adults, communications with adolescents are certainly not identical to interchanges with adults. In particular, although the verbal and cognitive abilities of adolescents are comparable to those of adults, adolescent life experiences, interpersonal relationship patterns, and stability of intrapsychic structures are not. The clinician dealing with adolescents can best be compared to an obstetrician for emerging identities who goes from exciting birth to exciting birth, while the clinician working with adults proceeds more like a family practitioner.

Basic Concepts of Adolescent Development

The clinician working with adolescents must take into account the nature of developmental changes in terms of both reaching a diagnosis and planning treatment. In particular, he or she should recognize that the span of adolescence, approximately ten years, is not a unified stage of life and behavior and thus, behavior that is appropriate for one phase of adolescence may be indicative of psychopathology in another.

The term *adolescence* generally covers the second decade of life and consists of three phases, demarcated for convenience by age: early adolescence (10–13 years), mid-adolescence (14–17 years) and late adolescence (18–20 years). Although there are individual differences within each phase of adolescence, and gender differences, with girls proceeding through the sequence more rapidly than boys, each phase carries with it some information as to what is normative and acceptable in a given society or context. For example, in the area of heterosexual relations, in some middle-class communities boy-girl parties and school dances are acceptable in early adolescence, going out on dates is not acceptable until mid-adolescence, and sexual explorations, if acceptable at all, are condoned only at late adolescence. In other communities such as African-American inner-city neighborhoods, the sequence can be earlier, with dating acceptable in early adolescence and sexual activity acceptable or at least normative in mid-adolescence. Yet in other communities, such as Mediterranean neighborhoods, opposite-sex relations occur relatively later, with dating unacceptable until after high school completion. Knowledge of community norms for each phase of adolescence permits a clinician to differentiate between "on-time" age-appropriate explorations of different roles and behaviors that may have risky consequences from genuine full-blown psychopathology. It is the social context of behavior that sometimes differentiates normal from pathological.

The developmental changes that occur during adolescence are extensive and affect virtually every domain of a teenager's functioning. Other than infancy, in no other stage in life do so many rapid changes take place. These begin with pubertal changes affecting appearance, behavior and mood, relationships with others, and risk-taking. We describe here, very briefly, a synopsis of some of the major changes and direct the interested reader to a recent volume with state-of-the-art reviews of adolescent development (see book by S. Shirley Feldman and Glen Elliott, 1993, for a developmental psychological perspective; and Iris Litt, 1990, for a pediatric perspective).

Pubertal Changes

Puberty brings marked changes in a teenager's appearance, with accelerated growth, weight gain, changes in body configurations, the maturing of the reproductive organs, and the development of the secondary sex characteristics such as facial and body hair for males and breast development for girls. These changes, mostly visible and external, serve as signals both to the adolescents themselves and to others of their more mature status and their reproductive abilities. The hormonal changes that underlie these developments are implicated in the increased moodiness of teenagers, their newfound interest in the opposite sex, sexual strivings requiring some acknowledgment, and perhaps an elevated level of aggression.

There is significant variation in the age at which children enter puberty, and this variation is significant in its effect on their functioning. Early maturers in the two sexes fare differently: girls who begin menstruation early and show the expected bodily changes are usually more at risk for teasing, inappropriate remarks, and associating with older peers and its attendant risk-taking (smoking, drinking, using drugs, and engaging in early sexual activity). Just at the time that early maturing girls are experiencing more conflict and feeling somewhat more distant from their parents, their bodies provide a strong and mostly unwanted attraction for attention from the opposite sex. To deal with this multitude of changes is a challenge at any age, but it particularly stresses the younger, inexperienced adolescent whose psychological structures are relatively weak. Not surprisingly, there is some evidence that early maturing females—that is, those who start their menses a year or two ahead of their peers—tend to have a higher rate of psychopathology (especially internalizing pathology such as anxiety disorders, Anorexia Nervosa, or depression) than their "on-time" classmates. In contrast, early maturing boys seem to be at some psychological advantage in that they are given more leadership experience; are judged more attractive by girls; are at a competitive advantage in sports, which gives them status in the peer group; are generally popular with peers; and date more.

For boys, it is the late maturers who have more trouble in being "off-time" in their development. To lack facial hair in mid-adolescence, to be small and skinny rather than tall and muscular, to look "child-like" when others look "adult-like" makes for a difficult transition. Late maturing boys often seek attention by becoming bossy or unduly talkative, or taking the part of the classroom "clown." The unintended result of these behaviors is generally to make the late maturer less popular with both same-sex and opposite-sex peers.

Cognitive Changes

Pervasive changes in cognitive functioning permit adolescents to deal with abstractions; project thought into the future; examine previously unquestioned attitudes, behaviors, and values; and to take themselves as the object of their own thought. David Elkind claims these changes precipitate a form of egocentrism in which adolescents act as if they are on stage, playing to an imaginary audience that is totally focused on them and on every nuance of their performance. Perhaps because they feel they are the focus of attention, adolescents come to construct a personal fable that they cannot be understood by others because their experiences are unique—no one else has suffered so agonizingly or experienced such exquisite raptures.

The Construction of an Identity

Erik Erikson has claimed that the major task of this age is to develop an identity, a sense of self distinct from that of others, particularly that of the parents. The sense of identity must be coherent and meaningful, acknowledging the full complexity of the individual, and consistent with abilities and potential. Adolescents experiment with new roles both at home and in the peer group to help them define who they are. Erikson claims that adolescents often appoint perfectly well-meaning people such as parents to serve as their adversaries. Thus, teenagers may assume an oppositional stance and refuse to do what their parents want. Later on, as adolescents become more confident and acquire more sophisticated tools of assertion, they are able to present themselves as distinct in more refined ways, that is, by their tastes and preferences, beliefs and attitudes.

New Peer Behaviors and Contexts

The relationships with friends and acquaintances assume new complexities as adolescents use the peer group to explore their identities and as the peer group changes in composition to include opposite-sex as well as same-sex youths. In addition, early in adolescence, youths leave the protected, familiar neighborhood schools and established peer groups and attend larger, more impersonal middle schools and high schools with more diverse peer groups. Teenagers often find they are unsure of how to conduct themselves in the new settings and with the expanded peer group. This insecurity increases their conformity to peer values and frequently promotes a rather rigid adherence to sex stereotypes. These behaviors ensure the individual that he or she will not stand out as inappropriate or be socially ostracized.

Dealing with Sexuality

Adolescents, for the first time, must deal with the full range of their sexuality, aspects of which have an insistent quality that intrudes on their everyday functioning. Sexuality is now manifest in erotic dreams, attraction to the opposite sex, masturbation, and for boys nocturnal emissions. Complicating this task is the fact that in our society parents rarely communicate openly and comfortably about the psychological aspects of sexuality, leaving such information to be gleaned from unreliable sources such as locker room talk from same-sex peers and pornographic magazines. Dealing with sexuality may be more complex for those youths who are out of step with their peers in terms of their pubertal development. The film *Revenge of the Nerds* is a clumsy but instructive introduction to that theme.

School and Achievement Pressures

On the academic front, life also changes significantly. Middle schools and high schools are much larger than the neighborhood elementary school; students no longer have a single teacher who knows them well and instead have different teachers every hour. There is a greater academic emphasis and more stress is placed on the pupil's performance. In addition to academics, adolescents have opportunities to excel in multiple arenas—sports, social clubs, extracurricular pursuits. The rhythm of daily life begins to resemble that of adulthood. Unmistakably, the stakes are higher, the consequences of success or failure have more direct implications for the future. Because college admission depends on a teenager's academic scores, academic pressures mount in high school. The school system by and large rewards the high achiever and the student invested in school-related sports and student-government activities.

Renegotiating Family Relations

The progressive path of development also demands a reworking of the adolescent's relationship with the family of origin, including new steps toward autonomy. The most palpable manifestation of this process is the teenager's greater need for privacy, frequently expressed by the closed or even locked door to the child's bedroom. Furthermore, adolescents, in contrast to elementary school children, express a clear preference for spending leisure time with peers rather than with family. Until children are about eleven years old, most parents know roughly 75 percent of their activities. By the time these children are eighteen, however, parents are lucky if they know 25 percent of what their sons or daughters are doing at school and with their friends. Adolescents use two approaches to limiting what their parents know about them: they withhold information about their daily activities and feelings, even in the face of patient and gentle questioning by parents. They answer questions by monosyllabic replies rather than an elaborated sharing of information. In addition, most adolescents report that they tell lies to their parents at least on occasion.

For most parents, such a profound withdrawal of contact and intimacy is difficult. At the same time that adolescents cease sharing their thoughts and feelings with parents, there is an increase in family conflict centering on daily aggravations of living rather than on value differences. Parents put increasing pressures on adolescents to be responsible (doing homework, keeping their room tidy, helping with housework) whereas adolescents put pressure on parents for increased privileges of adolescence and adulthood (a later curfew, more money, fewer restrictions on the type and amount of television viewing, and so forth). This conflict may serve positive functions in helping the adolescent differentiate from his or her parents, spend more time with peers, and develop greater behavioral autonomy and emotional independence. It is noteworthy, however, that protracted and very intense family conflict, with powerful negative emotions directed at family members, is not typical or age appropriate and usually signals pathology.

SPECIAL FEATURES OF PSYCHOPATHOLOGY IN ADOLESCENCE

Given these pervasive developmental changes, it is common to find that clinical cases typically contain aspects of the normal developmental tasks although magnified and perhaps distorted in nature so that they resemble psychopathology. Three aspects in particular present with some frequency: risk-taking that can be so marked as to jeopardize the life and well-being of the adolescent; problems with identity; and suicidality. In dealing with adolescents, these three aspects need to be considered as part of the case formulation regardless of the primary diagnosis. We present some case material to illustrate each of these themes.

Risk-Taking

Perhaps the most disquieting aspect of working with adolescents results from their exploration of the limits of their newfound abilities, skills, and social contexts. Experimenting and risk-taking are ubiquitous in this age group and may be necessary for further development. Failure among adolescents to experiment with new roles and behaviors and avoidance of all risks may indicate undue constriction and hamper appropriate growing up and dealing with the age-appropriate issues of autonomy and identity. The clinician must be prepared to work with adolescents who exhibit risky behaviors and must be able to help parents set appropriate limits if necessary. We describe some relevant scenarios that convey the complexity of the situation.

JOHN

John, a sixteen-year-old boy, was incarcerated at the California Youth Authority after he was adjudicated for grand theft auto and assault with a deadly weapon. He and some friends had been celebrating the victory of their baseball team. As a backup pitcher, his position on the team was somewhat tenuous, and to be fully included in the celebration was a matter of great importance to him.

As the party wore on, the group consumed beer liberally. Shortly after midnight, one of the boys suggested they make a beer run. However, they were without a vehicle, as they had wanted to avoid the temptation of driving while intoxicated. After a lengthy debate, one of the group suggested they take the neighbor's truck, which was unlocked in the driveway, keys in the ignition. There was some hesitation on everybody's part, but as soon as one of the boys pointed out that the neighbors were good friends, their worries dissipated, and they all agreed it would be inappropriate to wake the owners to get consent.

The group left, with several friends piled in the back of the truck, despite John's protests. The urge for more beer got greater, and so the truck left, driving slowly at first, but accelerating on the highway. They encountered friends in another truck, and there was joyful banter about the status of each group's engine, resulting in a challenge to race to the store. Shortly thereafter, John lost control of the vehicle, and several youths, including himself, were severely injured in the accident.

This case certainly has a familiar ring to it and conjures up many drag racing and "chicken" scenes from movies such as *American Graffiti* and *Stand by Me*. The gradual escalation of risk throughout the evening, without appropriate counterchecks by any member of the group, is quite typical of a group whose functioning is impaired by alcohol. None of the youths involved had a criminal record; most of them came from well-functioning families. None of them intended for the evening to end this way, but nobody came forward and pointed out that the next step— although it seemed small—was a huge escalation compared to the baseline behavior. Although this case has a distinct male flavor to it, girls are not immune to such events.

ANNE

Anne, a fourteen-year-old girl attending an adolescent medicine clinic, presented after she had been sexually assaulted by several boys. Following her parents' divorce, she initially lived with her mother. However, she did not get along with her mother's live-in boyfriend, so she moved to her father's home. He lived in a southern California community where she found herself somewhat isolated. In addition, her father was greatly upset by the unexpected divorce and less than able to deal with his own grief, let alone that of a daughter entering puberty.

Anne made one new friend at school, someone not part of the mainstream group. This girl introduced Anne to her brother, who turned out to be a charming individual with a past. His mother was quite dysfunctional, intermittently abusing drugs and alcohol. His father was a free spirit, who appeared and disappeared as he saw fit. The young man had formed affiliations with a local gang without becoming a full-fledged member, in order to help himself and his sister deal with the problematic family situation. Anne was acquainted with some of her new boyfriend's friends, although mostly from a distance. She found the group interesting and romanticized their antisocial exploits. She was impressed by their strong attachment to each other and the protectiveness they showed toward their own.

One day, as she was going home from school, several of the boys invited her to join them in their car. Facing a lonely afternoon at home and a surly father in the evening, she accepted the invitation. The trip led to several stops in amusement parks and fast-food places, terminating in a remote park, where everybody was invited to try some cocaine. Curious, Anne agreed. Following that, she was asked to "pitch in," but when she could produce no money, she was asked to perform fellatio on the boys. She refused, and the boys subsequently raped her.

Although this case has a more typical female theme to it, the gradual escalation of risk over time is similar. The increase of risk from one step to the next was modest, as when Anne went from the bus to the car, and from the amusement park to the fast-food place. But with each step she progressively put herself in the debt of an exploitive group. She was blinded to that realization by her own dependency needs, activated by the divorce in her own family, although she had heard her boyfriend describe beatings of gang members by other members when they were out of line.

Both cases illustrate risk-taking in this age group. It usually involves engaging in new, adult-oriented activities—to drive, to drink, to use mind-altering substances, to have sex, to face danger and survive, to perform in some way to impress others, to become in some form a primus inter pares—the first among the peers. Except in the most pathological cases, risky behavior is rarely an enterprise that is foolish or dangerous from the start. Most often, risk-taking is a series of small, incremental steps in which judgment is suspended sufficiently that the young people do not examine the whole picture—only its immediate constituent parts. Thus they fail completely to see how far they have come from the baseline of acceptable conventional behavior. Under normal conditions, neither of these two patients would have agreed to a car chase while they were drunk, or an evening in a park with gang members doing cocaine. However, the slope they were on was slippery, leading them to engage in behavior they would not usually condone, and into situations over which they had no control.

Often, adolescents find that they take unnecessary risks and get away without consequences or damage. At that point they usually reason that since nothing happened, some kind of immunity has been conferred on them, or conversely, that the adult estimations of risk were grossly exaggerated. Both the cases above show the limited ability of this age group to deal with probabilistic outcomes and to project into the future the possible risks and negative consequences of current actions and circumstances. From the adolescents' perspective, parents and adults are hopelessly out of date and as a result do not understand the realities of the adolescent's world.

In dealing with adolescents engaging in risky behavior, we need to give them calm and persistent reassurances that risk is risk, and probability is not certainty. Each scenario, such as the ones above, can be dissected to show the gradual accumulation of risk; this exercise is quite helpful to adolescents when they are able to reflect more rationally on the situation, that is, when they are not caught up in the heat of the moment or surrounded by peers on whose acceptance they depend.

As part of the routine assessment and periodically throughout treatment, we need to address issues related to risk-taking. A nonmoralistic, matter of fact, nonseductive approach is usually quite effective. Most adolescents, in the cool light of day, are quite able to examine properly the dangerous portions of their behavior and are grateful when the clinician shows interest and concern. The discussion is most easily begun by examining what happens in the leisure and recreation domain of the adolescents' life, what they do for fun, and how far they take it.

Care is needed, though, in how the investigation is structured. Sometimes patients clearly do not want to share some of this information for fear of self-incrimination and punishment. It is tempting for clinicians under these circumstances to offer premature guarantees of confidentiality to find out more, but such assurances can be tricky and counterproductive. For example, after the full extent of risk-taking becomes apparent, it may be necessary and in the patient's best interest to involve his or her parents, which, under the given guarantees, can happen only with the patient's consent. If he or she refuses, the clinician is left with the problem of either going ahead with the report to the parents and risk losing the working alliance with the patient, or of being unable to ensure that appropriate limits will be set by the parents and thus, perhaps, leaving the adolescent at risk.

Identity Crises

Adolescence is a time of taking stock of one's strengths and weaknesses, all that one possesses, all that one has been through, and all that one hopes for in the future. This process should lead to a reasonably accurate image of who one is and hopes to be in the future. The adolescent must be able to step back and appraise the self and the situation with some honesty and accuracy and summarize it accordingly. The cognitive advances of adolescence permit a majority of adolescents to perform this task, and thus it is during adolescence that issues of identity and self-examination first emerge in psychopathology.

Issues of identity need to be assessed as part of the initial diagnostic exam and again in the course of treatment, as major shifts can occur as a normal part of successful treatment. Such shifts, however, are usually experienced as somewhat threatening and anxiety producing; sometimes patients are tempted to return to their previous status because they are unable to cope with the ambiguity of the "psychological birthing process."

GAYLE

Gayle, a seventeen-year-old girl with Anorexia Nervosa, was initially diagnosed at age fourteen and has been in treatment ever since, first as an inpatient and then an outpatient. Preoccupation with weight and appearance have not been an issue with her for the past year. She is at a low normal weight, and although she is not menstruating, her body is beginning to show pubertal changes that indicate she could start regular cycling soon. In school, she has developed a new group of friends, and her academics have been—as always—quite success-ful. In treatment, issues such as applications to college, interest in certain boys in her class, and dealing with conflicts with her parents about privileges have been raised and are usually addressed fairly well. Nursing staff at clinic visits have made several comments on how "healthy" the patient looks, carefully avoiding other adjectives.

Three events, however, triggered a session in which the patient was intensely preoccupied with being "fat," a concern she had not voiced for more than a year. A boy asked her out to a formal dance; she was accepted into five of her seven college choices—some of them quite prestigious; and her clinic visits for weight check were reduced from once a week to once every three weeks. The explo-ration of her defensive stance led to a detailed discussion of her extreme discomfort with each of these changes in her life.

Gayle felt that her current successes would lead to a stream of increasing demands, which she would not be able to control, and thus she lost sight—again—of why she was striving so hard for suc-cess and who she was trying to please. She felt fragmented and torn, and experienced the reduction of clinic visits as a decrease of the treatment team's interest in her personally. Her parents also exhibited reduced concern and publicly voiced considerable relief at her recovery. Facing her imminent departure from a constricting, overly structured but well-known and familiar environment, she became increasingly anxious, and fled back to her former identity as an eating disorder patient, where all the trouble in the world could be reduced to a simple "I am too fat."

This case illustrates some typical dynamics around the issue of identity. The patient was aware that her old identity of a pseudo-mature, subservient, and unassertive young woman had allowed her to show only certain sides of herself. And although she was very much dissatisfied with such an existence, she could not withstand the simultaneous onslaught of becoming an independent, healthy, sexual, and high-achieving person in the eyes of others. The anxiety about continued expectations, which she was afraid she could not fulfill, was too much for her and she retreated to safety: back to the self who was simpler, lacked all these complex parts, and above all, was familiar. After continued intervention involving exploration of her fear of success and responsibility, rooted in her distorted self-image and lack of trust in her own abilities, she successfully continued her journey toward health.

To assess a young person's identity at any given point in treatment, clinicians must form a judgment as to how appropriate the youngster's appraisal is, how different from reality as judged by parents and other important members of the youth's circle. We can anticipate many problems if the gap between the adolescent's perceived and actual identity is too great, especially when there are discrepancies in most domains of functioning. The direction of the discrepancy leads to some important clues about the adolescent's status. Depression and related disorders usually lead to underestimation of abilities; psychosis and conduct disorders result in overestimation, sometimes to a grotesque degree; anxiety disorders are usually accompanied by excessive constriction of the self, with many important domains of functioning omitted from the appraisal; borderline adolescents exhibit a highly diffuse self-image, fragmented and markedly lacking integration. The most extreme cases of identity disturbance are the Multiple Personality Disorders—or Dissociative Identity Disorders as they are known in the *Diagnostic and Statistical Manual of Mental Disorders* (DSM-IV). In this rare variant, the individual has distinct *alters* at different times, and usually has little or no knowledge of the other identities residing within.

Suicide and Self-Harm

A serious feature of psychopathology in this age group is the potential for inflicting serious self-harm or even committing suicide. Suicide in adolescents ranks among the three most prevalent causes of death. Data show that for youths between the ages of eleven and fifteen, suicidal thoughts triple in frequency, parallel to the reported rise in attempted and lethal suicides. Some adolescents use suicide as a threat or a punishment for significant others including parents and romantic partners. The threat is formidable because the individual has the tools to follow through in such a manner that the outcome is guaranteed. Other adolescents see death by suicide as a solution to intolerable pain and suffering.

Self-destructive and suicidal behavior are part of a continuum rather than discrete states (that is, suicide versus nonsuicide). For Aaron Beck and his colleagues, suicidality can be assessed along two dimensions: (1) intentionality—the degree to which the patient wants to be dead, ranging from "not at all" to "definitely," with "possibly" and "probably" in between; (2) lethality of method used—what precisely was the method and what is actually known about the method's efficacy. Very often there is only a weak association between these dimensions. A Tylenol overdose, for instance, may be accompanied by very low intentionality for death, but because of the liver toxicity of the medication, it is lethal when untreated—a fact unknown to many patients who take such medicines. Hospitalization may be required to treat medical lethality or high intentionality or problems with both. In addition, attention needs to be paid to the temporal characteristics of suicide attempts. Often multiple suicide attempts are interpreted by inexperienced health care personnel as indicating a high degree of indecision on the part of the patient. Quite to the contrary, evidence suggests that the risk for lethal outcome increases as the number of attempts increase.

A proper examination of the psychopathological context in which the suicide occurs is mandatory. Suicide attempts usually occur in the context of disorders indicative of a profound disturbance of the self, such as conduct disorder, borderline syndromes, and psychopathology related to chronic traumatization. Depression is a clear risk factor, but these other syndromes are more commonly associated with suicidality. Usually there are clear-cut precipitants, most generally of an interpersonal nature. Prior to the suicide attempt there usually is a period of progressive social isolation from family and friends, during which multiple direct and indirect warning signs are left for others. Failure to receive an expected response from significant others gradually strengthens the patient's resolve to follow through with the suicide attempt. Very often, the attempt occurs following a breakup of an age-inappropriate, sexually and emotionally highly charged relationship, or in the case of conduct disorders in particular, of a legal transgression being found out, or appropriate limits (such as incarceration) being set.

ROBERT

One sunny California morning, Robert, a mid-adolescent boy walked south on the train tracks of a commuter line. It was the hour before school started, and many trains were expected. The boy walked as if in a trance, and as the train approached, honking its horn, blinking its light, the young man continued on the tracks. Shortly thereafter he was hit by the engine at sixty miles per hour, and his body almost totally disintegrated. The news of his death

spread rapidly through school, because the tracks were on the way
to the local high school, and the police had to close access to collect
his body and perform their investigation. The boy was well known
to the school authorities. Robert and a group of friends habitually
dressed in black. Two months before his death, he had published a
poem in the school paper, celebrating the "dark night" and extolling
his fearless encounters with it. He was learning disabled, not a very
good student, smoked heavily, and had a history of drug abuse. Several police charges had been filed against him but were usually
dropped. The family was disorganized and chaotic, and there was
suspicion of child abuse in his past.

The day prior to his death, his girlfriend, a twenty-five-year-old
woman with two children, had announced that he was no longer
welcome at her house as she had a new, older lover who could support her. This announcement followed months of stress and strain
in the relationship. Many of his friends knew of his morbid preoccupation; to some of them he had spoken openly about suicide.
None of them had taken the news elsewhere, as he had sworn them
to secrecy.

Subsequent to his death, many of these friends became suicidal
in thought. Some were hospitalized for their own attempts, many of
which were triggered by their burden of guilt: they had known about
Robert's preoccupation and had not been able to help because their
loyalty tied them to their word.

This case represents the classic adolescent example. The boy
showed a difficult combination of co-morbidity, including conduct disorder, drug abuse, learning disability, and dysthymia; lack
of age-appropriate support, and increasingly high lethality of
method and intent. The reaction demonstrated by his friends
has been well described in the literature and is known as suicide
contagion, also an age-specific feature, which at times can
assume epidemic proportions. As part of each suicide assessment
and psychological autopsy, it is necessary to establish who knew
of the attempt and their current mental health status.

Not all suicides occur with so many warning signs. Sometimes, there is an isolated suicide attempt that seemingly appears out of the blue. As shown in the following case study, closer examination usually reveals a long-standing social isolation and, although not necessarily overt psychopathology, prodromal features of internalizing disorders.

BILL

Bill was found dead by hanging in his parents' garage one morning. The family lived in a very affluent suburban neighborhood. The boy had been an excellent student and clearly was headed for one of the elite colleges in the United States. At home he spent his time building computers and related equipment, which he then would sell to his peers. He was very active in multiple sports, clubs, and other activities. He did not date or have close friends, although he had casual friendships with several girls. In his suicide note, addressed to his father, he apologized for causing so much pain, but said he could not stand the thought of having to present a C in one of his courses at school to his Dad. The father's expectations of the son's success were extremely high. A graduate of Harvard himself, he envisioned nothing but the best from his son. The father held a very high-level job in industry and was away from home a great deal. In his absence, the stepmother, whom the son did not get along with, was the boy's sole social contact. Although he showed no overt signs of psychopathology prior to the suicide, people described Bill as "bottling up" his feelings, especially negative ones, as unfailingly friendly and concerned for others, and as never cross or angry, even when stressed. Such behavior was strongly encouraged by his father whose favorite sayings were "never look back," "let bygones be bygones," and "don't dwell on it." The boy had a very strong attachment to his mother who had left him in his father's custody because "that way he was better provided for."

The young man in this case fit the profile of a repressor, that is, someone who habitually underreports negative emotions, much to his or her detriment. This kind of adaptive style is quite common in the general population, but in its extreme forms has been found to be associated with isolated explosive periods of violence or self-harm. Lacking the appropriate means to "mentally digest" adversity—in this case, abandonment by a strong attachment figure and affectless control and demands for excellence by another—he was unable to use negative emotions constructively to bring about change in his unhappy situation. Such a stance may then ultimately lead to the explosive discharge of anger in dangerous forms, either to the person or others.

A special word needs to be said about self-injury, especially such behavior that is habitual. Although relatively uncommon before puberty, self-harm becomes quite frequent in certain forms of pathology among adolescents. Most often it consists of cutting, stabbing, or burning oneself. The injuries are usually inflicted on arms and legs, although other, more rare sites are possible. Sometimes the behavior involves taking pills such as laxatives or diuretics to induce sickness. Although such behaviors are related to suicidality, it is best to consider them as somewhat different. Studies have shown that they are usually not meant to lead to death, at least not in the immediate future. Most often, they are linked to episodes during which the patient is extremely angry, disappointed, frustrated, or anxious about a separation. These behaviors have a highly coercive undercurrent to them, meaning that very often they are intended to force significant others to gratify some request of the patient. These patients claim that these self-inflicted injuries serve to soothe and settle them.

The origin of these behaviors is usually found in a past filled with abuse and neglect. Pain and pleasure have become solidly associated and are almost interchangeable. In their most extreme form, the behaviors appear as sadomasochistic sexual practices or fetishes. The most commonly associated syndromes are the trauma-related pathologies such as Posttraumatic Stress Disorder (PTSD), borderline disorders, and conduct disorders. Limit setting in the context of appropriate structures and supervision, and exploration of the origin of the pairing of pain and pleasure are the most effective ways of dealing with this behavior.

ISSUES IN DIAGNOSIS: DISTINGUISHING BETWEEN NORMAL ADOLESCENT BEHAVIOR AND PSYCHOPATHOLOGY

The distinction between normal and abnormal adolescent behavior is complicated. In the following subsections we give a case illustration of the difficulty in ascertaining whether the presenting problem is part of normal developmental issues or whether it represents serious pathology. In the second subsection we consider some of the factors that complicate making such a determination and give some suggestions for dealing with them.

KIRSTEN

Kirsten, a fifteen-year-old German exchange student, was brought to our eating disorders program by her "American host family" with whom she had been placed three months earlier. They observed in Kirsten some dietary restriction, some vomiting, rapid weight loss, some episodes of intoxication, and drug use. They described Kirsten as weepy and anxious but did not link this behavior to the absence from her family. Their immediate concern was to ascertain whether she was suffering from major psychopathology and whether to return her to Germany.

We employed two strategies to determine whether these episodes were indicative of an eating disorder or merely a perturbation of normal development. First, we obtained an extensive developmental history and looked carefully for antecedents that might have appeared previously and even required some intervention. A lengthy phone interview with the parents in Berlin revealed no such occurrence. The girl had always been an excellent student—responsible, friendly, with a wide circle of friends. She was usually careful in dealing with her bodily needs and sought appropriate advice from her physician parents. The parents seemed warm, supportive, and appropriately involved.

Second, we set up a contract with Kirsten for four consecutive outpatient visits to our clinic, when she would allow us to follow her weight and vital signs, and do blood and urine chemistries as deemed appropriate to rule out drug use and improper nutrition and hydration. In assuming responsibility for her care, we relieved the pressure on the host parents and reassured both the biological parents and the exchange student agency. Our hypothesis was that the eating problem resulted from normative experimentation with new behavior that had gotten out of hand because of the special circumstances in the situation.

The patient later confirmed our hypothesis: she completed the tracking period without problems and ultimately completed the whole student-exchange year successfully. The ingredient that had created some of the difficulty was that this European youngster was placed in an adolescent peer group that was socially one to two years ahead of her German peer group in terms of experimentation. Not being acculturated, she mistook the age-appropriate experimentation in the American peer group for license to experiment more seriously herself. Lacking the usual access to reliable parent figures and not wanting to appear "out of synch," she slipped into risk-taking that bordered on pathology; she responded quickly, however, once her host parents were apprised of the situation and appropriate limits were set for her.

Many of the fluctuations in adolescent functioning can be understood as a natural accompaniment to the acquisition of new skills: adolescents find themselves in possession of new abilities to think about problems and formulate solutions; they relate to others in new and exciting ways; they are eager to test themselves under pressure and without manifest adult supervision and support; and they achieve physically like never before in their lives. New competencies and new opportunities need to be tested, taken to the limit, and then reintegrated into a solid image of self. This substantial task takes several years, is rarely linear in its progress, and requires patient and flexible support from others.

Kirsten's case demonstrates temporary regression (the reemergence of separation anxiety) and precipitous progression (risktaking in terms of dietary behavior and drug use in someone who had no experience in these domains) induced by special external circumstances (separation from the family of origin, complicated by some transcultural complexities). As we reinstated age-appropriate supervision, the patient responded positively and cooperated well. Mere tracking rather than intervention was enough to bring this case to a successful outcome. To state the main point succinctly: when in doubt, wait, observe, and track the symptoms. Positive response to tracking differentiates developmental crisis from pathology in most cases and often tracking bypasses the need for unnecessary and costly treatment. Our motto should be *"primum nil nocere"*—first do no harm; sometimes treatment, if not needed, can be harmful.

In general, it is not a trivial task to ascertain whether presenting problems are part of normal experimentation of the age (perhaps gone awry) or are harbingers or actual manifestations of major pathology. The situation is complicated by the fact that the course of development is complex and there are many variants of normal development. Below we list some of the factors we need to keep in mind in assessing adolescent problems as a case formulation is developed.

The Nonlinear Course of Development

During adolescence, the course of development is not always linear or forward moving. Some development proceeds slowly and gradually whereas other aspects of development proceed with fits and starts in which there are lengthy plateaus punctuated by periods of rapid growth. In general, progression (orderly and regulated advancement of skills and functioning) is normative during the teen years and suggests that development is continuous over time. For example, we find that children with the best social skills continue to have them in adolescence, even when they change schools or peer groups and experience change in the nature of peer activities and the basis for friendships. However, progression is not the only form of normal development. Regression (backward movement to less complex, less mature forms of behavior, and abandonment of more advanced functioning) also occurs and can be normal. Normal regressions are usually temporary retreats in level of functioning, often made in response to major stress such as family dissolution or real or threatened separation from a significant other. In contrast, pathological regressions, as in schizophrenia, are generally long term and even permanent and involve profound dysfunction in one or more domains.

Intraindividual Variability in Functioning

The distinction between normal and abnormal in adolescent behavior is complicated by the fact that there may be different rates or patterns of development in different domains. For convenience, we classify important domains of adolescent functioning into five categories: (1) basic and body needs, which includes attention to health and hygiene; (2) interpersonal functioning, which includes ability and motivation to get along well with others including parents and same- and opposite-sex peers; (3) mental health functioning, which includes such relevant aspects as affect, mood, attachment status, self-esteem, motivation, conscience, defense and coping behaviors, and ability to observe oneself; (4) academic and vocational achievement with appropriate planning for the future; (5) recreation and leisure activity, which includes an ability to "recharge" one's batteries, relax and enjoy oneself, and utilize free, unstructured time.

Given the multiplicity of domains, it is not uncommon to find youths with different trajectories in different domains of functioning. For example, a student may make linear progress and achieve well in school and in planning for college and a professional career. At the same time, his interpersonal behavior might show regression with avoidance of intimacy and commitments and manifestation of risky sexual behavior. In the recreational domain the youth might show age-appropriate but excessive experimentation with alcohol and drugs. Finally, his relations with his parents might be turbulent at some points, but at other times there might be a reasonable accommodation between them. We are interested in how adolescents put all these domains together, how they succeed in constructing and maintaining a consistent and coherent sense of self, by observing how they function in these different domains.

Contextual Influences on Functioning

Adolescents find themselves in a variety of different social contexts including the school setting, the peer group, the family, the part-time labor force, and a variety of leisure and recreational contexts (on the sports field, in student government, at a party). Each of these settings makes different demands. Individual responses to these demands (expressed as adequacy of adolescent functioning) can be quite variable across diverse contexts.

For example, the student who works constructively in student government may spend hours crying after altercations with her parents. The altruistic high schooler who spends hours planning a fund-raiser for disabled children may draw graffiti on the school walls after learning that his parents are seeking a divorce. The adolescent who threatens to kill herself because her boyfriend has broken off their relationship may continue to be a soccer star on the playing field and a high achiever in the classroom. As a result, it is important to rely on multiple observers and to examine functioning in all relevant domains in assessing whether a teenager is suffering from problems requiring treatment or is simply showing the normative perturbations of adolescence. Teachers, classmates, close friends and partners, parents, and other family members all have somewhat different views of the adolescent's functioning; these all contribute in important ways to the formation of an accurate picture of the adolescent's strengths and vulnerabilities. When marked problems and compromised functioning emerge in multiple domains, it is more likely to be due to psychopathology than when problems are limited to a few areas or occur only in times of elevated stress.

The Importance of Developmental History

Psychiatric examination in adolescence must include a careful developmental history. Specific milestones should be reached by certain ages and there should be a general picture of continuity of development across ages. Developmental phases follow each other and to a large degree build on one another. The successful resolution of prior developmental tasks makes it possible for the individual to progress and take on new challenges of greater complexity. In order to run, one has to be able to walk. In order to relate successfully to peers, one has to relate reasonably well to parents and siblings. In order to do calculus, one has to master arithmetic and algebra. In order to anticipate possible outcomes of a course of action, adolescents have to be able to face facts squarely, without withdrawing from the situation or denying elements of significance. For example, the available evidence in Kirsten's case suggested such an orderly progression had taken place, thus reducing the likelihood that her current behavior was the sign of emerging psychopathology.

Not all skills and competencies are acquired in a linear and sequential fashion. Jerome Kagan, a Harvard developmental psychologist, has challenged the universality of the model of developmental continuity, using a series of elegant and important studies. Some skills appear *de novo*—out of the blue—in a kind of quantum leap. But the majority follow a predictable developmental progression and children and youths show considerable continuity in functioning over time.

The Need for Multidimensional Assessment

A perspective based on "developmental psychopathology," which takes account of the developmental tasks past and present, is useful for mental health clinicians, regardless of the age group with which they are dealing. But knowledge of normal development is indispensable for those who treat persons "under construction," as they become afflicted by a variety of psychiatric disorders.

To simplify thinking about a case, it is helpful to imagine a balance beam (see Figure 1.1) that represents healthy adjustment in the balanced position. After examining all the relevant domains in the patient's functioning, the clinician can construct a list of strengths and weaknesses and place these in their respective positions on the balance beam. Strengths might include the patient's intelligence, academic tenacity, ability to form rewarding relationships, and coping skills for dealing with adversity in a flexible manner. Weaknesses might include tendencies to withdraw from confrontation, inability to speak in one's own defense, and a tendency to isolate oneself from others when distressed. Then below the beam the clinician lists external stressors (such as recent losses and major transitions) and external supports (such as the adequacy of primary family relationships and degree of economic security). As treatment progresses, the balance of the beam is often upset—an expectable and predictable event. Periodically, during the course of treatment, the position of the beam balance should be rethought. Sometimes, especially in times of crisis, it is useful to ask the patient and his or her parents to construct the factors that impinge on the balance of the beam.

In summary, as part of the assessment, an extensive case formulation must be developed. This represents a first attempt to summarize and synthesize information, including diagnosis, developmental history, functioning in diverse domains, and manifest strengths and weaknesses. Hypotheses suggest causal connections that draw attention in a logical order to particular targets for treatment. In dealing with adolescents it is necessary to do the following:

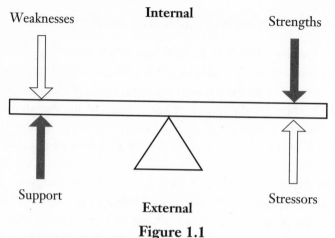

Figure 1.1
Healthy Adjustment in the Balanced Position

- Gather diverse information from multiple informants that covers a significant span of time.
- Avoid premature promises of confidentiality.
- Be honest about procedures, including the need to inform parents of dangerous activities.
- Focus first on observation and tracking that may sometimes be a sufficient intervention plan.

THE COURSE OF TREATMENT

In this section we address the general structure of a treatment program for an adolescent. We do not advocate a "cookbook approach" to treatment and recognize that individually tailored modifications will be required, depending on primary and secondary diagnoses. Nonetheless, there are some general principles that we describe here.

The Choice of Treatment

About forty years ago, Hans Eysenk, a British psychologist, challenged psychiatrists to prove that their interventions were effective. In response to this challenge, there are now data substantiating the efficacy of many forms of mental health treatment. Today, we have moved beyond the question of "Does therapy work" and focus instead on "How do treatments work" and on identifying which treatment works best for different problems. Recent summaries can be found in the authoritative volumes by Bergin and Garfield on psychotherapy, and Greene on psychopharmacology.

The belief, prevalent in early psychoanalysis, that one form of treatment is effective for a diverse array of disorders is clearly mistaken. So is the argument that different psychotherapies work equally well because of such nonspecific ingredients as the empathic quality of the therapist-patient relationship. A positive relationship is a necessary but not sufficient condition for success. Specific ingredients are at work in different therapies and the next decade will clarify their nature. What we know is that there is no single "best therapy." Instead, different kinds of treatments are effective for specific disorders. For instance, interpersonal problems (such as family conflict) are best treated by interpersonal therapies such as family treatment. Conduct disorders and delinquency are best handled by parent education and social skills training. Severe depression is most effectively treated by a combination of medication and problem-focused psychotherapy. Phobias respond best to exposure programs and desensitization in vivo.

Clearly, therapists require a rich armamentarium of interventions if they are to deal with a wide range of pathology. To know which therapy is likely to be effective, clinicians must collect some of the following information.

Duration of Disturbance. Short-term problems are likely to be "state" disturbances and require targeted approaches that deal with the presenting symptoms. Treatment is generally short term and contains many supportive ingredients. A classic example would be uncomplicated catharsis after trauma—such as the loss of a loved one, reaction to a car accident, or trauma induced by medical procedures. Long-term problems, such as Anorexia Nervosa, suggest a "trait" disturbance, which is more complicated to treat and which often entails a complex and changing therapist-patient relationship. Appropriate therapies contain exploratory elements designed to promote self-reflection, observation, and insight. Treatment is usually multifocal and involves building on existing psychological strengths as well as use of interventions such as social skills training intended to build "psychological muscle."

Patient's Psychological Mindedness. Patients differ in terms of their processing of psychological information. With psychologically minded patients who think in more abstract terms and are comfortable with mental categories, exploratory, insight-oriented approaches are likely to be effective. The detail-oriented behavior approach is likely to bore these patients. In contrast, patients who tend to be more detail focused and concrete, and have trouble with concepts such as "conflict," "emotion," and "insight" respond better to the use of a "bottom up" approach, where they track symptoms, precipitants of stress, and the like, and make connections between events only after psychoeducation by the clinician.

Extent of Impairment. When symptoms affect many areas of basic functioning, such as sleep, appetite, mood, and behavior, medication may be indicated. For an isolated symptom such as a specific phobia of snakes, a targeted behavioral approach utilizing desensitization or exposure treatment is often helpful. For problems of a very complex nature, such as underachievement or trouble selecting an appropriate mate, an exploratory psychotherapeutic approach may be the most helpful. Such an approach is broadly based and draws on a wide variety of experiences (such as fantasies, dreams, present and past behavior, and transference-countertransference observations) to detect maladaptive patterns in behavior.

The Clinician's Preferences. No single clinician is equally good at all types of treatments, and no single treatment is suitable for all kinds of problems. A therapy inappropriate to the problem can be outright dangerous. For example, exploratory therapy with severe delinquents is likely to be useless at best, dangerous to you at worst. Most clinicians build their practices around problems they are good at dealing with and feel comfortable treating. Practitioners of the future will reflect this trend even more.

The Treatment Setting

Treatment can be carried out in a variety of settings, depending on the safety requirements of the situation, the intensity or extensiveness of treatment needed, and the complexity of the problems to be addressed. Hospitalization is the most intensive, safe, but costly alternative. Partial hospitalization, day treatment, therapeutic schools, and outpatient care are all important alternatives. And as previously described, consultation and tracking can be an efficient way to deal with some problems.

The Treatment Contract

A treatment contract is planned after the clinician has reached a diagnosis and formulated a treatment plan. The treatment contract is negotiated in one or two sessions and has several different components. It includes communicating the preliminary diagnostic findings and treatment alternatives first to the adolescent, then to the family; giving the family time to decide jointly the treatment plan they wish to pursue; and then meeting with the family as a whole to establish the course of treatment, and sometimes even signing a real contract as to the number of sessions and the nature of the intervention.

Discussions with the Patient. The first step is usually to meet with the adolescent alone and review the contents of the case formulation. The information is tailored to the particular characteristics of the patient, taking into account defense structure coping skills as well as sensitivities and particular areas of conflict.

In general, it is helpful to begin with domains of strength and the least defended topics. For example, this may include asking the adolescent to describe relationships about which he or she feels unconflicted or areas of success (for example, academic achievement in a patient with Anorexia Nervosa).

It is necessary to approach more sensitive topics with "trial balloons." In patients with Anorexia Nervosa (who tend to defend tenaciously against aggression), the clinician might raise obliquely issues of assertiveness and anger by noting that the patient had said little about angry situations and wondering aloud what he or she would do with such an emotion when it arises. If the patient reacts with curiosity, the topic can be further pursued; but in the face of a blank stare or a noncommittal smile, the clinician might move on to the next area. In communicating the findings to the patient, it is helpful to give examples—preferably verbatim ones from interviews—describing specific problems and discussing possible explanations.

The clinician then suggests a plan of treatment, estimates duration of treatment, and notes alternatives and options. It is important that the patient follow the discussion and feel free to ask questions. The usual treatment package consists of weekly individual sessions complemented by family sessions every other week or so. Medication and conditions for hospitalization, where appropriate, are also discussed. The therapist describes the anticipated length of treatment together with the caveat that such estimates are preliminary and subject to revision based on periodic reviews of progress.

While staying firm about the need for intervention, the clinician will find it helpful to describe to the adolescents their options and choices regarding therapists, location of treatment, and split family assignment (whether the adolescents prefer that their parents be seen by a therapist other than their own). Because good patient-clinician matches lead to good outcomes and not every match works equally well, it is always important to take account of the patients' preferences. These may be influenced by clinicians' gender, personality or interpersonal style, or age. It is appropriate to offer your services but also to recommend other therapists, if required.

Discussions with the Family. Once patient and clinician have reached a reasonably clear understanding, parents are invited into the therapist's office and the discussion is repeated. After answering questions raised by the parents, the clinician asks the family to return in a week for the beginning of treatment or the finalization of referrals. He or she emphasizes that decisions about the treatment should be made jointly by the patients and their families in the privacy of their homes, taking into account their own psychological needs as well as such practical issues as money, time, and travel. Families should be encouraged to find the solution that will allow them to work in therapy for as long as necessary.

The Need for Family Involvement in Adolescent Treatment. It is usually necessary to involve the family in treatment unless the adolescent is emancipated or the problems are very circumscribed. There are at least three reasons parents should be involved. First, the adolescent frequently perceives them to be part of the problem. Even internalized problems (which can be treated on an individual basis) are often externalized to other family members and therefore require the parents to be involved in the therapy. Picking fights with one's parents is usually very effective for adolescents seeking to avoid awareness of their own intrapsychic conflicts. It is easier for teenagers to say: "My stupid parents won't let me go to this party (where there will be drugs and sex)" than to acknowledge "I don't want to go because I am afraid of how I am going to handle myself there." "My parents are lame" is easier to accept than the attribution "I am lame."

Second, adolescents' attachment to their families is usually strong, despite all their protestations to the contrary and their counterphobic avoidance of family members. Particularly in crisis situations, all but the most severely disturbed teenagers show considerable tendency to turn to their parents for comfort and support.

Third, since the family is the context in which recovery occurs, clinicians can help parents understand the nature of therapeutic progression and regression. For example, the clinician sees progress when an anorexic patient dares to go to a party, whereas an anxious overprotective mother sees this as acting out or a threat. Progress in psychotherapy is maintained only when supported by significant others such as parents, and thus parents need to become the allies of clinicians. The psychotherapy outcome literature is very clear on this point.

One of the great challenges in working with this age group is to forge and maintain good working alliances with both patients and parents without appearing to be ineffective, taking sides, or being "two-faced." This can be accomplished in a number of different ways. Some families are receptive to dealing with adolescent problems within a systems framework in which the child's disturbance is understood in terms of its function within the family. The basic idea is that symptoms serve to reestablish the homeostasis of family relationships when irritants and changes have been introduced. Other families are resistant to the systems perspective, and, in such cases, individual treatment augmented by some family sessions is useful. Both approaches have merit and neither is preferable in terms of results; the choice depends on the clinician's training and preference and the family's style of problem solving and level of functioning.

Resistance to Proposed Treatment. If there is resistance in the family to recommendations for treatment, it is necessary to determine which aspects of the treatment contract seem to be creating difficulties. For example, it may be finances, time involved, perceived stigma, or time diverted from school work. The clinician can highlight the importance of the intervention in preventing the problem from becoming chronic. If such an argument still fails to convince the family, it may be necessary to give them a referral for a second opinion. At times, an acceptable alternative is a contract for fewer sessions (most often ten) followed by a review of progress.

A knotty problem presents itself if the adolescent is clearly in need of intervention but the parents express vehement opposition. In such cases, more sinister forms of pathology such as severe marital problems, abuse, or family secrets may be suspected. Clinicians then need to redefine their role from being potential providers (those who will be part of the treatment team) to change agents (those who, without treating the problem, effect some change in the family). In such a situation, it is necessary to keep the adolescent's safety and health foremost in mind, even at the risk of total alienation of parents and family. Sometimes a brief period of hospitalization for the patient permits more intensive assessment and gives the clinician a chance to get to know the parents and form a better alliance with them. If the youngster is a clear danger to self or others, it will be necessary to proceed with involuntary commitment; in less clear-cut cases, contacting child protective services and reporting the situation as medical neglect is an alternative.

None of these situations is a particularly good solution to the problem, and such dispositions usually lead to termination of contact without good long-term prognosis. That is why formal contracting, after appropriate assessment, is still the best possible solution and should be regarded as the preferred standard.

The Phases of Treatment

The course of treatment with adolescents proceeds in somewhat predictable form, almost regardless of the diagnosis, with an early, middle, and terminal phase. The designation of early, middle, and terminal is given by the nature of the process in the sessions, the material covered, and the involvement of the parents rather than merely by the passage of time. Typically, but by no means invariably, the phases differ in duration: one to three months for early, four or more months for middle, and two to four months for terminal.

The Early Phase of Treatment.   In the early phase of treatment, individual and family therapy sessions occur regularly and family members "tell the whole story" with some cathartic effect. Old family facts, interpreted in a new light by the therapist, typically lead to new understandings, and the patient's symptoms often recede or improve. An adolescent is usually gratified that a powerful and important adult takes great interest in his or her life and helps to navigate tricky situations with parents. Parents, in turn, are relieved because they observe progress and the situation at home settles down. Transference is usually positive and there is a sense of optimism in the family.

Countertransferentially, the clinician must be careful not to respond to the praise and appreciation of the patient and parents; narcissism can easily get in the way and push clinicians to collude with the family, who at the end of this phase sometimes request termination of treatment.

The observed change in the adolescent patient and the family is real but superficial; it occurs because an "interpersonal carbon rod"—that is, the therapist—has been introduced into the usual nuclear reactions of the family. With the removal of the interventions such changes rarely last, for they are not based on new interactions in the family or new psychological structures in the patient.

The Middle Phase of Treatment.   If catharsis is the code word for the early phase, drudgery is perhaps the best way to summarize the middle phase. It is hard work to bring about lasting changes. In transference, patients and parents bring into the consulting room and enact with the therapist the very problems that plague them with each other at home. This fact can be interpreted positively: rather than being dependent on secondhand accounts of problems, clinicians are now able to observe firsthand and work directly with the problems.

How does this change in the therapy process come about, and how do we detect it? In general, behaviors and emotions are organized around significant others and as the therapist becomes part of the patient's emotional orbit, his or her emotions, beliefs, and attitudes will come to refer to the clinician. Psychoanalysis was the first to systematically label and describe this process of transference and eventually utilized it in the treatment of patients. From a psychoanalytic perspective, transference is always the expression of infantile antecedents, but not all clinicians endorse this viewpoint. We count ourselves among the dissenters.

From our perspective, although some of the mental and emotional states patients exhibit in the consultation room are repetitions of past states, many are not. The difficulty is to distinguish whether a given behavior, expectation, or demand the patient makes of clinicians in fact fits with an old behavioral program (which had some utility to the patient in the past) or whether it is about the present. The clues for such a distinction come from the patient's developmental history, the case formulation, and the clinician's own reactions to what the patient brings into the consulting room. Again, it was Sigmund Freud's genius to recognize the importance of the clinician's own mental states as possible sources of information about patients. He labeled these reactions countertransference. A small but solid body of evidence, beginning with the landmark studies of David Malan, supports the notion that transference-countertransference material is important in treatment; therapists who utilize such interventions achieve better results for their patients in terms of symptom reduction and general level of functioning than therapists who do not.

What does transference behavior look like? Usually, the shift in the therapeutic process is heralded by a change in emotional tone in the session. There appears to be an extra emotional charge that was absent before. The tone can be positive (erotic) or negative (angry), with all possible shadings in between. For example, in the clinical practice of one of us (H.S.), a young bulimic patient came to a session dressed and made up in a manner that contrasted starkly with her previous appearance (which sought to conceal all evidence that she was a young woman).

Thus she brought into the session for the first time sexual behavior that was a source of considerable conflict in her home and which, to that date, had been described only by her parents. In response to questioning about her change of attire, she acknowledged her intent to test the clinician's reaction. This led to a long exploration of her sexuality that ultimately revealed molestation at the hands of her father.

Not infrequently, additional problems, often located in the unconscious, are uncovered in the course of treatment. An increase in problems sometimes frightens patient and parents, and progress needs to be titrated accordingly. A good strategy to keep in mind is that therapeutic information can be presented in terms of the treatment relationship (transference), the patient's past, and relationships outside the consulting room. In this middle phase, concentration on the treatment relationship will intensify affect and accelerate progress, while discussion of the other two domains generally will make affect more manageable but slows down progress. Repeated discussions are necessary for proper working through of important issues. Very often, it is useful to give homework and assign diary duties to the patient. Clinicians can consult the family's baby books, videos or films, and photo albums to help reconstruct key experiences in the patient's life. The general attitude to be fostered in treatment is that of a joint effort at solving a major jigsaw puzzle: the patient by and large can produce the pieces, while the clinician tends to know where to put them to help a meaningful picture emerge.

Requests for termination are sometimes precipitated by a reemergence of old problems or the discovery of completely new ones. In such situations, some families and patients react with hopelessness or fear of the unknown. These emotions and responses on the part of the family need to be anticipated and dispelled, and realistic assurances given that the next phase will bring the opportunity for true realignment in the family and positive psychological growth in the patient. The majority of families respond to such assurances and continue in their quest for betterment.

The Terminal Phase of Treatment. Parental contact may be reduced as patients do more significant work on their own, but parents need to be kept informed and prepared to deal with key changes in their adolescents. Two factors determine the frequency of contact with the parents at this point: the age of the patient and the progress in treatment. Contact with parents may be reduced earlier for older patients and for those whose treatment is proceeding in accord with expectations that have been communicated to parents. If progress is very rapid, so there are numerous changes in a short period of time, parents need close contact with the clinician lest they confuse emergence of new problems with the manifest progress.

As new competencies emerge in the adolescent, he or she takes and masters new risks. Gradually, the developmental trajectory begins to normalize itself (if the primary deficits are not too great). The realization that this is taking place is both exhilarating and scary for the patient. Often, the transition into the last phase of treatment—the termination phase—is signaled by a negative therapeutic reaction, a precipitous, completely surprising, and sometimes even profound abandonment of gains in treatment.

This reaction is usually induced by patients' fears of ever-increasing demands by parents, teachers, and friends for normal progression, and by doubt on their part that such progress can be maintained. Success is the threat, not failure. Most adolescents do not have a realistic expectation of what is in store for them as adults; they project steeper increases of demands into the future than they are likely to encounter. Such a crisis often induces regression and a reemergence of original symptoms. Parents then once again doubt the lasting nature of progress and may doubt the competence of the clinician. The patients also rework old fears, and remnants of attachment problems appear, precipitated by the pending separation from the treatment team. The transference often assumes negative dimensions, with the following concerns often implied or expressed: "Why haven't you fixed this or that," "Maybe you are a charlatan after all," and

"Our money was wasted." The countertransference problems consist of the clinician's temptation to give concrete examples of progress and false reassurances that all will be well for the rest of the patient's life. Patient and persistent examination of termination issues and integration of progressive solutions into the patients' and parents' structures remains the best way to proceed.

If a patient does not progress through these phases, it signals that it is time for reassessment and reconsideration of the treatment plan. Was the diagnosis correct? Should other diagnoses be considered? Was anything missed in the initial formulation? Are more sessions per week needed? Is medication needed? Are the parents undermining progress because their child is changing too fast? Is there a need for an intensification of the treatment by increasing the level of care to day treatment or even hospitalization to get beyond the current impasse? Sometimes, consultation with a colleague is helpful.

In this chapter we have outlined some general issues in treating adolescent patients. Specific issues in the treatment of particular disorders are dealt with in subsequent chapters. Clearly, the nature of the clinical intervention is strongly influenced by the primary and secondary diagnosis and the entire case formulation, but we anticipate that the template we have provided in this first chapter will be useful in designing the "battle plan" for all the syndromes we describe in this book. It is true, the treatment of youth in the second decade of life is a complex process, but it is, from our perspective, the most rewarding and intellectually stimulating activity in the mental health field. We hope that we have succeeded in stimulating your curiosity.

NOTES

P. 3, *A recent volume with state-of-the-art reviews of adolescent development:* Feldman, S. S., & Elliott, G. (1993). *At the threshold: The developing adolescent.* Cambridge, MA: Harvard University Press.

P. 3, *for a developmental psychological perspective:* Litt, I. F. (1990). *Evaluation of the adolescent patient.* Philadelphia: Hanley & Belfus.

P. 5, *these changes precipitate a form of egocentrism in which adolescents act as if they are on stage:* Elkind, D. (1967). Egocentrism in adolescents. *Child Development, 38,* 1025–1034

P. 5, *The Construction of an Identity:* Erikson, E. (1963). *Childhood and society* (2nd ed., especially chapter 7). New York: Norton.

P. 7, *Dealing with sexuality may be more complex for those youths who are out of step with their peers in terms of their pubertal development:* Metcalfe, T. (Writer), & Kanew, J. (Director). (1984). *The revenge of the nerds* [Film].

P. 10, *This case certainly has a familiar ring to it and conjures up many drag racing and "chicken" scenes from movies such as:* Lucas, G. (Writer/Director). (1973). *American graffiti* [Film]; Reiner, R. (Director), & Gideon, R. et al. (Writers). (1986). *Stand by me* [Film].

P. 16, *For Aaron Beck and his colleagues:* Beck, A. T., Risnik, H.L.P., & Lettieri, D. J. (1974). *Prediction of suicide.* Bowie, MD: Charles Press.

P. 19, *Sometimes, there is an isolated suicide attempt that seemingly appears out of the blue:* Pfeffer, C. R. (1986). *The suicidal child.* New York: Guilford Press.

P. 20, *This kind of adaptive style is quite common in the general population, but in its extreme forms has been found to be associated with isolated explosive periods of violence or self-harm:* Weinberger, D. A., & Schwartz, G. E. (1990). Distress and restraint as superordinate dimensions of self-reported adjustment: A typological perspective. *Journal of Personality, 58,* 381–416.

P. 20, *A special word needs to be said:* van der Kolk, B. A. (1987). *Psychological trauma.* Washington, DC: American Psychiatric Press.

P. 26, *Not all skills and competencies are acquired in a linear and sequential fashion:* Kagan, J. (1989). *Unstable ideas, temperament, cognition and self.* Cambridge, MA: Harvard University Press.

P. 29, *Recent summaries can be found in the authoritative volumes:* Bergin, A. E., & Garfield, S. L. (1994). *Handbook of psychotherapy and behavior change* (4th ed.). New York: Wiley; Greene, W. H. (1991). *Child and adolescent clinical psychopharmacology.* Baltimore: Williams & Wilkins.

P. 36, *How does this change in the therapy process come about, and how do we detect it?:* Strupp, H. H., & Binder, J. L. (1984). *Psychotherapy in a new key: A guide to time-limited dynamic psychotherapy.* New York: Basic Books.

P. 37, *A small but solid body of evidence, beginning with the landmark studies of:* Malan, D. (1976). *Toward the validation of dynamic psychotherapy.* New York: Plenum Medical Book Company.

2

DISRUPTIVE BEHAVIORAL DISORDERS

James Lock

Almost all adolescents have problems with rules and following instructions from time to time. Usually this is something that is intermittent or passes quickly. Sometimes, however, they develop patterns of responding to adults and authority figures in ways that get them in trouble with schools, their families, and even the law.

In this chapter we discuss how to treat some problems that adolescents have that can get them into this kind of trouble. As we will see, some of these problems develop because of a genetic propensity whereas others are probably caused by difficulties of one kind or another in the home. Psychiatrists have grouped these kinds of problems under the heading of disruptive behavior disorders and include the following types of diagnoses: Attention Deficit/Hyperactivity Disorder, Conduct Disorder, and Oppositional/Defiant Disorder.

Sometimes these disorders are called "externalizing" disorders. In practical terms, this means the symptoms are initially experienced as more of a problem for those outside the teenagers than for the teenagers themselves. With these teens there is little internal structure, so external structure is applied to keep them functioning. Such problems usually begin early in life but magnify in adolescence when capacities to engage in aggressive and sexual ways in society develop more fully. All domains of their lives are affected and a variety of approaches are required to treat such teenagers successfully.

ATTENTION DEFICIT/HYPERACTIVITY DISORDER

At one time, children with Attention Deficit/Hyperactivity Disorder (ADHD) were believed to outgrow it. Now we know differently. About a third of children with ADHD will continue to have the full syndrome in adulthood, and about two-thirds will be significantly bothered by at least one of the major symptoms—inattention or impulsivity.

In my experience, I have found that it is often necessary to approach the teenager with ADHD differently from the way I work with a child. To begin with, if the teenager has been diagnosed and treated for ADHD since childhood, new issues about taking medications, drug abuse, and other developmental struggles complicate the ongoing treatment. On the other hand, sometimes teenagers receive the diagnosis for the first time and this helps put into perspective problems they have been having for years.

I will explain my approach to these two different situations and the kinds of problems I usually have in the treatment process. To begin with, though, I'd like to briefly review a little about the process of making the diagnosis of ADHD in general and with the teenager specifically.

The Origins of ADHD

ADHD is not a new diagnosis at all. References to overactive and impulsive children can be found going back to the 1800s, and children with such problems have been scientifically studied since the early 1900s. Unfortunately, some of this study and the variety of ideas about it have led to misconceptions and confusions about ADHD. Children have been referred to as "mad idiots" and suffering from "impulsive insanity"; more scientific but equally damaging rubrics such as "minimal brain damage syndrome" and "minimal brain dysfunction" have also been applied to such children. This history has stigmatized the illness and made many families initially reluctant to accept the diagnosis or to accept treatment.

The core kinds of problems that a person with ADHD has are a short attention span, difficulties with impulsive behavior, and a pervasive restlessness. These lead to problems in paying attention to what is being said to them by friends, family members, and teachers, and makes them subject to social rejection, disciplinary problems, and school failure.

ADHD is a fairly common problem in children and is thought to occur in 2 percent to 6 percent of all children. It appears throughout the world and affects about four times as many boys as girls. No one is sure what causes ADHD, but like many psychiatric illnesses, a combination of genetic and social factors is probably involved.

Most studies indicate a genetic aspect to the etiology of ADHD. Some studies suggest that children of parents with ADHD are twice as likely to have ADHD as are other children. On the other hand, exposure to certain toxins, such as lead, have also been implicated in the development of behavior problems like those found in ADHD. Similarly, certain kinds of subtle abnormalities in the brain, either structural or neurochemical, may also be involved. What has not been proven, though many parents I see continue to think otherwise, is that food additives, dyes, and sugar in particular, are related to the development or maintenance of ADHD.

Social influences also play a role in the development of ADHD. Studies have shown that family stress and a negative mother-child interaction can be found among even very young children with symptoms of ADHD. Sometimes this is also associated with lower socioeconomic status where certain family stresses—including fewer resources in time and money—are prevalent. It may be that a genetic vulnerability is exacerbated in such a setting, leading to worsening behavior and attention problems.

Unfortunately, there was a period not long ago when the diagnosis of ADHD was extremely common and made without a thorough diagnostic assessment. This led to an abuse in both the diagnosis and the treatment of ADHD, especially in regard to using medications. A backlash from families and educators about treatment of children with ADHD followed. I often run into this type of negative prejudice and it can be a significant impediment to a patient's getting proper treatment. Now we understand that the diagnosis of ADHD requires a comprehensive evaluation before any form of treatment is initiated.

Diagnosis

To determine whether a teenager has ADHD, I find it necessary to see the patient, interview the family and schoolteachers, and if possible observe the teenager in a group or school setting. I do not find it sufficient to assess a patient based solely on his or her behavior in an office setting. I have had some teens in my office who ultimately were diagnosed with ADHD but who seemed quiet and subdued in that setting because they are nervous or shy. Other times I have thought certain adolescents clearly had ADHD only to find they actually had an anxiety disorder, or had experienced some kind of trauma that made it appear they were unable to pay attention or sit down.

When I assess a teenager for ADHD I start by interviewing the teenager to identify the target symptoms. I ask the adolescent to relate the symptoms to situations in which they occur. I try to elicit any particularly difficult situations where symptoms are worse as well as situations where symptoms are minimal. In addition, I evaluate the teen's mood for depression, anxiety, or lability in case these are the reason for the symptoms or are complicating ADHD. In addition to the remainder of the mental status exam, I spend extra care in taking a history of family relationships, friendships, social functioning, and academic functioning with special emphasis on the possibility of a learning disability.

Next, I arrange to interview the parents to review the teenager's developmental history, the age of onset of symptoms, the situations where symptoms occur, the medical history, the learning history, the presence of family stresses, the type of disciplinary measures taken, the familial ADHD history, and any recent changes in the family that might be affecting the adolescent. Since ADHD begins in early childhood, this history can help me a lot in making a definitive diagnosis. I like to conduct this interview with the teenagers present. Sometimes they can elaborate, correct, or clarify what parents report. I also find that teenagers prefer to know what is being said about them and if I am going to continue to treat them, I want them to be assured that I take their perspective seriously.

Often I find it helpful to interview the family as a whole to see how the behavior that is being considered consistent with ADHD emerges. Often brothers and sisters can assist in identifying problem behaviors. This type of involvement can also serve as an opportunity to begin educating and helping the family to help the patient. In one case in particular I remember that it not only helped to clarify the diagnosis of ADHD in the teen but also identified ADHD in a younger sibling as well.

When discussing with the family the behavior of a teenager who may have ADHD, I find it important to ask the family members to identify the situations where they notice the behavior that concerns them. For example, people with an anxiety disorder or phobia may seem distracted, physically agitated, and even disobedient when near a person or situation that makes them anxious or frightens them. A depressed person may also have difficulty paying attention, show increased problems with friends, and have problems doing well in school. The person with ADHD, however, is most likely to display the symptoms in an indoor group setting or environments with multiple input stimuli—like school or clubs—when other teenagers are able to sit and focus on work. Teens with ADHD often seem to do a little better in unstructured settings, but even there they remain impulsive and sometimes cannot follow the rules of the game or get along well with others.

These patterns usually are noted by parents to have begun by age three. It's likely that they've become more pronounced as the demands for focused attention, work, and work with and alongside others increase; the start of preschool or kindergarten is often a time when children are first referred for evaluation for ADHD. Sometimes because they do not understand what is happening around them or are unable to follow the rules, they hit other children or try to avoid being in places where their difficulties are likely to be noticed. This may cause them to seek being sent out of class or excused from school, which is at first a relief to them. Many times these kinds of patterns have persisted without treatment and complicate the presentation of a teenager being assessed for ADHD for the first time.

Girls with ADHD sometimes appear differently from boys. They tend to be somewhat less physically active, behaviorally intrusive or aggressive, and therefore present less obvious problems for parents and teachers. As a result, they are often not diagnosed until much later, if at all. Nonetheless they still have all the problems with attention, screening stimuli, and organizing that boys have.

I also ask about behavior at home. Parents consistently report that teens with ADHD have trouble following directions and leave things they are asked to complete unfinished or broken. Parents tell me they find themselves constantly reminding these children to do this thing or the other only to find it still not done when they check yet again. Because of their inattention and impulsive behavior, these children can be accident prone and get hurt or damage things easily and often.

If at all possible, I ask that the family send me any educational testing that has been done prior to my first visit. This helps me identify even before the child comes to the office any additional tests I am likely to want. It is important that educational testing be done to assess other concomitant learning problems that may be causing, exacerbating, or complicating the behaviors. Records of school performance are of great assistance, especially when they report both academic and behavioral aspects, and I always request them when conducting a diagnostic evaluation for ADHD.

Instruments. To assist clinicians in evaluating persons who might have ADHD, a number of instruments have been developed for use by parents and teachers to rate children's behaviors. The most common one in use today is the Connors Behavioral Checklist. This instrument is a compilation of behaviors listed in columns; it allows the rater an opportunity to grade the teen using a range of scores on a variety of behaviors commonly associated with ADHD. If the scores are high enough, the teen is more likely to have ADHD if the rest of the information one has gathered also fits this picture. In addition, there are specialized tests to quantify thought processing and sequencing called continuous performance tasks; these tests are available in some areas to assist clinicians in particularly difficult cases. I have seldom used them and find that I can make good diagnostic assessments without them in the vast majority of cases.

The Connors or similar instruments can also be used to monitor the progress of patients with ADHD during treatment to learn whether an intervention is producing a positive, negative, or no effect.

Diagnostic Examples

Here are two case examples to illustrate the points I am making about the diagnostic process in teens with ADHD:

LARRY

Larry was an energetic thirteen-year-old who had already been held back one year because of not learning and behavioral problems in the first grade. Larry was friendly and loud. He was often intrusive physically with others and got into minor scrapes with his peers on the playground. Although he was a good athlete, Larry didn't play sports well because he would drift off in the middle of the game and others kids would get angry at him. In class, he was often seen looking off as if in a daze or constantly getting out of his chair and talking to his neighbors when they were trying to work. Larry did poorly in all subjects although his IQ suggested a greater-than-average capacity for learning. Larry's parents had been told to have him evaluated for learning difficulties and ADHD. They did the former and found none, but they were reluctant to seek psychiatric evaluation for ADHD. As they saw it, Larry was just like his father was at that age and he had turned out all right. In fact, the father had enormous difficulty with school and even now struggled with problems related to inattention at work. In the end, Larry's parents kept him out of treatment for ADHD and he continued to have school difficulties and not achieve up to his potential.

SARAH

Sarah was always an active girl. Even at three she was turning over tables and getting into everything, usually all at once and all over the room. Her mother tried to get her started in a preschool, but she was always disruptive to even the most simple group activity. Sarah was dismissed from three schools before her mother decided she had best keep her at home. When Sarah started kindergarten, her mother had hoped things would be different. By the time Sarah reached age fourteen she had become such a disappointment that her mother was almost ashamed of her. She was constantly having to admonish Sarah who originally became angry about all the negative comments she received, but now had become more sad and withdrawn. She remained very active and she was still unable to pay attention or complete any work, but in addition she slept less, cried easily, and began to lose weight.

Sarah's mother asked a close family friend what she should do. The friend suggested that she contact the school psychologist and ask for assistance. Sarah was evaluated by the psychologist who observed her behaviors in class; interviewed Sarah and her mother, alone and then together; conducted a Connors; and screened Sarah for learning disabilities. The psychologist concluded that Sarah suffered from ADHD but also now had developed a depression. She recommended that Sarah see a child psychiatrist for a full evaluation. Sarah was seen and started on a regimen of low dose psycho-stimulant and family therapy.

Associated Problems

My experience has shown that many teenagers who have ADHD develop other kinds of problems in addition. Two of the most common are Oppositional/Defiant Disorder and Conduct Disorder, both of which we discuss later in this chapter. It is estimated that at least 40 percent of children diagnosed with ADHD will develop Conduct Disorder and most of these would be diagnosed with Oppositional/Defiant Disorder at an earlier age. Other kinds of problems that teens with ADHD have include learning disorders of all types. Naturally these problems complicate the treatment of the person with ADHD and make school performance even more difficult.

Anxiety Disorder, depression, and substance abuse can also be part of the clinical picture of an adolescent with ADHD. Sometimes these other problems occur independently of the ADHD, but often they can be viewed as at least partly a consequence of it. Serious behavior problems can naturally grow out of impulsive and inattentive ones. Teens with ADHD can become angry at all the negative things they experience and try to find ways to struggle with this. Sometimes these are not very productive and they become violent and assaultive. Other teens can become anxious or depressed as a result of their ADHD. Because of their failures and lowered self-esteem, they may become worried about everything they do, leading both to excessive anxiety and often lowered self-esteem. Teenagers with ADHD do sometimes become seriously depressed and often are not diagnosed as such because of their other ADHD presentation.

Looking at the problem from the other side, many psychiatric diagnoses also occur with ADHD. Adolescents with Tourette's, a disorder that involves both motor and vocal tics, have ADHD between 20 percent and 34 percent of the time. Between 30 and

50 percent of oppositional/defiant and conduct disordered children also have ADHD. About 30 percent of adolescents with mood disorders have ADHD, as do about 25 percent of adolescents with anxiety disorders or learning disabilities. About 27 percent of adolescents with ADHD have more than two of the above diagnoses.

TREATING ADOLESCENTS WITH ADHD

Treating a teenager with ADHD requires that the clinician take a multimodal approach. This is true because ADHD dramatically affects all aspects of a person's life. As in the evaluation process, treatment requires attention to the individual, family, and school.

Medication

Studies of the varieties of treatment available demonstrate that medications are the single most effective treatment. The most common medication used to treat ADHD is methylphenidate or Ritalin. It has been found effective in up to 75 percent of children with ADHD and helps with symptoms of inattention, distractibility, and hyperactivity; it also improves short-term memory, motivation, accuracy, and speed of problem solving. In addition, it appears to help decrease aggression and oppositional behavior and improve peer social interactions.

As the use of Ritalin has apparently doubled every four years since 1971, there has been increasing concern about the widespread use of such psychostimulants. There are now parent organizations struggling against the use of these medications so that it is sometimes difficult for a caring mother or father to know what to do. I know in my practice it's unusual for a parent not to ask if it is necessary and to struggle with this issue almost as much as the teenager.

For these reasons I am especially careful in discussing medications with both teenagers and their parents. I also discuss the issue with any referring clinician when I'm asked to evaluate a teen who is under someone else's care for a trial of medication. Certainly medication should be offered only to a teenager who has been thoroughly evaluated, and its benefits, if any, should be documented on a regular basis to ensure that the medication continues to be helpful. I make such assessments both verbally and in writing during each medication visit.

Psychostimulants, and especially Ritalin, are some of the most thoroughly studied medications available to the clinician. They are also among the safest. I communicate this to the teenager and the parents, but I have to admit it sometimes falls on deaf ears. I also tell them that at this time there appear to be no long-term side effects of stimulant medication when given in proper doses and appropriately monitored. Parents are sometimes legitimately concerned about effects of the medication on a child's growth, tics, and psychotic thought problems and I address these in any consent process. Other problems I commonly see with Ritalin include appetite suppression, abdominal pain, sleep problems, and cognitive blunting or confusion. There are a number of other agents that I also use to treat ADHD and some of these come into play with adolescents, especially if I suspect any potential for substance abuse. These are discussed in more detail below.

As mentioned in Chapter Eight on treating affective disorders, the consent process offers an opportunity for building rapport and trust with both the teenager and the parents. Though medication is only a part of treatment, it's important for this part to go well since it is so often crucial to success. In those cases where I am involved in this aspect of care only, I communicate with the other professionals working with the teen about the potential side effects and send them copies of notes from my visit. I also try to talk with these other clinicians regularly to see what impression they have of the impact of the current medication treatment.

Medications are not a cure-all for children with ADHD. Short-term efficacy of medications has been demonstrated, but not long-term effects. This may be because many secondary problems develop as a result of ADHD that are not helped by these kinds of medications. I discuss a few of these that come up regularly in my therapeutic work with teenagers who have ADHD. They include treatment compliance issues in adolescence, self-esteem issues, family struggles, drug abuse, and severe behavioral disturbances.

Treatment Compliance

The issue of adolescents' compliance with treatment is germane to all aspects of therapeutic work. I experience compliance problems around appointment times, scheduling conflicts, medications, and family work. Resistance can be overt: "I'm not taking your damn meds, Doc!" or covert "I ran out and my mother forgot to get it and besides it doesn't taste good." Compliance, or the lack of it, can signal treatment problems—"I'm never coming back here. I'm the cause of all the problems and you don't help"—or treatment progress—"I used to not take the medicine, but pretend I did. I still don't take it. It scares me to take those pills."

When I feel I am having a problem with compliance with the teenager, I first evaluate the situation in terms of its meaning, then likely etiology; last, I try to change the behavior. Here's an example of this process:

One young man who had severe ADHD suddenly dropped out of treatment after having attended sessions for several months. He had, by all reports, benefited from his treatment. When I called his home, his mother was shocked to find that he hadn't been coming. When confronted, he had little to say, but did agree to come to his next appointment.

He did come—about ten minutes late—and reluctantly told me what was up. It turned out that he had recently made friends with another boy at school who also had ADHD and his friend had convinced him that he should stop seeing me. My evaluation of the meaning of this for the young man was that his need for approval from his peer was so important to him that he was willing to jeopardize his own progress to have it. This fit well for him because he had been ridiculed and unpopular all through elementary school and was very anxious that he not have that experience again. He was able to see that the approval of this one friend might lead to a recurrence of the behaviors that had caused his earlier unpopularity and decided to continue treatment.

Other ways that compliance problems commonly reveal themselves are in transference reactions to the authority of the clinician in lieu of that of the parents. Other times, the narcissistic injury of the illness becomes too great for teenagers to tolerate and they rebel against it by being noncompliant. I find that several of these issues can be operative at once.

Self-Esteem

In noting that narcissistic injury can lead to noncompliance, as in the vignette above, I am also suggesting something of the importance of self-esteem management in working with teenagers who have ADHD. I find that most teenagers I work with are readily capable of ranging from grandiose exaggeration of their capacities to anxiety-ridden depreciation of their gifts. Teenagers who have a psychiatric illness are particularly vulnerable to veering into a negative appraisal.

Teenagers who have ADHD often have a history of school failure, social failure, and problems at home. One very bright sixteen-year-old with ADHD said that ADHD "has ruined my life" and from his experience at the time, he was not far off the mark.

When I work with self-esteem issues in teens with ADHD, several key points almost always recur. The first is usually concerned with academic failure. This may be disguised or actively denied, but the shame associated with difficulty or failure in this area is usually long-standing. To address the problem, I try to put ADHD in perspective as an illness. This is tricky at times because the idea of having an illness is rarely more acceptable than the school problems to most teenagers. Still, if I can initiate the idea of recovery or rehabilitation, I find that teens invest more in the hope that things can change at school. I also use feedback from external sources—like teachers' reports and grades—to mark progress.

There are often dramatic improvements at school that teachers report after a student begins treatment; however, the presence of learning disabilities and negative patterns of behavior might still persist, so an effort to evaluate and assist with these is also important. When they are present, I develop a program with teachers to address them. This might involve specialized instruction or alternative work at times.

Sometimes these teens feel especially isolated at school. Their history of being called "dummies" and being ostracized fuels both anger and depression. Families and teachers can work together to address this isolation. I always recommend that the family meet with teachers to help them understand the child's problems. I also volunteer to speak to teachers myself. Some teachers have a hard time accepting the diagnosis of ADHD in adolescents, so some educating can go a long way toward improving their working relationship with such students. It is also important to support alternative learning strategies that help students with ADHD to succeed. Often this requires assistance from special education instructors who know such techniques as overlearning and repetitive patterning approaches for mastering academic material. As a therapist, I try to help the teen with the frustration and anger involved with having to do this "extra work" because of the attentional problems.

Another common area where self-esteem issues and ADHD collide is the result of chronic peer relationship problems and rejection. I use several different approaches to this. In individual work I emphasize the opportunity for a change in how peers relate to one another in adolescence compared to earlier years. Encouraging and supporting teens to try out new opportunities and ways of relating is my fundamental strategy, as opposed to interpretation or confrontation.

I also try to involve the more difficult cases in group therapy with other teens. Not all members of the group need to have ADHD, but it helps for the teen not to be the only one. The adolescent with ADHD can also benefit from social skills training and groups to assist with changing how they interact with other age-mates and thereby improve their overall social functioning. Especially when an adolescent is between fifteen and seventeen years old, when peer relations are paramount, the use of group therapy with patients who have ADHD can help improve their lowered self-esteem.

Family Therapy

Even if medication and individual and group therapy help, families must deal with the residual patterns, expectations, and negative attitudes that have accumulated over the years. In these cases, family therapy can be useful in helping the family to understand and support the teen with ADHD as well as work through some of the feelings that may be present about the high level of energy that these children require from parents.

I often work with families in which ADHD behaviors have been experienced as the norm for a number of years. In these cases there may often be a feeling of exhaustion and hopelessness about any possibility of change. Such comments as "He is impossible. He has been since he was three years old. He was hyperactive in the womb!" have been said to me by parents during many evaluations. With this in mind, I try to spend time alone with the parents early in the treatment, to help them express these negative feelings. I find that if I don't do this, the overwhelming negativity derails any therapeutic opportunity now available. I have had teenagers storm out of family sessions never to return, so I am careful about trying to download these negative feelings before bringing the whole family together.

When I do bring in the family as a whole for therapy, I set a number of ground rules. The first is that we are working on current issues, not the past. I let them know that I will help them to keep this task in mind. In addition, depending on the level of sophistication of the family, I may start with educational and cognitive instructive sessions where I try to help the family to better understand ADHD. For example, I will talk about the history of the illness, discuss how this has nothing to do with intelligence or being good or bad, how medications help, and so on. This often sets a tone of a shared enterprise that makes it possible to move past the negatives and entertain the possibility of change.

If I am able to get the family to see the possibility of change, I usually work on an assignment model that will allow them to explore or test for improvements. For example, I will ask them to track or chart a particular behavior that causes problems, such as leaving things half finished, constantly interrupting, or not following through on a requested chore. This cognitive strategy has the advantage of being measurable and reinforcing. Of course, there have been occasions when this backfires. At these times, I retrace my steps and look for something else to chart.

Only after the family has been able to understand ADHD and has seen ways that behaviors can change and improve do I begin the process of reintroducing the emotional issues of having a teen with ADHD in the family. At this stage, it is safer to bring out the emotional history that has been kept back while the more therapeutic atmosphere has been created. The issues that have accumulated through years of criticism, feeling like a failure, and experiencing low self-esteem can now be brought to the surface with the family. Even with adequate preparation and education, though, I have had things come apart at this juncture, so I seldom undertake this more in-depth work until I feel that the teen is ready and agrees to try it.

Drug Abuse

Unfortunately, some of the medications used to treat ADHD have street value and this can lead to problems. Sometimes teens sell their medications for money, or give them away to gain popularity with their peers. Sometimes even siblings or parents may steal or borrow the teen's medications. I am very vigilant about this possibility and if I suspect any of the above, I either do not prescribe psychostimulants or do so only in very small amounts. Alternatively, I use medications that have no value to others— such as Cylert or Clonidine.

If the question is bigger than this—that is, if I think that the teen is abusing drugs—I develop a treatment plan to address this. It is not acceptable not to treat ADHD if it is present, so I'll use all the means I have discussed above, try to use medications sparingly, and prescribe only those that are of little or no interest to individuals in the drug culture. Usually, I am a lot less worried about the teens abusing a psychostimulant themselves than I am that they will use it to trade for other drugs. Please see Chapter Three on drug abuse in teenagers for more help with this problem.

Severe Behavioral Problems

Adolescents with ADHD also appear to be at risk for developing Antisocial Personality Disorder but it is unclear whether this is so because of ADHD or other factors. Some studies have shown that problems with Oppositional/Defiant Behavior and Conduct Disorder were present at the time of initial diagnosis in those who later developed Antisocial Personality Disorder. If this was not the case, their risk for developing Antisocial Personality Disorder was no greater than normal. My approach to working with this aspect of treating teens with ADHD differs little from what follows in the section on Oppositional/Defiant Disorder and Conduct Disorder.

Oppositional/Defiant and Conduct Disorders

Gangs and teen crime are often in the headlines. Many people see this growing population of teenagers in trouble as evidence of a society falling apart. Most reports focus on teenagers who seem to have little hope or direction for the future. Other reports in the last few years have cited a trend toward increasing use of psychiatric hospitals and medications to try to control these teenagers. Reports of success and failure of the programs are still preliminary. What is evident from these kinds of reports is a growing use of jails, prison, detention facilities, and psychiatric facilities to contain, limit, and perhaps help these troubled teenagers.

Aggressive and delinquent behavior has long been a part of mental health concerns. Unfortunately, there has also been a great deal of disagreement and confusion over how best to think about these kinds of problems. Today, the most severe forms of this behavior in adults is called Antisocial Personality Disorder, while in younger children and adolescents it is called Oppositional/Defiant Disorder and Conduct Disorder.

In many ways Oppositional/Defiant Disorder (ODD) can be considered a precursor to Conduct Disorder as Conduct Disorder is considered a precursor for Antisocial Personality Disorder. As with Conduct and Antisocial Personality Disorders, Oppositional/Defiant Disorder does not necessarily develop into Conduct Disorder.

Diagnosis

The DSM-IV describes ODD as a recurrent problem with defiance, disobedience, and hostility toward authority figures. Problems with these behaviors must last at least six months and include at least four of the following: often loses temper; often argues with adults; defies authority; deliberately annoys people; blames others for own mistakes; is touchy, angry and resentful, spiteful, and vindictive. In addition to six months' duration, these behaviors cannot occur exclusively during a mood disorder or psychosis. The behaviors must lead to impairment in school, home, or social functioning.

The etiology of Oppositional/Defiant Disorder is not known. It is supposed that the genetic, familial, and social injuries are less than those associated with Conduct Disorder (CD). Here's an example of a typical presentation of a teen with Oppositional/Defiant Disorder.

BILLY

Billy was aggressive with peers starting as early as three years of age. He hit his little sister and challenged his mother and father on every point. He was sent home from friends' houses on a regular basis as a result of fighting or disobeying rules. He was sent home from several preschools and did not do any better in kindergarten. Billy often was a bully at school but whined and complained about how others treated him. He said the teacher didn't like him and that she taught him wrong.

Billy's teacher asked for a conference with his parents and she discussed with them the problems Billy was having. She suggested that he be taken out of school and perhaps started again in a year when she hoped he would be more mature. Billy's parents listened to these reports with an increasing understanding that Billy's problems might need more help than time alone could provide. They sought out the advice of a behavioral therapist and a family therapist who together worked out a treatment plan for Billy that would assist him through a positive reward system and also help the family find more effective ways to manage him.

Conduct disordered teenagers lie, steal, cheat, destroy property, and struggle with authority—parental, school, and societal. The number of teenagers affected by the disorder is unclear. Estimates vary by country, socioeconomic status, and geographical locales—city versus rural settings. Estimates run from about 4 percent in rural settings to 8 percent in cities, with an overall rate of 6 percent.

No one is sure what causes these problems of conduct. Some studies have suggested a genetic basis. Researchers holding this view suggest that aggression might be heritable. Chemical problems in the brain have also been implicated, but no hard evidence is available for either of these possible etiologies.

Psychological and social reasons for these behavior problems have also been considered. Some theorists believe that aggression can result from attempts by teenagers to avoid feeling powerless or helpless. Others believe that such teenagers might be trying to cope with a past trauma. Certainly psychological factors play a role in maintaining conduct disordered behaviors even in the face of powerful incentives to change.

Social theorists have suggested that poverty, abuse, neglect, and poor parenting all contribute to the development of conduct disorders. Parents of conduct disordered teenagers have often been found to be severe disciplinarians, irritable and demanding, with few abilities to empathize with their children's experience. They have also been noted to suffer in a greater-than-expected degree from psychiatric disorders, especially depression and psychotic disorders. Substance use and abuse is also a common part of these adolescents' family history. Other specific factors that have been identified include parental deviance and criminality, poor parenting, marital discord, and large family size.

Taken together, a variety of possible pathways lead to a teenager's developing a conduct disorder. A genetic vulnerability, compounded by an abusive and neglectful upbringing, with few models for coping with stresses other than through violence and substance abuse, combined with a psychological unwillingness to manage these stresses in other ways, converge in the teenager with Conduct Disorder.

The DSM-IV organizes the diagnosis of Conduct Disorder in a new way—each new addition of this manual has made fairly significant revisions in diagnostic criteria for this disorder, suggesting that it remains in many ways one of the more difficult to define using the descriptive approach of the DSM. In this iteration, in addition to demonstrating a repetitive pattern of behaviors that infringe on the basic rights of others, the child or teenager must be doing so in at least three ways over a twelve-month period and at least one of those ways must have been present in the most recent six months. The behaviors are grouped under four major types with a total of fifteen possible specific behaviors. The groups are aggression toward people or animals, destruction of property, deceitfulness or theft, and serious violation of rules. These behaviors must also lead to an impairment of social, academic, or work functions.

Although few younger children meet the criteria for Conduct Disorder—most are in late childhood or early adolescence and few have an onset after age sixteen—the behaviors that ultimately result in a diagnosis of this disorder can be traced back to earliest childhood. In the youngest age group—three to six years old—parents report argumentativeness, stubbornness, and temper tantrums. As the child enters school, more oppositional behaviors are noted and fire-setting and stealing may begin. Some girls may have a late onset of Conduct Disorder that is usually associated with promiscuity and alcohol and substance use in the early teens.

Many teenagers who are diagnosed with conduct disorder have other psychiatric problems as well. Some of the most common include major depression, schizophrenia, substance abuse, Anxiety Disorder, Attention Deficit/Hyperactivity Disorder, and Posttraumatic Stress Disorder. These other psychiatric problems complicate the diagnosis and treatment of Conduct Disorder, but sometimes treatment of them goes a long way toward helping to resolve the Conduct Disorder as well.

Diagnostic Examples

Here are two case examples that demonstrate something of the range of behaviors and presentations consistent with a diagnosis of Conduct Disorder.

MATTHEW

Matthew was always in trouble. He began stealing in the second grade, had been held back two years in elementary school, and now was failing ninth grade. He seldom went to class and had a small group of similarly minded peers who smoked dope and drank together. He had been arrested twice for assault and once for breaking into a storage locker. Matthew lived with his single mom and his two younger sisters. Matthew's father had disappeared about five years before. He had been a harsh disciplinarian and drank to excess. Matthew had been sent many times to see the school counselor, but he was silent or openly hostile to any help offered there. Matthew's mother was at her wit's end and called her brother to take Matthew to Oregon to live with him on his farm. While there, Matthew burned the barn and ran away in a car he stole from a neighbor.

I met Matthew in a juvenile hall. He related his story casually and openly, but continued to refuse psychiatric assistance. He was released from juvenile hall when all charges were dropped against him. He and his family refused all follow-up or referral.

MAGGIE

Maggie had matured early and had started dating by age thirteen, usually much older guys. She used drugs and alcohol frequently and had on occasion exchanged her body for favors or money. Maggie shoplifted regularly, had been arrested, and had spent several weeks in juvenile detention. She had fights with her female peers—usually over a boy—and broke curfew on a regular basis. Maggie lived with an aunt who had raised her since her mother had disappeared shortly after Maggie turned three. The aunt had never been able to discipline Maggie and suffered from depression herself. Maggie ran away from home and lived on the street for a time. While staying in a shelter, she was approached by a social worker to see if she would be interested in finding other teenagers on the streets who needed help. Maggie was hesitant at first but agreed and found herself feeling useful and helpful. Gradually she stopped using drugs altogether and worked in a soup kitchen and shelter to get by.

TREATING SEVERE BEHAVIORAL PROBLEMS IN TEENAGERS

Treating severe behavioral problems in teenagers takes patience, persistence, creativity, and hope. The approaches I describe in this section are ones that I employ and that work most of the time for me. Many therapists are reluctant to take on such teens, but I have found them to be among the most rewarding to work with when I do find a way to engage them in therapy.

Treating Oppositional/Defiant Disorder

Approach to the treatment of ODD is usually multifaceted. Medications are not indicated unless the child also has another psychiatric disorder. Some of the most common ones that such a child might experience are depression, ADHD, and anxiety disorders. If these other psychiatric conditions are treated, many of the ODD behaviors dissipate in intensity in some cases.

The mainstay of treatment for ODD is individual and family therapy. I find that in individual therapy with an oppositional child, the first hurdle is making a treatment alliance with the patient. This sometimes requires extraordinary patience and perseverance on the part of the therapist. I have had to tolerate tantrums, name calling, and worse. Sometimes it simply does not seem to be possible, but when it is, much progress can be made when the underlying issues—usually feelings of inadequacy, powerlessness, and poor self-esteem—are brought out in the safe environment of play therapy, or supportive or insight talk therapy. I can illustrate this with an example.

TOM

Tom first came to see me when he was eleven years old and I continued to see him for about two years on a weekly basis. His divorced, single-parent mother brought him in because of worsening disobedience and escalating complaints from his teacher. When I came in to greet him he made a face and turned away in his chair. He did eventually come to my office after being coaxed by the idea of possibly getting to play with things there. Once inside, though, he quickly lost interest in almost everything and sat spinning in an office chair throwing bits of construction paper about the room.

I spent this and the next five to eight sessions tolerating his behavior and setting only necessary limits of safety. My goal was to let him know that I would listen to him and even tolerate some misbehavior without getting angry at him, but at the same time making certain that we were both safe and my office not destroyed. I did this by playing games with him and complimenting him on his abilities, steering clear at all times from critical appraisals of any limitations. I find that games in this kind of patient are a particularly good tool because the analogy of following rules ultimately fits nicely into the struggles they are having.

As time passed, Tom's capacity for using insight increased. He was also better able to comment on his own behavior. Throughout this process, I maintained a warm, but neutral position. What Tom had too much of was criticism. He had more or less determined that he was a hopelessly bad character, so why bother? My interest and support was experienced by him as less conflicted than that of his mother and my demands on him were comparatively less burdensome as well. As a result, he was able to see that he could perform well and even make mistakes without having to get into a power struggle with me.

This last point is the key to individual work with oppositional defiant persons: stay out of the power struggle. Opportunities will abound to get into it and the therapist may be sorely tempted—especially when picking up paper wads off the floor after the patient has flown the coop. Patience, clear boundaries, and toleration of some negative behavior are critical.

Progress in individual therapy of children with ODD is usually limited by the issues that have likely generated much of the problem in the first place. Families are unreliable and don't bring the child to scheduled appointments, pull them from treatment, move from place to place, and do not or cannot invest in their child's treatment. Enlisting families in the work is therefore key to any possible success with the ODD child. Again, this is not an easy thing to do. In order to begin building such an alliance, I start with educational material about behavioral problems. Next, I move to a discussion of disciplinary practices in the home. Finally, I approach how parental histories and emotional problems may contribute to the teenager's behavioral difficulties. Let me continue with Tom as our example.

Tom's mother worked to support the two of them. She appeared harried and depressed in our interview. She was extremely critical of Tom and described him as uncaring and unappreciative. It was clear her own emotional needs were not being very well met. She described her disciplinary style as "strict," but in fact what she described was an inconsistent pattern—being lenient when she was too tired and extremely punitive at other times. She described using long time-outs when he was young, and now restricting him to home for months on end.

In my work with Tom's mother I found myself up against both her personal history of having had poor parenting herself and her ingrained set of negative expectations and appraisals. In some ways the teen with ODD has a "bad reputation" and—as when working with an adolescent with ADHD—we try to establish a new starting point with their parents. Also similar to my work with parents whose children have ADHD, I begin with an educational approach. Usually I give them reading materials on disciplinary strategies and information about how a change in parenting can affect their teenager's behavior. Parents frequently laugh at me, but most of this information is simply tolerated. I refer again to it later when I ask them to attempt some simple strategies. I also reinforce basic principles of discipline: be consistent, be timely, and make the punishment fit the infraction. Of course, I also help them develop a reward system for positive accomplishments, but this takes a bit more trust and that takes a bit more time.

Tom's mother was able to recognize her inconsistency and unreasonable punishments. She began to work on this in family sessions by negotiating with Tom around the behaviors that bothered her and deciding together with him what was an appropriate consequence. More important, we developed a positive reinforcement plan that involved Tom's earning increased freedoms for such things as not talking back, doing chores without being asked, and doing his homework. This positive reinforcement plan was reworked several times over the year and the consequences plan was used less and less.

Tom was also able to discuss with his mother some of the feelings he had about not having a father around. He felt it was too much for him to take care of her, but still felt he should. His mother acknowledged that she did need him a lot, but that she could take care of herself and would make an effort to do better at it so he didn't feel so much pressure to do so. At this point Tom's self-esteem and confidence had improved markedly and his behavior problems were well within the normal range.

Laying the groundwork for family therapy through education, a concrete behavioral plan, and reviewing and revising those plans made it possible for a deeper trust to develop between Tom and his mother. This allowed them to take better care of themselves and each other.

Sometimes families with teens with ODD want a quick fix and ask for a "pill" to cure their child—usually a psychostimulant like Ritalin. This can be a real dilemma for the therapist. The patient may indeed have ADHD, but the family structure may be one where the medication might be misused either by overmedicating the child or by one of the adults using or selling the medication. Sometimes an arrangement can be made to work with the school to dispense the medication, but most often a medication with less street value and no immediate high should be used—such as Cylert or an antidepressant.

The prognosis of children with ODD depends a great deal on how they respond to the continuing demands of adolescence and their changing capacities to manage the stresses in their lives with intellectual and emotional insight. Sometimes they do grow out of it in this way. Those who make successful alliances with therapists and experience a more nurturing and supportive relationship with an authority figure—like a big brother or surrogate father figure—also stand a better chance of making the transition to more successful social functioning. Those who progress to Conduct Disorder have a poorer prognosis.

Treating Conduct Disorder

Treatment of Conduct Disorder is at this time an unproven territory. Studies of hospital interventions, medications, family work, and individual and group psychotherapies have not been proven. Any of these or a combination of them might help in a specific case, but none is guaranteed.

Acute Management

Often when I receive a referral of a teen with Conduct Disorder, there is an acute crisis. Someone has been beaten up, the school has expelled the adolescent, or the police have placed the teenager under arrest. In my experience there often needs to be a cooling off period. Sometimes the courts arrange this for you. Other times relatives can take the teen into their home for a brief period. In some communities there are crisis homes available for these kinds of emergencies and their use can prevent hospitalization. Often, though, psychiatric hospitalization is needed.

Hospitalization of adolescents with Conduct Disorder has been a major type of treatment intervention. No studies have proven it to be beneficial in the long run, but it does allow for a certain amount of control and some opportunity to evaluate the teenager more carefully than is possible in an outpatient setting. In some cases, it's the only way to approach chaotic social and family situations.

If it's a new patient or information is hard to get, hospitalization can also be critical in helping to identify other psychiatric illnesses that can be more effectively treated. The behaviors that teenagers with Conduct Disorder sometimes engage in can put themselves and others around them at serious risk, so the hospital may be the only place that's safe for a period. I do not hesitate to use hospitalization in the initial phase of treatment when there is a clear danger to the teen. I try to use it sparingly as treatment progresses, because in my experience there are usually diminishing returns with subsequent hospitalization.

A stay in a psychiatric hospital for a teen with Conduct Disorder can be challenging for everyone involved. Most often the hospitalization is against the teen's wishes and much of the initial part of treatment is my attempt to work with the anger and injury associated with this. In order to build a rapport with such teenagers, I approach them respectfully and attend carefully to any limitations they set. I set my expectations fairly low. Just getting them to meet briefly in a somewhat cordial way can be a major accomplishment.

My goals for therapy in such a setting are also limited. I want to get as much information as I can and to settle the acute situation down sufficiently for the teen to return home. When these criteria are met and if there are no other psychiatric illnesses that require acute intervention in the hospital, I discharge the youth to a less acute setting for care as soon as possible. Sometimes I will initiate a medication trial in the hospital, which we'll discuss in a later section.

Adolescents with Conduct Disorder cannot generalize the structure of the hospital and its interventions and apply them to their lives. In other words, a hospitalization will not cure a teen with Conduct Disorder. External structure does not automatically become internalized no matter how long the stay or how good the therapy. Instead, hospitalization is an acute intervention in the context of an extended intervention plan that includes the use of almost all modes of intervention at one time or another. Sometimes it even includes stays at juvenile halls. These are often viewed by families and therapists as failures, but in my experience they can precipitate a crisis that leads to the start of meaningful work for the first time.

Medication

A variety of medications have been tried—almost all classes of psychotropics including neuroleptics, mood stabilizers, and benzodiazipines. Neuroleptics and mood stabilizers have been the most promising in managing acute and chronic irritability and aggression. Teenagers with Conduct Disorder are rarely compliant with medication approaches, however, and are therefore unusually poor candidates. Sometimes medications can be a helpful addition to other approaches.

I use the same basic strategies that I use with ADHD teens to enlist them in the use of medications: empowerment, consent, information, and careful follow-up with special attention to side effects.

Individual Therapy

Most teenagers with Conduct Disorder do not take kindly to mental health professionals. For a variety of reasons they usually prefer to identify with their peer groups and anything that might stigmatize them—like mental health treatment—is particularly unacceptable. Therefore I approach individual work with conduct disordered teens judiciously.

Many times these teens are likeable and can make a very good first impression. I have been fooled by their charms. Still, if they can be engaged, it is usually by appealing to their narcissism. Although they may act tough, they usually are quite fragile emotionally and feel insecure about almost every aspect of themselves. I keep this in mind in each interaction to keep my anger in check at some of the noxious things they say or do. An example of how I worked with one fifteen-year-old boy may serve to demonstrate how I approached this:

T Y

Ty was a handsome boy. He was fastidious in his clothing and could be especially charming when he wanted. He also was volatile, constantly fighting at school and running away from the group home where he had lived since he was removed from his mother's care at age eleven. I met Ty when he was hospitalized for beating up another peer in his group home and for depression with suicidal ideation.

Ty refused to see me at first. I persisted and made myself available to him at several different times during the day. This made him feel special and valued, something he seldom experienced, so he eventually agreed to meet. He said he had nothing to say. Life was trash. He was going to get a gun and steal a sports car and get a girlfriend to run away with.

In this case, I used a device not always available but one that turned out to be helpful. A student who wanted to observe therapy was rotating in the hospital so I asked her to join us. I explained to Ty that she needed to learn about teens and that together he and I could teach her. This appealed to his narcissism and also empowered him in a way that made him feel less vulnerable. He was teaching this grown-up. From that point forward, sessions were more lively as Ty shared much of what his inner experience was like. We were able to build a significant enough rapport that he was willing to try a mood stabilizing medication. These two interventions along with some work with the group home staff helped to stabilize Ty and he was able to return to school. His outpatient therapist picked up where we had left off and Ty continued to make progress.

Group Work

Teenagers with Conduct Disorder who refuse or fail individual therapy may do better in teen groups. I would note, though, that many times the problems they have with authority and bullying make them difficult group members. In addition, I find myself always walking a fine line therapeutically—one needs to confront the teenagers about their behavior but also be prepared to deal with rapid and sometimes severe decompensations. This requires that the therapist be able to support and challenge at the same time. The following short example illustrates this.

BILL

Bill is a seventeen-year-old with Conduct Disorder who had been hospitalized twice and been in juvenile hall once. He had started individual therapy but began skipping sessions more often than he attended. To try to keep him in treatment, I proposed a trial of group therapy. He was reluctant but agreed, partly because he had enough rapport with me for him to feel that I was invested in his future. He agreed because he didn't want to disappoint me and partly because he thought it might "be better than talking in this office."

The group Bill attended was one with teens who were recovering from depression, anxiety, and family problems as well as other behavioral problems. He started off by arriving late to his first meeting. He then monopolized the conversation. He interrupted others and made comments under his breath. In short, he did all he could do to be rejected. The group was patient with him, though, and at first put up with his behavior. It's possible he took the heat off the others, which some didn't mind for a while. Bill enjoyed the attention and being allowed center stage so he kept coming.

During about the fourth group session, I asked the group to talk generally about how they experienced one another. This allowed some members to express their anger at Bill for how he treated the group. Bill defended himself and threatened to leave. They encouraged him to stay and listen. Bill managed to stay, but skipped the next two weeks.

Bill returned and made excuses for his missing two weeks. Someone asked why he came back. He was truly surprised by the question. He wasn't sure. This allowed me to facilitate a discussion of why anyone came to the group. In this context, Bill was able to acknowledge that he recognized that the group had "put up with his obnoxiousness," but had also let him know how they experienced it in a way that he could hear. Bill's work in the group became more personal after this. Bill had experienced the group's confrontation of him as supportive, a shift that allowed him to respond to them with less hostility and defensiveness. This realization allowed him to become more aware of his real need for the group and to begin to value it. Eventually he returned to individual therapy where he was able to be more productive than before.

Family Work

Working with the family system has so far been found the best way to work with these teenagers, with a number of programs demonstrating some success. Unfortunately, the chaotic, abusive, and neglectful nature of these family systems makes traditional family therapy unworkable. Approaches that visit the family and do interventions in the home setting have had more success.

In other respects, working with families or parents with adolescents who are conduct disordered differs little from the principles I use in working with families of teens who have ADHD or Oppositional/Defiant Disorder. I would say, though, that my experience supports the research findings—that even more patience, flexibility, and creativity will be required to create a therapeutic family environment.

Prognosis

The prognosis for teenagers with conduct disorders might be presumed to be particularly poor. In some ways it is and other ways it is not. Only about 25 percent of such teenagers go on to develop adult Antisocial Personality Disorder, which might be the worst long-term outcome. Nonetheless, it is clear that even those teenagers with better outcomes grow up to be adults with severe problems. They are subject to other psychiatric disorders—depression, psychotic disorders, and substance abuse in adulthood, marital problems, financial and educational under-achievement, and poor occupational histories.

Perhaps more than with any other group, I feel it is imperative not to succumb to my rescue fantasies. It is not helpful to add my expectations to the list the teen already feels unable to meet. On the other hand, avoidance or hopelessness are not helpful therapeutic stances, either. We do not yet know exactly who among these adolescents will get better, but some will get a little better, some a lot better, and some will recover fully. My current markers for therapeutic hope include a treatable co-morbid psychiatric diagnosis, past trauma, and an intact family. Any one of these makes me more optimistic about my ability to work effectively with a particular adolescent.

Working with adolescents with behavioral problems can be unusually rewarding. Their recoveries can be dramatic and inspiring. For the most part, though, keeping an eye on the bigger picture and the extended plan is required to prevent feeling overwhelmed or disappointed about a current downturn. Expect to "be had" from time to time—it's part of the deal when you work with these teens. Persistence, even tenacity, along with patience, flexibility, and a general attitude that is firm and warm but that allows for challenges, demands, and limit setting is crucial to successful treatment of teens.

NOTES

P. 49, *The most common one*: Connors, C. K. (1985). Rating scales and checklists for psychopharmacology. *Psychopharmacology Bulletin, 21, (1989).* 809–815.

P. 51, *Looking at the problem*: Bukstein, O. G., Brent, D. A., & Kaminer, Y. (1989). Comorbidity of substance abuse and other psychiatric disorders in adolescents. *American Journal of Psychiatry, 146*(9), 1136–1137.

P. 59, *Some studies have shown that*: Gittelman-Klein, R., & Mannuzza, S. (1987). Hyperactive boys almost grown up, III. *Archives of General Psychiatry, 45,* 1131–1134.

P. 60, *Reports of success and failure*: Lock, J., & Strauss, G. (1994, October). Psychiatric hospitalization of adolescents with conduct disorder. *Hospital and Community Psychiatry,* pp. 925–928.

P. 62, *Estimates run from*: Bailey, G. W., & Egan, J. H. (1989). Conduct disorders. In J. M. Oldam et al. (Eds.), *Review of Psychiatry* (Vol. 8, pp. 182–186). Washington, DC: American Psychiatric Association Press.

P. 62, *Other specific factors*: Offord, D. R. (1989). Conduct disorder: Risk factors and prevention. In D. Shaffer et al. (Eds.), *Prevention of mental disorders, alcohol, and other drugs* (pp. 273–307). Washington, DC: U.S. Department of Health and Human Services.

P. 63, *The DSM-IV organizes: Diagnostic and statistical manual of mental disorders* (pp. 90–91). Washington, DC: American Psychiatric Association Press.

P. 63, *Some girls may have*: Robins, L. N. (1991). Conduct disorder. *Journal of Child Psychology and Psychiatry, 32,* 192–212.

P. 69, *Treatment of Conduct Disorder*: Offord, D. R., & Bennett, K. J. (1994). Conduct disorder: Long-term outcomes and intervention effectiveness. *Journal of the American Academy of Child and Adolescent Psychiatry, 33*(8), 1069–1078.

P. 74, *Working with the family*: Patterson, G. R., Chamberlain, P., & Reid, J. B. (1982). A comparative evaluation of a parent training program. *Behavior Therapy, 13,* 638–650.

3

SUBSTANCE USE AND ABUSE

Rebecca A. Powers and Robert Matano

"Crash Kills 8 Contra Costa Youths. 2 injured as pickup, 4-wheel-drive vehicle collide; beer containers found at accident scene." Eight young teenagers and adults from the age of 15 to 21 were killed in a head-on collision when they swerved into oncoming traffic while traveling about 60 mph, none of them with seat belts. One victim's brother was stunned: "I don't know how it happened. We always have a designated driver. It was a freak accident. I love my brother, man. I loved all of them. They were good people." The California Highway Patrol Sergeant at the scene, Barry Koven said, "When you've got teens of your own, it gets to you."

Alcohol and other drugs contribute to and often are the reasons for the three major causes of death to young people in the age group of fifteen to twenty-four years. In the United States of America, accidents are the leading cause of deaths in adolescents. Motor vehicle accidents, falls, fires, drownings, and poisonings are the main types of accidents, and many of these occur when the teenagers are under the influence of alcohol and other drugs. Of all adolescents who die, more than 30 percent are killed in motor vehicle accidents. Half of those accidents involve a person who is driving under the influence of alcohol.

Homicide and suicide are the second and third causes for these tragic losses. More specifically, homicide is the second most frequent cause of death in all adolescents, and suicide is the second most frequent cause of death in *white* adolescents. Alcohol and other drugs play a primary role in homicides and suicides. Fist and gun fights, self-hangings, overdoses, and other violent actions erupt under the disinhibiting effects and changes in perception created by alcohol and other drugs. Completed adolescent suicide has tripled in the last thirty years, and 50 percent to 70 percent of those suicide victims had a history of substance abuse as well.

There *is* a problem here. Alcohol and other drug use in adolescents is a major public health problem, for it leads to devastating effects on millions of individuals, families, communities, and the U.S. economy. Moreover, alcohol and other drugs contribute to the formation of other severe psychiatric problems, such as mental health disorders, school dropouts, delinquency, and incarceration. Given that this is a national crisis, it is tragically under- or undiagnosed.

Many of these victims with abuse problems have been in contact with a health care provider within the last year. But these providers are missing the diagnosis. Even though schools, social services, and the courts are the most likely referral sources, they still do not do an adequate job in detection. Primary care professionals, and *all* health professionals, have key roles in prevention and treatment, and they must incorporate screening as part of the routine history.

EPIDEMIOLOGY

A series of studies beginning in 1975, including the Monitoring the Future surveys and the National Household Survey on Drug Abuse (NHSDA), examined trends in the use of illicit drugs *other than alcohol and cigarettes* by young people in the United States. The Monitoring the Future surveys are done yearly in high schools with seniors, and the NHSDA is a periodic survey of households across the United States. A key trend noted was a long-term decrease in the number of America's youth using drugs. The peak of annual use (drugs used *in the past year*) of any illicit drug in high school seniors was in 1979, when 54 percent reported use. By 1991, that figure had dropped to 29 percent; this is still a huge number of adolescents, but at least it's a number that is decreasing. Lifetime prevalence was the highest in 1982, at 66 percent, meaning that two-thirds of that graduating class had used *sometime in their life*. In 1991, the number was 44 percent—so it is dropping. On the other hand, lifetime prevalence of alcohol use in seniors of today is over 90 percent, and most seniors have smoked cigarettes as well.

The National High School Senior Drug Abuse Survey of the 1994 Monitoring the Future study shows a rise in illicit drug use among eighth, tenth, and twelfth graders. The increase is most dramatic for marijuana, with use by eighth graders at 16.7 percent compared to 12.6 percent in 1993. Increases are also shown in the use of lysergic acid diethylamide (LSD) and other hallucinogens overall, inhalants, stimulants, barbiturates, steroids, alcohol, cocaine, and crack cocaine. Emergency room visits for drug-related incidents have also increased. The rise is secondary to teens' beliefs that the drugs are not dangerous. In fact, only about half our youth think there is any danger in using marijuana occasionally and trying cocaine, phencyclidine (PCP), or heroin.

Illicit drugs for adolescents are different from those for adults. Illicit substances are controlled substances. Alcohol and tobacco are recognized as licit or legal chemicals for adult consumption, but not for adolescents in most jurisdictions. Therefore, when reference is made to illicit substances in this review of use by adolescents, alcohol and tobacco are automatically included. Additionally, please refer to the *Diagnostic and Statistical Manual of Mental Disorders*, Fourth Edition (DSM-IV) by the American Psychiatric Association, 1994, for the definitions of the different types of abuse and dependence disorders for the various types of drugs. You should also be familiar with each street drug, its common street name, and its effects.

So What Drugs Are We Talking About?

Marijuana is the most prevalent illicit drug, other than alcohol or cigarettes, used by high school seniors. In 1979, 51 percent of seniors reported use in the past year, but in 1991 that amount decreased to 24 percent. Today, the number is increasing again, and the marijuana used now is ten times more potent than that used in the 1960s and 1970s. If an adolescent uses marijuana, the chance that he or she will also use cocaine increases by eight times. Major point: there is no such thing as "just marijuana." Marijuana use *is* a big deal in adolescence.

In the late 1980s and early 1990s, high school seniors used some drugs less than they did in the 1970s. This list includes marijuana, cocaine, amphetamines, barbiturates, hallucinogens including LSD, and opiates including heroin, codeine, opium, Demerol, and morphine. The decrease over the years in use of the above drugs is secondary to the perceived risk of harm associated with regular use. Because of education, the annual prevalence of use has gone down since 1978, as the perceived risk went up, but the perceived availability remained about the same.

Legal psychoactive substances that are used illicitly by adolescents include over-the-counter stimulants, which are used like amphetamines. The use of these stay-awake pills, which often contain phenylpropanolamine or caffeine, has nearly doubled from an annual prevalence of 12 percent in 1982 to 22 percent in 1991. Anabolic steroids are also abused by adolescents, not to get high, but to get big. About 2.1 percent of mostly male seniors reported a lifetime prevalence of use.

After adolescence, nicotine will cause more deaths for today's teens than other drugs. In 1991, high school seniors used cigarettes more each day than any other substance (18.5 percent compared to 3.6 percent who drank alcohol daily, 2 percent who smoked marijuana daily, and 0.2 percent who used other drugs on a daily basis). Cigarette smoking has declined since 1977 when 29 percent of the seniors smoked daily, but this decline is still smaller than one would expect given the publicity against the habit in several recent years.

Even though a "war on drugs" like crack and heroin has been declared, and lost, alcohol has always been and is still the most often abused drug in the adolescent age group, and consequences of alcohol use result in more deaths in adolescents than all the other drugs combined. Although daily use is relatively infrequent, episodic or binge drinking is much higher: about one-third of teenagers reported drinking five or more drinks in a row once or more during the last two weeks of the interview in 1991. And over 90 percent of high school seniors have used alcohol at some time. So remember, it can take just one time to cause that "freak accident."

Keeping up with these data is important. The knowledge lets us in the mental health and education professions know the points to push. We would be foolish to ignore the trends and wait placidly as the patients come knocking on our doors. If we don't fulfill our role as educators, for both our individual clients and the community, we are not doing a complete job.

Other Important Characteristics of Today's Adolescent Drug Abuser

Over the last few decades, particular trends have been noted in the demographics of the adolescent alcohol and drug user. These bits of data are important to know if we are going to help our youth with this significant health problem. In the past, for instance, we would not commonly have been suspicious that a nine-year old boy was using drugs, and in an evaluation may not have asked about it readily. Today, it is considered neglectful if a health care professional doesn't ask every child and adolescent about alcohol and drug use.

1. *Age of Initiation.* Retrospective reports from 1975 to 1991 show trends in patterns of age at which initiation of drug use occurred. A very small number of adolescents tried illicit drugs

prior to entering high school in the 1950s, and less than half tried alcohol. The age of initiation is now significantly declining for alcohol and other drugs. It is common for kids to be using by grade nine. Therefore, education and effective preventive strategies must begin early in the schools, home, and community.

2. *Sex Differences.* Male adolescents use illicit drugs more than females, and the differences become greater at the higher frequency levels. This is the general rule except for the use of amphetamines, barbiturates, and tranquilizers, which females use at about the same level as males. Additionally, females use over-the-counter diet pills more than boys, and they use anabolic steroids less than boys. Females beat the males in nicotine use in 1987, but in the early 1990s, males surpassed the girls once again.

3. *Socioeconomic Status Differences by Parental Education.* The use of alcohol and other drugs is about the same across all socioeconomic levels. With higher parental education, there is slightly more marijuana and alcohol usage but slightly less of cigarettes among seniors. Kids that dropped out of school before the twelfth grade are not counted among the seniors. Dropping out tends to be higher among the lower socioeconomic status groups, so if those kids were still in school at the time this study was done, the statistics would be different.

In the eighth grade, significantly less substances are used by the kids whose parents have more education, a finding that would support the above "dropping out" supposition. The children in lower status groups may be more precocious in development and begin taking on adult roles, like using drugs and alcohol, at an earlier age. Moreover, non–college-bound seniors use more of all the illicit drugs, alcohol, and nicotine, than college-bound seniors.

4. *Urban Versus Rural Use.* Illicit drug use has spread widely throughout our nation. The differences were small in 1991 in use of all drugs and alcohol in all types of areas. Addictions to alcohol and other drugs are just as common in the suburbs as in

the ghetto. Regional differences have more variation. Overall, illicit drugs are used less in the South, and alcohol and cigarettes are used less in the South and the West.

5. *Racial and Ethnic Comparisons.* It is very difficult to generalize across minority groups. For example, within the group of Hispanics, there is considerable variation among Mexicans, Puerto Ricans, Cubans, and other Latin Americans. Overall, white high school students report the most use of all substances, followed by the Hispanics. African Americans use alcohol and other drugs the least. However, Hispanics drop out of school more than African Americans or whites. When eighth graders were compared, Hispanics used drugs more than whites, who used more than blacks.

6. *Adolescents Entering Treatment.* Whites who enter treatment lead in the use of multiple drugs, with an average of 4.3 different drugs used regularly. If they use marijuana, which is their primary drug of choice, there is a higher risk for poly-substance use. Most who use marijuana use alcohol. Alcohol is the second most common primary drug of choice for adolescents entering treatment, then amphetamines, and then cocaine. Whites are more likely to use amphetamines, and barbiturates or sedatives, than other races as their primary drug of choice. Hispanics use the low-cost, highly available inhalants.

ETIOLOGY AND RISK FACTORS

We have now covered the who, the what, and the how much. Now we must address the how come. The etiology for alcohol and drug use in adolescents is different from that of adults. We all know some of the major causes of adult use, but most of us are not aware of the causes in adolescents. How can we begin to treat this major health problem if we don't know why it exists?

It is not simply enough to "Say no to drugs." We have to get deeper, or treatment will be futile. This discussion of etiology can get complicated, so we'll try to keep it simple and at the same time hit on the key risk factors. As we do any kind of assessment on an adolescent, we must keep all the following factors in mind. This focus will help us determine whether there is a possibility of a problem, the type of problem(s), and the appropriate type of treatment(s). More specifically, it directs treatment to the main underlying issues important in the life of the adolescents and their families.

Genetic Theories

An inherited component appears to figure in vulnerability to substance abuse. This means some people may suffer a direct effect of substance use by their parents independent of psychosocial variables. Studies of twins, adoptees, and siblings raised apart show a genetic component in the development of alcohol abuse. A major gene effect is likely for some types of alcoholic families, although that gene has not been identified. Data are less conclusive about a genetic cause of other drug abuse.

Alcoholism runs in families, and there is also a close association between alcoholism and other psychiatric illness. Antisocial behavior and a family history of problem drinking are often found together. Conduct Disorder, severe alcoholic complications, mental illness, and sociopathy are more prevalent in relatives of patients who have a strong family history of alcoholism than in problem drinkers without such a history. Family studies also show a link between depression and alcohol dependency.

Male offspring of an alcoholic father have a four to five times greater rate of alcoholism than the general population. Twin studies have reported significant concordance for illness in monozygotic twins of patients with suicidal tendencies, alcoholism, and illicit drug dependency. Adoption and cross-fostering research studies have tried to separate the contributions of nature and nurture by studying individuals reared by people other than their biological parents. These studies have shown significant correlation of the genetic etiology and alcohol abuse, but environmental influences and gene-environment interaction also remain implicated in the genesis of alcohol problems.

Psychosocial and Psychodynamic Theories

In the past, classical theorists have suggested that alcohol and drugs are masturbatory equivalents, a defense against homosexual impulses, or a manifestation of oral regression. Recent theorists, on the other hand, suggest a relationship between substance abuse and depression, a symptom of disturbed ego functions, or a self deficit.

Psychodynamic theorists have suggested that alcoholics have a different background from other drug users. Those with other drug abuse had more childhood trauma and often use substances to self-medicate. Consequently, individual psychotherapy has focused on teaching more healthy types of coping mechanisms to replace the unhealthy ones patients learned just to survive a tough childhood environment.

Psychosocialists suggest that there is a societal role in the formation of a drug culture, and study how that culture impregnates areas of urban poverty. Children are brought into those ways of life at an early age. But there must be other factors, because not all kids who grow up with other drug users end up having that Axis I diagnosis.

Family members have a lot to do with etiology and promotion of the illness. Co-addiction or codependency occurs when one of a couple is responsible for maintaining the addictive behavior of another. The relationship and behavior are perpetuated by both of them, and denial by each supports this unhealthy partnership. Both the enabling and denial must be addressed in treatment.

Are the behaviorists right to suggest a drug-seeking behavior? After all, the behaviorist would argue that we have all the elements for a good behavior principle behind the problem. We have both the positive reinforcing qualities, even after only a one-time use of many drugs, and the adverse effects that can act as deterrents to continued use. A person can distinguish the drug of abuse from those without abusive properties, and there are additional cues associated with alcohol and other drug use.

Psychosocial factors are not easily or clearly understood as an etiology for alcohol or other drug use. Alcohol and other drugs are a swift, convenient, and cheap way to "feel good." If an adolescent has behavioral traits like rebelliousness, delinquency, and poor school performance or social skills, one can easily deal with this by just downing or popping a pill. If there is depression, low self-esteem, anxiety, or lack of self-control, why not put a fast damper on it with something right around the corner? Thrill- and novelty-seeking have been connected in research with the development of alcoholism. If the adolescents believe there is nothing wrong with use of the drug—they're young, impulsive, and daring anyway, and it makes them feel good—they will try it.

Other factors include lack of social responsibility and little religious commitment. Additionally, mental obsessions, emotional compulsions, negative attitudes, rigid defense mechanisms, and delusions can affect the use. If there is little identification with viable role models or family, and inadequate interpersonal skills, such as communication, cooperation, negotiation, empathy, listening, and sharing, a teenager may be more prone to turn to alcohol or other drugs. Weaknesses in judgment come out as crises in sexual, drug, and alcohol environments as a type of self-destruction.

Tie all the above with the mind of an adolescent: "It'll never happen to me. I will just try it, but I won't get hooked." "I'm invincible." "I have no fear."

Psychological Factors. Following is a list of psychological factors that often predate the use of alcohol and other drugs in adolescents. These factors are important in users as opposed to nonusers:

- Some adolescents have psychological disturbances—problems such as affective disorders or anxiety, attention deficit with or without hyperactivity, learning disorders, eating disorders, and psychosis; users may also be victims of physical, sexual, or psychological abuse; they may have thoughts of suicidality, increased seclusion and withdrawal, be more irritable, or have labile moods.

- Adolescents often feel a need to be different from the way they are: they need insight and understanding, they desire a "high" or a "low"; they want to feel less uptight around friends or be more creative; they want less boredom and have more curiosity.

- Adolescents need to "fit in": those who are disabled, are members of a minority, have school problems, look or act a little different from their peers, are smarter, are getting better grades than their buddies, are less bright, excel at sports, or can't do sports well, all could be at greater risk for using.

- Adolescents often have less ability to manage their feelings: they may have difficulty controlling anger, disappointment, or embarrassment.

- Some adolescents may exhibit more antisocial behavior than normal: they may be rebellious and oppositional; they may argue and yell, blame and annoy others, defy rules and regulations, be spiteful and vindictive, give lots of excuses for staying out late, intercept the mail, split parents, sell their own things, steal others', set fires, be cruel to animals, get in fights, use weapons, run away from home, destroy others' property, become more defensive, be abusive to others, or have to deal with pregnancy.

- Adolescents may have difficult personality factors: these may be low self-esteem, lack of self-control, less maturity, alienation from conventional goals, or a high tolerance for fighting and lying.

These tendencies can all be displayed with physical signs of the disturbance such as sleeping more, appearing to be in worse physical health overall, and undergoing a change in personal appearance. Don't ignore the obvious drunk, high, or low.

Social Factors. Following is a list of social factors that often predate the use of alcohol and other drugs in adolescents. These factors are important in users as opposed to nonusers:

- Unique socioeconomics: the adolescents may be economically disadvantaged (even among the "advantaged," watch out if there are sudden money urgencies)
- Poor school performance: they may have poor grades, spend less time reading, spend less time doing homework, have low value on achievement, or be a dropout.
- Legal problems: these teenagers may exhibit delinquency, criminal activity, or a history of problems with the police.
- Unique and risky peer involvement: they may be involved with gangs, spend lengthy time "hanging out" with peers, or have more satisfaction with the amount of friends or social contact; *initial* substance use is most common from peer interaction than at home, and teens use more if they have using friends (ask specifically about friends and acquaintances); normalization of drug use in peers is also a significant risk factor.

Family Factors. Following is a list of family factors that often predate the use of alcohol and other drugs in adolescents. These factors are important in users as opposed to nonusers:

- Significant negative behaviors in the family: such behaviors include arguments, fights, stealing, conflict, family crisis, or high stress.
- Unique familial situations: mothers and older brothers and sisters have a larger influence than others; other factors

include less shared authority, poorer communication, and less shared problem solving.

- Parental examples and influences:

  Use of alcohol or other drugs in parent

  A teetotaling, overdemanding, or overprotective parent

  Parents that fight normalization of drug experimentation, and use intimidation and threats to get the kid to stop, therefore pushing the child closer toward the using friends, and farther away from the parents

  Adolescent's perception that parents approve of alcohol and drugs

  Absence of a parent

  Excessively passive mothers

  Unconventional parents (stepparent, parent and partner living together unmarried, multiple partners)

  Lack of closeness by parent to child

  Lack of perceived closeness of the adolescent to the parents

  Perception by adolescents of less love and support from parents, especially fathers

  Strict controls imposed by parents or parental disagreement about discipline

  Parents with legal problems or antisocial behaviors

  Discrepancy between how the parents would ideally like their children to be and how they perceive them actually to be

  Use of ineffective coping mechanisms (avoiding anger; having lower competence to display feelings appropriately)

  A greater tolerance for deviance and lower behavioral control

  Continued use more dependent on parental interactions than peer relationships

  Use of alcohol and other drugs as a family coping function (For example, a parent comes home and says "I've had a rough day at work"; as he heads for the refrigerator, he says, "Oh, I really need a beer to relax now." The kids pick up quickly on this quick fix for a hard day.)

Neurochemical Theories

Particular neurotransmitters, neurotransmitter receptors, and pathways have been examined extensively in research and are related to alcohol and other drug dependency. For example, people who either lack endogenous opiate activity or have too much opiate antagonist may be at risk for developing a dependency on opiates. Even when these systems are in balance, if a person uses the opiates for a long time, eventually the receptor systems in the brain can be modified. In due time, the brain could require exogenous sources of opiates just to maintain homeostasis. Tolerance could also be developed in a similar way. Additionally, addiction has been linked with several neurochemical and brain pathways involving the pleasure center. C. Robert Cloninger has studied and found some correlation among certain neurotransmitters related to behavior and different types of alcoholism.

On the other hand, the disease model of addiction is not usually emphasized for adolescents. Physical addiction, loss of control, and health problems related to alcohol and other drugs are not as prevalent for adolescents as for adults. Therefore, the disease model might have little value when abuse or dependency problems in adolescents are being treated.

Multifactorial Basis of Addiction

Our experience has shown that addiction to alcohol and other drugs is a multifactorial problem. It is driven, in various combinations, by all the previous etiologies described. Different people experience different amounts of these etiologies and in different magnitudes, but every individual can have a serious problem regardless of what etiologies are exerting influence. Consequently, in order to be effective helpers, we need to learn as much as we can about the relationship between the client and each type of factor: genetic, physiological, social, environmental, spiritual, or psychodynamic. It is often impossible to separate these multifactorial causes of alcohol and other drug abuse and dependency. The definitive cause is unknown. No particular reason, or cause, applies to any particular drug or alcohol, or any particular user of drugs or alcohol.

The Process of Dependency

In addition to the etiologies and risk factors above, the spiral of addiction and the process of dependency is also a major factor in adolescent alcohol and other drug abuse. Addiction has its own dynamics, which shape the psychological, familial, social, and biological world of the addict. Drug use usually occurs in a sequence of stages. The prior drug stage acts as a possible gateway to the next stage. Users usually progress from legal to illegal, and from less to more serious drugs. These stages are often followed regardless of the user's gender, his or her ethnicity, the size of the community of residence, or the region of the country where the user lives.

Experimentation

The first stage of use is experimentation, when a teen may still be using in a situational or recreational circumstance. Experimental use means just using once or twice with no *intention* of continuation. This is when the adolescent first learns how to use alcohol and other drugs, and the teachers are usually other peers, or occasionally the teen's parents.

The "gateway drugs" are generally the first ones tried, and most often include alcohol—beer or wine, then hard liquor—and cigarettes. Not all these drugs are used before the experimenter goes on to the next types, but at least one is commonly used. The first drugs then lead to marijuana and cocaine,

hallucinogens, heroin, and opioids. The user generally continues with the old gateway drugs, and the new drugs are added on.

Remember, experimentation is common and considered the
usual for most adolescents. More than 90 percent of adolescents
use alcohol or other drugs of some kind but do *not* become
addicted. *But,* experimentation can still cause significant problems for an adolescent. For example, it only takes one "gateway"
drink for an adolescent to be in a fatal motor vehicle accident.
In this age group, adolescents' systems have not yet kicked into
the tolerance stage, so a little of this drug may cause signs of
intoxication, poor judgment, and perceptual disturbances.

Occasional, Social, or Recreational Use

During this stage of substance use, the adolescent does not go
out to buy the alcohol or drug but somehow comes across it,
seeking out situations where he or she can use it for pleasure,
such as at parties or just gatherings after school with friends. Parents may be chuckling about the increased disappearance of John
after school, as they say, "Oh, he's probably off having a good
time with his friends, and maybe even starting to try some beer,
you know, like we used to." Again, this can be a very dangerous
stage for an adolescent in and of itself because it can lead to an
accident as well as be the stepping stone for later drug use.

Regular Use or Abuse

In this stage, adolescents maintain their own supply of the drug
so they are able to use it often or have it readily available for
their friends. The liquor cabinets at home need to be locked now
or parents better start to be aware of evaporating liquor from the
fifths of hard stuff tucked away up high.

This period usually marks the beginnings of conflict with family, money problems, and peer group changes. This is the time
when mom starts saying to dad, "Honey, have you noticed John
is not involved with us as much any more? He goes off with that

new friend Bob all the time, and he's not even letting us know where, like he used to. Besides, Bob seems a little different from the rest of John's friends, and I'm not sure if I like him, but I'm not sure why." Problem drinking usually comes after marijuana, and before heroin and cocaine. The grades may be dropping now, and the school might be starting to wonder about the increased absences. This is the beginning of a big problem, and we better try to stop it before it goes on to the next stage.

Dependence

Now we're really worried. Whoops, it got out of hand, just like that! Substance use is now a major factor in John's life. The family, school, his past dreams, religion, and even his friends, unless they are helpful to his habit, are not as important as the booze or drugs. He will probably not be able to discontinue on his own unless he hits bottom. But remember, the bottom can be avoided if the parents are right there to pick up the pieces.

SCREENING AND EVALUATION

Every adolescent uses a substance for a combination of reasons. If we can detect even one of those reasons, we can relate to it a motivator for discontinuation. So we need to find the clues that will help with change. We can use these clues in all facets of treatment, especially individual, family, and group therapies.

Key Points for a Thorough and Necessary Evaluation

Regardless of the setting in which you first see an adolescent, you need to address certain issues. These detailed questions can be put into paper and pencil form or asked verbally. They are all pretty heavy-duty questions, for an adolescent especially, so try to start with the least invasive ones.

There is a high correlation of reliability in self-reporting and true alcohol and drug use in adolescents. So the time spent for this thorough evaluation is justified, as early identification and treatment can be lifesaving. The following is a list of necessary items an evaluation must cover. Caregivers and adolescents alike are sources for much of the evaluation information.

- *General Identification/Demographics:* age, race, sex, where the adolescent lives, who he or she lives with, in what kind of a dwelling, and how long there, usual transportation, phone numbers and cities of all important contacts including personnel at school, and signed consents from parents to talk with each referral source.

- *Chief Complaint:* in adolescent's words the main reason he or she is there. (Parents should also provide this information separately.)

- *History of the Chief Complaint and Main Problem:* time line of the problem with significant life events and how long it has occurred; describe the problem in detail with all symptoms, what makes it worse, what makes it better, precipitating factors, what the adolescent has tried, how it affects his or her and others' lives, what significant others have tried to do to help the adolescent, their view of the problem. (Parents should also provide this information separately.)

- *Pregnancy, Birth, and Development History* (from parents alone): pregnancy history with the adolescent (wanted, planned, family life then, medications, problems); birth (date, weight, problems, where); postdelivery issues; how raised; temperament; development milestones and issues; feeding; sleeping; walking; talking; toilet training; speech; hearing; vision; coordination or clumsiness; what client was like at infancy, preschool, school age, and adolescence.

- *Past Medical, Surgical, and Injury History* (from parents): name and phone number of primary care physician, and signed consent to talk with him or her, past and current medical history, past and current surgical history, injury history (especially head injury and loss of consciousness, any head imaging studies done), hospitalizations, medications past and current and their effects, special diets, sleeping, general physical health, change in personal appearance.

- *Family Medical History* (from parents).

- *Allergies* (from parents).

- *Current Medications* (from parents and child), including over-the-counter medications.

- *Past Psychiatric History* (from parents and child): diagnosis, therapists, hospitalizations, medications and their effects, other treatments, suicide attempts.

- *Family Psychiatric History* (from parents and child): diagnosis, including alcohol and other drug use, how it affects the user, how it affects the patient and others, therapists, treatment, medications, hospitalizations.

- *School* (from parents and child): present school, highest grade attained, best subject, worst subject, other school activities, school history, truancy, time spent on reading in general, time spent on homework, attention or concentration problems, special education testing, school changes.

- *General Family Questions* (from parents): parental ages, occupations, marriage and divorce history, custody and visitation issues if applicable, how they get along with each other (their own perception and the adolescent's), adolescent's background (relationships with parents, especially what it was like for parents at the age the adolescent is now), siblings' ages, relationships with them, where they are living now; grandparents, relationships with them, where they are living now.

- *Relations with Family Members* (from parents and child): discipline, support, parental discord and violence in the home, arguments, fights, stealing, family crises, stress at home; feelings about rules and regulations; running away, staying out late; adolescent's view of parental listening and concern; view of parental approval of alcohol and other drug use; comments about discipline (and ask the teenager to include the types); legal concerns of parents or other adults in the home; how adult role models deal with stress; changes parents have noticed in their adolescent lately, including mood, affect, behavior, dress, lying; family belongings missing, adolescent's prized possessions missing, money missing; personal hygiene; drug paraphernalia around the home, suspicious smells; stealing, shoplifting, or other legal encounters; school performance changes, truancy, conflict with coaches or teachers; abusiveness to family members; talk about suicide or running away; anything else different or questionable.

- *Relations with Friends in General* (from parents and child): who, how many, what type, how they spend their time together, adolescent's perception about how she or he compares with peers.

- *Alcohol and Other Drugs* (from parents and child): alcohol (be specific regarding all the types), nicotine (smoked or chewed), caffeine (ask about specific types), marijuana, and other drugs—don't forget inhalants, amphetamines, methamphetamines, cocaine, opiates, LSD, PCP, psilocybins (mushrooms), barbiturates, benzodiazepines, steroids, over-the-counter stimulants, diuretics, prescribed medications. Remember to use common street names.

- *Usage of Each Drug and Alcohol:* How did adolescent get started, age at first use, length of use, how often, how much, the last use. Ask parents, teachers, referral sources, and any other person involved in the life of the adolescent about that adolescent's use.

- *Consequences of the Use of Each Drug:* legal ramifications, effect on family relationships, peer relationships, money, school, health, feelings, appearance, specifically asking about how the drug helps, and how it hurts. Can adolescent drink more alcohol than most of his or her friends? Did adolescent have to increase the amount he or she drinks, from the first time, to get the same effect? Include specific questions about intoxication including blackouts, amnesia, withdrawal. Has the use put the adolescent in a high-risk situation (climbing to the top of a flagpole while high on PCP, driving under the influence, sexual encounter, fight with a friend)? The CAGE (control, annoyance, guilt, eye opener) to be done verbally.

- *Use of Alcohol and Other Drugs by Significant Others and Friends* (from parents and child): how these affect the user and the adolescent.

- *Legal Concerns* (from parents and child): number of and reasons for arrests, time served, lying, stealing, fire-setting, cruelty to animals, difficulty with authority, gang involvement.

- *Violence* (from parents and child): past involvement, problems with temper control, physical fights, parents' abuse of adolescent, weapon availability, carrying, or use.

- *Sexually Transmitted Diseases (STDs):* knowledge, education, symptoms in themselves or others, the idea that one may have a STD without symptoms, confidentiality in treatment, and condoms.

- *Pregnancy and Sexuality:* sexual activity and past education; past or present intercourse; sexual practices, such as masturbation; preferred sex of a partner; past or possible present pregnancy; abortions; response to past pregnancy or fathering and school dropout; parents' responses to questions about or actual pregnancy and birth control.

- *General Social Problems, Changes, and Concerns:* money problems, religion, hobbies, short-term goals, long-term goals.

A Mental Status Exam must be done on every adolescent verbally. The following is a list of the key features.

- *Feelings and Mood in General:* adolescents' feelings about themselves and self-worth, feelings of boredom, and how much and how often; questions about emotions including sadness, crying, withdrawal, depression, irritability, mood changes, anxiety or nervousness; sleepwalking, nightmares, eating problems, decreased or increased fears, rituals, habits, superstitions, strange or bizarre behavior, impulsivity, soiling, bed wetting, maturity; any abuse history—physical, sexual, verbal; any separations from father or mother, including hospitalization, staying with other relatives.

- *Questions About Suicide in the Adolescent:* wish to die, wish not to be alive, plan and intent to kill themselves (these are different, and adolescents need specific questions), their own ideas and thoughts about being alive and dead, self-abuse (cutting, head banging), family or friend history of attempts or completion, any losses in their life, and the who, when, what, and why about these.

- *More Data in the Mental Status Exam:* Don't miss general appearance, attitude, relation to examiner, behavior and movements, eye contact, speech, gait, mood, affect, thought processes (goal directed, logical, spontaneous), thought content (suicidal and homicidal ideation; auditory, visual, olfactory, and tactile; hallucinations, thought insertion, broadcasting, or withdrawal, paranoid ideation, delusions, obsessions or compulsions); sensorium and cognition exam (conscious state, orientation, memory, concentration, calculations, cognitive abilities, fund of knowledge); similarities and proverbs to test concrete or abstract interpretation, insight, and judgment.

Medical Considerations in the Evaluation

"Fatigue, sore throat, cough, chest pain, conjunctivitis, headaches, and school or behavioral problems are the most common symptoms of drug use." It is possible, therefore, that the pediatrician or family practitioner will be the first one to assess the child. You may be a referral from that source, or you may be the first one to assess an adolescent for behavioral problems and then need to refer him or her to primary care. Nevertheless, every alcohol- and drug-using adolescent needs a thorough physical examination.

Acquired immunodeficiency syndrome (AIDS), AIDS-related complex (ARC), and seropositivity with the human immunodeficiency virus (HIV) have become major public health issues. Their acquisition has been highly correlated with the use of illicit drugs, especially intravenous use. Additionally, a high-risk group is individuals who are sexually active without protection, and teens are in this group.

Moreover, the physician needs to be aware of and help stop alcohol and drugs in potentially pregnant females, and teens are in this group also. Not only HIV but several other ailments related to alcohol and other drugs can be passed on prenatally to the developing fetus including brain damage and retarded physical and mental growth patterns. Full fetal alcohol syndrome comprises a triad of growth retardation, central nervous system dysfunction, and craniofacial dysmorphology. The adverse effects of prenatal alcohol exposure exist along a continuum, so another term, *alcohol-related birth defects*, is useful to describe less distinctive aspects of the illness.

Prenatal alcohol exposure is one of the leading known causes of mental retardation in the Western world. Drug abuse during pregnancy can cause miscarriage, low birth weight infants, and increased infant mortality. Neonatal addiction is a significant problem, with withdrawal a dangerous complication for babies at birth.

Structured Interviews and Questionnaires

Some practitioners prefer to use a questionnaire to uncover data. Several types are available, including direct and indirect measures of alcohol and other drug use and dependency.

Direct Measures. A number of instruments use direct measures for asking detailed questions about use and dependency. A structured interview to uncover "negative consequences" is the

Michigan Alcoholism Screening Test (MAST), which has been studied in college-age students but not adolescents. It seems to indicate current drinking habits reliably. The Addiction Severity Index (ASI) and the Adolescent Expectancy Questionnaire both measure beliefs about alcohol use.

Other structured interviews are Questions Concerning Drugs for the School-aged Child: A Screening Tool; the "HEADS" Organized Interview (Home, Education, Activities and Affects, Drugs, and Sexuality); Open-ended Questions Intended to Provide a Basis for Further Exploration of Advanced Substance Abuse, and Guidelines for Substance Abuse Interviewing.

Rapid Direct Measures. There are also some rapid screening types of direct measures. CAGE is generally accepted by clinicians in the field for a quick and easy test. It has not been studied in adolescents, but for adults it is not very intimidating and usually doesn't seem intimidating for adolescents, either. The format follows the initial inquiry "Have you ever . . ." with extensions such as "felt the need to cut down?"; "been annoyed by criticism about drug use?"; "felt guilty about your drug use?"; "had a morning eye-opener?" Because the most common precipitating factor leading some to seek substance abuse treatment is realizing personal shame, questions must also be asked about this. To recognize the existence of shame, you can ask about the 5 F's: Fatigue, effect on Finances, effect of the use on relationships with Family and Friends, effect on Future plans, and Follow-up (do you want to change your situation?). These, and other psychiatric components must be addressed.

Questionnaires that have found favor with health professionals for screening include the Symptom Checklist for Substance Abuse, Questionnaire Items Relevant to Substance Abuse, Questionnaire for Adolescent Patients Suspected of or Known to Be Abusing Drugs and/or Alcohol, Questionnaire for the Parent(s) of the Adolescent Suspected of or Known to Be Abusing Drugs and/or Alcohol, the Adolescent Assessment/Referral System (AARS) Manual, the Problem Oriented Screening Instrument for Teenagers (POSIT), Substance Abuse Subtle Screening Inventory (SASSI), Drug Use Screening Inventory (DUSI), and the NIAAA Treatment Handbook Series 2: Alcoholism Treatment Assessment Research Instruments.

Indirect Measures. Indirect tools for alcohol and other drug evaluation usually uncover personality traits that could be significant for the development of an addiction. These indirect measures also may be more likely to elicit a positive response than the direct measures because they do not ask specifically about drugs and alcohol. Direct questions about these topics could make the person questioned resistant to answering, and so the responses could be somewhat unreliable. Our experience suggests that the clinician should never depend on an answer from one of these scales as a sole diagnostic tool. An example is the MacAndrews Alcoholism Scales (MAC), which can identify a psychological tendency toward dependence on alcohol or other drugs, but doesn't help with current use. Additionally, the Millon Clinical Multiaxial Inventory (MCMI) can be used for this identification purpose along with other evaluation.

Evaluation Related to Confidentiality, Informed Consent, and Reporting

Confidentiality issues must be addressed at the initial interview as at the very beginning collaterals are often involved. If we deal with them early, several pitfalls can be avoided. Confidentiality must be assured except when there is a threat of harm to self or to others, or when modification can be made because of reporting laws. The reporting requirement varies from state to state, but usually includes child or elder abuse and violence in the home. A nonjudgmental but reasonable assessment must always be made.

If a parent shares a drug or alcohol concern with the therapist, that concern must be shared in an appropriate way with the adolescent. Each of us must assess individually how much can be shared with the parents, and the state laws in this regard must be adhered to. The adolescent must also be aware of the clinician's limitations and respect for confidentiality.

Basically, whatever the adolescent shares with you must be kept in confidence, except for the above exclusions, but what a parent shares with you can be told to the adolescent. If you learn something from the adolescent that affects his or her safety or the safety of someone else and you feel that you must share this with the parents, discuss it with the adolescent first. You should explain this procedure at the beginning of any interaction with the adolescent and parents.

Legal matters have to be considered before initiating treatment with an adolescent. You should not sit down with an adolescent until you know the laws for your state. Some states are more liberal than others in requiring informed consent for treatment of adolescents. Some say we need informed consent from the adolescent before treatment begins. It is not legal in some states to commit an adolescent to treatment against his or her will unless there is a demonstrated need for involuntary admission. On the other hand, some states allow involuntary admission to a treatment program if the parent consents. In these cases, a teenager could actually be put on a plane by the parents, taken to one of a few states, and involuntarily admitted for treatment. One should consider the therapeutic value of such a maneuver very seriously, especially in how it will affect the adolescent's trust of his parents in the future. Additionally, in such a situation, the family cannot work with the treatment team and the adolescent, as is normally done and recommended, unless they can afford to stay for the duration of treatment in the other state.

On the other end of the spectrum, an adolescent can consent to treatment for substance abuse. Of course, the parents might not agree with the treatment, may not agree to pay for it, or may not offer the support needed for effective treatment. Some cases requiring parental involvement may be counterproductive to effective treatment, but we should always encourage that involvement. If the adolescent refuses the involvement of the parents, his or her wishes need to be respected; at the same time, you can continue to make gentle recommendations for their inclusion. If the clinician does not feel comfortable with such an arrangement, he or she may refer the adolescent to another confidential program if one is available. If there is a possibility of serious health threat when parental involvement is recommended (for instance, serious abscess with IV drugs), disclosing the problem to the parents is ethically justified but not necessarily legally justified, depending on the situation or the state the teenager is in. If there will be a breach of confidentiality to the parents, the minor must be told the reasons prior to the act. Legal counsel should be consulted when there are any questions.

To get around these legal matters, a parent may make deals with the adolescent in a coercive way. How much coercion is legal by parents to get adolescents into a voluntary treatment center? Therapeutic and legal concerns must again be addressed according to the individual's larger clinical picture and the state in which he or she lives. A parent could refuse to let the adolescent drive the family car until the teenager agrees to regular drug testing or treatment. A better way to accomplish this is for the adolescent to refuse the keys voluntarily because he or she wants to get help with the alcohol or drug problem.

The results of testing should be confidential, as is the therapy. If the adolescent has given the informed consent for testing, sharing the results is permissible; but care must be given to the manner in which they are delivered. Don't use the results as a weapon but as an additional piece of the total picture.

Informed consent can be obtained by the parents alone, because of poor judgment of the adolescent, or danger in the condition, as determined by two physicians. Then the results must be shared with the parents and the patient. In these cases, the child has already been judged to be in a life-threatening situation, and it is the responsibility of the clinician and parents to protect the patient's health at the risk of confidentiality. Again, when there are any legal disputes, doubts, or concerns, please consult with legal counsel.

Involvement with the patient's primary care physician is always in order during every step of the treatment process. This includes the beginning investigative stages, the planning stages, and the treatment stages. Primary care physicians are responsible for and concerned about the overall care of their patients. For us to leave them out of the process would be neglectful. Again, however, because of confidentiality, we cannot contact the primary care physician without consent.

The Issue of Paternalism in Treatment

Medical practice of the treatment of adolescents for alcohol and other drug problems must not be based only on scientific knowledge but also on the sociocultural climate, and what is morally right. When do the health care professionals step in with a paternalistic stance to treat adolescents without jeopardizing the effectiveness of the treatment? Dr. Tomas Silber believes paternalism can be justified in the case of a minor when "the principle of protection of life tends to outweigh the principle of autonomy," and "there is reasonable evidence that the minor's capability for autonomy is impaired." If we as clinicians find out about alcohol or drug use in the adolescent, we have to decide whether to tell the parents. No matter what we decide, we must discuss it with the adolescent before taking action.

First ask whether the situation is potentially dangerous in the teenager's life. The use of alcohol and drugs may get worse, and we need to consider where the adolescent is and where he or she is realistically headed on the "process of dependency" continuum. Remember, the parents are legally responsible for the teenager. Additionally, treatment depends on parent collaboration, and if they don't know cooperate, effective follow-up may not happen. Payment from the parents is usually an additional issue.

We may extend the privilege of the confidential relationship on the condition that the adolescent demonstrates responsibility. Confidentiality is an integral part of the doctor- or therapist-patient relationship. There are humane alternatives to the physician's telling the parents: helping patients share the truth, being the spokesperson for the adolescents with them present, or having the teenagers involved in treatment programs that will lead them to tell their parents.

If we have to tell the parents, inform the adolescent first that "it would be wrong of me as a professional to do something different from what I know is best for you." Occasionally, the worst nightmare comes true, and there is no choice but to tell the parents against the wishes of the patient, and thus deprive the patient of privacy and liberty.

Dr. Silber stresses an invaluable principle: "Paternalism can only be justified when the evil prevented from occurring to the person is greater than the wrong caused by violation of the moral rule and, more importantly, if it can be universally justified under relevantly similar circumstance always to treat persons in this way."

TREATMENT BASICS

Current approaches to treatment of adolescents with alcohol and other drug abuse have been fraught with problems. Recently, we have seen the rise and fall of extensive inpatient adolescent alcohol and drug treatment, as much of the recent treatment for adolescent alcohol and drug abuse has been driven by a profit motive. An example of that abuse is the total consumption of a $250,000 lifetime psychiatric benefit for a single acute care inpatient treatment episode for one adolescent. At the time, treatment had been focused on an inpatient model, often neglecting other important and effective approaches.

We are just now beginning to develop these other resources, which can not only be more therapeutic and appropriate for the individual patient but also more financially feasible. This evolution has occurred in the absence of any research or professional development in this area, a key problem in the current approaches to adolescent treatment. Much more research needs to be done in this vital area.

Chemical Dependency Approaches

Adult chemical dependency approaches have traditionally tended to group all alcoholics and all drug addicts under one umbrella, deemphasizing the differences among them. This treatment has been applied on both an outpatient and inpatient basis.

This traditional type of treatment has focused on the disease model that emphasizes genetic and physiologic factors as the cause for the addiction, therefore taking away from the patients some responsibility for their actions. The interpersonal and psychological problems are not viewed as a significant cause of the problem. The treatment then focuses on the loss of control as a central theme, and deemphasizes the underlying individual psychological, interpersonal, cultural, familial, and social variables. We believe, however, that if these issues are not addressed and treated, the patient may continue with the same problems, and in fact, these problems can contribute to relapse.

In a similar fashion, adolescents with a drug or alcohol problem have been grouped with other adolescents with a drug or alcohol problem, regardless of individual differences. Often this type of approach has been done in an inpatient or outpatient setting depending on what is available, not always what is best for the particular patient with his or her particular problem.

There are many strengths in this traditional chemical dependency treatment approach. The first is an easy bonding around the experience of addiction. People who are addicted have similar experiences with loss of control, guilt, and shame. In some ways, the individual differences are overshadowed by the universal trauma of addiction. The positive and negative effects of the use of alcohol and other drugs can be shared in a useful way. Another strength is the emphasis on recovery from addiction as a priority. This dimension is made much clearer if people are grouped. Alcohol and drug treatment should take priority over other psychiatric treatments in the beginning stages. Grouping can help share some coping strategies that have worked or not worked with others having similar problems.

However, this "traditional" approach can fail to address the individual differences among patients. Specifically, if an adolescent is socially phobic and we place him or her in a group, the anxiety from that experience can be overwhelming. The patient may leave. The traditional dependency program may confront patients like this as though they are in denial, when in fact they must deal with the underlying phobia before they can benefit from the group experience.

In other cases of adolescent chemical dependency, the alcohol and drug use is symptomatic of an underlying psychiatric problem. This is more so than in adult alcohol and other drug dependency. Each adolescent has different interpersonal processes, different family systems, different psychiatric complications, different levels of anxiety, and different levels of depression. Therefore, it is important to be less uniform and more individualized in approaching adolescent alcohol and other drug treatment.

Psychiatric Approaches

On the other end of the spectrum, the psychiatric approaches to adolescent care have often deemphasized and neglected alcohol and drug abuse as a weighty variable in formulating treatment. In fact, the psychiatric difficulties are often viewed as primary, when they are no more important or debilitating than the alcohol and drug problem.

The alcohol and drug experience itself can generate psychiatric symptoms and be a major contributor to the psychiatric difficulties. Furthermore, evaluating, initiating treatment, and providing therapy of any kind in the face of continued alcohol and drug use is countertherapeutic and usually useless. We feel that this is a fundamental failure in traditional psychiatric approaches to adolescent care and one major reason for our chapter.

A Treatment Team Is the Only Way

We do not recommend individual, sole provider attempts to treat substance abuse. The individual practitioner lacks the resources to manage this complex treatment, and treatment must occur in the context of a structure. This structured management and treatment should be delivered by a team. The ideal treatment team consists of psychiatrist, psychologist, pediatrician, counselor, nurse, teacher, and specialized therapists—recreational, occupational, art, and speech—if needed. This team can manage the many complex difficulties of treating adolescent alcohol and drug abuse. For example, the team is best suited to help manage transference and countertransference issues, and healing and resolving the splitting that occurs in treatment.

The other vital parts of the team include the patient and family members. Sometimes these are the only team members other than the primary care provider. When possible, a teacher, school counselor, and primary care physician should be involved. Other team members might be a police officer or other caring individual who has been and continues to be involved with the adolescent.

In the following pages we recommend an approach that combines the traditional chemical dependency alcohol and drug treatment and the principles of traditional psychiatric care. Each treatment alone is inadequate. We feel the traditional alcohol and drug treatment focuses on the commonalties and similarities among substance abusers. The traditional psychiatric approaches, on the other hand, focus more on individual differences and evaluating the individual psychopathology of adolescents. We propose to combine the two, and use the team approach to carry out the work.

Our treatment approach focuses on the primacy of the alcohol and drug addiction while at the same time looking at the psychiatric underpinnings of the alcohol and drug problems. This model can be used in any kind of a treatment setting—outpatient, residential, or inpatient. We would like to stress the importance of using the particular setting that would be appropriate for the individual based on a thorough and proper assessment and evaluation. And we would like to do all this in the most economically feasible and fair way.

TREATMENT GUIDELINES

To accomplish this integrated approach, we suggest that clinicians observe the following guidelines in the treatment of adolescents with alcohol or other drug abuse problems.

1. EVALUATE, EVALUATE, EVALUATE. Evaluate the adolescent substance abuse first. Evaluate the role the substance abuse plays in the family system second. Evaluate the relationship of substance abuse with psychiatric co-morbidity third. These assessments must be done to formulate a case for treatment of adolescent alcohol and drug abuse.

Adolescents are different from adults, and in particular, adolescent alcohol and drug abuse is different from adults' alcohol and drug abuse in several key ways. The differences include age, development, family connections, awareness of responsibility, legalities, diagnosis criteria, and relationships to others. These vital differences are discussed in the following guidelines and must be addressed to treat adolescents appropriately and differently from adults.

2. TREAT THE ALCOHOL AND OTHER DRUG PROBLEMS FIRST. This step is vital, as alcohol and other drug addiction can cause psychiatric difficulties. Without addressing the dependency problems first, the rest of the treatment is futile. Moreover, recovery from alcohol and other drug addictions takes priority over other forms of treatment, with only rare exception. For example, if an adolescent walks in with an alcohol dependency and a social phobia, he or she must first be stabilized off alcohol before the social phobia is treated.

Second, when a person is off alcohol or other drugs, the psychiatric symptoms may improve. That is, abstinence may decrease the adolescent's anxiety levels, depression, and so on.

Third, alcohol and other drugs may be masking psychiatric difficulties, and with abstinence, other psychiatric problems may then emerge. Psychopathology often leads to alcohol and drug abuse. Evaluating those psychiatric problems, then treating them is the next vital step in adolescent care. All the time we are addressing the alcohol and other drug problems, we must be watching closely for suicidality or any number of serious psychiatric issues that may emerge. Frequently, adolescents have additional diagnoses besides the chemical dependency, including affective disorders, posttraumatic stress, learning disabilities, personality disorders, and eating disorders. Additionally, they often have a history of physical or sexual abuse or assault, suicidal ideation or attempts, and poor self-esteem.

We must first discover all the problems (alcohol, other drugs, and other psychiatric diagnoses), thoroughly evaluate the whole picture, then treat appropriately. This is a never-ending process, which goes on continually throughout treatment. We must never think we have the whole picture at the beginning of treatment, as it continues to develop throughout the *entire* process.

3.   BE AWARE OF THE LIFE-THREATENING ASPECTS OF BOTH THE ALCOHOL AND DRUG PROBLEMS AND THE PSYCHIATRIC ILLNESS. Life-threatening aspects in each adolescent need to be treated accordingly. It is our fundamental position that both alcohol and other drug dependencies and psychiatric illnesses are serious and can be deadly. Certainly not all psychiatric illnesses are life threatening, but most do have high morbidity and mortality. Suicidality, homicidality, and poor life functioning are all serious consequences of many of these ailments. Hospitalization in a locked unit may be necessary for the adolescent's safety, the initiation of abstinence, and individual and family treatment.

4.   DO NOT TREAT ADOLESCENT ALCOHOL AND DRUG ABUSE OUTSIDE THE CONTEXT OF THE FAMILY SYSTEM. The family system influences adolescent substance abuse, and the substance abuse influences the family system. There must be a family commitment for treatment of the adolescent, for steady

involvement in the adolescent's care, and for effective treatment outcome. There are, on the other hand, adolescents who have been separated from their family, either because of the chaotic family system, the alcohol or drug problem in the adolescent or other family members, the existence of psychiatric difficulties, or a combination of the above. Clearly, these adolescents still need intensive care, even if the traditional family approach is not available. In this kind of situation, a residential treatment setting could substitute for a familial environment.

5. GEAR TOWARD THE ONGOING POWER DYNAMICS THAT ARE OPERATING IN THE ADOLESCENT'S COMPLEX LIFE. Adolescents have acting-out power, the power of compliance, and the power of succeeding or failing as an individual patient. On the other end of the spectrum, they often lack financial power and most legal power. All these issues can alter the course of treatment and must be addressed very quickly if an effective treatment plan is to be formulated for adolescent alcohol and drug abuse. Failure to address this is to render the treatment ineffective.

Parents hold financial power, legal power, driving power, loving power, disapproval power, criticism power, and abuse power. Parents also have role-modeling power. Sensing, evaluating, and working with the power is vital in formulating a treatment and care plan. A goal of treatment may be to renegotiate the power dynamics; this would involve the development of a whole new life system, based on trust. So who is really in charge of the car keys?

6. IF YOU SEE YOURSELVES ON THE ROAD TO BECOMING RESPONSIBLE FOR THE ADOLESCENT, PULL OVER AND JUMP OFF! RESPONSIBILITY MUST BE DEFINED. The therapist is not the adolescent's parent. There may be difficulties between the adolescent and the parent, and there may be deficits with respect to parenting. That's why power dynamics and the family systems issues must be addressed. The "corrective emotional experience" and "unconditional positive regard" can still be accomplished in the therapeutic process, especially because the therapist is *not* the parent.

Our job is to help *improve* the adolescent's relationship with the parents, not to replace it. Regardless of how hard the adolescent will pull for you to become a parent, or the parents push for you to take on the parenting role, do not be sucked in. We have to resist taking the steering wheel. Keep in mind, too, the therapist does not care for the adolescent twenty-four hours a day, as do the parents.

Neither accept the adolescent nor reject the adolescent, as a parent might. This is a general goal in adolescent treatment. Often the transference of the adolescent toward the caregiver, or the specific countertransferences that develop with respect toward adolescents, entail treatment. Are we going to be sucked into the parenting role where we are responsible for the care of the child, and fight and devalue the parents? Will we become the "good parent" for the adolescent, and actually believe the adolescent will suddenly conform to our recommendations? Will we let our guard down enough to enter into an alliance with the cunning and manipulative adolescent, so that we are actually working against the parents, and forget their important role in the child's proper treatment? Will we be on the side of the parents, where we may end up just as angry and frustrated with the adolescent as they are? Will we say, as the parent might, "If you take another drink, I will never see you again"? Can we avoid the deleterious effects of countertransference by attending to the defensive styles, and working with them to manage the therapeutic dyad?

As therapists, we often meet the needs of adolescents in treatment by providing structure in their lives, giving them ideas on how to do things differently and more effectively, and supplying attention. In hospitalization, we provide food, a bed, and structure, even to the point of telling the teenagers what they need to do in a day. Meeting these basic needs does not mean the therapist becomes the parent. Rather, it means that the adolescents at that particular time are not able to meet their own needs so we provide the overall environment and structure. We must never assume the role of Mrs. Cleaver, Mommy Dearest, Nurse Ratchet, or Florence Nightingale.

7.   REMEMBER THE PARENTS' RESPONSIBILITIES. The financial responsibility is rarely that of the adolescent. The parents are the ones who purchase insurance if that's what covers the fees. Can you imagine an adolescent paying a therapist $100 an hour? Not likely. Even if the adolescents were expected to pay for our services, they probably would not feel that it was the best way to spend their hard-earned, or given, money. Because they are not financially responsible, their motivation may not be very strong to elicit help; if it is made available to them, they may not use it as productively as if they had to pay for it themselves.

With adolescents, parents usually pick up the pieces. The parents bail the child out of trouble with the law. They usually pay for the damage done by a drunk driving accident. They call the school with an excuse of illness the "morning after." The parents *prevent* the adolescent from experiencing "bottom," and then treatment. If the adolescent has not hit "bottom," he or she may be resistant to treatment. If there is no pain, why bother? It is usually "bottom" that brings adults into treatment. There are often multiple bottoms, and multiple treatment efforts, before they are on their feet again. But because *they*, no longer their parents, are responsible for what happens to them, they must take care of the consequences from their addiction.

If we as health professionals think the traditional "bottom" will bring the child to treatment, we are being fooled. It will be something else, like problems at home or school, and the alcohol or drug use may not be apparent. The parents are responsible for preventing their child from hitting bottom because they are responsible for the child's safety. They are also responsible for noticing when a child is not well and needs help. The parents are responsible for observing a different kind of "bottom," described by behavioral changes that create dysfunction in their adolescent's life.

Therefore, the parents are forced in a way into a codependent role with the abusing adolescent. They can't really kick the kid out of the home—that would be neglect. They are obliged, for some time, to be the enabler, without infringing on the separation-individuation of the adolescent, that stage in life when the teenager is trying to become independent from the parents. What a tough situation to be in! When is it still safe for the adolescent to use? When do the parents step in? When do we step in?

The family is usually involved with the problem. They have been affected by it and often are related to many of the causes. It is imperative that the family be committed to and involved in whatever treatment plan is chosen. The child cannot do it alone, if he or she is still in the same environmental situation as when the condition began. Recent research by the AMA Council on Scientific Affairs identifies alcohol and drug use as common *responses* to family violence and victimization. So family chaos can contribute to the problem, then the problem can cause more family chaos. On a more positive note, a common occurrence is for the child who is being treated for an abuse problem to succeed in getting an abusing parent into treatment.

8.   DON'T TREAT ADOLESCENTS LIKE ADULTS. DON'T TREAT THEM LIKE CHILDREN. THEY ARE ADOLESCENTS. DSM-IV criteria do not distinguish between adults and children and adolescents in the diagnosis of alcohol and other drug problems. But there are several challenges unique to the treatment of adolescents because they *are* different from adults. This is important to remember and to use in the treatment of this different group of people. We have quite a bit of experience with treatment of adults with alcohol and other drug abuse problems, and we can use some of the data acquired from this treatment— but not much of it. Therefore, we must understand the basic differences of the ages in order to understand what is behind the illness and then the treatment. If we think we can simply take the common models of treatment for adults and apply them to adolescents, we are fooling ourselves and short-changing the people who desperately need our help.

Early signs of alcohol and drug abuse problems in teenagers are most often behavioral rather than physical. Alcohol and other drug use cannot be easily detected in a physical exam. Unlike adults, adolescents rarely develop physical dependence.

Adolescents can be difficult to manage, as they often act out their feelings rather than verbalize them. Adolescents are often more impulsive than adults. They may have more of a compulsion or uncontrollable impulse to drink or use other drugs. They have less ego strength and are more vulnerable to peer culture. Adolescents are especially vulnerable to experimentation which is, by the way, "normal." If one figures that most adolescents have experimented with drugs or alcohol, that means it's customary behavior, although still often dangerous.

9. REMEMBER THE DEVELOPMENTAL DIFFERENCES IN ADOLESCENTS. Adolescents are at very different levels of development from adults and consequently our assessment and treatment ought to be geared to these differences. Adolescence is marked by pronounced biological, psychological, and social changes. Besides the complexities of regular adolescence, the timing, length, and definition of adolescence is different from culture to culture, and there are several different cultures in America.

Watch out for puberty! Hormonal changes can lead to massive mood changes. Estrogen decreases in girls can affect the development of depression, and testosterone in boys is correlated with aggression and impassivity. Adolescent boys and girls view sexual intercourse very differently from the other sex, and from adults. Additionally, adolescents are more sensitive to peer opinions and constantly compare themselves to others.

If you were to offer adults a medication that "would make you feel lots better," they would likely accept your professional opinion and help. With adolescents, it's different. They probably don't want any medication that some doctor wants to give them, or that their parents are excited about trying as a quick fix. They'd rather do what their friends are doing to make them "feel better." The peer culture must be contended with. There is no use fighting it; that's the way it is, and that's the way it's supposed to be. So, how can we help these adolescents live safely in this different culture?

Erik Erickson says the major task in adolescence is to achieve ego identity. The *normal* struggle during that time is between *identity*, or the secure sense of self, and *confusion*, or identity diffusion, which is a failure to develop a cohesive self or self-awareness.

Oppositional tendencies reappear, often with statements such as "No, you can't make me!" This normal negativism will gradually decrease as the adolescent works through this difficult stage of life. These growing people attempt to let others know they have their own minds, and "Don't tell me how to use it." They *try* to let parents know it every chance they get, questioning parents' choices constantly. Parents become people at home base, and peers are where the real world is.

Another task to be accomplished by the end of adolescence is separation-individuation. Parents exclaim, "What's happening to my nice little Johnny," as he won't wear the shirt mom bought him but insists on wearing the one he picked out. Different parents react differently to this conflict. Some do a great job of limit setting and formation of individuation; others don't. Some actually act out *their* hidden fantasies through their children. A crucial task that must be consummated is for the parents to deal appropriately with the sexual anxiety their teenagers may be experiencing but which is not apparent. Risk-taking is usually increased at this exciting stage, as adolescents try to relate to counterphobic acting out, inadequacy fears, and the need to affirm their sexual identity while dealing with ongoing peer pressure.

Morality and ethics are internalized in an organized way if all is successful at the end of adolescence. The young adults will have a pretty good idea of who they are, what they believe, and where they are going. If this stage of development is not properly or adequately settled, they may experience role confusion. Examples of this confusion may be turmoil, truancy, running away from home, or mental illness, including substance use, abuse, or dependency. Adolescence is a tough time for the teen and for the parent, and drugs or alcohol can and do creep in at many opportune times during the struggles or chaos.

10. EVALUATE THE PEER CULTURE FOR ALCOHOL, DRUGS, AND VIOLENCE. The setting where alcohol and drugs are used can be very different for adolescents compared to adults. The adults can use in the privacy of their homes or those of their friends. Kids don't have the luxury of using in their own homes

because they are often hiding the use from the other people who live there. The adults also have more control over their environment than do the kids. The kids have to sneak from school or home in order to use. A favorite spot is the local mall. When we are assessing or treating, we have to keep in mind those possible sneaking places or times, and monitor them. By the time we see these adolescents, they have become extremely skilled at sneaking and will try to fool everyone, including us.

The peer culture of today can itself be very dangerous. "Punk slamming" happens only when kids get together with others and attack some innocent person. The level of violence in and out of the dance hall and rock concerts is far too high with or without alcohol or drugs.

11. IF THE ADOLESCENT NEEDS TREATMENT AND IS REFUSING IT, DECIDE FOR HIM AND HELP HIM GET IT IN AN EFFECTIVE WAY. Alcohol or drug use commonly causes many fights in the home. The parents may decide on treatment for the adolescent against the teenager's will, but this has clear problems. Even the best of treatments would probably not work under these circumstances. It's important for the patient to say, "I need and want some help to assist me with this problem, because I can see how it is affecting my life." Self-directed treatment can positively affect the therapeutic process. Unfortunately, adolescents may not be self-directed for treatment *until* they get into treatment, and are clean and dry. In that case, the persistent parent or health care professional who got them into treatment may have saved their lives. There are all kinds of treatment available at this stage. The different types and indications are addressed later.

12. CONSIDER ALCOHOL AND OTHER DRUG TESTING WISELY. Testing urine or other body fluids may be an alluring alternative to interviews and physical examinations, and it is common for mental health professionals to ask physicians for such a test. Interviews are much more time-consuming, and some health professionals may even feel uneasy about questioning a person about such matters. Nevertheless, interviews are the major assessment techniques. Drug testing generally should be

used only at later stages in treatment, as it can be very problematic if used as an assessment tool.

Drug testing must be done by a qualified professional and physician who is familiar with the different tests available, the limitations and advantages of each, and the interpretation of the results. Testing can sometimes be used in addition to the interviews and physical exam. But a positive result is only one part of a more complex picture, and the use of the result must be integrated into a comprehensive clinical assessment. The screening test is also different from the confirmation test; this is the test the laboratory does to identify the particular type of opiate if the screening test was positive for opiates. There are actually no definitive screening tests available, so they must be used with a great deal of care for several reasons. There are moral, ethical, philosophical, practical, psychological, therapeutic, medical, and legal considerations that must be addressed. Body fluid testing can prevent or damage a therapeutic alliance with an adolescent and is one major reason the procurement of body fluid tests is controversial.

Body fluid testing for alcohol or other drugs is *not* justified when

- An examiner does not trust the adolescent.
- Only the parent requests or demands it.
- It is part of a routine medical workup.

Adolescents can refuse screening for drugs if they are competent, and the laws in their state allow this action. Schools cannot involuntarily test for drugs because they are subject to the Fourth Amendment, the constitutional right of individuals for protection against unreasonable searches and seizures. Urine tests are searches and can be reasonable only if the person has violated the school's lawful drug policy. One must be careful to ensure that a search is reasonable and not an invasion of privacy.

The following are *indications* for body fluid testing:

- With informed consent proper for the state.
- For adolescents with psychiatric symptoms.
- With high-risk adolescents.
- For those with mental status changes.
- With acute onset of behavior changes.
- With recurrent respiratory ailments.
- With recurrent accidents.
- With unexplained somatic complaints.
- As part of an abstinence program with known monitoring.
- If an adolescent is out of control, incompetent, with obvious dysfunction or inability to participate in informed consent, and two physicians feel it is a necessity. The arena is either the emergency room or other emergency setting, and in these cases the test may be done with parental consent only.

Every clinician ordering these tests needs to be aware of the common laboratory methods of toxicological analysis, including the advantages and disadvantages of each and how to order, understand, and interpret the results. The results then need to be correctly interpreted and shared with the patient, families if appropriate, and consultants.

A negative screen does not really mean much. It doesn't mean the patient has not recently used as the timing of the test can affect the results. Nor does a positive screen necessarily mean the patient has recently used, as some drugs hang around a long time in the system. Drug interference by other pharmacologically active agents can cause problems for accurate interpretation. Prescribed medications, unprescribed medications, and illicit drugs taken in combination can interfere with accurate results. Interpretation of these and any other laboratory results must be done by a skilled clinician knowledgeable about medicine, pharmacology, drug kinetics, and drug effects.

13.   REFER TO A CHILD PSYCHIATRIST WHEN IT IS
NEEDED. The time for a referral to a pediatric psychiatrist
varies from case to case. Generally, referral is necessary when

- There are any questions about assessment or treatment recommendations as a thorough biological, psychological, and
social assessment is always necessary.
- There is a concern for safety because of suicidality, homicidality, or any other type of harm the adolescents might do to
themselves or others.
- A question exists about the possibility of another psychiatric
diagnosis as a pediatric psychiatrist is trained to handle all
aspects of dual diagnosis.
- If there are any concerns about withdrawal or other medical
complications with the alcohol or other drugs.
- If hospitalization is a possibility.
- You see the necessity of body fluid testing.

14.   CONSIDER WHEN A PATIENT MAY BE APPROPRIATE
FOR THE ADOLESCENT PROGRAM VERSUS THE ADULT PRO-
GRAM. This is a real problem. Technically, a person is an adult
when he or she reaches eighteen years of age. In real life, many
individuals who are eighteen, nineteen, and even twenty are not
acting in any way like adults. Equally important, most drug and
alcohol dependent people are stuck at a much younger development age level. We have seen several thirty-year-old people in
treatment who have not gotten past the age of fifteen based on
the way they function in life.

Many use the argument, "He still acts like an adolescent, so
he should be in an adolescent treatment program." Of course,
that does not work for the thirty-year-old who consistently and
rightly ends up in the adult program. We also don't want to promote the person's dependency and help him or her stay at
the adolescent level if the person would really benefit from moving on. We want to provide the treatment that will be most ben-

eficial for a particular person, and that is what we will do, regardless.

Ideally, we could have treatment divided for adolescents, young adults, middle-age adults, and older adults as each age group has very different developmental issues to consider for treatment. For each individual in the "age gray zone," we need to consider all the factors with that one person. Where do most mental health professionals draw the line for adolescents and young adults? Each state differs, but for an example, where a person is considered an adult at the age of eighteen, the usual guidelines are these:

- If a person is younger than eighteen, he or she is an adolescent and needs an adolescent program.
- If a person is eighteen or nineteen, still in high school, and living at home, he or she is considered an adolescent and should be in an adolescent treatment program.
- If the person is eighteen or nineteen, has graduated from high school or is working toward a general equivalency diploma (GED), and is still living at home and dependent on his or her parents, that person should be treated like an adolescent.
- If the person is eighteen or nineteen, has graduated from high school or is working toward a GED, is still living at home with his or her parents but is working at a job, this person is usually treated like an adult.
- If the person is eighteen or nineteen, has graduated from high school or is working toward the GED, and is not living at home, that person should be considered an adult.
- If the person is younger than eighteen, is emancipated and living as an adult, the person should be treated like an adult in an adult program.

As you are involved with the treatment of an adolescent, remember that every case is a struggle. Most of these cases involve many different people; some of them are not stable and are at different levels of mental health. Don't worry if you're frustrated. It's not you; it's the tough case. That's a normal feeling.

THE TREATMENT

Current treatment programs have not paid sufficient attention to age and developmentally appropriate services. Again, adolescents are very different from adults, and thus must be treated differently. An adolescent would feel very much out of place in a group with adults for good reason. Treatment in this manner would be mostly ineffective. Separation of adolescents and adults varies across all types of treatment systems depending on the director. Usually systems do appropriately separate for psychiatric treatment in general. But the line is easily muddied when it comes to treatment for alcohol and other drugs because treatment programs are limited in most settings, and to save money, many times all ages are combined.

A high quality of treatment must be maintained at the same time costs are conserved. Patients must be matched to the levels of care that meet their needs, and the different levels of care must be attainable to most people. Selection criteria must be clinically sensible, yet cost conscious.

Treatment Levels of Care

"Medical necessity" is not enough to assess needs for care. One must look at the biological, social, and psychiatric parts of the whole picture. If the traditional payers are in charge of treatment necessity, they may insist on nasal abscesses in a cocaine user or significant withdrawal before approving an inpatient stay. They may also accept suicidality as a psychiatric concern warranting intensive treatment. But an adolescent may be in big trouble with alcohol or other drug use without exhibiting anything nearly this acute. He is in big trouble, having severe arguments in the family, taking his mother's silver and selling it, failing to attend school, and not keeping up with his school work. This bigger picture must be looked at to determine proper treatment.

Treatment also depends on the resources in the area where patients live. Sometimes it is more important to be in their home town and near family so family members can be involved in treatment, rather than to be in the best of treatment programs. Sometimes patients have undergone multiple treatments that have failed, and now they need more intensive care. These patients may receive more benefit from a top-notch program several miles away than one near home. The benefits must always must be weighed along with the risks.

For a complete treatment program, ideally the staff should be a multidisciplinary team with psychiatrists, psychologists, pediatricians, counselors, nurses, teachers, and specialized therapists—recreational, occupational, art, and speech—if needed. Members should join the team as appropriate depending on their areas of expertise and the patient's needs at each level. You could be a member of a multidisciplinary team or the primary case manager who started off as the original therapist. It all depends on your expertise and the resources available for each area—and these are usually scant for this significant mental health problem.

We need to be on the watch and treat as necessary acute intoxication and/or potential withdrawal, biomedical conditions and complications, emotional and behavioral conditions and complications, treatment acceptance and resistance, relapse potential, and the recovery environment. Moreover, each type of treatment is expected to occur in a drug-free environment.

In the next sections we describe the ideal. Six levels of care are discussed, with each dependent on the patient's individual needs. Table 3.1 indicates the types of treatment needed for each level of care.

The text that follows presents treatment plans for several types of patients with different care needs. Each type of alcohol and drug adolescent patient you may encounter in a usual therapeutic setting is considered and used as an example. For each level of care, six in number, a patient is described, and then the level

Table 3.1
Types of Treatment in Each Level

Treatment Modalities	Level					
	1	*2*	*3*	*4*	*5*	*6*
Agreement to remain sober	x	x	x	x	x	x
Psychosocial evaluation and cognitive approach	x	x	x	x	x	x
Psychiatric evaluation and appropriate treatment	x	x	x	x	x	x
Physical exam and treatment	x	x	x	x	x	x
Individual psychotherapy	x	x	x	x	x	
Psychoeducational: All aspects (individual)	x					
Unstructured drop-in center available	x	x	x			
Psychoeducational: All aspects (group)		x	x	x	x	
Group therapy: Open ended		x	x	x	x	
Multiple family group		x	x	x	x	x
Case manager for team		x	x	x	x	x
Provide school (can lead to H. S. certificate)			x	x	x	
Community meeting		x	x	x	x	
Recreational therapy, occupational therapy, art, ropes			x	x	x	
Male/Female tracking (optional)		x	x	x	x	
Psychodrama			x	x	x	
Anger management			x	x	x	
Journal and homework time			x	x	x	
Food services			x	x	x	x

appropriate for that person. The treatment components for each level are described in Table 3.1. Before addressing the six levels, we describe a patient we commonly encounter who is *not* in need of a specific adolescent alcohol and drug treatment program at one of the six levels, but who needs continued mental health treatment and monitoring. That person is at "Ground Zero."

Ground Zero: Normal Experimentation. Normal experimentation means using drugs without any consequential dependence or dysfunction. No alcohol and drug treatment is necessary yet.

Table 3.1 *(continued)*

Treatment Modalities		Level					
	1	*2*	*3*	*4*	*5*	*6*	
Treatment in the day, home at night			x				
Twenty-four-hour shelter				x	x	x	
Restraints/seclusion/quiet room			x	x	x	x	
Designated visiting hours			x	x	x	x	
Privilege system (step system)		x	x	x	x		
Recreation activities (movies, cards, and so on)				x	x		
Weekend activities (music, sports, social)				x	x		
Psychiatric/medical attending			x	x	x	x	
Nursing			x	x	x	x	
Locked/unlocked capability				x	x		
Life support						x	

Patient-Specific Treatment Modalities
Continue with outside therapist
Individual family therapy
Toxin screens
Alcohol, narcotics, cocaine anonymous
Al-Anon, Nar-Anon, Alateen
Further psychological testing
Signed agreements for treatment and next higher level if needed

LYNNE AND JOYCE

Fifteen-year-old Lynne and thirteen-year-old Joyce came to me after their mother called frantically because they weren't adjusting to their new school. They had just moved back with their mother from Saipan, where their maternal grandparents had been caring for them for the last two years. Throughout the girls' lives, they had been shuffled back and forth between the grandparents in Saipan and the mother in the United States. Mother had sent them there before coming back to the United States this time because she was very busy with her work and having troubles with her second husband, and she felt the girls would receive better care on the island. Finally, the mother married a third time and sent for the girls once again.

This current marriage was rocky; the stepfather was from yet another country and had beliefs about women, discipline, and religion that were different from U.S. norms. He was quite strict, and the girls found it more comfortable to be outside the home with their new friends. They were both very bright but were beginning to skip school. Once when they skipped, they had tried marijuana with some friends. Three times they tried crank (methamphetamines) and they regularly smoked cigarettes—about three per day. Additionally, they had drunk some alcohol a few times with their friends. The two girls stuck together in all respects because each found the other to be the only consistent and reliable figure in her life. Therefore, they used drugs and alcohol together, they skipped school together, and they had the same friends at the same time.

I did a complete evaluation, and we started meeting regularly in psychotherapy. We discussed drug education, safe sex, school, and friends. We also discussed the primary problem, which was the chaotic home life. Mom and stepdad had to agree on something—*anything* would be good. Naturally, with all the arguing at home, it was not a very pleasant place to be. Because they found more comfort, attention, and happiness with their friends, they used their friends for an escape.

Mother had no idea they were using any alcohol or drugs at all. She was sure she had taught them at some point that that was "very bad; people in our country drink a lot and I'm sure they realize how bad it is." She didn't find out they were using experimentally until one of the times they were truant; the truancy officer from the school said they had been found with their friends using crank. She was furious. She demanded I do a drug screen immediately. I instead met with them all and told her I did not find it necessary to do a screen since they had already admitted to using the drugs. They were using drugs in an experimental manner with their friends only, and they had no intention of continuing their use. This was also not the most important problem.

The major problems were those at home, and these were the items that needed work first. We are still in the process of working through problems in individual psychotherapy with the girls and in family therapy as well on an outpatient basis. I continually monitor them for drug and alcohol use, and they are still not using. They did have a nicotine dependence; that was given attention, and they are no longer smoking. They continue to be at high risk because they have some identity questions; problems at home; and trouble fitting in at home, their new school, and culture in general.

Level 1: Outpatient Alcohol and/or Drug-Focused Psychotherapy. Some programs call this level "pretreatment" when in reality it *is* treatment. So when is this level of care appropriate for an adolescent?

KRAMER

Kramer was a fourteen-year-old white boy from a middle-class family in which both parents worked hard and had fairly good insurance. Unfortunately, things were not so great at home, though it appeared as if they were. Kramer's father was usually a little out of control when he was married to Kramer's mom. He spent money he didn't have on cars and trips; he didn't work regularly because he was off preaching about God, a topic about which he talked incessantly. You may recognize some of these symptoms as describing a man with mania. Kramer's mother and biological father were divorced, and mom married a second man with similar symptoms. Fortunately, he was taking lithium and "is a really nice guy" but still somewhat out of control. Mom and her second husband divorced—and all this time Kramer was growing, and learning.

Mom married her third husband a few years ago. Kramer saw his guru biological dad when they could connect, but this certainly did not happen reliably or consistently. He adored his first stepfather, and he and Kramer had a great time together; but the man didn't help with any responsibilities. Kramer could not stand his current "Nazi" stepfather who was a Vietnam veteran who lived by the motto "You do as I say or I'll beat you up" (not necessarily physically but certainly mentally). As you can see, mom chose quite a different type of mate that time, and Kramer was becoming an adolescent. What a mix! Mom was the only consistent figure; she basically managed everything, including the emotions in the family. Unfortunately, these emotions were on overload in everyone's life so she was always screaming, yelling, and crying.

Kramer was a great student. Well, occasionally. His erratic academic behavior was the reason his mom brought him to see me. She was certain he had the symptoms of Attention Deficit/Hyperactivity Disorder (ADHD), for which he was diagnosed earlier. At the same time, he had symptoms of mania like his biological dad, which made sense, because there is indeed a genetic tie with that illness. During the investigation, I learned that he had smoked marijuana for a few years, and lately had done it more regularly—three to four times a week. Additionally, he would go out on weekends with his buddies and get plastered on bourbon. This all helped him "be more mellow and relaxed," like a type of self-medication.

We had several options at this point. Mother was encouraging me to start medications for his underlying psychiatric concerns, which I still hadn't seen without the muddiness of the marijuana and alcohol. (If you are not a pediatric psychiatrist, you should ask for a medication consultation if you have any doubts.) I did intensive family therapy with them and individual therapy with Kramer. He agreed to lay off the drugs and alcohol. He understood that he could not start any medications until I saw that it was necessary—when I saw what the *real* Kramer was like—for I had discovered that the substances cause him to have significant mood swings and loss of control. (I knew it all along, but discovering this helped him.) He was still safe as an outpatient. He wasn't acting too dangerously yet; he was not suicidal, and remember, he had agreed to stop the drugs and alcohol.

When he was clean and dry, he brought his grades up to A's and B's. The whole family was getting along better (with many fewer yelling matches and battles, with Kramer coming home less often late at night and banging on the door to get in). Mom still insisted on starting medications, but I continued to say, "Well, he's doing great now, and functioning well; medication doesn't make sense."

The old tension came back at home. Things were rocky, and Kramer began to use alcohol and drugs even more than before. Remember, it really helped him feel better, and it didn't really cause *that* many problems; besides, he still liked those friends who use. Moreover, "It's *just* beer and marijuana!" Mom was frantic now, and very angry at Kramer: "How can he do this to me!" It was time for an intervention. Interventions are used at every level to get a person into whatever kind of care is needed. The whole family came in together to say individually how they were affected by the drinking and marijuana, and specifically the effects from the substance. There was a lot of crying, and I was the only one there on Kramer's side. He was shocked and hurt by what his family said about him, and now really felt lousy that he could be such an awful person and hurt so many important people in his life.

He continued to self-medicate. He did not agree to go to the Level 2 care, a full outpatient recovery program, which is what I recommended. He said he could stop. Therefore, we all agreed on Level 1 care that included his agreement to stay sober; physical exam and treatment as needed; continued psychosocial, educational, and psychiatric evaluation; individual cognitive and supportive psychotherapy; and continued family therapy as needed (see Table 3.1).

Level 1 care would also have been appropriate if Kramer had not needed more intensive care. Here it was useful because he was not committed to more intensive care, but the option gave him some autonomy to choose. If he failed this treatment program, he agreed to go into the Level 2 care. This strategy is also useful if there is a waiting list for the more intensive Level 2 outpatient care.

If he remained abstinent during this period, he could stop the alcohol and drug focus of treatment but might agree to continue

Alcoholics Anonymous (AA) twice or more per week, and he could now resume once-weekly individual sessions. He might agree to contract for random urine drug screens as seen appropriate by the therapist. He was functioning well, and needed no medications.

Level 2: Structured Outpatient Evening Care.

Kramer had a rough day at school. He had to take a final exam that he had not prepared for adequately. He knew he hadn't done well on the test, so he went out with his buddies after school to the shopping center. They all decided to have a joint and a few beers. No big deal, except to Kramer. He felt guilty and came home with the smell of booze on his breath and body, and his parents got a whiff. His parents called me the next day, as I am his primary therapist. I saw him individually, and he whined about all his problems, apparently not able to cope without his friends, beer, and marijuana. He had committed to a contract, agreeing to go up to the next level of care if he used, and thus knew he was headed for Level 2. He put up a fight, to which I listened attentively. Nevertheless, he had agreed.

Next he began the program described in Table 3.1 for Level 2 care, including continued agreement to stay sober; continued psychosocial, psychiatric, and medical evaluation; continued individual and separate family therapy as appropriate; group psychoeducation, group therapy, and multiple family group; meeting with the case manager for the team and a community meeting daily; and a step privilege system (see Table 3.1). Again, the full treatment team is often a luxury depending on where the treatment is and who is covering the costs (managed care, individual private pay, or county, for example). Much of the group work may have to be done by AA, Narcotics Anonymous (NA), Al-Anon, or a general group therapy setting for adolescents in the area. The other work may have to be done by the primary caretakers, including the therapist and pediatrician.

Treatment took a lot of time and money for Kramer and his parents. If parents can't commit to all of it, there can be modifications in the signed agreement. These alterations can be made among the family; me, the primary therapist; and the case manager from the multidisciplinary team. This treatment is so important, however, that some of it must be mandatory and minimal. It can also be life-saving, so even if it takes time away from some other activities, the time will be well spent.

If he remains abstinent during this period, Kramer can stop the organized treatment after the agreed-on period of time. He might then continue AA twice or more per week, and he might resume my once-weekly individual sessions. He may agree to contract for random urine drug screens as seen appropriate by me and the treatment team for the structured program. He is functioning well and still needs no medications.

This type of outpatient treatment may also be used for a patient who is coming out of the hospital (day or full) as a transition period of treatment, before the patient goes back to the least intensive care. It all depends on the stability of the patient at the time of discharge.

Level 3: Partial or Day Hospitalization.

Now Kramer is still "*just* using marijuana and alcohol," but he is skipping school part of the time to use drugs with his friends, his grades are dropping, and he's angry with his parents most of the time. He even threatened to take a baseball bat to his stepfather. Moreover, when he gets into these arguments, he leaves the house, goes over to his somewhat older friend's house down the road, and they drive somewhere and use drugs. He can't stay with his parents, and he can't stay away from his friends. At this point he definitely needs Level 3 care, if not Level 4, depending on finances, contractibility, and family commitment. Level 3 would be less costly; he would not be able to skip school to use drugs; he could go home every night and work on straightening out his life in the day treatment.

SALLY

Another example is Sally. Fifteen-year-old Sally just moved from Ohio with her mom, who just divorced Sally's father. Mom can get a better job here. She is busy settling into a new job, a new city, and a new relationship. Mom is a very busy lady.

With Sally, we're talking about a small-town girl coming to a fairly racy city in California. In Ohio, Sally used alcohol on weekends with her friends and marijuana for the last year—about three times per week. She smokes about a pack of cigarettes per day. She is a very pretty, fair-skinned girl who was popular in her high school back home. Her mom was always busy then, too, but she regularly attended the school plays Sally was in. Sally was also on the school girl's soccer team and enjoyed horseback riding on weekends. The high school in California is much larger than the one she was used to back home. There is much more competition for spots in the school plays and on the soccer team. She still tried, and actually managed, to keep her grades up for a while. She had a difficult time fitting in because she was new, and didn't feel like she belonged yet.

She finally met Joe, who was quite a hunk and on the football team. They dated. She started drinking with him at parties and found he also used marijuana regularly. It was easy for her to get back into smoking marijuana. Joe introduced her to crack cocaine, and then she experimented with crank. Along the way she tried PCP and LSD, but didn't really like them well enough to continue. She especially liked the cocaine and used crack regularly. She had intercourse with Joe regularly by that time; he was her first.

Mom and Sally touched bases occasionally, and Mom knew about Joe's drinking and marijuana use, but not the rest. She figured it was all right for Sally to continue the relationship until she discovered that Sally did not come home occasionally and her grades were dropping. She started having a lot of nasal congestion and seemed to be sickly. She was tired, coughing a lot, and also complained of headaches. Mom took her to the doctor, who, as Mother suspected, found she had mononucleosis. He also discovered nasal lesions and suspected nasal cocaine use. He questioned Sally about cocaine use; she admitted the problem minimally, and the doctor referred her to me.

I did an extensive evaluation. Mom was still aware of only the alcohol and marijuana use by her daughter, but that was enough to work on in treatment. There was a lot of friction at home because Sally felt she was being neglected, and "Mom didn't care." She knew she should stay away from her new drug-using friends at school but couldn't, and she went out with them regularly after school, too. She didn't want to lose the only friends she had. Her dilemma was to figure out how could she get help with her drugs (by now she could tell they were damaging her health) and still keep her friends. The fact is, she couldn't.

I considered the Level 2 outpatient program, as that is all she agreed to at first. She even tried it for a while, but she was still using regularly at school and cutting class consistently. She finally agreed to day treatment to help her stay away from her usual friends and to focus only on herself. Luckily, there was a day treatment program in her city of residence. Her treatment consisted of the Level 3 items listed in Table 3.1. In addition, the program included a twenty-four-hour shelter, recreational activities besides the recreational therapy, and weekend activities because on weekends she will be at home. Day treatment does not have locked unit capabilities, but most programs do have a quiet room for an emotional outlet. Some are safely padded so that a person can vent physically as well.

Unfortunately, although this level of treatment may be the best, an adolescent may not be able to receive it as most cities are not able to offer such care. Part of the main benefit is working on problems during the day in an intensive treatment setting, and trying new strategies in the evening at home with the family. Again, a lower level of care can be tried, but if it is not adequate, the patient may die. In a case like this, it may be well worthwhile for the primary care provider to argue with somebody in a management position of an insurance company, even if the manager doesn't have a medical background, to get a patient like Sally the lifesaving care she requires. It is up to the primary care provider to convince the person on the other end of the phone, who has not met Sally, that she needs certain care. Sometimes, a residential treatment program, Level 4, may be decided on if day treatment cannot be appropriately instituted, if the nearest day treatment program is one hundred miles away. Sometimes this battle can't be won, and the primary care provider must work with what is available.

The work at Level 3 is continued by the same multidisciplinary team at the same or another facility, depending on the resources for the area. Many insurance companies are beginning to favor day treatment to save the costs of inpatient care. Moreover, the classes offered are given by the people who do them for the hospitalized patients. Day treatment is also effective, because adolescents can live through several problems in the evening at home, and get support and work on them during the day. Day treatment may also be the step after hospitalization, as a transition to outpatient care, depending on the stability of the patient's condition.

Level 4: Residential Treatment Center (RTC).

Level 4 care is for the Sally who was not fortunate enough to have a day treatment program near home. We had attempted the intensive Level 2 structured outpatient program, but Sally lost ground quickly, and I could not hold onto her any longer. She was not suicidal, homicidal, or psychotic, but she was into cocaine severely and bacteria from her nasal abscesses were seeding her blood so that she had continued septicemia. She required hospitalization for lifesaving intravenous antibiotics. She did not feel she could control her habit with the available treatment options in her city or with what was offered at the hospital. Because she was not "sick enough" to require inpatient treatment, the insurance company agreed on a residential treatment center approximately two hundred miles away from her home. She lived in the center with twenty-four-hour monitoring and appropriate care. The care included all the items in Table 3.1, except for life support and family involvement in her case. Obviously, family therapy was a necessary part of her treatment, but the risks were too high for her to stay in any kind of a setting other than one that could offer full-time treatment, care, and monitoring. Her mother and I each had continued contact with Sally and the treatment team at the RTC. I continued working with her mother at home while Sally was working far away on similar issues. The distance apart proved beneficial in the long run, as each discovered new ways of coping, caring, sharing, and living.

Sally received less education than she would have received in an outpatient or day treatment program, but she was given occupational and vocational training appropriate for her age instead. This is common for RTCs. She was with several teenagers referred by the legal system who had previously been through several other treatment episodes. Most of her peers there used drugs other than marijuana, such as heroin, other opiates, cocaine, hallucinogens, and barbiturates. These adolescents lived together, so they worked out their problems together; also, there is a strong emphasis on more group than individual counseling in RTCs.

Residential treatment centers are often the placement immediately after hospitalization for those who need to live in a therapeutic community. They can also be appropriate for some as the first treatment for the problem, depending on medical necessity, as medical care is limited. RTCs have a great deal of structure and close supervision. They are designed for the adolescent with additional psychiatric concerns, significant behavioral problems, and such severe social and family problems that the teenager cannot have a successful outpatient or day treatment program. He or she may have tried going home from an inpatient program, but it did not work. The RTC is between inpatient care and day treatment, and the only alternative for many teens. The length of stay is longer than the stay for a hospital inpatient, and usually shorter than for someone in day treatment. Of course, outpatient treatment can last a varied amount of time depending on the patient's needs.

State codes may be different in defining residential care facilities (RCFs) and residential (or community) treatment facilities (RTFs). The latter is equivalent to a residential treatment center (RTC). We also have facilities called social rehabilitation facilities (SRFs). It is important to know what you are referring your patients to, to be sure they get the amount and level of care appropriate for their needs. The specific differences are these: a residential care facility is the least restrictive family or group home for twenty-four-hour nonmedical care if a person needs supervision, protection, assistance, or personal services for the activities of daily living. A residential treatment center or residential treatment facility is a residential facility that offers mental health treatment services to children in a group home setting. A social rehabilitation facility is a residential home that provides social rehabilitation for no longer than eighteen months in a group setting to adults recovering from a mental illness, including alcohol or other drug dependencies, and who need assistance, guidance, or counseling temporarily.

Level 5: Medically Monitored, Inpatient Psychiatric Care, Locked or Unlocked.

Level 5 is for Kramer if he can't manage going home at night. He is really hooked. He may even need a *locked* unit with these same capabilities. He may have reached the point where the mental health professionals have to keep the drugs in the facility away from him. It may be that his parents are so angry that they can't manage their temper with him at night when he's home. You may just have to skip Levels 1, 2, 3, and 4 and go directly to this level for a short time, with a close holding environment. This facility also has a padded blue room where Kramer can safely vent his anger when he wants or needs to.

SAM

Now it's time to meet Sam. He's a sixteen-year-old Asian boy from Singapore. He's comparatively tall and quite attractive. He's also very smart and cunning. His parents are extremely wealthy. Of course, dad's high-powered job is the reason he could visit with Sam only twice per month, by appointment. In the meanwhile, mom was attempting to raise him, but very busy with her social life, and a nanny cared for him daily. He was quite an aggressive little guy growing up. He pulled dogs' eyes out and twisted birds' heads off. Maybe this was in response to his mother's discipline. She put him out on the porch for a night at a time if he was "bad," but said that was nothing compared to the hot iron she got on the back of her hand when she was young. To be sure, he did his homework when she stood over him with a cane in one hand and held his ear with the other. The canes broke as he grew, so she was continuously buying new and bigger canes.

Sam's recreation was "rave" parties—all-night dance sessions, usually in England, where he went to school. They were nightly events. There he used all his favorite recreational substances, including the best PCP and LSD money could buy. He smoked cigarettes and marijuana regularly every day. Alcohol and sex was always mixed with his drugs at the raves. What more can I say? He used everything several times. His private school was concerned, but he managed to buy grades and was able to squeak by. He obviously could not manage on any kind of an outpatient basis, and when he came into the hospital, he had drugs hidden in the heel of his shoes so he wouldn't be deprived of anything he wanted. He actually needed a locked unit because he was at high risk for running away and for obtaining drugs. A locked unit would also be indicated for someone who is suicidal, homicidal, or actively psychotic.

MARK

Sam is an extreme case of an adolescent in need of a locked inpatient unit and care. A more common example would be Mark, who is a sixteen-year-old white boy enrolled in a typical high school and living with his biological parents. His parents referred him against his will. He used most drugs, but his primary drugs of choice were nicotine and marijuana; he also snorted crank (methamphetamines) regularly. He was sexually molested by his uncle, and even though both parents appeared to be average American citizens who each worked, his dad beat his mom regularly. Dad was also an alcoholic and cigarette smoker. Mark easily said, "My parents don't care about me."

Mark is a person who could get by with an unlocked psychiatric unit. He needed intensive treatment for his drug use, but other serious life events were adding to his already difficult life. Recently Mark's best friend had been shot to death in a drive-by shooting, and he went to two different girls for comfort in the way of regular sexual activity. His school was ready to expel him because of his truancy. He had recently been released from juvenile hall where he had spent time for breaking, entering, and theft. He said he had always been depressed, and life really wasn't worth living. He wasn't, however, actively suicidal. His parents confirmed the long-standing depressed mood.

Mark certainly did not agree to inpatient treatment. But because he was in great danger and was passively suicidal, I could have put him in the hospital against his will. I basically said, "I must hospitalize you with or without your consent because of the danger you are in." He reluctantly agreed to hospitalization with consent. He could contract against self-harm and manage in an unlocked psychiatric unit. He required continual assessment and treatment and close monitoring.

Sally, whom we discussed earlier, may need this level if her problem continues or worsens. A patient in need of this care may have a great potential for relapse, may have a poor environment for recovery, and may require observation. The use of intravenous drugs or other signs of serious dependency would be enough indication for treatment this intensive. Additionally, a girl who is prostituting probably needs inpatient care.

The inpatient unit, whether it needs to be locked or unlocked as indicated previously, has all the components listed in Table 3.1 except life support. If the psychiatric unit is a part of a general hospital, life support is nearby and readily accessible.

Level 6: Closely Medically Monitored, Intensive Inpatient Medical Care.

RACHEL

Meet Rachel. She is an attractive seventeen-year-old girl with reddish-brown hair. She's slim, and some would even say skinny. She was admitted to the hospital for a knee abscess. The reason for the abscess was her daily intravenous use of heroin. Prostitution provided the funds for her habit. She had moved away from her mother's home in Northern California, leaving her two-year-old daughter in her mother's care. She had dropped out of school up north, and started beauty school here. She had to drop out of beauty school because she often could not concentrate on anything but getting a fix. Money ran out anyway.

Rachel was first hospitalized on the medicine unit because of her acute medical needs for the severe knee abscess. The medical team was not accustomed to patients having withdrawals from heroin and of course requested psychiatric consultation. Additionally, Rachel kept trying to escape because she wanted and needed a fix of heroin. Rachel required a one-to-one sitter around the clock. She had that on the medical unit, but the nursing staff were not used to this type of patient, who would constantly complain and try to escape, so they were not able to manage her, even with the sitter. The psychiatric treatment, as described above, was not instituted consistently at first, as she still needed the intensive medical treatment. The psychiatric group therapies came gradually, as she became able to participate more and actually be transported from the medical unit to the psychiatric unit for groups. The group treatment was instituted much faster than Rachel thought it should be.

She was transferred as soon as possible to the medical/psychiatric unit so she could get both types of intensive treatment. Most hospitals do not have a medical/psychiatric unit, so the decision for the type of service has to be made based on the priority at the time. In this case, a psychiatric unit was needed as soon as she could be transferred from the straight medical unit with psychiatric consultation, because of her risk of running away and her dangerous drug habit. Also, because of her withdrawals, she needed to have continued and immediate medical management. The medical necessities could be managed on the psychiatric unit at that time, with close medical management as well as psychiatric care.

Depending on the staff and treatment available, the psychiatric unit might be able to provide adolescents with the intensive medical treatment they would need for withdrawals and any other medical problems they might have. In other situations, patients may not be able to get into the full psychiatric program at first because of their medical limitations. The psychiatric unit would have to be locked or unlocked based on the same criteria for a locked unit described under Level 5.

Occasionally, a patient may require strictly intensive medical care because of the acuity of the medical problems. Joe is an example of that.

JOE

Joe was drinking at a fraternity party one night when his fraternity brothers saw him pass out (not the first time). This time, however, he was not responsive, so they rushed him to the emergency room. He had aspirated his own vomit, was unconscious at that point, and was not breathing. Emergency services had to provide life support and send him to the medical intensive care unit. He survived, was removed from life support, and was sent to the medical unit for clearance. After he was medically stable, he did not require a locked inpatient psychiatric program but did need inpatient psychiatric services because of the high-risk and near fatal alcohol-induced event. He went from a short stay there to an intensive day treatment program, as his family could offer support at night and join in the treatment process as well.

Level 6 care is usually used for a short time for an alcohol- or other drug-addicted adolescent. It provides essentially medical treatment as offered in any inpatient setting, with the inclusion of psychiatric consultation and management. Outside the medical arena, family therapy has begun for patients at this level, and usually a primary case manager has been chosen to help determine the next level of care. Many times, the adolescents can go directly to day treatment, but sometimes they require inpatient psychiatric care before day treatment. If being at home is too risky, residential treatment may be the next step after intensive medical care, providing the person does not need inpatient psychiatric care first.

Aftercare

Aftercare is a type of outpatient care used as follow-up to inpatient treatment. It may be a residential treatment care center, partial/day hospitalization program, or outpatient care; it is not as intensive as inpatient care, depending on the need of the individual.

Aftercare is critical to help adolescents avoid the temptations they will be faced with after being involved in intensive monitoring. How well will they be able to avoid the slippery places? An adult may be able to drive down a different street and not go near his or her favorite bar. But many adolescents do not drive and often have absolutely no "say so" as to where the car is driven. They may have to return to the same school they just came from, and be required to see the same kids each day. Self-help groups such as AA, CA (Cocaine Anonymous), and NA (Narcotics Anonymous) will be important, but they may not be sufficient. Again, these adolescents live with and depend on several other people ordinarily, so they will need from these other people to do the things that will help rather than hinder them at this time when they are very vulnerable.

Practical Treatment Considerations

For all the types of treatment, some practical considerations are necessary to help determine the appropriate care for each individual. Who is responsible? Are the parents committed enough to get the adolescent to treatment on time, and regularly? Can the program provide the transportation? Is every level of management available in the area, or are you limited to certain programs? Movement along a continuum is significant. Is the overall program set up so a patient may go back and forth between programs appropriately?

There must be a manager for each patient. This could be the regular pediatrician, psychiatrist, psychologist, social worker, or counselor. Someone needs to be sure the patient is getting the appropriate care and to act in their behalf. Are all the needs of each individual being met? For example, if a person has a learning and reading disorder, can management take that into consideration, and can the treatment plan fit the needs of that person? If the usual treatment plan requires reading, can the adolescent handle this alone, or does he or she need someone to help with the reading? What kind of financial support and care is available for the patient?

A substance-abusing parent, guardian, or other family member may also need attention to improve the prognosis for the teen in treatment. It could be futile to treat only the adolescent. He or she might be able to succeed in treatment if the significant other is using, but it is unlikely. On the other hand, if the adolescent is ready for help, and the family isn't, you must work with the adolescent to access all available help. A good role model is important. Sometimes the adolescent in treatment opens the door for the other family members to get help. Besides alcohol and other drug use by family members, other psychiatric diagnoses need attention as well.

Overall, treatment must be therapeutic rather than punitive, and the adolescent and parents need to know that. Much education needs to be done with the family as well as the teen. The treatment team deals with the adolescent as a human being and responsible young person in a nonpunitive manner. It would not be beneficial, and could be detrimental, if at the same time the parents are treating the young person in exactly the opposite way.

OUTCOME

Recovery is not an all-or-nothing process. If a person needs ten people to help him or her decide to quit smoking, and you're the seventh one in that path, your help will put the person one step closer to quitting. Some use of alcohol or other drugs doesn't necessarily equal failure; abstinence alone does not necessarily equal success. A person needs to work through the stages of the recovery process while he or she is learning to live a comfortable and substantial life, clean and sober. The already complex assessment and treatment picture gets more complex as one considers the fact that dual diagnosis issues can interfere with recovery at any step.

The developmental tasks of adolescence are already a tough process to master, and part of recovery must address the process of working through the psychosocial developmental phase arrested or modified by alcohol or other drug use. The issues around and through identity, independence, intimacy, conflict, choices, social skills, impulse control, and coping mechanisms are all hard without drugs, especially at the age of adolescence.

Can we help discover useful substitutes for alcohol and other drugs? Can modifications be made effectively in the person's entire lifestyle that do not involve the use of alcohol and other drugs? We had better try to work on these things for successful treatment outcomes! At the same time, we need to remember that addictive disorders are chronic; they can be managed but not cured! As we say, "Once an addict, always an addict." It is vital to start where the patient is and set realistic goals for that individual and his or her family.

Posttreatment Continuation of Care

Posttreatment continuation of care is paramount. Of course, in reality this is still treatment. It is extremely critical, as temptation is greatest right after a person returns to the old environment. Aftercare has been described above. The type of aftercare depends on the type of treatment the adolescent has already received, where the person is in the way of progress, the financial coverage for care, and the support he or she will have on discharge from that treatment program. Aftercare is normally a step down from the previous level of care. A major point is that adolescents have *lower* rates of total abstinence than adults during the year after completing treatment. Forty percent of adolescents remain abstinent after completing an inpatient alcohol and other drug treatment program, compared to a rate of 50 percent to 60 percent for adults. It is the posttreatment care, or aftercare, that determines the success rate.

Some may argue about the definition of successful treatment. Does success mean abstinence, controlled use, or simply adequate life functioning? Society, after all, has the idea that the norm equals some drinking of alcohol, and there is not a problem with that unless a person's functioning is affected negatively. Would that norm be applicable for an adolescent who has already had trouble with alcohol or other drugs? There is a good chance that a teenager would have problems again if he or she started using again. On the other hand, the person may be able to control his or her drinking successfully as an adult. Even the definition of *relapse* is debatable. We would say that it depends on individual factors, beliefs, and the ability to function. You need to look at the entire picture of that individual person.

Continued abstinence is dependent on several factors. Don't forget the basic developmental growth an adolescent is going through at the time of treatment The adolescent may not be using alcohol or other drugs any more, regardless of what you or I have done. There are no data on that subject from which to glean an answer.

We do have data on other factors that determine success in treatment. The most significant factor related positively and strongly to continued abstinence is the regular continuation of attendance at support groups. These are AA, CA, NA, Al-Anon, and Nar-Anon. Abstinence is significantly higher if the patient attends meetings of these groups twice or more per week for a full year.

Parents' participation is related positively to adolescents' success, not only for continued abstinence but for continued participation in support groups. Their involvement is essential, and they must talk about it and work through the problem. The number of friends who use alcohol or other drugs also affects the adolescent's success. The more friends who use during the first six months after the teenager's treatment, the worse the young person's recovery will be. This is one reason, with data to support it, for encouraging an adolescent to develop healthy relationships after treatment. Finding a whole new crowd is a tough process and the teenager will need help with this. But it is crucial.

Some favorable outcomes from residential treatment centers (RTCs) include a reduction in the use of opiates and criminal activities. RTCs are more effective than drug-free outpatient programs (DFOPs) in decreasing marijuana and alcohol use, but both decrease criminal activity. One year after discharge, RTC patients said they were more satisfied with treatment than DFOP clients.

Some outcomes are not so favorable: neither types of treatment programs significantly decrease the use of marijuana and alcohol. Marijuana use showed no significant change among whites, and there was even an increase among blacks. Moreover, alcohol use increased among blacks. The longer a teenager is in a DFOP, the more problems he or she has being productive in school, home, work, and life in general. If the adolescents are in the protective environment of a RTC, they are better able to restructure their lives and become productive. These statistics were found with or without decent aftercare, according to the authors, but the type of aftercare was not discussed. Again, it is vital to have proper aftercare to better these types of statistics.

Other Positive Results

The schools, criminal justice system, and society as a whole benefit from continued success of treatment for adolescents with alcohol and other drug problems. If they remain abstinent, statistics show that they require fewer school disciplinary actions than if they continue to use.

Moreover, if abstinence continues, these young people have fewer arrests for any type of offense. The same person will often have fewer than half as many arrests as he or she did before treatment. These benefits are just as meaningful as abstinence to the individual, his family, and society. In fact, these consequences are probably of greater interest to society. The public doesn't have to worry quite as much about a robbery for drug money if there are fewer kids out there with that need.

Dependency in later stages of life will become more chronic and debilitating if not caught early. Like adults, many adolescents in treatment will relapse, but many improve after repeated failures and treatments. Work with and help for the family is an integral part of treatment. You must develop a strategic alliance with the family and the adolescent. You must work with the healthiest part of the family system first to get help for the entire system. Sometimes that happens to be the abusing adolescent; if the teenager is the strongest link, use him or her to help the rest of the family.

Prevention Is Key

Prevention is a key in adolescent alcohol and drug use. The major emphasis must be on preventing the initiation of alcohol and other drug use in the first place. "Affective education," "affective-humanistic education," and "Just Say No" models have shown only minimal effectiveness.

The most promising preventive measures focus on the psychosocial etiologic issues that promote drug use. Parental, peer, media, and other pressures, and the teaching of coping skills to deal with everyday pressures are items to focus on. Smoking cessation programs using these types of techniques have had good results. Personal and social skills training must be implemented in schools and homes. Teenagers need to be taught problem-solving and decision-making skills. Instruction, demonstration, reinforcement, rehearsal, and assignments can help young people learn cognitive skills for resisting social pressures and improving their self-control, self-acceptance enhancement, coping alternatives, interpersonal skills, and assertiveness training.

Studies have shown that the best results come from a combination of personal-social skills training and social influence techniques. These techniques are working effectively for the reduction of cigarette, alcohol, and marijuana use.

WE HAVE A RESPONSIBILITY TO OUR YOUTH

Substance abuse in adolescence is a major public health problem and affects many people. We have a lot of work to do in these two groups. We do not know the definitive cause of adolescent use, nor the definitive treatment, but we do know some things that can be helpful for our youth and thus society. We know about etiology, epidemiology, and the progression from and to types of drugs. We know the risk factors for adolescents. We also know some developmental issues that play a part. We know that family work is integral to effective treatment, and we know a lot about treatment techniques that are recommended at this time. Consequently, we must put every effort to helping those in need with these things we do know. We are also aware of the need for further research in this extremely important area of medicine.

The distressed youth of today are distressed adults of tomorrow, and anything we can do to help prevent more suffering is beneficial. Stressing prevention is better than succumbing to a false economic argument: we can pay some now, or pay a lot later. Cost is always a consideration, but no treatment at all is the most expensive of all the options.

NOTES

P. 77, *Crash Kills 8 Contra Costa Youths:* Cooper, C. (1991, August 11). Crash kills 8 Contra Costa youths. *San Francisco Examiner, Metro,* pp. B-1, 6. Reprinted by permission.

P. 77. *accidents are the leading cause:* Kaplan, H. I., & Sadock, B. J. (Eds.). (1994). *Synopsis of psychiatry* (7th ed.). Baltimore: Williams & Wilkins, p. 1121.

P. 77. *Of all adolescents who die:* Gans, J. E., & Shook, K. L. (1994). *Policy compendium on tobacco, alcohol, and other harmful substances affecting adolescents: Alcohol and other harmful substances.* Chicago: American Medical Association, p. 3.

P. 77, *Homicide and suicide are the second:* Kaplan, H. I., & Sadick, B. J. (Eds.). (1994). *Synopsis of psychiatry* (7th ed.). Baltimore: Williams & Wilkins.

P. 78, *other severe psychiatric problems:* Gans, J. E., & Shook, K. L. (1994). *Policy compendium on tobacco, alcohol, and other harmful substances affecting adolescents: Alcohol and other harmful substances.* Chicago: American Medical Association.

P. 78, *Many of these victims:* Schydlower, M., & Rogers, P. D. (1993, June). *Adolescent substance abuse and addictions.* Philadelphia: Hanley & Belfus, p. 378.

P. 78, *A series of studies beginning:* Schydlower, M., & Rogers, P. D. (1993, June). *Adolescent substance abuse and addictions.* Philadelphia: Hanley & Belfus, p. 378.

P. 79, *By 1991, that figure had dropped to 29 percent:* Schydlower, M., & Rogers, P. D. (1993, June). *Adolescent substance abuse and addictions.* Philadelphia: Hanley & Belfus, p. 378.

P. 79, *the 1994 Monitoring the Future study:* Hudson, J. (1995, February). Drug abuse increases among U.S. teenagers as beliefs about drugs' dangers soften. *Psychiatric Times,* pp. 35–36.

P. 80, *Marijuana is the most prevalent:* Schydlower, M., & Rogers, P. D. (1993, June). *Adolescent substance abuse and addictions.* Philadelphia: Hanley & Belfus.

P. 80, *The decrease over the years:* Schydlower, M., & Rogers, P. D. (1993, June). *Adolescent substance abuse and addictions.* Philadelphia: Hanley & Belfus.

P. 80, *Legal psychoactive substances that are:* Schydlower, M., & Rogers, P. D. (1993, June). *Adolescent substance abuse and addictions.* Philadelphia: Hanley & Belfus.

P. 80, *In 1991, high school seniors:* Schydlower, M., & Rogers, P. D. (1993, June). *Adolescent substance abuse and addictions.* Philadelphia: Hanley & Belfus.

P. 81, *Even though a "war on drugs":* Schydlower, M., & Rogers, P. D. (1993, June). *Adolescent substance abuse and addictions.* Philadelphia: Hanley & Belfus.

P. 81, *over 90 percent of high school:* Jellinek, M. S., & Herzog, D. B. (1990). *Massachusetts General Hospital, psychiatric aspects of general hospital pediatrics.* Salem, MA: Year Book Medical Publishers, p. 332.

P. 81, *Retrospective reports from 1975 to 1991:* Schydlower, M., & Rogers, P. D. (1993, June). *Adolescent substance abuse and addictions.* Philadelphia: Hanley & Belfus.

P. 82, *Male adolescents use illicit drugs:* Schydlower, M., & Rogers, P. D. (1993, June). *Adolescent substance abuse and addictions.* Philadelphia: Hanley & Belfus.

P. 82, *Socioeconomic Status Differences:* Schydlower, M., & Rogers, P. D. (1993, June). *Adolescent substance abuse and addictions.* Philadelphia: Hanley & Belfus.

P. 82, *Illicit drug use has spread:* Schydlower, M., & Rogers, P. D. (1993, June). *Adolescent substance abuse and addictions.* Philadelphia: Hanley & Belfus.

P. 83, *It is very difficult to generalize:* Schydlower, M., & Rogers, P. D. (1993, June). *Adolescent substance abuse and addictions.* Philadelphia: Hanley & Belfus, p. 243.

P. 83, *Entering Treatment:* Beschner, G., & Friedman, A. (1985). Treatment of adolescent drug abusers. *International Journal of Addictions, 20*(6&7), 971–993.

P. 84, *Studies of twins, adoptees, and siblings:* Powers, R. (1994). *Primary prevention in psychiatry; A focus on prenatal care.* Stanford, CA: Stanford University Hospital, pp. 13–16.

P. 86, *Thrill- and novelty-seeking have:* Rogers, P., Silling, S. M., & Adams, L. (1991). Adolescent chemical dependence: A diagnosable disease. *Psychiatric Annals, 21,* 91–97.

P. 86, *Additionally, mental obsessions, emotional compulsions:* Lawson, G. W., & Lawson, A. W. (1992). *Adolescent substance abuse, etiology, treatment, and prevention.* Gaithersburg, MD: Aspen Publishers, p. 7.

P. 89, *a greater tolerance for deviance:* Wills, T. A., Schreibman, D., Benson, G., & Vaccaro, D. (1994). Impact of parental substance use on adolescents: A test of a mediational model. *Journal of Pediatric Psychology, 19*(5), 537–553.

P. 91, *followed regardless of the user's gender:* Bailey, G. W. (1989). Current perspectives on substance abuse in youth. *Annual progress in child psychiatry and development.* Reprinted with permission from *Journal of the American Academy of Child and Adolescent Psychiatry, 28*(2), 503–531.

P. 91, *The first stage of use is experimentation:* Schydlower, M., & Rogers, P. D. (1993, June). *Adolescent substance abuse and addictions.* Philadelphia: Hanley & Belfus.

P. 93, *Problem drinking usually comes after marijuana:* Bailey, G. W. (1989). Current perspectives on substance abuse in youth. *Annual progress in child psychiatry and development.* Reprinted with permission from *Journal of the American Academy of Child and Adolescent Psychiatry, 28*(2), 503–531.

P. 94 *There is a high correlation:* Bailey, G. W. (1989). Current perspectives on substance abuse in youth. *Annual progress in child psychiatry and development.* Reprinted with permission from *Journal of the American Academy of Child and Adolescent Psychiatry, 28*(2), 503–531.

P. 98, *"Fatigue, sore throat, cough, chest pain:* Rogers, P., Silling, S. M., & Adams, L. (1991). Adolescent chemical dependence: A diagnosable disease. *Psychiatric Annals, 21*, 91–97.

P. 99, *alcohol and drugs in potentially pregnant females:* Powers, R. (1994). *Primary prevention in psychiatry: A focus on prenatal care.* Stanford, CA: Stanford University Hospital.

P. 99, *A structured interview to uncover:* Bailey, G. W. (1989). Current perspectives on substance abuse in youth. *Annual progress in child psychiatry and development.* Reprinted with permission from *Journal of the American Academy of Child and Adolescent Psychiatry, 28*(2), 503–531.

P. 100, *Other structured interviews:* Schydlower, M., & Rogers, P. D. (1993, June). *Adolescent substance abuse and addictions.* Philadelphia: Hanley & Belfus.

P. 100, *Because the most common precipitating:* Powers, R. (1994). *Primary prevention in psychiatry: A focus on prenatal care.* Stanford, CA: Stanford University Hospital.

P. 100, *Questionnaires that have found favor:* Schydlower, M., & Rogers, P. D. (1993, June). *Adolescent substance abuse and addictions.* Philadelphia: Hanley & Belfus.

P. 102, *an adolescent can consent:* Schydlower, M., & Rogers, P. D. (1993, June). *Adolescent substance abuse and addictions.* Philadelphia: Hanley & Belfus.

P. 103, *The results of testing should:* Gans, J. E., & Shook, K. L. (1994). *Policy compendium on tobacco, alcohol, and other harmful substances affecting adolescents: Alcohol and other harmful substances.* Chicago: American Medical Association.

P. 104, *Dr. Tomas Silber believes paternalism:* Silber, J. T. (1989). Justified paternalism in adolescent health care. *Journal of Adolescent Health Care, 10*, 449–453.

P. 105 *"Paternalism can only be justified:* Silber, J. T. (1989). Justified paternalism in adolescent health care. *Journal of Adolescent Health Care, 10*, 449–453.

P. 106, *Adult chemical dependency approaches:* Matano, R., & Yalom, I. (1991). Approaches to chemical dependency: Chemical dependency and interactive group therapy—a synthesis. *International Journal of Group Psychotherapy, 41*(3), 269–293.

P. 106, *This traditional type of treatment:* Matano, R., & Yalom, I. (1991).

Approaches to chemical dependency: Chemical dependency and interactive group therapy—a synthesis. *International Journal of Group Psychotherapy, 41*(3), 269–293.

P. 106, *The treatment then focuses:* Matano, R., & Yalom, I. (1991). Approaches to chemical dependency: Chemical dependency and interactive group therapy—a synthesis. *International Journal of Group Psychotherapy, 41*(3), 269–293.

P. 110, *Frequently, adolescents have additional:* Schydlower, M., & Rogers, P. D. (1993, June). *Adolescent substance abuse and addictions.* Philadelphia: Hanley & Belfus.

P. 110, *Additionally, they often have:* Schydlower, M., & Rogers, P. D. (1993, June). *Adolescent substance abuse and addictions.* Philadelphia: Hanley & Belfus.

P. 114, *the AMA Council on Scientific Affairs:* Gans, J. E., & Shook, K. L. (1994). *Policy compendium on tobacco, alcohol, and other harmful substances affecting adolescents: Alcohol and other harmful substances.* Chicago: American Medical Association.

P. 118, *Schools cannot involuntarily test:* Lawson, G. W., & Lawson, A. W. (1992). *Adolescent substance abuse, etiology, treatment, and prevention.* Gaithersburg, MD: Aspen Publishers.

P. 136, *State codes may be different: California Community Care Facilities Act. California Health and Safety Code Section 1502.* (1973). Sacramento: Department of Social Services, pp. 610–612.

P. 144, *adolescents have lower rates:* Schydlower, M., & Rogers, P. D. (1993, June). *Adolescent substance abuse and addictions.* Philadelphia: Hanley & Belfus.

P. 145, *The most significant factor related:* Schydlower, M., & Rogers, P. D. (1993, June). *Adolescent substance abuse and addictions.* Philadelphia: Hanley & Belfus.

P. 146, *Some favorable outcomes from residential:* Beschner, G., & Friedman, A. (1985). Treatment of adolescent drug abusers. *International Journal of Addictions, 20*(6&7), 971–993.

P. 146, *The schools, criminal justice system:* Schydlower, M., & Rogers, P. D. (1993, June). *Adolescent substance abuse and addictions.* Philadelphia: Hanley & Belfus.

4

DEPRESSION

James Lock

Over the past several years the media have begun to report extensively on the problem of suicide among adolescents. Stories about the rising rates of suicide and group suicide pacts have raised our level of concern about what might be contributing to this problem.

Adolescence is often considered to be a time of turmoil, with the stress of making friends and planning for a job in the future sometimes becoming overwhelming for some teenagers. Adolescence is also known as a time of testing new waters and of experimentation, but these challenges can also lead to feelings of uncertainty, to fears of being unable to meet these challenges, and to feeling unattractive to friends and potential mates. Adolescents often fight off these feelings with drugs, reckless behavior, and flight—running away. And many times an adolescent who behaves this way is seriously depressed and in need of help from a professional.

Forms of depression occur in a range of illnesses. Major Depression is the most severe on the spectrum of these disorders. Others include Bipolar Affective Disorder, Dysthymia, and Cyclothymia. We discuss each of these in this chapter. What they all share in common, though, is—to a greater or lesser degree and for various periods of time—a feeling of sadness and an inability to manage school, work, or social activities as before.

DIFFERENTIAL DIAGNOSIS

In my experience as a child and adolescent psychiatrist, I find that other disorders may sometimes resemble one of the clinical syndromes of depression. An important part of my initial treatment is to make sure I have not mistaken one of these other disorders for a depression.

Adjustment Disorders

The most common of these is what is called an Adjustment Disorder with Depressed Mood. Adjustment Disorder, as the name implies, is a response or adjustment to a change or stress. The hallmark of adjustment disorders is the clear identification of a specific stress or significant change that corresponds in time to the onset of a depressed mood and decreased ability to work, play, or study. To meet the criteria, according to the DSM-IV, the stressor or change must have occurred within three months and the degree of impairment in social and school domains must not be severe enough or of long enough duration to meet criteria for Major Depression or other affective disorder, as illustrated in the following case study.

TOM

Tom was a high school debate team leader and above-average student in a public high school when he was in a car accident, breaking a leg and arm. He missed over three weeks of school and was in a great deal of pain for a short period immediately after the accident. When Tom returned to school, his friends noticed that he seemed more withdrawn and did not want to participate in their group activities as he had before. His girlfriend also told his parents that Tom was worried about driving his car and had asked her to drive him. When Tom's parents inquired about how he was feeling, he freely admitted that he worried about driving and was taking his life more seriously. He denied having problems with sleeping now that he was no longer in pain and was putting on some of the weight he had lost from being at bed rest.

The family consulted a therapist who found Tom to be suffering from an adjustment reaction and recommended several weeks of individual therapy to allow Tom to explore how the accident had affected his life. Tom agreed to this and after about three months of individual therapy reported that he felt more confident about driving and less worried about things.

Normal Bereavement

Another kind of stress that may lead to a change in mood is the sadness and loss of social and school functioning after the death of someone close to the adolescent. In this case, normal bereavement might for a short time look like an affective illness, but usually it is not. At times, bereavement does lead to a major depression, so if the process of grieving becomes extended and the symptoms or behaviors more pronounced or if a person's self-esteem or self-image are negatively affected, then further evaluation is warranted. But here is a case of normal bereavement:

EMILY

Emily was a popular and energetic thirteen-year-old high school freshman when her older brother was diagnosed with cancer. A year later he died. Emily had been close to her brother and had discussed his death with her family. During the first two weeks after his death, Emily cried frequently and complained of not sleeping well; her school work declined. Over the following two weeks, Emily showed progressive improvement with fewer crying spells and her sleep and appetite also improved. Her friends said that she talked about her brother's death less often and seemed to be "getting a handle" on it better. Her parents were concerned for Emily at first, but she continued to improve over the following months. A psychologist friend of the family, on hearing of Emily's early difficulties, comforted the family by telling them that Emily's reactions were within the norms for human grief.

Separation-Anxiety Disorder

Separation-Anxiety Disorder is another kind of problem that can look like an affective disorder. This disorder is associated with a fear of separation by a child from someone to whom they are attached. It results in such symptoms as sadness, excessive worry, sleep problems, feeling physically ill, and trying to stay home.

These kinds of problems are also associated with an affective disorder, but the difference here is that all the problems described are ways of trying to keep the attachment figure (usually a mother or father) close at hand. They are strategies to stay home and to get attention, or responses to fears that the attachment figure might not always be there. This distinction is sometimes hard to make, so we must sort out whether the problem really is about separation anxiety or a depressive syndrome or even both. Here's an example of the former:

MELISSA

Melissa had often been ill as a young child. Because her parents were divorced and her father lived in another state, she spent a great deal of time with her mother who took care of her. Although Melissa was now perfectly healthy in her adolescence, she would often feign illness to stay home from school. She also became very angry and threw tantrums whenever her mother, who mostly worked at home, had to go out for a necessary business meeting.

The problems worsened when her mother started to see a new man. When her mother would go out for the evening, Melissa would cry incessantly and not be able to sleep or eat until her mother returned home. The problems accelerated to the point that the school recommended that the mother seek assistance for Melissa. Melissa was diagnosed with Separation-Anxiety Disorder and began therapy structured to assist the whole family.

AFFECTIVE DISORDERS

When a teenager comes to my office or hospital with symptoms that suggest problems with mood, I carefully consider the kinds of problems and diagnoses discussed above. If I find that none of them adequately describes the patient I am seeing, I review the affective disorders.

In the following few pages, I provide a brief review of these disorders and a short clinical vignette to illustrate key points that I use in making my diagnoses. To me, making the correct diagnoses will get me halfway to success in treatment. I hope these are helpful.

Major Depression

Major Depression is arguably the most severe of the affective disorders. The consequences of untreated Major Depression in adolescents include suicide, school failure, alcohol and substance abuse and reckless, life-endangering behavior.

Major Depression is a common problem among teenagers. Some estimates state that 5 percent to 7 percent of teenagers experience a major depression, compared with adult rates of 10 percent in men and 20 percent in women. Depression apparently increases with age, as about 1 percent of preschoolers are depressed and only 2 percent of school-age children. The first significant rise in Major Depression is associated with adolescence. Teenagers with a history of or current medical problems are also at increased risk for Major Depression. Studies of pediatric patients have demonstrated that 7 percent to 30 percent of hospitalized children are suffering from depression. Major Depression also seems to be rising in each generation.

Other risk factors include a family history of alcoholism or depression. There is approximately a 10 percent to 13 percent increase in risk for individuals with close relatives who have Major Depression. Rates are higher for fraternal (dizygotic) twins and highest for identical (monozygotic) twins. Risk for a major depression is also increased if a child loses a parent through death before the child is thirteen years old. Some studies have found that persons from lower socioeconomic circumstances are also at slightly increased risk.

Other factors that increase the likelihood that a teenager will become depressed include chronic illness, stressful life events such as trauma and abuse, and family factors such as divorce, marital discord, and ongoing parent-child conflicts. Any of these variables in combination with other risk factors greatly increases the likelihood that a major depression might develop. Depression in females increases at puberty to a greater degree than in males. Some have suggested that this is related to the relative value placed on boys' pubertal advancement and the associated social status. Studies have shown that on the whole, boys experience puberty with improved mood and body image, whereas girls feel more unhappy, anxious, and unattractive. According to the DSM-IV, there is little difference for the child, adolescent, or adult in terms of how a major depression is supposed to look. This is partly because the DSM-IV attempts to describe clinical syndromes from an atheoretical basis so such factors as age often don't figure prominently except in illnesses clearly associated with only one age group.

The DSM-IV states that for teenagers to be diagnosed with Major Depression they must have a depressed or irritable mood, or a decreased interest in previously pleasurable activities for two consecutive weeks. They must also no longer be able to work, do school work, or engage in social activities as they did earlier. In addition, they must have four of the following symptoms: sleep disturbance, weight or appetite disturbance, problems in concentration, suicidal ideation or thoughts of death, observable increased or decreased activity, fatigue or loss of energy, feelings of being worthless, or inappropriate guilt.

In spite of the DSM-IV criteria, however, we often see that the ways children and teenagers present with Major Depression *do* vary in some ways with age. Decreased mood, difficulty concentrating, sleep problems, and suicidal ideation occur equally in all age groups. With increasing age, on the other hand, there is a general decline, with depressed appearance, complaints of feeling physically ill, increasing occurrence of inability to enjoy things that were once pleasurable, a worsening of mood as the day continues, hopelessness, decreased physical activity, and delusions.

Among teenagers specifically, some kinds of symptoms increase and become predominant. Depressed teenagers may begin abusing drugs and alcohol, and become more rebellious and challenging of authority figures at home and at school. They often have increased difficulty in all aspects of school functioning, become sexually more active and promiscuous, become more sensitive and easily slighted, especially by friends or lovers. In addition, their hygiene may deteriorate and they tend to have more problem with increased sleeping and weight fluctuations than do younger children or many adults who suffer from Major Depression.

Here are two examples of how teenagers with Major Depression have appeared in my office:

TONI

Toni was a fourteen-year-old girl who had been shy since starting school but who had become more withdrawn and avoidant of all her friends since starting the ninth grade. Toni's family noticed that she skipped school and slept at home as much as possible. She stopped showering every day and left her hair uncombed—something she had never done before. She stopped inviting her friends over and they in turn slowly stopped calling her. Her grades went from B's to D's. Toni's English teacher called to tell her parents that she felt Toni was in danger of failing her class.

Toni's parents were concerned that she was using drugs but Toni steadfastly denied this. The parents also thought that her behavior might be a "phase," but after about three months they took Toni to her pediatrician to learn whether she had any medical problems. When the pediatrician had finished her examination, she told Toni's parents that Toni had no medical problems but appeared to be depressed; the pediatrician recommended that they consult with a psychiatric colleague of hers. This meeting was arranged with some protest on Toni's part. The psychiatrist confirmed the pediatrician's suspicion and began individual therapy to assist Toni with her problems. He also said that a medication might be needed, but that he would not start that until therapy had been given a trial.

MAX

Max had always been something of a troublemaker. He had never liked school and had begun experimenting with drugs early in high school. His crowd often skipped class and he had been suspended many times during his high school career for unexcused absences. Still, he was just getting by when during his senior year his behavior worsened to the point that he was expelled from school. Max was found drinking on school property and fighting with his friends. He had broken up with three different girls in rapid succession.

Max's mother had died when he was a young child and now he lived with his father and younger brothers. At home he was slovenly, rude, and constantly defying his father. More recently, though, he had stopped eating—very unusual for Max—and looked haggard and physically unkempt. His father was sure Max was doing hard drugs. Max denied this, but admitted he was depressed and felt hopeless about his future.

Max's father consulted with the priest at his parish who knew the family well. He recommended that Max see someone for his emotional problems. Max reluctantly agreed to see a social worker at the community mental health center who told the father that Max was depressed. He scheduled an appointment with the center psychiatrist who confirmed the diagnosis and recommended family and group therapy for Max as a beginning. After much resistance, Max ultimately was tried on an antidepressant and his depression began to abate.

Dysthymia

Another disorder of mood that can resemble Major Depression is called Dysthymia. Dysthymia happens when a teenager has a depressed or irritable mood for more days than not for about a year. The difference between Dysthymia and Major Depression has mostly do with the severity of the symptoms—Major Depression is more severe—and the persistence of the symptoms—most Major Depression remits after a few months whereas Dysthymia by definition continues. It is important to note that Dysthymia is not a little Major Depression. Instead, it seems to be a pattern of lowered mood and results in longer-term patterns of depressive behaviors.

The DSM-IV describes Dysthymia in children and adolescents as consisting of a depressed mood for most of the day for most days for a year. In addition to depressed mood, adolescents must have at least two of the following symptoms: poor appetite or overeating, insomnia or hypersomnia, low energy or fatigue, low self-esteem, poor concentration or difficulty making decisions, feelings of hopelessness. Teenagers must not have suffered a major depression within a year or have ever had a manic episode. These symptoms must not result from a medical condition or from the use of alcohol or drugs. Together the symptoms must result in impairment of social, school, or interpersonal relations.

Dysthymia is often difficult to diagnose in teenagers because many are guarded and secretive about their mood states. They often try to keep adults and siblings from seeing how they feel. As part of trying to separate from their parents, this strategy often leads to isolation and worsening of problems for teenagers. Additionally, the difficulties associated with going through puberty, dating, and being in high school often cause brief but routine feelings of sadness, frustration, and irritability. Distinguishing among normal and abnormal responses usually requires that clinicians look at a variety of sources of information. They must talk to teachers, coaches, friends, families, social groups, and of course the teenagers themselves to get a comprehensive view of how things are really going. Although this procedure is necessary for any evaluation of a child or adolescent, it is especially so for chronic conditions like Dysthymia, which can be hidden or can resemble normal developmental struggles.

Mitchell is an example of a sixteen-year-old dysthymic teenager:

MITCHELL

Mitchell arrived in my office dragging his bookbag. He looked tired and slightly disheveled. He spoke in a monotone and made generally poor eye contact with me. He described his life as "boring" and "pointless." He denied depression, but admitted to feeling listless, lacking energy, and often being unhappy. He said he had felt this way for a long time—"Maybe forever, but at least since I was twelve." He had been a chronic underachiever since about age twelve as well. His school performance was uneven, but it was generally below what would have been expected of him. He had no overt conflicts with his parents or older sister. He had few friends and socialized rarely. He said that he had tried marijuana, but didn't use any drugs.

I treated Mitchell with a combination of individual and family therapy and he responded to a certain extent. However, when I was able to get him involved in a group of other teenagers with emotional problems, he really began to improve. He continued to struggle with his mood at times, but his school and social functioning were much less affected.

The consequences of untreated Dysthymia are not unlike those associated with Major Depression. The chronic and persistent nature of the symptoms may actually lead to a major depression—a so-called double depression. In this case, treatment of the depression is often protracted and more difficult as there is less likely to be a remission of all symptoms with the passing of the Major Depression. Chronic feelings like those associated with Major Depression can lead to a depressive pattern of interacting with others, neglected school work, and a hopelessness about the possibility of change in the future.

Bipolar Affective Disorder

Bipolar Affective Disorder or Manic Depressive Disorder is another relatively common psychiatric illness associated with problems of mood. In this case, there is a fluctuation of mood, often called mood swings, characterized by highs and lows. Bipolar Disorder affects about 1 percent of the population and is considered to be inherited, though exactly how this occurs is not well understood. About 20 percent of Bipolar Disorder is thought to have its onset during a person's adolescence, but it is often not diagnosed until much later because of the mixture of symptoms that characterize the illness.

According to the DSM-IV, Bipolar Affective Disorder is divided into two major types—I and II. Bipolar I and Bipolar II are further subdivided into subtypes depending on the character of the most recent presenting symptoms. Bipolar I Disorder in general requires a manic episode or a mixed manic and depressed episode and may also have had a period of depression.

A manic episode is a period of expansive or irritable mood lasting at least one week and is further characterized by at least four of the following symptoms: inflated self-esteem or grandiosity, decreased need for sleep, increased talkativeness, flight of ideas or subjective feeling that one's thoughts are racing, being easily distracted, an increase in goal-directed activity (either socially, at work or school, or sexually), psychomotor retardation, or excessive involvement in pleasurable activities that have a high potential for painful consequences (shopping sprees, sexual indiscretions, foolish business investments). Manic episodes cannot be related to any other thought disorder such as schizophrenia nor as a result of intoxication with alcohol or other drugs. These symptoms must lead to an impairment significant enough that the person is no longer able to function as he or she did earlier at work, socially, or in a school setting.

Bipolar II Disorders are similar to Bipolar I Disorders, but in these disorders, it's not necessary to have a full manic episode. Instead, what's called a hypomanic episode is intermixed with periods of major depressive symptoms. A hypomanic episode, as the name suggests, is a manic upset of somewhat lesser severity. In this case, it may be of shorter duration (four days or so) and does not cause marked impairment in school, work, or social relations. As with a manic episode, these symptoms cannot be the result of another psychiatric condition or the influence of alcohol or drugs. The distinction between Bipolar I and II is of clinical interest only to the extent that knowing if there is true mania will affect treatment planning. In my experience, patients with Bipolar I are more likely to require hospitalization, need more aggressive medication intervention, and have more legal problems because of the sequelae of their manic symptoms.

Most clinicians now believe that Bipolar Disorder usually begins in adolescence but has often been incorrectly diagnosed as schizophrenia, Schizo-Affective Disorder, and Conduct Disorder in teenagers. The reason for this relates at least partly with how the illness usually begins. In teenagers, Bipolar Disorder can present as a sudden onset of bizarre symptoms including psychotic thinking—disordered and incoherent expression of thoughts—strange beliefs or delusions that no one else shares, substance use, over- and under-sleeping, and hallucinations. When someone presents this way, many clinicians believe the symptoms most resemble a schizophrenic illness and so it is diagnosed as such. Others see the symptoms as probably part of an intoxication and withdrawal syndrome associated with various drugs and alcohol use, and still others see many of the symptoms as common to adolescents with severe emotional problems who are responding to these stresses.

Recently, however, three clinical features have been recognized as more likely to be associated with Bipolar Disorder. These are sudden onset of symptoms, psychomotor retardation, and psychotic thinking; in addition, pharmacologically induced hypomania and a three-generation family history of Bipolar Disorder are also strong indicators.

Here's an example of a typical bipolar presentation in the middle teenage years.

SAMUEL

Samuel was the bright and handsome son of a wealthy family. He was popular in school and had done well in sports. In his sophomore year he became depressed, did less well in school, and withdrew socially. These symptoms subsided without treatment in about three months and he resumed his normal activities. His parents and he passed this episode off as being his response when his best friend moved away. He graduated from high school with honors and as a reward his family offered him a trip to Australia.

Sam flew from New York to Australia. He felt great for someone who had not slept in twenty-four hours and immediately went out to see the city. He forgot his luggage at the curb at the airport and arrived at his hotel looking disheveled and very confused. He checked into his room with some difficulty and ordered an expensive meal with several bottles of wine, which he consumed readily. He was found in the lobby at three in the morning with no clothes on and making lewd comments to the hotel staff, who called the police. Sam was taken to the emergency room of a local hospital where the doctor on call found him to be incoherent and babbling about being a rock star and wanting to have sex with everyone.

Sam was sedated with a mixture of benzodiazepine and a neuroleptic. He was thoroughly examined but he showed no evidence of intoxicants and was otherwise physically healthy. The family was contacted and they confirmed that Sam's uncle and grandfather both had Bipolar Disorder and had required treatment.

Sam was started on Lithium and continued on low-dose neuroleptics until his acute symptoms remitted. The psychiatrist explained to Sam that sometimes a prolonged period of not sleeping can trigger an episode like this and that he would likely require medication assistance for some time to come.

Cyclothymia

A disorder similar to but not as severe as Bipolar Disorder, is called Cyclothymia. As the name suggests, in this disorder there is a cycling of moods as in Bipolar Disorder, but the severity and chronicity of the mood changes is different.

For a diagnosis of Cyclothymia, the DSM-IV requires that the patient has experienced what is called a hypomania numerous times over a one-year period as well as periods of numerous depressive symptoms that don't meet the criteria for a major depression. In children and adolescents, there can be no more than a two-month period without mood problems during a two-year period, and no manic episodes or Major Depression experienced during the first two years of the mood cycles. These mood cycles must lead to a disturbance in social, work, or family relations and cannot be due to a physical illness or secondary to the use of alcohol, drugs, or medications. Of course, the teenager cannot be suffering from a psychotic or other mood disorder. Here's an example of a fifteen-year-old cyclothymic girl.

REBECCA

According to Rebecca's parents, who brought her to my office, she had started becoming moody about three years earlier. They reported several periods when Rebecca would sit in her room, refusing to go out for several days at a time. At these times she was tearful and her grades at school plummeted. These periods had never lasted long and her parents had assumed her behavior was just a phase. They became more concerned when during the last eight months Rebecca had on three occasions stolen her mother's credit card and stayed out with people she barely knew until very late at night. Rebecca stated that she didn't understand why she had done these things, but she was clearly remorseful and regretted worrying her parents.

Rebecca began individual therapy reluctantly, but over time she trusted me enough to discuss the many ways her mood changes had caused problems in her life. She initially refused to take medications but finally agreed to try Lithium. This medication, in conjunction with her individual and family therapy, helped Rebecca improve sufficiently to graduate from high school and attend a local college.

A BIOLOGICAL APPROACH TO TREATING AFFECTIVE DISORDERS

Treatment of affective disorders in teenagers can be very challenging, with a variety of possible approaches. The one we ultimately take can depend on what we believe to be the most important factors in a particular case. I illustrate my approach to these patients in a general way with case histories, but also include several specific problems encountered in some diagnostic groups.

Medications

As a child and adolescent psychiatrist, I am often asked to evaluate a depressed teenager for a medication trial of antidepressants. I always begin such an evaluation by having a frank discussion with the referring clinician, the family, and the teenager about our limited knowledge of antidepressant use in teenagers. I tell them that a variety of such medications have been tried in adolescents. Those that have been most carefully studied have not been shown to be more efficacious than placebo medications. This does not mean that medications have never helped a teenager with depression—this is not the case; but studies of these medications in controlled trials with adolescents have not supported their general use with this group, unlike the results of similar studies with adults.

After reporting this information, I discuss the range of current antidepressants, their respective side effects, and why I might recommend one over another in a particular case. Such variables as past allergies and cardiac, kidney, or liver problems are common considerations. Family history and particular side effects are always additional important concerns. The side effect of dry mouth, for example, may not be a concern to one person, but to another, it may be intolerable. A more common side effect that often troubles teenagers is the possibility of gaining weight. Many times the decreased self-esteem associated with this side effect can seriously dampen the antidepressant's usefulness. In young girls in particular, I have had to change medications for this reason alone.

I also tell my adolescent patients that some of the newer antidepressants, which many of them have heard of and which psychiatrists are prescribing for adults, have yet to undergo rigorous trial in teenagers. Ultimately, these new agents—such as Prozac or fluoxetine, Zoloft or sertraline, and Paxil or paroxitene—may provide a promising treatment for adolescent depression as they've been shown to be effective in some adults with depression that resembles adolescent depression. These kinds of depressions are associated with rejection sensitivity, mood lability (more irritability), increased sleeping, weight gain, and increased incidence among women. Other agents that are sometimes used to treat these depressions are called monoamine oxidase inhibitors (MAOI). But persons who take these medications are required to follow a fairly strict diet so teenagers are seldom good candidates for these antidepressants.

In my office, I always go over a written consent with both the parent and the teenager. I usually ask both to sign it. Experience has shown me that teenagers do not like to take medications of any kind, and ones they feel will affect their minds or feelings are particularly repugnant. They often experience them as intrusive and can therefore get them mixed up in struggles for independence from parental authority.

One young man said to me: "I don't want to take anything that will change me," expressing both his anxiety about his identity as well as his worry about side effects. Another young woman in a battle with her mother about her independence said directly: "I will only take the medication if my mother doesn't want me to."

I use the process of sharing information about the limitation of medications and signing the consent as a way to establish a sense of respect for the teenager that I hope will help with compliance problems down the road. When I start a medication, I spend a great deal of time enlisting the teenagers in the process by helping them identify the changes or gains they hope to achieve as a result of taking the antidepressant. Many times these goals are not the ones I might set, but I find that by tracking them, I increase compliance and understanding of a particular teenager's struggles with depression.

In terms of medications, Bipolar Disorder is one of the more treatable of psychiatric disorders, even among adolescents. In fact, unlike psychopharmacological treatment for Major Depression or Dysthymia, it appears that adolescent onset and adult onset Bipolar Disorders have similar response rates to medication. The types of medications used to treat Bipolar Disorder are called mood stabilizers and some of the most common are Lithium, Tegretol, and Valproate. Sometimes longer-acting benzodiazepines are also used. Lithium has been shown to be effective in adolescents. For reasons that are not entirely clear, some patients, adult or adolescent, respond better to one medication over another. In addition, each of these medications has significant side effects and risks associated with them; the decision about which to use and how to monitor is an important medical decision, one in which a psychiatrist should be involved. Proper medication management over the long term can help prevent the number and severity of manic or depressive episodes, leading to better overall emotional and psychosocial functioning in the patient.

Often teenagers who have Bipolar Disorder struggle with their diagnosis. The behaviors that helped to establish a diagnosis—such as recklessness, promiscuity, drug use—have caused them a great deal of embarrassment and sometimes legal and emotional problems. Helping the adolescent to accept the diagnosis as well as the medications required to treat it are important ways therapists can assist teenagers to manage their illness more successfully. There is considerable resistance to taking medicine because of side effects, especially sleepiness or fuzzy-headedness at times as well as the need for frequent blood level checks. Teenagers often have trouble believing that they are still ill and will discontinue their medications. This often leads to a resurgence of their symptoms and more problems at home and school as a result. Individual therapy can help support teenagers as well as increase their compliance by encouraging the development of insight and understanding about their illness.

During the entire treatment with medications, I make it a special point to ask about side effects, to make every attempt to limit them, and when this is not possible, to support the adolescents' decision to continue to take them by talking with the teenagers about the long-term goal of getting over the depression. Because of the short-range future orientation of most teenagers, this can be difficult; but in my experience, if they believe that you are interested in their future, they can borrow on this to help weather many of these compliance problems. One young girl who had failed one trial of medication required almost daily phone calls from me for about two weeks to help her through a rough change of medications. Fortunately, she used my support effectively and ultimately responded to this second medication.

In addition to spending time convincing teenagers and their parents to try medications when these are indicated, I also discuss with them frankly the limits of medications. None of them is a panacea, and often the patient's wish to have a quick fix with a pill can undermine other aspects of treatment. Helping other clinicians understand these limits is also something I often find myself doing. So although medications can be helpful in many cases, I find that getting them started, continuing them in the face of side effects, and convincing patients not to have unrealistic expectations about their efficacy require constant attention on my part.

Other Biological Approaches

Other biological approaches to depression in teenagers are used less commonly and their effectiveness is unknown. These include electroconvulsive therapy (ECT), photo-therapy, and a variety of medications used to treat mood instability. If I believe my teenage patient will require any of these kinds of interventions, I attempt to arrange for a hospitalization to initiate and evaluate them.

I seldom find the biological approach alone sufficient for treating affectively disordered teenagers. Most often, unless it is a clear case of Bipolar Disorder or severe depression, I start with therapy and if this proves inadequate, I consider a medication trial.

THERAPEUTIC APPROACHES TO TREATING AFFECTIVE DISORDERS

Many of the issues associated with teenage depression can be seen as a part of adolescent development. Difficulty in mastering this developmental hurdle can result in the symptoms of depression. I use a combination of individual, family, group, and cognitive approaches. As a starting point, I try to determine the developmental issues and how they may be contributing to the depression.

Adolescence can be divided into three phases: early (ages twelve to fourteen), middle (ages fourteen to sixteen), and late (ages sixteen to nineteen).

- The early phase is when the teenager is most concerned about issues of puberty and physical maturity and the task is to accept the growing and changing body.

- The middle phase is dominated by increasing importance of peers and increasing abilities to distinguish self from others, especially one's parents. The task is to separate one's ideas and feelings from those of one's parents and to venture out into the world of peer relations as an individual.

- The late phase is dominated by issues of consolidating a sense of identity. The task is to work out plans for school and vocation and establish a pattern of interpersonal relations of intimacy and friendship. The kinds of issues addressed in each may affect how one approaches depression in the teenager.

The Early Phase

When working with an affectively disordered teenager in the early phase, I initially focus on the self-esteem issues associated with the physical changes of this period. With girls, concern about weight and attractiveness are predominant. Boys focus on body size, comparisons with male peers' athletic prowess, and increasing competition in all spheres. I find this early phase one of the most challenging to work with because teenagers in this period are usually remarkably labile. They can be as needy and concrete as school-age children or as aggressive and sexual as young adults. Their lability is uncomfortable to them and adds to their sense of feeling that they do not have much control. When a depression complicates this picture, simple direct information about the realities of physical change and development is generally well received. Information of this sort is supportive and can help.

One depressed thirteen-year-old boy was so relieved to learn that he could expect to grow another three to four inches in the following years that he was willing to stay in therapy long enough to work on why this was so important to him. Another young girl felt she was too tall and therefore unattractive. She used the information that she was unlikely to grow much taller as a starting point for exploring other, deeper issues of her feelings of diminished self-worth.

In the early phase, adolescents are usually still deeply involved in their families and only beginning to experience much ambivalence about them. With these young teenagers, I involve the family early and keep them involved during the treatment more than I do with older teenagers. Here's an example of how that worked in a fourteen-year-old boy:

MATT

Matt's mother had died two years before he had begun to experience decreased mood, irritability, decreased school performance, sleep problems, and weight loss. When Matt came to my office he did so with great reluctance. He spoke little at first and my efforts to engage him were repulsed. He refused to consider taking medication and made it clear that he didn't trust doctors, especially those that "messed with your head."

I was finally able to get somewhere when I asked him to draw a kind of blueprint of his house. While doing this he was able to discuss his family members and his relationship to them more openly. This strategy worked because the concrete activity of drawing helped Matt organize some of his feelings. I used this strategy again when we did a similar drawing of Matt's room and its contents. With this procedure, Matt slowly let me into his world and the problems contained in it.

Matt was protective of his family and seemed to feel that I would blame them for his depression. He was therefore not willing at first to have his family come in for therapy. After the elaborate blue-printing, however, he agreed that it might be helpful if they too came in and discussed their blueprints. This is exactly what we did. Each family member went through an abbreviated version of blue-printing, which helped everyone to see in rather direct and concrete terms some of the ways the family had contributed to the feelings of worthlessness and powerlessness Matt had generalized during his depression. Doing drawings or blueprints of this sort matched the developmental and emotional limitations of the early-phase adolescent. They were neither too abstract nor too emotionally threatening.

The key points of working with the early-phase depressed adolescent are to (1) build a rapport based on supportive information-sharing about the realities of adolescent physical development; (2) use a strategy to engage the adolescent that recognizes both cognitive strengths and limitations of the early adolescent; and (3) involve the family.

Many times a teenager who develops Bipolar Disorder has been a high-achieving, affable, and treasured child. The development of the kinds of problems associated with Bipolar Disorder are often devastating to families. Mothers and fathers are often the object of abuse and what appears to be uncontrollable anger. Siblings often are embarrassed and simply do not understand what is happening to someone in their family. Sometimes there are actual physical and property types of injuries that result from symptoms of the illness.

All this suggests that there can be an important role for family therapy when a teenager has developed a bipolar illness. Family therapists often also have to deal with guilt on the part of parents or grandparents who also suffer from bipolar illness; they feel as if they have passed it down and feel guilty about this. Sometimes there has been resistance to making this diagnosis in some other family member or treatment has failed or was not complied with. Consequently, feelings about how a teenager will be treated after having similar problems brings up ghosts from the past.

Family therapists need to be able to provide information about the illness, be supportive of the changes that having a teenager with Bipolar Disorder make in a families' hopes and fantasies, and also be able to conduct some reparative work on damages actually suffered.

The Middle Phase

Although many adolescents may have an episode of depression in the early phase, it may often be missed or not identified until it occurs in the middle phase. In my experience, family members often write off the lability and moodiness of early-phase depression as normal. Consequently, I see more adolescents with depression in the middle and late phases.

For me, the middle phase is in some ways easier to work with and in some ways harder. It is easier because usually the teenagers have an increased capacity for and interest in insight and that makes therapy more interesting to them. The increased importance of peers and their judgment, on the other hand, often makes it harder for middle-phase teenagers to trust adults. I work with these variables as flexibly and agilely as possible. I do this by always trying to stay aware of the adolescent's experience of therapy: Did he or she experience that remark as too confrontational? Or infantilizing? Or authoritarian? Then I attempt to regulate my subsequent comments to maintain the equilibrium of our discussions. This kind of vigilant course correction helps the two of us to maintain an optimal distance and allows the adolescent to continue in the process by limiting his or her experiences of intrusiveness and abandonment.

An example of this effort to find and maintain an optimal distance is found in the therapy of a sixteen-year-old boy whose depression was complicated by sexual orientation issues. Exploration of his thoughts and feelings required that I be unusually sensitive to the possible narcissistic injury that any direct questions about sexual fantasies or behaviors would have on him. If I was too direct, he would shut down or change the subject. If I remained too indirect, he would become sullen and hint that I wasn't interested in anything except his taking medication. Only over time did it become safer for me to explore how his anxieties about sex contributed to his low self-esteem and depression.

Another technique I use to keep optimal distance with teenagers is cognitive therapy. Cognitive therapy often appeals to teenagers because it allows them to experience therapists as less intrusive, especially in regard to deeply personal issues. Cognitive therapy depends to a certain extent on the teenager's capacity to use abstract thinking, to generalize, and to see patterns in behaviors, beliefs, and approaches. This is usually possible by the middle period of adolescence and can provide an opportunity to explore in a nonjudgmental way many of the issues that may be contributing to the adolescent's feeling of depression. I use cognitive approaches in a way that is similar to the blueprinting technique I described in early-phase treatment. A cognitive approach is a kind of developmental extension of that more concrete strategy. It involves less visual and more intellectual activity, but still uses a structured way of exploring potentially emotionally charged issues.

I used a cognitive approach with a fifteen-year-old depressed girl to explore how her depression had negatively colored her view of her friends, family, and school. We began by making a list of all the negative factors she could identify in each of these areas. Her follow-up assignment was to make a list of at least half as many positive elements for each area. As we discussed each of the possible negatives, we were able to use the possibility of the positive elements to explore how the patient contributed to a negative development through her own behavior. This helped us to identify specific ways she could try change in a direction that she herself had identified as desirable.

It was clear to me that even though she was depressed, she became invested in the process largely because of her own sense of control over the contents. My experience is that the challenge this kind of assignment implies must be timed when the depression is just beginning to resolve. If I attempt it too early, patients find it too difficult and are resistant to even trying it.

Family work is perhaps most difficult in the middle phase. Still, I always attempt it at the beginning if only to add to the information gathered during evaluation. The reason that family work is difficult is because it runs completely counter to the adolescent's struggle for emancipation and peer identification that is the focus of this phase. Teenagers in this phase need desperately to feel some increased identity outside the family. Reintroducing the family connection can just make matters worse. In the family meetings I have in this period, I focus on very practical matters. Issues such as clear communication of expectations, rules, and safe conduct are typical themes. It is seldom possible to work through a depressive illness in a teenager without dealing with some of these family struggles, but much of the family work goes better in individual or group therapy.

Teenagers, as we have noted, are beginning to move out of the family and into a world of peer relations. It makes sense that approaches that take advantage of this fact would likely be helpful for depressed teenagers. Groups or milieu can provide opportunities for depressed teenagers to test out new roles with their peers. A group can also be a source of support when others relate their similar experiences and difficulties. Assumptions and attitudes can be expressed in the group and responses to them assessed. In this way, depressed teenagers can explore their ideas and feelings with their peers; these experiences can lead to increased insight, more appropriate reality testing, and support through identification.

Group work for affectively disordered teenagers is not used as much as it might be because these groups are difficult for the individual clinician to organize and sustain. This is unfortunate because the group format works especially well with teenagers in the middle phase. Such groups support individual teenagers in continuing treatment, continuing medication, and helping to destigmatize emotional problems. Again, group work in my experience is most helpful after the most acute phase of the depression is past. Depressed teens are unlikely to benefit prior to this, though sometimes such groups can help kick-start a reluctant patient. I believe group treatment will develop more in the future as we try both to manage medical resources better and to deliver effective care.

When I work in a group, I limit the number to six to eight and work with a co-therapist. I try to have a mixture of sexes and a fairly narrow age range. This helps to recreate something like the outside peer group of the teenagers and tends to lower their resistance to attendance and talking. Encouraging depressed teens to talk is not always easy, so I use trust-building exercises and role-play in the early sessions. I find that later they are able to better manage a less structured session. Groups should last from eight to twelve weeks and usually begin after the most acute phase of the depression has subsided.

The Late Phase

Working in the late phase of adolescence most resembles work with young adults. In this phase, most of the struggle with parental figures is resolved, though particular issues with a parent might remain. In my experience, the teenager who becomes depressed during this phase is particularly vulnerable to major setbacks in personal and professional achievements. Scholastic tests, early college courses, and more serious intimate relationships can all be compromised.

When I work with teens in this late phase, I focus my work initially on getting them back to their normal activities to keep them on the school or vocational track they have started. It is usually easier in this phase for the teens to appreciate the consequences of their depression and to work to change it. Unlike my work with the early or middle-phase depressed teens, I seldom need to rely on a structured strategy to get them talking. When I do find myself using such an approach, it signals to me that there are likely still middle-phase issues I will ultimately need to watch for. Compliance with treatment and medication, when it is used, is usually less an issue as well, though with severely depressed teens I find that despair and hopelessness can be complicating issues regardless of the phase.

Individual therapy in the late phase is the mainstay of my work even if I use medications as well. Issues of identity, intimacy, and work always complicate depressions in this period. For example, a seventeen-year-old young woman who became depressed after breaking up with a boyfriend said: "He was how I spent my time. I don't know who I am without him." Another male teen just getting ready to graduate became depressed after a fight with his father and said: "He hates me and I am really nothing anyway. He says so, too."

These kinds of remarks underscore the uncertainty of identity that leaving home can exacerbate. During treatment, the young woman who made the first statement was ultimately able to explore how she used her boyfriend as a way to avoid growing up. In the second case, the young man gradually came to understand that he had adopted his father's perspective on him rather than question it. He had failed to really work through the middle phase, and when he headed off to college, he did so with a conscious intention to free himself of his father's opinion.

If family treatment is used in the late phase, I use it sparingly and in a very focused way. Usually, I get a family in to try to support the independent striving of the late adolescent by helping the family identify the ways they may be interfering with this effort. For example, a depressed girl who had been accepted into an out-of-state college was about to abandon her plan because her mother needed her. In fact, the mother did seem to need her because she was also depressed, but she had been able to get treatment. Family work identified this issue and allowed both mother and daughter to get help with their separate problems and move on with their lives.

Managed Care

Like most practitioners today, I operate in a managed care environment where there is increasing review of my clinical work by a variety of insurance and utilization personnel. Their involvement extends from initial authorization to completion of treatment. I begin my relationship with these organizations with the longitudinal perspective in mind. I want my patients to be able to get the treatment they need, so I go prepared to discuss cases with these reviewers with an eye to what they are interested in.

Usually they want a clear diagnosis, a treatment plan with time frames and goals, and a clinical rationale for the approach I am taking. I find that if I provide these, especially at the outset, I can usually maximize the benefits the patient has. I try to avoid confrontation and argumentativeness with these reviewers as I have never found this to help. This does not mean that I always agree with them nor am I hesitant to request a clinical review at a higher level in their organization. I find that 80 percent to 90 percent of my requests are approved if I follow these kinds of guidelines; I feel this is an area of future clinical development for all of us.

Suicidal Behavior

One of the most important parts of working with teenagers with an affective disorder is suicide. Suicide is the third leading cause of death for persons eighteen or younger. There are 2,000 completed suicides a year among children and adolescents under the age of eighteen, and 5,000 a year for persons under the age of twenty-three.

Suicide is a problem of both girls and boys, but boys complete suicide three to four times more often than girls. Girls, on the other hand, attempt suicide about three times more frequently than boys. Most of these suicides occur in persons over the age of twelve. Levels of suicide have been rising since the 1960s in each successive generation of teenagers. Certain teenagers are at even higher risk. Teenagers who are gay or lesbian, are Native American, are depressed, use drugs or alcohol excessively, or have had a family member die or commit suicide are at especially high risk.

Although this chapter is not concerned specifically about the management of suicidal behavior, I think it is so common and so important a problem in depressed teenagers that I want to say something about my approach to it.

I always include direct and thorough questions about suicide in my interviews. If there is any question about suicide in subsequent treatment, I am equally persistent. If I find that a teen is actively suicidal and has a plan and the means to hurt or kill himself or herself, I arrange for immediate emergency inpatient treatment. In this area, I err on the conservative side. That is, I do not hesitate to hospitalize a suicidal teen. It may not be for long and it may sometimes be damaging to my therapeutic alliance, but this doesn't prevent me when my concern is great enough.

Sometimes such hospitalizations are involuntary. Where I practice, it is possible to detain a minor for evaluation against the child's wishes, even if parents disagree. Minors do have a right to a clinical review of their confinement in this situation. Parents can also sign a teenager into a hospital and consent to treatment. There are many gray areas surrounding a teenager's civil liberties, so I do my best to respect the developing autonomy of adolescents while still recognizing both parental and statutory limitations on that autonomy. I try to avoid involuntary treatment and minimize the use of such detentions, but it is necessary at times to protect teenagers from the consequences of their suicidal feelings.

In other circumstances less acute or severe, I develop contracts with depressed teens, which I ask them to sign. These contracts specify that the adolescents will tell me of any suicidal thoughts, plans, or actions. Breach of these contracts may mean the end of treatment with me, but this has rarely come to pass. I find that teens like to negotiate contracts, and I find I must be on my guard as the letter of the contract is often emphasized over the spirit in some questionable situations. I also use contracts to address reckless behavior and substance abuse when needed. I make our contracts short term and end their use when the teen and I agree they are no longer needed.

RELATED PROBLEMS

Many teenagers who are depressed also have other psychiatric problems. Some of the most common include alcohol and substance abuse, Conduct Disorder, and anxiety disorders. Patients who have both Major Depression and are dysthymic are called "double depressives"; they are especially difficult to treat. Usually they require a full complement of psychopharmacologic interventions as well as a variety of psychotherapeutic interventions.

Substance Abuse

It is almost impossible to treat a major depression or Bipolar Disorder if there is a substance abuse problem active at the time. It is therefore imperative that the substance abuse issues be treated simultaneously or before the Major Depression. Many times, withdrawal and substance abuse itself can mimic depression. Consequently, a period of time must pass before a more definitive diagnosis and treatment of Major Depression or Bipolar Disorder can be initiated.

Conduct Disorder

Conduct Disorder is the most common diagnosis of adolescents. Sometimes conduct-disordered behaviors can be a part of a depressive syndrome. Some studies have shown that in these cases, if the depression is treated, many of the behavior problems dissipate. Where there is a true diagnosis of Conduct Disorder and Major Depression or Bipolar Disorder, the patient is at severe risk of death by suicide or reckless behavior. Most of these patients require some form of high-security residential treatment to get the help they need. Unfortunately, many of them are routed into the juvenile justice system and don't get this kind of assistance.

Chronic Medical Conditions

Teenagers with a severe or chronic medical condition may develop a depression. Many reasons for this can be considered, including increasing insight into the impact of the disease on their quality of life and future hopes. Sometimes medications, treatments, and missing school and social opportunities complicate these teenagers' lives and they experience a decreased feeling of self-esteem. They feel more dependent on their families and on medical systems than they would like to as teenagers trying to make a start on their own. This realization can also lead to depression.

Sometimes the treatments themselves, especially certain drugs, can cause a pharmacologically induced depression. In all these cases a close relationship with the medical team and the recognition of these problems as they begin to emerge will likely help the course of treatment.

༄

The prognosis for Major Depression in teenagers is not well understood. We do know that there is a high rate of spontaneous remission, but we also know that most follow-up studies of depressive disorders that start in childhood or adolescence show that these recur.

The cumulative probability of recurrent Major Depression within five years of onset was 72 percent in the only major study that has been done. In addition, 84 percent of those experiencing depressive symptoms in childhood or adolescence developed a similar episode in adulthood. Social functioning has been found to diminish even after remission and the patient's return to normal functioning at school or in a vocation.

In my experience, I find a somewhat more hopeful clinical outcome. Many teenagers who have been depressed or have had Bipolar Disorder do continue to have difficulties in their early adulthood, but many get better and learn to manage well their ongoing symptoms and the treatments they continue to require.

Although it is clear that teenagers with Bipolar Disorder are likely to have a variety of problems, their overall prognosis is good. If they continue on medications and get proper assistance with the social and academic problems that may stem from the illness in one way or another, they are likely as a group to do fairly well. Unfortunately, it often takes a number of episodes of depression and mania for them to get real acceptance of their illness and their need for treatment.

Working with adolescents with affective disorders is challenging. There are times when I feel overwhelmed with the range of difficulties they exhibit. Sometimes this makes me feel inadequate and can affect the treatment relationship in a number of different ways. I have found myself struggling with rescue fantasies—if only I could take the teen out of the school or family; or, conversely, angry feelings that tempt me to try to avoid the patient. The latter may show itself by my seeming bored in therapy, being late, or forgetting an appointment. In order to prevent these countertransference feelings from interfering with my treatment, I try to stay aware of their possibility and monitor my behaviors and feelings. Sometimes I have found it helpful to discuss my frustrations with colleagues who treat similar kinds of patients.

Even with the limitations of our current treatments and the challenges that working with adolescents necessarily involve, I find it rewarding to work with teens who suffer from affective

disorders. Such teenagers are often sensitive, reflective, and ide-
alistic. Sometimes these are qualities that contribute to the
depression. Helping to transform these qualities from ones that
often make the adolescents feel hopeless and vulnerable to ones
that enliven and empower them is a great therapeutic pleasure
for me. Essentially, this is the return of hope. Adolescence can
be such a time when things go well. All the emotional, social,
and intellectual efforts of childhood culminate here, and by
returning depressed teenagers to this hope, we can change how
they will approach all aspects of their adult lives. When this happens, and it happens often, you will experience deep gratification with your work. And it will add to your own feelings of hope
as well.

NOTES

P. 154, *To meet the criteria:* American Psychiatric Association. (1994). *Diagnostic and Statistical Manual of Mental Disorders* (4th ed.). Washington, DC:
American Psychiatric Press, p. 626.

P. 157, *Studies of pediatric patients:* Kashani, J. H., Barbero, G. J., & Bolander,
F. D. (1981). Depression in hospitalized pediatric patients. *Journal of the
American Academy of Child and Adolescent Psychiatry, 20,* 123–134.

P. 159, *With increasing age:* Ryan, N. D., Puig-Antich, J., Ambrosini, P., et al.
(1986). The clinical picture of major depression in children and adolescents. *Archives of General Psychiatry, 44,* 854–861.

P. 165, *These are sudden onset of symptoms:* Hanna, G. L. (1992). Natural history
of mood disorders. *Child and Adolescent Psychiatric Clinics of North America,
1,* 169–181.

P. 180, *One of the most important parts:* Shaffer, D., Garland, A., Gould, M., et
al. (1988). Preventing teenage suicide: A critical review. *Journal of the American Academy of Child and Adolescent Psychiatry,* pp. 665–687.

P. 181, *Sometimes such hospitalizations are:* Please see Chapter Eight, "Schizophrenia and Psychotic Disorders," for further discussion of involuntary
treatment.

P. 183, *The cumulative probability:* Asarnow, J. R., Goldstein, M. J., Carlson,
G. A., et al. (1988). Childhood-onset depressive disorders. A follow-up

study of rates of rehospitalization and out-of-home placement among child psychiatric inpatients. *Journal of Affective Disorders, 15,* 245–253.

P. 184, *Social functioning has been found:* Puig-Antich, J., Lukens, E., & Davies, M. (1985). Psychosocial functioning in pre-pubertal major depressive disorder: II. Interpersonal relationships after sustained recovery from affective episode. *Archives of General Psychiatry, 42,* 511–517.

5

ANXIETY DISORDERS

Chris Hayward and Julie A. Collier

The experience of anxiety during adolescence is common. For most adolescents, feelings of anxiety are transitory and harmless, or related to a specific stage of development. However, for some adolescents, anxiety interrupts their pursuit of developmentally appropriate goals such as intensification of bonds with peers, exploration of emerging sexuality, and increasing independence from family. Mental health practitioners need to differentiate so-called normal anxiety from pathological anxiety, and anxiety symptoms from anxiety disorders.

Adolescents with anxiety disorders usually are not aware that they have a disorder, much less a treatable one; therefore, most do not receive appropriate treatment. The consequences of untreated anxiety disorders include depression, suicidality, and substance abuse. Furthermore, early onset of anxiety disorders is associated with worse outcome. Because the potential for preventing the negative outcomes of anxiety disorders is greatest in adolescence, the recognition and treatment of adolescent anxiety disorders is a public health priority.

This chapter reviews the assessment, diagnosis, and treatment of anxiety disorders in adolescence, focusing particularly on Panic Disorder, phobias, Obsessive-Compulsive Disorder, and Generalized Anxiety. Although it is classified in the *Diagnostic and Statistical Manual* (DSM-IV) as an anxiety disorder, Posttraumatic Stress Disorder is considered by many to be a dissociative disorder and is not covered in this chapter (see Chapter Nine).

ASSESSMENT

For many adolescents who are seeking treatment, anxiety is a common complaint. One task we have as clinicians is to determine whether the symptom of anxiety represents a transient reaction to a recent stressor or developmental phase, or is a manifestation of a more serious psychiatric disorder. Anxiety can often be the first manifestation of severe depression, Obsessive-Compulsive Disorder, Panic Disorder, Separation Anxiety Disorder, and even occasionally, impending psychosis. Thus, it is important to do a complete diagnostic assessment of current and past symptoms to learn the extent to which the symptoms are interfering with the patient's current functioning.

In general, the process of assessing adolescent anxiety disorders does not differ from any thorough psychodiagnostic assessment for any other disorder or problem. However, a few areas, highlighted below, are of particular relevance to the diagnosis and treatment of anxiety disorders.

Medical History

A very important first step is obtaining a thorough medical history, including family medical history, and ascertaining when the adolescent last had a physical exam. A number of medical conditions can be associated with anxiety symptoms. Hyperthyroidism, for example, can present with anxiety as the primary symptom. In addition, medications prescribed for medical illnesses can cause or exacerbate anxiety. One adolescent evaluated in our clinic complained that she felt "nervous" and "jittery." A careful review of her symptoms and medical history revealed that her anxious feelings occurred most frequently when she was taking steroids for severe asthma. Not every adolescent who first presents with anxiety requires a medical evaluation. However, if there are any new medical complaints in addition to the symptom of anxiety, or a family history of medical problems that com-

monly have anxiety as a symptom, a complete medical evaluation is warranted.

Substance Abuse

Careful assessment of substance use and the potential for abuse
and dependence is also important. The use of alcohol, stimulants, marijuana, and other illicit drugs can induce anxiety states,
during episodes of both intoxication and withdrawal. The presence of active substance abuse makes accurate diagnosis of any
other Axis I psychiatric disorder difficult until the adolescent has
been drug free for an acceptable period of time.

Although substance abuse or dependence may not be an issue
for a particular adolescent, evaluation of patterns of "recreational" substance use may help to clarify an anxiety disorder
diagnosis. Some adolescents "self-medicate" prior to entering
situations that trigger anxiety.

Additional substances to inquire about include caffeine consumption and use of over-the-counter medications. Excessive
caffeine intake has been associated with increased levels of anxiety and can trigger panic attacks. Over-the-counter medications
such as cold medications or diet pills can have similar effects.

Family History

A thorough family assessment is essential; it should cover family history of mood and anxiety disorders and the typical
responses of the parents to displays of anxiety or fear by the adolescent. Evidence from a number of studies suggests the strong
possibility of genetic heritability of anxiety disorders. However,
it is difficult to distinguish the contribution of genetics from the
effects of growing up in a family with anxious relatives who
model fearful behavior. In addition, the response of the parents
to the fearful behavior of a child can further shape, reinforce,
and maintain the teenager's maladaptive behavior.

As an example, twelve-year-old Jason presented for treatment of school phobia related to Separation Anxiety Disorder. The family assessment revealed that Jason's mother had a particularly difficult time encouraging age-appropriate independent behavior in her child. Her fear that Jason would be "too overwhelmed" by his anxiety led to counterproductive "rescue" attempts by her that maintained his anxious state of dependency.

Additional areas to be covered in the assessment that may be relevant to complaints of anxiety include increased family discord, such as marital conflict, separations, and divorce, and any recent losses or perceived threats of loss. Similarly, exposure to frightening situations in school or in a child's neighborhood, such as violence or gang activity, can precipitate a new onset of anxiety symptoms. Of course, traumatic events, such as physical or sexual abuse, are frequent causes of anxiety.

Adolescents may be reticent to discuss the traumatic or stressful events that underlie their symptoms, and they will not necessarily make psychological connections between external events and internal anxiety states. Thus, it is important for the mental health practitioner not only to understand the events in the adolescent's life that may be contributing to the symptoms but also to document carefully the timing of events with relation to the onset of symptoms.

To further complicate the assessment process, many adolescents view their symptoms as weird, bizarre, or crazy, and they may not readily volunteer certain aspects of their experience. Questions such as "Is there anything you are afraid of which others aren't?" or "Do you ever get scared all of a sudden for no particular reason?" can be useful leads to uncovering symptoms.

If an individual reports a severe fear or phobia, the clinician should always assess for the presence of panic attacks. Similarly, if adolescents describe clear panic attacks, it is likely that there is associated phobic avoidance. The presence of an anxiety disorder warrants follow-up questions regarding depression and suicidality, as there is a high degree of association between mood and anxiety disorders.

SYMPTOMS AND DIAGNOSIS

In the following section we review the characteristic symptoms and criteria for diagnosing Panic Disorder, specific phobias, Social Phobia, Agoraphobia, School Phobia, Generalized Anxiety Disorder, and Obsessive-Compulsive Disorder.

Panic Attacks and Panic Disorder

The cardinal feature of a panic attack is sudden onset of intense fear associated with a multitude of bodily symptoms that have no apparent explanation. For example, individuals with Panic Disorder describe sudden bursts of fear associated with a belief that something is terribly wrong or that something dangerous is about to occur when there is no obvious external source or object of fear. Panic symptoms include rapid breathing, a sense of difficulty swallowing, a feeling that one's heart is pounding or beating rapidly, perception changes (objects seeming closer or farther away, the sensation that one is outside one's body, that limbs are detached from one's body), light-headedness or dizziness, cold and/or clammy extremities, and heat flush.

Panic attacks are frequently associated with catastrophic thoughts about dying, having a sudden heart attack, fainting, having a stroke, or going crazy. Adolescents are particularly troubled by and have difficulty admitting fears that they are "going crazy" or "losing it."

Panic attacks can occur spontaneously without provocation or can be cued. Cued panic attacks occur in predictable situations while the person is anticipating a frightening situation such as crossing a bridge, giving a talk in class, or entering a crowded, closed place such as a theater, church, or elevator.

In epidemiologic studies of adults diagnosed with Panic Disorder, they most often remember their first panic attack occurring during adolescence. Prior to puberty, panic attacks appear to be quite rare. There are only a handful of case reports of Panic Disorder in prepubertal children. Thus it appears that puberty marks the period at which the risk for panic attacks increases. Panic attacks and Panic Disorder are also more common in adolescent girls than in adolescent boys, with panic symptoms occurring two to three times more frequently in girls. This is also consistent with the prevalence of Panic Disorder in adults: Panic Disorder is approximately twice as common in women as in men.

It is important to distinguish between panic attacks and Panic Disorder. Panic attacks can occur in bunches or can be isolated events and occur once in someone's lifetime and never again. Some 30 percent of adults are estimated to experience a panic attack at some point in their life, and approximately 10 percent of adolescents of high school age have experienced a panic attack at some point during their adolescence. In contrast, only 1 percent to 2 percent of adults meet the full criteria for Panic Disorder, and estimates are that less than 1 percent of adolescents have Panic Disorder.

To receive a diagnosis of Panic Disorder, an individual must experience recurrent panic attacks, at least one of which is followed by at least one month of persistent concern about having additional attacks, worry about the implications of the attack, or a significant change in behavior related to the attacks, such as avoidance of feared situations or self-medication using illegal substances.

The diagnostic process for Panic Disorder includes careful assessment of the factors related to the experience of panic attacks. If attacks are temporally associated with the ingestion of caffeine or cold medications, both of which are known to trigger panic attacks, a diagnosis of Panic Disorder is not given. The diagnosis of Substance-Induced Anxiety Disorder is given instead. Likewise, panic episodes may be related to an underlying medical condition. The correct diagnosis in this case is Anxiety Disorder Due to a General Medical Condition. The common feature of both types of presentations is the assumption that removal of the underlying panic precipitant (for example, elimination of caffeine or medical treatment of the thyroid condition) should reduce significantly or eliminate episodes of panic.

Panic Disorder can co-occur, and frequently does, with other anxiety disorders, including Social Phobia, Agoraphobia, and Generalized Anxiety. In addition, Panic Disorder and Major Depression are frequently diagnosed simultaneously in individuals who suffer from panic symptoms.

Because of the wide variety of somatic symptoms associated with panic attacks, some adolescents with Panic Disorder or isolated panic attacks present initially to their pediatrician because of concern that something is wrong with their bodies. We recently received a referral of a sixteen-year-old girl who was certain that the experience of pounding heart and light-headedness meant that she had a serious heart condition. In light of a negative medical evaluation and the presence of several recent stressors, the pediatrician referred this patient for a psychological evaluation. She was subsequently diagnosed with Panic Disorder.

Although to date there are no objective physical findings or laboratory tests associated with the diagnosis of Panic Disorder, those who have Panic Disorder seem to be more sensitive to the panic-producing effects of some substances, including carbon dioxide, lactate infusions, or caffeine. Thus panic attacks can be precipitated in the laboratory in those with Panic Disorder by administration of these substances exogenously. There is also some evidence that those who suffer from Panic Disorder have more frequent diagnoses of mitral valve prolapse, a common, benign heart murmur found more commonly in women than in men. The significance of this possible association between Panic Disorder and mitral valve prolapse remains unclear.

The first episode of panic attacks frequently occurs after stressful life events. These events may include loss of a loved one, separations, moving to a new location, changes in schools, parental separation or divorce, or turmoil in a romantic relationship. The timing of the panic following the life event may vary, with the panic attack occurring a few days to months after the life event. Frequently the panic sufferer doesn't relate the life event to the panic attack because the panic attack is interpreted as a physical problem and the life event is an emotional event in the person's life. An example is the case of Matt.

MATT

Matt was fourteen years old when he experienced the first of three panic attacks. The first episode of panic occurred about one week after the death of his uncle. Matt's parents had divorced when he was two, after which he had little contact with his father. Over the years, his uncle had become a very important figure in his life. The panic attack was described as "a horrible feeling that something bad was going to happen." Matt also experienced light-headedness and shortness of breath. The second attack occurred about two weeks later at his brother's high school graduation. After the third attack, Matt told his mother what had been happening. She recognized the symptoms as similar to those experienced by her mother fifteen years earlier, and she sought psychological treatment for Matt.

Therapy initially focused on education about panic attacks. Matt found it very reassuring to hear that he was having panic attacks and not "going crazy." Over the next eight weeks, Matt explored his reactions to his uncle's death and other upcoming stressors (such as his brother leaving for college), and learned strategies to manage his panic episodes.

Another common feature of Panic Disorder, particularly in later adolescence, is the use of alcohol in the hope of preventing the attacks. High school or college students, for example, may drink prior to a social gathering or an important event to reduce their social anxiety and therefore potentially prevent panic attacks during the event.

MEGAN

This was the case for Megan, a nineteen-year-old college freshman who was in treatment for Anorexia Nervosa and depression. She had never been diagnosed as having panic attacks. When she was questioned about her alcohol use prior to social gatherings, however, it became apparent that the reason she drank prior to these events was to prevent the occurrence of a panic attack during the gathering. Although her attacks were predictable in the sense that she knew they would occur in a social situation, she was unsure at what point during the event they would occur, an uncertainty that left her feeling terrified that she would be noticed and would behave in some socially unacceptable way. When possible, she would avoid social situations for fear of having a panic attack. When avoidance was not possible, she would drink alcohol prior to any gathering she attended.

The Origin of Panic Attacks and Disorders. The etiology of Panic Disorder remains controversial. There are two competing hypotheses. The biological hypothesis argues that Panic Disorder is analogous to a seizure disorder and represents a physiological dysfunction in the brain. This dysfunction in the brain is thought to be related to the noradrenergic and serotonergic neurotransmitters. Support for the biological hypothesis includes the potential genetic heritability of the disorder. Evidence suggests that adolescents having one biological parent with Panic Disorder are five times more likely than other adolescents to develop Panic Disorder. Twin studies also support the possibility of genetic heritability. Further support for biological explanations of Panic Disorder include the possibility of inducing panic attacks using external substances, and the response to medications that occurs in those suffering from panic.

The competing hypothesis, although not necessarily mutually exclusive, argues that panic attacks represent a misinterpretation of bodily signals. For example, in adults there is evidence suggesting that increased awareness and attention to internal bodily cues, such as one's heartbeat or breathing patterns, can trigger anxious responses to normal bodily perturbations.

The demonstration of this tendency to overreact to bodily perturbations has been demonstrated in a number of elegant experiments. In these experiments, patients with Panic Disorder and controls without Panic Disorder are put in a laboratory environment in which they are allowed to hear an amplified version of their heartbeat. The experimenter then artificially increases the rate of the heartbeat so that the subjects think their heartbeat is suddenly much faster when in fact it hasn't changed. Those with Panic Disorder will frequently become very anxious and have panic attacks. The control group, on the other hand, remain unaffected by the false information of an elevated heart rate. These types of studies indicate that individuals with Panic Disorder have anxious responses to perceived bodily symptoms that they view as threatening.

This cognitive model of Panic Disorder proposes a vicious cycle, beginning with an anxious response to internal cues leading to fear. The fear produces more abnormal bodily sensations such as shallow breathing, rapid heart rate, and other autonomic nervous system symptoms, which are again interpreted in an anxious fashion, increasing the fear even more in an ever-revolving cycle. This cognitive appraisal occurs very quickly and presumably unconsciously so that the sufferer is not aware of the role of cognitive appraisal of bodily symptoms in the development of panic symptoms. The diagram that follows illustrates the Cognitive Model of Panic Disorder as articulated by David Clark (Figure 5.1).

Specific Phobias

JOE

Twelve-year-old Joe was brought to therapy by his parents who were distressed by his persistent fear of the dark. Though he had always

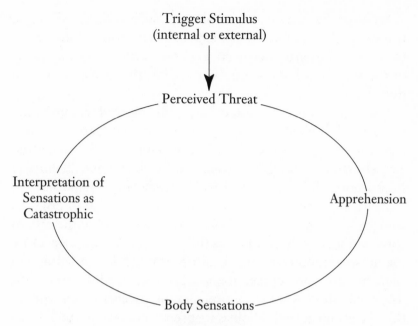

Figure 5.1
A Cognitive Model of Panic Disorder

Source: Reprinted from *Behavior Research and Therapy, 24,* Clark, D. M.
A cognitive approach to panic, p. 463, copyright 1986, with kind permission
from Elsevier Science Ltd, The Boulevard, Langford Lane, Kidlington
0X5 1GB, UK.

been fearful of the dark, his parents had expected him to "outgrow"
his fear. Now that he was entering adolescence, his unwillingness to
go upstairs alone at night unless someone had preceded him to turn
on the lights, and his need to sleep with a small nightlight in his
room was beginning to appear increasingly inappropriate.

Fears and phobias are common complaints among both children and adolescents. Not all irrational fears become phobias,
however. By definition, a phobia entails marked avoidance of the
feared object. For example, an adolescent might fear the dark,
but we would not call this a true phobia unless he or she refused
to enter a dark room alone, as in Joe's case.

Some of the more common phobias, such as fear of the dark, fear of heights, and fear of spiders, may have had adaptive value from an evolutionary perspective. In fact, primates exhibit many of the same phobic responses to snakes that are observed in humans.

Fears and phobias change during different developmental periods. Thus children often "grow out of their fears" but these fears can often be replaced by more age-appropriate fears. From a recent study of fears in normal youths, the ten most common fears among children aged 11 to 16 are shown in Table 5.1.

Fears appear to be more common in girls than in boys. In some studies, girls have demonstrated nearly twice the rate of fears exhibited by boys. Phobias (fear with marked avoidance) are the most common psychiatric disorder in adults, and although there are not good epidemiological studies in adolescents, it is likely that phobias are the most common psychiatric disorder in this age group as well. Phobias that represent fear and avoidance of a circumscribed object or situation are called Specific Phobias in DSM-IV. This represents a change in title from Simple Pho-

Table 5.1
Ten Most Common Fears, Children Ages 11–16
(in descending order of frequency)

- Being hit by car/truck
- Not being able to breathe
- Bombing attack/being invaded
- Fire—getting burned
- Falling from high place
- Burglar breaking into house
- Earthquake
- Death—dead people
- Getting poor grades
- Snakes

bia that was used in DSM-III-R. This diagnostic category can be broken down into subtypes (see Table 5.2).

Social Phobia and Agoraphobia. Rarer types of phobic disorders in adolescents include Social Phobia and Agoraphobia. Social Phobia is characterized by a severe fear of social or performance situations in which a person feels that he or she is the object of scrutiny by others. Individuals with Social Phobia worry about being embarrassed and believe that others will think badly of them. They worry about blushing, shaky hands or voice, losing control of their bowels or bladder, sweating, or just appearing anxious in front of others. These fears lead to avoidance of public situations, particularly when there are strangers or authority figures present.

To meet DSM-IV criteria for Social Phobia, the symptoms described above must persist for longer than six months in those younger than eighteen years of age. Individuals with Social Phobia often do poorly in school because of performance anxiety, even though they may be good students. Social Phobia frequently begins during adolescence, but there is evidence that a history of shyness or social anxiety during childhood often precedes Social Phobia. In addition, Avoidant Personality Disorder is believed to be associated often with Social Phobia. The case of Sally illustrates the significant degree of distress and life disruption associated with Social Phobia.

Table 5.2
Specific Phobias

Type	*Example*
Animals	Snakes
Natural environment	Lightning
Blood injection/injury	Needles
Situational	Airplanes

SALLY

Sally was an accomplished high school senior who had a part-time job after school. She came to the clinic for treatment of symptoms that had begun to interfere with her job performance.

Sally stated that she had been shy for most of her life and blushed very easily. She said that her fair skin and red hair made her face look like a "light bulb" when she blushed. She had become increasingly self-conscious about blushing at work. In addition, when she became nervous, her hands trembled slightly. She was extremely embarrassed about this and felt that people noticed and thought that she was scared. She was particularly concerned about handing hot drinks to fellow employees, especially her boss. She feared that her hand would become so shaky that she would spill the drink—even though this had never happened. These symptoms had become so troubling to Sally that she avoided her boss, confined herself to her office as much as possible, and had even called in sick.

Another phobic disorder that can occur in adolescents, although rarely, is Agoraphobia. Agoraphobia represents a fear of places or situations from which escape may be difficult or viewed as unsafe. Agoraphobics often experience frequent panic attacks and tend to practice extreme avoidance for fear of having a panic attack. Agoraphobics are often afraid of being in crowds, traveling far distances, or going over bridges and through tunnels. Someone suffering from the most severe form of Agoraphobia will not even leave the house. The anxiety associated with exposure to these feared situations is so great that agoraphobics "allow" their lives to be completely dictated by their pervasive fears. Agoraphobia is more common in women than men and its onset typically occurs between late adolescence and mid-life.

Both Social Phobia and Agoraphobia are very debilitating disorders. The lives of those who suffer from these disorders are extremely limited; they often resort to alcohol use for symptom relief. In addition, both Social Phobia and Agoraphobia are associated with depression and suicidality. These combinations of disorders can represent a difficult treatment challenge.

School Phobia. Although School Phobia is not listed as a diagnosis in DSM-IV, it is a common clinical presentation of anxious adolescents. School-phobic adolescents represent a subgroup of all adolescent school refusers. Adolescents may refuse to attend school for a variety of reasons, many of which are not anxiety based. For example, school refusal may be related to oppositional behavior (such as truancy) or to other psychological disorders such as depression.

Anxiety-based School Phobia can be related to Separation Anxiety Disorder or some other school-specific fear, such as fear of public speaking, dressing or undressing in gym, or fear of physical harm. When School Phobia is secondary to Separation Anxiety Disorder, adolescents' fears are most often related to the possibility that a terrible accident or illness will befall their primary attachment figures or themselves if they are separated. With any case of School Phobia adolescents typically exhibit a number of symptoms on school days that they hope will precipitate their parents' agreement to keep them at home. These symptoms include extreme fearfulness, emotional upset, temper tantrums, somatic complaints, and oppositional behavior.

GEORGE

George was a ninth grader with a cognitive neuromuscular disorder that caused him difficulty with speaking and walking. Over the past year he had gained considerable weight and felt increasingly self-conscious about his appearance and coordination. Simultaneously, he began to miss school. Initially he told his parents he was sick, but after missing more than half his classes during one quarter, his parents and school personnel became very alarmed.

Although reticent to discuss his reasons for not wanting to attend school, George finally admitted that he felt isolated, embarrassed, and ashamed of his appearance. He felt that he did not fit in with his peers, and although he was not mistreated by the kids at school, he was convinced they did not like him. The more he became convinced of this, the more anxious he became, and the harder it was for him to return to school.

The frequency of occurrence of School Phobia is difficult to estimate, although some believe that it affects 3 percent to 5 percent of school-age children and 5 percent of clinic-referred children. School Phobia tends to occur equally in both girls and boys and can occur during the entire range of school years. Normally it peaks at ages five to six and ten to eleven. In addition, there is no relationship between intellectual function and School Phobia; in fact, School Phobia can occur in those of above-average intelligence equally as commonly as in those with average intelligence. School Phobias often follow severe life events such as death of a family member or friend, parent illness, mental illness, an accident, or a move in location or school district.

Nonattendance at school for a period of time can lead to severe educational impairment, with long-standing effects on social functioning in later life. Thus, it is a very important symptom to treat before it persists for any extended length of time.

Generalized Anxiety Disorder. In DSM nomenclature, the diagnosis of Over-Anxious Disorder was available in DSM-III-R. This disorder was defined as excessive worry or anxiety exhibited by a child or adolescent. These children tended to be self-conscious, focused on future events, worried about injury, and worried about involvement with peers. In addition, they tended to obsess about meeting expectations of others, ruminate over past events, and have physical complaints with no known medical explanation. The child or adolescent tended to spend a large amount of time inquiring about safety of situations and required considerable reassurance.

In the DSM-IV, this Childhood Anxiety Disorder diagnosis has been subsumed under the category of Generalized Anxiety

Disorder. Generalized Anxiety Disorder is a disorder of adults that now includes Over-Anxious Disorder of Childhood. It is characterized by the same degree of anxiety and worry and is associated with restlessness, difficulty concentrating, irritability, insomnia, and preoccupation with immediate and past events. The extent of the worries is far out of proportion to what the situation warrants. Children and adolescents may also worry about catastrophic natural disasters such as earthquakes, floods, and hurricanes. They tend to be perfectionistic, and though quite competent, may be unsure of themselves and their performance. In adults this presentation is more common in women than in men; and in adolescents, there appears to be a higher proportion of adolescent girls than boys with these symptoms.

Although the frequency of adolescents who meet all diagnostic criteria for Generalized Anxiety Disorder may be low, a number of adolescents may have some features of the syndrome. Many adolescents present to mental health workers with one or more anxiety symptoms that have begun to interfere in the adolescent's life. For example, a teenager may focus on a particular bodily symptom and believe that something about the symptom requires continued medical attention or that the symptom should prevent the subject from attending school or participating in usual or regular activities. On the other hand, some adolescents just appear to be nervous, high-strung, and preoccupied about what others think of them. These adolescents may not have a diagnosis of Generalized Anxiety Disorder, but nevertheless, from a spectrum point of view, they are more anxious than their peers.

Anxious adolescents frequently have one or both parents who are equally afflicted by the propensity to worry, anticipate future events, and have concerns about their performance. Thus it is not clear if this is a learned behavior or a behavior for which there is a biological propensity. Similar to the indicators of other anxiety disorders, these symptoms of anxiety can often begin after a loss, a trauma, or a change in the external environment that the adolescent finds threatening. In this case, identifying the precipitant and helping the adolescent differentiate the reality of the situation from what is feared becomes an important part of assessment and treatment.

FRANK

The case of twelve-year-old Frank exemplifies the onset of Generalized Anxiety Disorder in an adolescent. Frank's grandfather, living in another state, had recently suffered a heart attack that required Frank's mother to visit him. Frank had always been prone to experience anxiety in response to new situations, but he had previously been able to manage these feelings. During his mother's absence, however, Frank became convinced that his mother was dying. When asked what she was dying from Frank said, "Her heart."

When his mother returned, she reassured him; but Frank still became morbidly concerned about heart attacks, death, and the loss of his mother. These themes consumed his conversation, play, and imagination. At the same time, Frank began reporting physical complaints to his parents. After a thorough pediatric evaluation, no explanation of these symptoms could be offered.

Obsessive-Compulsive Disorder. Obsessive-Compulsive Disorder (OCD) is characterized by intrusive thoughts, urges, and images that cause significant distress or anxiety. To relieve the sometimes intolerable distress, individuals with OCD perform rituals that can be either behavioral or mental. In its most severe form, OCD can be an extremely debilitating disorder.

CAROL

Carol was sixteen years old when she presented for treatment of OCD. Over the previous year, her symptoms had worsened. Her grades had dropped and she was becoming increasingly isolated. Carol reported that she experienced frequent intrusive doubts about having completed certain tasks, such as turning off the stove, the iron, or light switches. Once she began to doubt having followed through, for example, on turning off the stove, she would experience catastrophic thoughts and images about the potential consequences, such as seeing the family home on fire. She would become overwhelmed with anxiety, which prompted her to check the stove repeatedly to reassure herself that she had completed the task. Much of the time, a single check provided only brief relief from her anxiety. The intrusive doubts would quickly recur, leading to subsequent "checking" behavior.

Carol was becoming increasingly distracted by her doubts, leading to a decline in her academic performance. On several recent occasions, she had feigned illness at school so as to return home early to check something. She described her intrusive thoughts as "crazy," and labeled her anxiety-reducing rituals as "nuts," but she felt powerless to resist them.

The vast majority of individuals with OCD exhibit both obsessions and compulsions. Although very uncommon, "pure obsessionals" (individuals who experience obsessions causing marked distress but do not perform anxiety-reducing rituals) do exist. Listed in Table 5.3 are the most common obsessions and compulsions.

Table 5.3
Obsessions and Compulsions Associated with OCD

Obsessions
- Contamination
- Repeated doubts
- Need for order

- Aggressive or horrific impulses
- Sexual imagery

Compulsions

Behavioral:
- Hand washing
- Ordering
- Checking

Mental:
- Counting
- Praying
- Repeating words silently

As in the case of Carol described above, individuals with OCD generally recognize their obsessions and compulsions as excessive and unreasonable. This may not necessarily be the case for younger children, however, because their level of cognitive development may limit their judgment.

OCD is surprisingly common in children and adolescents, affecting approximately one in every two hundred. Of all adults with OCD, about one-third report the onset of their symptoms during childhood. The average age of onset typically occurs earlier for males (peak onset occurs at thirteen to fifteen years) than females (peak onset occurs at twenty to twenty-four years).

Family studies suggest a genetic link for the development of OCD. Approximately 20 percent of children with OCD have a family member with the disorder, and many more have relatives with affective, anxiety, or tic disorders.

It is very common for adolescents with OCD to receive additional psychiatric diagnoses, with other anxiety disorders and the depressive-spectrum disorders being the most common co-morbid conditions. OCD also frequently occurs with eating disorders and Tourette's syndrome.

Although psychological theories have been proposed to explain the development of OCD, current thinking about the etiology of the disorder is primarily neurochemical and neuroanatomical. Researchers suspect that the neurotransmitter serotonin is involved in the development of OCD. Much of the support for this hypothesis comes from studies of the efficacy of serotonergic drugs in the treatment of the disorder. Neuroanatomical studies have suggested that many individuals with OCD have some deficits in frontal lobe functioning.

Despite the hypothesized neurobiological basis of OCD, behavioral treatments, with or without the concurrent use of psychotropic medication, are very effective. It has been estimated that 65 percent to 75 percent of patients treated with behavior therapy improve and continue to function well at follow-up.

TREATMENT

Treatment of adolescent anxiety disorders often requires a combined approach utilizing individual and family therapy, and in some cases the use of group approaches and psychopharmacology.

Individual Therapy

Our approach to treatment is based primarily on a cognitive-behavioral model. However, our work is also informed and enhanced by psychodynamic theory and technique. For many patients, treatment can be thought of in two phases:

> Phase I: Psychoeducation, symptom relief, understanding the symptom precipitant, and training in anxiety management techniques.
>
> Phase II: Exploration of "deeper" issues.

Much of the literature on treatment of anxiety disorders is based on a cognitive-behavioral model. In our experience, augmenting the problem-focused, cognitive-behavioral approach with more traditional exploratory techniques may help adolescents gain insight about their relations with others, their family of origin, and their own defenses used to manage emotions, and may ultimately lessen their long-term susceptibility for symptom return.

An example of the use of both approaches was provided in the discussion of Matt, the fourteen-year-old male who developed panic attacks following the death of his uncle. The cognitive-behavioral approach used early in his treatment to educate him about the nature of panic and teach him strategies to manage his anxiety eventually gave way to the use of exploratory techniques to examine the meaning of loss in his life, both the death of his uncle and the upcoming departure of his brother for college.

The successful blending of both phases described above is dependent on a solid case formulation and on the goals and expectations of the adolescent. Case formulation plays a vital role in any successful course of therapy. It provides a synthesis of the factors hypothesized to underlie a patient's problem. It reflects an understanding of the influence of multiple domains on the patient's functioning: cognitions and underlying assumptions about self and the world, family dynamics, adaptive style, stage of development, and so on. This understanding suggests priorities for treatment and guides the timing and choice of interventions.

Not all adolescents with anxiety symptoms are interested in an insight-oriented approach, preferring instead to remain very problem focused. This was the case for a sixteen-year-old girl who presented with a needle phobia. Her allergies had worsened and her physician was recommending regular allergy shots, a prospect that caused her great distress. She responded very well to systematic desensitization for her needle phobia (and subsequently tolerated her injections with little difficulty), but she was uninterested in continuing therapy to explore a number of other concurrent stressors in her life that she had mentioned during the course of the phobia treatment.

Even when adolescents are curious about the context and meaning of their anxiety symptoms, their primary concern on initiation of therapy is usually symptom relief. Ignoring this urgency can lead to their noncompliance with treatment or their stopping treatment altogether.

Following completion of the assessment, the first step is education about the specific anxiety disorder diagnosis and the cognitive-behavioral conceptualization of anxiety. Patients are also oriented to the collaborative nature of the therapeutic relationship, and are informed of the importance of exposure to feared stimuli and the necessity of practicing their new skills between sessions.

The introduction to the cognitive-behavioral conceptualization of anxiety focuses on the three ways in which anxiety is manifested:

1. Bodily reactions, such as rapid heart rate, difficulty breathing, light-headedness
2. Cognitions or thoughts, such as "They'll make fun of me if I talk in class," "I might do something really embarrassing"
3. Actions or behaviors, such as avoiding feared objects or events

Treatment focuses on each of the three areas, utilizing a combination of cognitive and behavioral techniques, such as relaxation training to help with the somatic manifestations of anxiety, cognitive techniques to alter anxious thought patterns, and gradual exposure to feared stimuli that is based on construction of a fear hierarchy.

Listed in Table 5.4 are a number of cognitive and behavioral techniques that are commonly used in the treatment of anxiety disorders.

The decision about which techniques to use and when is dependent both on the case formulation for that particular

Table 5.4
Cognitive and Behavioral Techniques

Cognitive Techniques
- Keeping daily record of dysfunctional thoughts
- Identifying cognitive distortions
- Examining evidence for maladaptive thoughts/beliefs
- Looking for alternative explanations
- Teaching relationship between maladaptive thought and underlying beliefs

Behavioral Techniques
- Relaxation training
- Activity scheduling
- Modeling and role-playing
- Exposure (imaginal and in vivo)
- Systematic desensitization

patient and the nature of the specific anxiety disorder. Although most anxiety disorders respond best to a combination of cognitive and behavioral techniques, there are differences in the degree of patients' responsiveness to certain techniques. For example, the mainstay of phobia treatment is exposure to the feared object or situation. The exposure can be gradual, based on a fear hierarchy, or can be more prolonged and intense (flooding). Exposure can be conducted in vivo, or it can begin with the use of imagery. Our experience is that in vivo exposure is more effective than imagined exposure. Relaxation techniques can be used to augment the exposure process, as with the classic technique of systematic desensitization. However, when teaching relaxation, you do not want to send a message to the client that anxiety is bad and is to be avoided at all costs. Rather, the point of relaxation is to help patients cope with anxiety so that intense anxiety no longer becomes a reason to engage in avoidant behavior. While cognitive techniques can be very useful adjunctive interventions, particularly with Social and School Phobias, successful treatment of any phobia is dependent on some type of exposure.

Exposure-based treatments are also common aspects of the treatment of Panic Disorder. However, because of the role of cognitions in the misinterpretation of bodily sensations, cognitive restructuring techniques are an essential part of the treatment. The exposure component of treatment generally includes exposure to feared situations (situations where panic attacks might occur) but also includes exposure to interoceptive cues. As with the phobias, relaxation techniques can also be useful components of treatment.

Generalized Anxiety Disorder differs from the other anxiety disorders in that the fears and concerns tend to be much more global and diffuse, as compared to phobias and Panic Disorder, in which the feared stimuli are quite specific. The treatment targets for Generalized Anxiety Disorder are the excessive, uncontrollable worry and its accompanying persistent physiological overarousal. Cognitive techniques are key, and target the anxiogenic cognitions associated with the persistent worry. Relaxation techniques alleviate the physiological component of the anxiety. Exposure can also be part of the treatment, but it differs from the traditional approaches used with phobias. "Worry Exposure" entails using imagery to expose patients to their principal worry spheres. For example, adolescents who are preoccupied with worries about terrible catastrophes befalling their loved ones would be told to concentrate on their anxious thoughts while trying to imagine the worst possible feared outcome related to that particular sphere of worry.

Exposure also underlies what is considered the most effective nonpharmacologic treatment for Obsessive-Compulsive Disorder. However, exposure alone does not automatically eliminate compulsive rituals. In addition to being exposed to the feared object or situation, patients are instructed to slowly increase the time during which they refrain from all ritualistic (anxiety-reducing) behavior during the exposure period. This is called response prevention. For OCD, however, unlike the other anxiety disorders, studies examining the efficacy of including cognitive techniques with exposure and response prevention have suggested little benefit from the addition of cognitive therapy. Even so, the studies conducted to date have been small, making it difficult to draw clear conclusions. Relaxation interventions are generally not effective for most patients with OCD.

In summary, the choice of which cognitive and behavioral interventions to use with an anxious adolescent is driven, in part, by the nature of the particular anxiety disorder. Table 5.5 provides an overview of the various anxiety disorders and the techniques considered most effective for each one.

The case of eighteen-year-old Sally illustrates the combined use of cognitive and behavioral techniques for treatment of Social Phobia.

Following the initial assessment and diagnosis, Sally was asked to keep a daily record of her anxiety symptoms and automatic thoughts associated with anxious feelings. It quickly became clear that Sally

Table 5.5
Cognitive-Behavioral Techniques for Specific Anxiety Disorders

Panic Disorder
- Identification and restructuring of dysfunctional thoughts and cognitive distortions
- Relaxation techniques
- Breathing retraining
- Exposure to feared situations, including interoceptive cues

Phobias
- Primarily exposure:
  Flooding or gradual
  In session and between sessions
- Relaxation techniques
- Systematic desensitization (combination of imaginal exposure paired with relaxation)
- Identification and restructuring of dysfunctional thoughts and cognitive distortions

Generalized Anxiety
- Identification and restructuring of dysfunctional thoughts and cognitive distortions
- Relaxation techniques
- "Worry exposure"

Obsessive-Compulsive Disorder
- Exposure and response prevention

experienced a variety of catastrophic cognitions on entering any situations requiring social interaction.

Examples of her thoughts included these: "Others can see right through me," "People will think I'm weird," "People will wonder why I'm so embarrassed," "People know that I don't have any self-confidence, and they don't like me." Sally experienced physiological symptoms when she was anxious, such as blushing and trembling hands, which exacerbated her anxiety and, in turn, created greater physiological arousal.

Sally began learning a form of progressive muscle relaxation to reduce overall physiological arousal and increase a sense of control or mastery. The therapist began cognitive restructuring, which entailed teaching Sally how to identify and challenge cognitive distortions and other maladaptive thoughts and beliefs. The exposure component of her treatment began in session and involved her engaging in feared social interactions, such as exchanging a hot cup of coffee with the therapist.

Once Sally began to experience some success with managing anxiety in these interactions, she and the therapist set goals for exposing her to anxiety-provoking social situations between sessions. Exposure goals were based on her fear hierarchy and began with situations that evoked mild to moderate levels of anxiety, and then progressed to situations that triggered more severe reactions.

When Sally ended treatment, she was no longer avoiding social events and gatherings, and although she continued to experience some anxiety during certain interactions, she was able to manage the anxious feelings using the cognitive strategies she learned in therapy.

Family Therapy

Family sessions are an important part of anxiety disorder treatment for most adolescents. However, the frequency and focus of the sessions varies considerably depending on the nature of the issues in a particular family and the way in which family dynamics are influencing the adolescent's difficulties.

In some cases, the focus of family sessions is on psychoeducation regarding the nature of anxiety and the necessary components of treatment. Periodic family sessions are scheduled to provide parents with feedback about their child's progress, discuss changes in the adolescent's behavior observed by the parents, and explore the impact of these changes on overall family functioning. Older adolescents, because of their developmentally appropriate greater degree of independent functioning, may require fewer family sessions than younger teens.

A greater degree of family involvement may be indicated in cases where it is clear that the response of the parents to the anxious behavior reinforces and maintains that behavior. This dynamic can be seen with any of the anxiety disorders, but tends to occur most frequently with Separation Anxiety Disorder and associated school refusal.

Earlier we mentioned Jason, the twelve-year-old with School Phobia secondary to Separation Anxiety Disorder. Jason's mother demonstrated great difficulty encouraging age-appropriate independent behavior in her son. Fearing that Jason would be "overwhelmed" by his anxiety, she went to great lengths to spare him unnecessary suffering, which led to a pattern of overprotection. Clearly, working individually with Jason using cognitive and behavioral interventions was not going to be successful without intensive intervention with the parents. Weekly family sessions were held to address the ways in which the mother's efforts inadvertently undermined Jason's attempts to function more independently.

We attempt to adopt a collaborative stance with families that is respectful of their strengths. We work with the family as a team to map the influence of anxiety in their lives and identify ways in which the family can take a stand in opposition to the negative influence of anxiety and support the normal development of their adolescent.

Jason and his parents were able to talk about the way in which anxiety had them all "cowering." When anxiety would pay the family a visit, it assumed control of Jason, but also of his parents. Everyone shared the concern that anxiety was "robbing" Jason of a normal adolescence. Jason's parents decided that in order to help their son, they needed to take the lead and make a stand against the anxiety. They were able to see that doing this would sometimes mean allowing Jason to experience his anxiety so that he could learn to master it and eventually fight it on his own.

We were able to capitalize on the mother's "exquisitely developed mother's intuition" about what her son needed and to support her in recognizing early signs of anxiety in Jason so that she could encourage his use of the new anxiety-management skills he was developing in individual therapy. Without this new perspective, it would have been difficult for the parents to assist Jason during the exposure portion of his treatment (gradually returning to school).

Group Therapy

Group therapy can be a useful format for many adolescent issues and disorders. This is particularly so for treatment of Social Phobia. A group format offers several potential advantages over individual treatment, including vicarious learning, seeing others with similar problems, the availability of multiple role-play partners, and a range of people who can provide evidence to counter the patient's distorted thinking. Because of the availability of multiple group members for role-playing, the group format facilitates the exposure component of treatment for social anxiety in a way that individual therapy cannot.

Debra Hope and Richard Heimberg have suggested that several factors should be considered in determining the appropriateness of a particular patient for group treatment of Social Phobia. Patients should be excluded from consideration if they are likely to be disruptive to the group process or to experience such severe anxiety in the group setting itself that they will not be able to tolerate it.

In addition, Social Phobia should be the primary problem for which a patient is seeking treatment. Co-morbidity should be assessed and the nature of the primary problem carefully determined. The patient's level of depression should also be assessed thoroughly, as depression is a predictor of negative outcome in group treatment of Social Phobia. Finally, patients with severe deficits in social skills may not benefit fully from group treatment for Social Phobia. Most social phobics perform poorly in social situations because of the disruptive nature of their anxiety, not because they do not possess adequate social skills. For some, however, their fears are realistic in light of their severely deficient social skills. These patients may benefit from a social skills group rather than a group for social phobics.

Medications

In some cases, anxiety symptoms persist or have severe consequences—for example, the patient who is having frequent panic attacks is convinced that she has a brain tumor and refuses to go to school. This individual may need additional symptom relief before longer-term therapy can be initiated. This can be achieved with the use of medications. Both anti-anxiety agents and antidepressants are effective for anxiety symptoms in adults and are probably equally so in adolescents.

In general, the antidepressant medications have one advantage over the anti-anxiety medications in that they create no physiologic dependence. On the other hand, their onset of action is much longer: two to four weeks versus one to two days. The best choice for antidepressants is one of the newer types called SSRIs (selective serotonin reuptake inhibitors), such as Prozac. The tricyclic antidepressants have many more side effects and can be lethal in overdoses. Medications, listed by class of medication, for each disorder are shown in Table 5.6.

SOME FINAL THOUGHTS

Cognitive and behavioral treatment of adolescent anxiety disorders can appear deceptively straightforward. In reality, cognitive and behavioral treatment is fraught with the same complex interpersonal dynamics that influence the course of any type of psychotherapy.

Progress in treatment can be affected by a variety of issues. One of the most important factors in working with adolescent anxiety disorders is the nature of the therapeutic relationship. Unlike most adults who seek treatment, many adolescents, even those who are experiencing a significant degree of anxiety, are

Table 5.6
Medications Used to Treat Anxiety Disorders

Medication	Panic Disorder	Social Phobia	Generalized Anxiety Disorder	Obsessive-Compulsive Disorder
I. Antianxiety Medication				
Benzodiazepine				
• High Potency				
Lorazepam (Ativan)	2		2	
Alprazolam (Xanax)	2		2	
Clonazepam (Klonopin)	2	2	2	3
• Low Potency				
Diazepam (Valium)			2	
Chlordiazepoxide (Librium)			2	
Many Others			2	
Buspirine (Buspar)			1	
II. Antidepressant Medication				
Tricyclic Antidepressants				
Imipramine (Tofranil)	2		2	
Amitriptyline (Elavil)	3		2	
Clomipramine (Anafranil)	3		3	1
Many Others	3		2	
Monoamine Oxidase				
Inhibitors (Nardil)	2	2		
Trazodone (Desyrel)	3			
Bupropion (Wellbutrin)	3			
Serotonin Reuptake Inhibitors				
Fluoxetine (Prozac)	1	1		1
Paroxetine (Paxil)	1	1		1
Sertraline (Zoloft)	1	1		1

1=First-line agents
2=Equally effective but have worse side effects
3=Less well-studied or second-line agent

not necessarily motivated to enter therapy. They are commonly brought to therapy by their parents and may be struggling with feeling pressured into a process about which they are quite ambivalent. Younger adolescents may feel they have less of a choice than older adolescents, but issues around autonomy and trust are common in working with all adolescents.

A strong therapeutic alliance is key to any successful course of therapy. With adolescents, it is important to monitor the development of the therapeutic alliance closely. It is easy to overlook this element and rush prematurely into setting goals and assigning "homework." It is sometimes easy for therapists to get caught up in the "aura" of cognitive and behavioral interventions that are commonly billed as providing rapid symptomatic relief, leading to relatively brief courses of therapy, and move too fast.

If the adolescent does not experience the therapeutic relationship as a supportive, trusting one, compliance with treatment is likely to be problematic. Special attention should be given to engaging the adolescent in a collaborative process around setting goals, constructing fear hierarchies, and designing between-session tasks. In the long run, it is better to proceed slowly in the initial sessions, carefully tracking motivation, rather than moving ahead too quickly and discovering that the adolescent's reactions to the process have been left behind.

Another factor that potentially influences motivation is high levels of anxiety. Although some adolescents may come to therapy willingly, some balk at the idea of having to expose themselves to stimuli that trigger extreme anxiety. Careful attention must be given to construction of an appropriate fear hierarchy. Noncompliance with exposure tasks between sessions may be a reflection of a fear hierarchy that is not gradual enough. Revision of the hierarchy is indicated in these cases so that high levels of anxiety do not interfere with progress in treatment.

Other factors besides high anxiety can interfere with follow-through on between-session tasks. Compliance with homework in cognitive-behavioral treatment can be as much of an issue with some adults as with adolescents. However, in general, adolescents tend to be a little more difficult to engage in follow-through with activities such as practicing progressive muscle relaxation or completing thought records and bringing them to sessions. A variety of factors may contribute to the compliance issue.

Some adolescents may not fully understand the rationale for a particular strategy and may see little use in completing the task. For other patients, the problems that prevent them from carrying out homework assignments are similar to problems that prevent them from doing other things in their lives. For example, patients with perfectionistic tendencies may have difficulty completing many things because they feel inadequate and unable to do a perfect job. Related to perfectionism are fears of failure, which may lead to such behaviors as doing the assignment but forgetting to bring it to the session so that the therapist will not be able to see the flaws. Patients with strong needs to please others may be so concerned with pleasing the therapist that they are reluctant to tell the therapist during the goal-setting process that they don't want to try a particular approach and would like to try something else as the assignment. Therapists must review the noncompliance in the context of the case formulation, carefully evaluating the range of factors that may be contributing.

We must also keep in mind the differences between younger and older adolescents, and tailor interventions accordingly. It may be quite appropriate, for example, to assign the task of completing a daily record of dysfunctional thoughts to a seventeen-year-old patient. Expecting the same of a twelve- or thirteen-year-old is probably unrealistic. In general, younger adolescents do better with tasks that are briefer in duration and more concrete. It may be more appropriate to enlist the aid of parents in completion of some homework tasks for younger adolescents than it is for older adolescents. Many younger adolescents, for example, benefit from a reminder by their parents to practice their relaxation. Older adolescents should be able to function more independently.

With careful monitoring of the above issues, the treatment of adolescent anxiety disorders can be a rich therapeutic experience. Unlike many adolescent disorders, the treatment of anxiety disorders can be accomplished effectively and efficiently, result-ing in a significant reduction in suffering and reduced risk for the dangerous consequences of untreated symptoms. In addition, the skills that adolescents learn for anxiety management are skills that can generalize, leading to enhanced coping efforts in all other areas of their lives.

NOTES

P. 187, *For most adolescents, feelings of anxiety:* Keller, M. B., Lavori, P. W., Wun-der, J., Beardslee, W. R., Schwartz, C. E., & Roth, J. (1992). Chronic course of anxiety disorders in children and adolescents. *Journal of the American Academy of Child and Adolescent Psychiatry, 31*(4), 595–599.

P. 196, *The diagram that follows illustrates:* Clark, D. M. (1986). A cognitive approach to panic. *Behavior Research and Therapy, 24,* 463.

P. 198, *Ten most common fears:* Ollendick, T. H. et al. (1989). Fears in children and adolescents: Reliability and generalizability across gender, age and nationality. *Behavior Research Therapy, 27,* 19–26.

P. 205, *"pure obsessionals":* Riggs, D. S., & Foa, E. B. (1993). Obsessive com-pulsive disorder. In D. H. Barlow (Ed.), *Clinical handbook of psychological dis-orders.* New York: Guilford Press.

P. 206, *OCD is surprisingly common:* Greist, J. H., & March, J. (1995). Clinical advances in OCD. In D. R. Pray (Ed.), *Psychiatric Times, 12,* Supplement No. 4.

P. 206, *The average age of onset:* Rasmussen, S. A., & Eisen, J. L. (1990). Epi-demiology of obsessive-compulsive disorder. *Journal of Clinical Psychiatry, 51,* 10–14.

P. 206, *Approximately 20 percent:* Greist, J. H., & March, J. (1995). Clinical advances in OCD. In D. R. Pray (Ed.), *Psychiatric Times, 12,* Supplement No. 4.

P. 206, *Much of the support:* Riggs, D. S., & Foa, E. B. (1993). Obsessive com-pulsive disorder. In D. H. Barlow (Ed.), *Clinical handbook of psychological dis-orders.* New York: Guilford Press.

P. 206, *Neuroanatomical studies have suggested:* Riggs, D. S., & Foa, E. B. (1993). Obsessive compulsive disorder. In D. H. Barlow (Ed.), *Clinical handbook of psychological disorders.* New York: Guilford Press.

P. 206, *It has been estimated:* Riggs, D. S., & Foa, E. B. (1993). Obsessive compulsive disorder. In D. H. Barlow (Ed.), *Clinical handbook of psychological disorders.* New York: Guilford Press.

P. 208, *This understanding suggests priorities:* Wilkes, T.C.R., & Belsher, G. (1994). The initial phase of cognitive therapy: From assessment to setting goals. In T.C.R. Wilkes, G. Belsher, A. J. Rush, & E. Frank (Eds.), *Cognitive therapy for depressed adolescents.* New York: Guilford Press.

P. 208, *three ways in which anxiety is manifested:* Silverman, W. K., Ginsburg, G. S., & Kurtines, W. M. (1995). Clinical issues in treating children with anxiety and phobic disorders. *Cognitive and Behavioral Practice, 2*(1), 93–117.

P. 210, *The treatment targets for Generalized Anxiety Disorder:* Brown, T. A., O'Leary, T. A., & Barlow, D. H. (1993). Generalized anxiety disorder. In D. H. Barlow (Ed.), *Clinical handbook of psychological disorders.* New York: Guilford Press.

P. 211, *"Worry Exposure":* Brown, T. A., O'Leary, T. A., & Barlow, D. H. (1993). Generalized anxiety disorder. In D. H. Barlow (Ed.), *Clinical handbook of psychological disorders.* New York: Guilford Press.

P. 211, *unlike the other anxiety disorders:* Riggs, D. S., & Foa, E. B. (1993). Obsessive compulsive disorder. In D. H. Barlow (Ed.), *Clinical handbook of psychological disorders.* New York: Guilford Press.

P. 215, *several potential advantages:* Hope, D. A., & Heimberg, R. G. (1993). Social phobia and social anxiety. In D. H. Barlow (Ed.), *Clinical handbook of psychological disorders.* New York: Guilford Press.

P. 215, *Debra Hope and Richard Heimberg:* Hope, D. A., & Heimberg, R. G. (1993). Social phobia and social anxiety. In D. H. Barlow (Ed.), *Clinical handbook of psychological disorders.* New York: Guilford Press.

P. 219, *the problems that prevent them from carrying out homework:* Persons, J. B. (1989). *Cognitive therapy in practice: A case formulation approach.* New York: Norton.

6

EATING DISORDERS

Mary J. Sanders

a little black
Devil
sitting on my shoulder, whispering
whispering
SCREAMING
into my ear
He is
mad
I have ignored him; He doesn't
know
that the only way I can
LIVE
(my life) is by ignoring
Him

MEGAN PARKER, THE BAD DAYS

The treatment of adolescents with eating disorders is quite challenging for several reasons. The effects of the eating disorder are extremely serious, sometimes leading to acute medical instability, chronic disability, suicidality, and even death. Although the effects of this problem are quite severe, adolescents may be ambivalent regarding their desire to give up the problem and may deny the seriousness of the situation. Thus, the therapist may find himself in the difficult position of supporting the adolescents' health and self-reliance while the adolescents attempt to hold onto the eating disorder despite its serious consequences. Although treatment tends to be quite lengthy and arduous, it may also be quite rewarding as many of these adolescents are able to reclaim their lives and appreciate their competence.

Adolescence tends to be the prime developmental age for the onset of eating disorders. School-based surveys indicate that approximately 80 percent of high school students report a desire to lose weight. Over half the girls report engaging in dieting, and approximately 20 percent have used dangerous weight loss methods. Girls with higher weights are more likely to engage in binge/purge behaviors.

The ideal of a slender body is reflected by the phenomenal growth of the weight reduction industry and the increased number of books and magazines dealing with weight control. A survey of six popular women's magazines indicated a significant increase in the number of diet articles over the past twenty years. Adolescents may be especially vulnerable to this quest for the "ideal" as they struggle for self- and other acceptance.

Girls outnumber boys approximately 10 to 1 in presentation of eating disorder symptoms. Boys dealing with anorexia or bulimia may be more at risk for not receiving treatment, possibly because they don't want to be seen as having a "female" disorder. Some of these boys may display feminine identification, and approximately 30 percent may be homosexual or report sexual anxiety.

Girls are invited by Western culture to value thinness and a deferential lifestyle. As they mature, they find that they are not the gender in power and that women are invited to "be for others." Carol Gilligan found that when girls hit their teens they begin to "not have a voice," and to respond "I don't know" when asked questions that they were previously able to answer in their younger years. It is interesting that this is the prime time in a girl's life for the voice of anorexia to make itself known.

THE VOICE OF
ANOREXIA OR BULIMIA

So what is it that these adolescents experience? In my work over the past decade I have asked this question of the adolescents I see in an attempt to understand their experience. Many times what I hear is such statements as "Being fat means I'm lazy, dirty, stupid, worthless," "I'd rather be dead than fat," "The only time I feel good about myself is when I feel empty," or "when I lose weight," or "when I can close my hand around my upper arm."

These thoughts are described as constantly nagging: "If you eat 1,000 calories today, you will have to run three miles." "You ate too much again. Now you have to take laxatives." "You can't eat today, because there will be no opportunity to throw up." One person described these thoughts as being similar to living in a police state. The thoughts are also quite demeaning and cruel: "You are fatter than everyone else. No wonder no one likes you." "You are stupid for being hungry."

Despite extreme weight loss at times, the voice of anorexia does not let up. One adolescent said that the only time she felt some relief from the nagging thoughts was when her body fat was .3 percent and she was at risk for death.

Dealing with Appetite

Although *anorexia* means loss of appetite, this is not true for those dealing with this problem. Quite the contrary. It seems that when hunger is the strongest—which tends to follow restriction—so grows the voice of anorexia. Needless to say, these adolescents attempt to find creative ways to quiet their appetite while appeasing the voice of anorexia. The methods used are (1) eating low calorie/low fat foods, (2) drinking noncaloric fluids such as diet soft drinks and water, (3) eating very slowly so that meals last a long time, (4) attempting to talk themselves out of hunger, or (5) eating and then engaging in compensatory behaviors such as excessive exercise, vomiting, or use of laxatives or diuretics.

As these adolescents eliminate foods from their diets, they tend to develop rules regarding "feared foods." Over time they may limit themselves to a very narrow range of choices and may be eating exactly the same menu daily with the fear that if they diverge, they'll gain weight. The distinguished English authority on eating disorders, Arthur Crisp, discussed how certain foods may become phobic objects for these adolescents.

Some adolescents may engage in a period of overeating or bingeing following a period of restriction. They may allow themselves to eat some of their feared foods. Once started, they may say to themselves, "Oh well, I have lost control. I will have to eat the whole thing, because I can't stop now."

Sometimes they may eat what is available or plan to have some time alone to bake and consume what they have baked. Sometimes adolescents will not necessarily overeat but may still consider any meal to be a "binge" and thus engage in purging behaviors or restriction following meals. Many times adolescents feel shame regarding these binge/purge events, and this sometimes leads them to restriction, purging, secrecy, and continued enslavement by bulimia.

Reliance on External Validation

Many times, adolescents who are dealing with eating issues rely on various "numbers" to "feel safe." These numbers may be the amount of calories or grams of fat they consume daily or the numbers on the scale when they weigh themselves. Many times adolescents who reported feeling good about themselves prior to being weighed in clinic would quickly become tearful and sometimes suicidal as a result of finding they had gained a pound. This reliance on external validation is evident in other areas as well. Many times adolescents report that an A is not a good enough grade, because they know they could have made an A+.

Frequently, the adolescents report an "all or none" quality to their thoughts about the numbers, especially regarding their weight. Some have told me that if their weight goes over a certain number (which tends to be extremely low), they feel they have lost complete control and feel they are then "fat," which (to them) means the same as "worthless." Some adolescents have told me that their rules are very strict because they feel that if they let up they will lose control. For them, this does feel like an "all or none," life or death situation. Some of these adolescents view any attempts to help them gain weight as a lethal attack. The rules tend to become stricter and stricter until there is little room for anything or anyone else.

Social Restriction

What first appears to be a means of attaining social approval and self-worth through weight loss tends to take these adolescents from their social group. Some adolescents isolate themselves during meals; they don't wish to be observed eating very little, or listen to others comment on their food combinations, or be seen eating at all, as they may see eating as a shameful activity. Also, they may become very absorbed in activities like exercising, meal planning and eating, and studying for grades. This isolation may result in social anxiety and promote further isolation.

DIAGNOSES

The *Diagnostic and Statistical Manual* (DSM-IV) describes the core diagnostic feature for patients with either Anorexia Nervosa or Bulimia Nervosa as being unduly influenced by body weight.

For Anorexia Nervosa, the criteria include refusal to maintain adequate weight, which is not a necessary criterion for the diagnosis of bulimia. For bulimia and for the binge-eating/purging type of Anorexia Nervosa, binge eating is present, involving both the consumption of a large quantity of food and the feeling of being out of control. Currently, both diagnoses also include the possibility of compensatory behaviors. These may include activities such as overexercise, vomiting, or diuretic or laxative use.

A diagnosis of Eating Disorder, Not Otherwise Specified refers to subthreshold situations in which eating problems are identified but not all the diagnostic criteria for either Anorexia Nervosa or Bulimia Nervosa are met. This diagnostic category may be particularly relevant for adolescent populations, as ideally, many of these patients would be identified and begin treatment at relatively earlier stages of the disorder.

ASSESSMENT

Sometimes the adolescent coming into your office does not always indicate that she is having eating problems. The presenting problem may be difficulty with schoolwork, peers, family, or decreased self-esteem. Eating concerns may not surface initially. It is my experience, however, that as I gather information regarding the presenting problem, material indicative of eating issues emerges.

For example, one adolescent came in complaining that she had made a C in one of her classes and was devastated by this event. She began to describe how important it was for her to be the best she could be in all areas of her life. I asked her what other areas were important to her, and she told me that she was not pleased with her appearance and gave a history of restricting her diet and engaging in excessive exercise. Thus, you may find that eating concerns may surface later in the interview or even later in the therapy. As the evaluating or treating therapist, you might then ask specific questions regarding the presence of eating disorders.

A complete clinical interview will include both an individual and a family interview, and possibly the use of some self-report measures. Both the family and individual interviews will attempt to cover the basic clinical interview information, with the addition of some specific questions focused on eating issues.

Individual Interview

In this section, I describe important areas to cover in an evaluation of the adolescent and family and present some specific questions that may be helpful in assessing these areas. The questions are directed to the adolescent but may be modified to obtain similar information from the parents. The first attempt is to learn the adolescent's attitude toward the evaluation itself.

1. What were you told about the evaluation today?
2. What are your expectations for this evaluation?

It may be helpful to be aware of how the adolescent views the evaluation in order to assess the type of data you receive from the interview. I have received quite a range of responses to this query, such as "I have a deal with my mother that if I come to this, I can go out with my friends this weekend," or "I was told we were going shopping, so I'm not going to tell you anything," or "I feel I can't control my weight loss, and I think I might have to be put in the hospital today."

It is also important at this time to explain the privilege and limits of confidentiality. The adolescents should be made aware that their communication with you will be shared with the treatment team as part of a team evaluation and that the information is confidential except for information that suggests that abuse may have occurred.

Presenting Problem. In the first portion of the interview, I like to hear what the adolescent perceives to be the problem and obtain as complete a description of these problems as possible. This is an opportunity for the adolescent to be heard as well as a chance for the therapist to get a history of the problem. It is during a discussion of presenting problems that an inkling of eating issues may emerge. Questions may be asked as follows.

1. Would you please describe the problems you are currently experiencing yourself? In your family?
2. How is (the problem described) a problem for you?
3. Would you please describe when (the problem described) first became a problem for you?
4. What was the course of the problem over time? What do you see as contributing factors to the problem?
5. Please describe other important chronic stressors or changes that have occurred that you feel may or may not have contributed to your present symptoms.
6. What other problems or concerns would you list as important in your life?

Weight and Body Issues. I ask the adolescent to tell me about the time she decided to lose weight and what prompted this decision. It's helpful to know what the initial motivations for weight loss were and if they changed or evolved over time so that you can have a fuller understanding of what the adolescent hoped to gain from losing weight. I ask whether the adolescent has set a specific goal weight for herself and how she may react if told she may need to gain more than this weight. This knowledge is helpful in assessing how powerful the number is and how strongly the adolescent feels about weight gain.

I then ask the adolescent about how others reacted to the weight loss, including reinforcements received from others. Many times, the initial reaction of others is support for weight loss and healthy eating. However, as weight loss progresses, sometimes parents become quite fearful, helpless, and frustrated. This occasionally leads the parents to bribe, entice, or threaten the adolescent about her eating behaviors, sometimes leaving the parents and adolescents feeling they are in a power struggle.

1. Do you have any concern about your body weight or body image? If so, in what way?

2. What prompted your decision to lose weight?

3. When did you first notice you were engaging in weight loss techniques?

4. What were your highest and lowest weights? How did you feel about these weights?

5. If you feel that you were not trying to lose weight, to what do you attribute your weight loss?

6. What is your preferred weight?

7. How would you feel (and what would you do) if told that you needed to gain more than the weight you see as your preferred weight?

8. Who noticed your weight loss and what was their reaction? What was your response?

9. If no one noticed your weight loss, to what do you attribute this? (for example, hiding under baggy clothes)

10. (If weight loss was hidden:) Why did you feel it was important to hide your weight loss?

Weight Loss Strategies. By asking the adolescent how she went about losing weight, I receive a full account of weight loss strategies the adolescent has used. If the adolescent restricted calories, did she count calories, and, if so, what was the calorie count and why? These questions help me assess the amount of energy the adolescent gives to learning calorie counts and how "controlled" the adolescent feels by the numbers.

1. Describe the course your weight loss took.

2. Did you restrict calories, and if so, did you count calories or grams of fat? What was your allotted calorie or fat gram count? If you had an allotted number, what would you do if you went over this number?

3. Do you engage in regular exercise, sports, or dance? Amount? How do you feel if you are unable to do your regular amount of exercise?

4. Have you ever engaged in purging (vomiting), and if so, what techniques have you used to help yourself throw up? How often do you purge? What are the triggers? Have you ever noticed blood in your vomit?

5. Have you ever had a time in which you ate a large number of calories at one time and felt that your eating was out of control? What did you do after this? How often has this happened? This is sometimes referred to as a *binge*. What would you consider to be a binge in regard to calorie amounts?

6. Have your ever used drugs such as appetite suppressants, diuretics, laxatives, or amphetamines to encourage weight loss? Which drugs? How much? Triggers?

Physical and Emotional Effects of Weight Loss. When the medical and nutritional assessment information has been obtained, we are able to have some idea of the current physical effect of the eating disorder on the adolescent's health. When this information is communicated to the adolescent, the therapist is then able to discuss the teenager's reactions to the information.

In working with this age group, the clinician should assess how the eating problem affects the adolescents' thoughts and feelings about themselves and their bodies. Many times adolescents will report that they initially felt good about the weight loss but find that they have difficulty feeling they have lost "enough" weight to feel good about themselves.

1. (For girls): At what age did you begin your menses? Have you lost your menses? At what weight did you lose your menses? (If she has not begun menses): At what age did sisters or mother begin menses?

2. (If menses were lost): How did you feel about having lost your menses?

3. What other physical changes have you noticed as a result of weight loss, purging, and so on?

4. If your bone density studies indicate serious bone loss requiring the curtailing of high-impact sports or dance, what would be your response?

5. How do you feel about yourself? What is the importance of weight loss in your view of yourself?

6. If you feel that you have not lost enough weight, or if you have gained weight, how do you feel about yourself?

Effect of Weight Loss Focus on Activities and Relationships. We should assess how the adolescents' experience with the problem has interrupted their life activities, such as school, hobbies, and socialization. Many times adolescents report that a negative effect of the eating issues is increased isolation from their friends and a decrease in activities they formerly enjoyed. Some report that they have begun to avoid social activities so they do not have to eat with others. They also report feeling compelled to decline social invitations to reserve time to exercise or engage in other weight loss activities.

The therapist should assess current and past stressors that the adolescent feels may or may not have contributed to a focus on weight loss. Many times adolescents report that being teased about their weight or development contributed to their desire to diet.

1. Do you have friendships that are important to you?

2. Do you feel that these friendships are going well? If not, what do you feel is getting in the way of these relationships?

3. How has a focus on weight affected your relationship with others?

4. How has a focus on weight affected your studies? How are you doing in school, and have there been changes in your performance?

5. How has a focus on weight affected your hobbies or interests?

6. What other stressors have occurred in your life that may have contributed to your desire to lose weight?

7. Did any significant changes occur around the time you decided to lose weight? Losses? Pubertal changes? Family changes or stressors?

8. Are there any problems in your family that you feel contributed to your desire to lose weight?

Past Individual and Family Psychiatric History. This portion of the assessment allows the therapist to gather information that may relate to eating concerns as well as past history of other problems that the adolescent has faced in her life. A psychiatric examination of the adolescent may be helpful in the evaluation of possible co-morbidity of other psychiatric conditions in addition to the eating disorder. Gathering a history regarding past treatment may be helpful in understanding what the adolescent found to be helpful and not helpful in past therapies.

The adolescent may be at risk for depression or self-harm. It is important to assess current risk for self-harm and to determine whether the adolescent may need extra support or even hospitalization for risk to self.

A family history should include information on past or present psychiatric, weight, or health problems for other family members as there may be either a genetic predisposition or familial experiences that may have influenced the eating problems.

1. Have you or anyone in your family ever been treated for any psychiatric problems in the past? If so, what problems were you experiencing? When, where, and what treatments did you receive? Did you find these treatments beneficial?

2. Have you ever thought about hurting yourself? Have you ever attempted to harm yourself, or has anyone in your family attempted self-harm? If so, when and what methods did you use? Do you feel you are currently in danger of harming yourself? If so, do you have a plan?

3. Do you or anyone in your family drink alcohol or engage in drug use? If so, how much do you (or family member) drink or use drugs in a week's time? Do you believe there are any problems or stressors as a result of the alcohol or drug use?

Medical and Developmental History. A general assessment of medical history and development is useful both in gathering these data for completeness of treatment and in understanding how the health of the child is perceived in the family. For example, is this an adolescent who has been viewed as medically fragile, perhaps due to birth complications, or is this a child who has done quite well in her development until the onset of the present problem?

1. Are you currently on any medications? Please list?
2. Do you have any allergies you know of?
3. Have you been treated for any significant medical problems? If so, what were these problems; when and where were you treated?
4. Has anyone in your family been treated for any significant medical problems? If so, what were these problems? When and where were they treated?

(For parents):

1. How would you characterize the pregnancy and delivery of this child?
2. Were there any early feeding or attachment problems?
3. Please describe sibling and peer relationships over the course of development.
4. When were important developmental milestones reached (such as walking, talking).
5. How has this child performed in school over the years?

Sexual and Possible Abuse History. Sometimes therapists become somewhat uncomfortable about taking a sexual history. I have found that being sensitive to the privacy of these issues while being matter of fact and straightforward about asking these questions tends to be a very good approach. Certainly, this is information that may be very helpful in the treatment of the adolescent and may address some of the adolescent's concerns that she may have trouble bringing up on her own.

Also difficult is asking questions regarding the possibility of abuse. Again, being sensitive and straightforward is a good approach while also reminding the adolescent your need to report allegations of abuse. It has been my experience that when allegations of abuse need to be reported, this is a very difficult situation for families. Most of the families I have worked with have continued with me in an attempt to provide a safe environment for the adolescent.

1. Have you ever engaged in sexual relationships? How did you feel about these relationships? What type of protection was used? Do you have any concerns about pregnancy or sexually transmitted illness?

2. Have you ever been in a situation in which you felt you were touched in a way that violated you or in a way that you did not like?

3. Have you ever been in a situation in which you were called names or felt that you were emotionally mistreated?

Mental Status Examination. A mental status examination helps the therapist determine domains in which the adolescent may be experiencing problems. By assessing the adolescent's current mood, behavior, and cognitive state, the therapist is more attuned to how the teenager is currently functioning globally. For example, on several occasions, we have determined during the mental status examination that an adolescent is having significant cognitive problems, apparently due to a severely malnourished state. On a few occasions, it was during this aspect of the assessment that the adolescent also became aware of the severity of the cognitive impairment.

1. A mental status examination includes the observation of the adolescent's appearance. Does she appear groomed, dressed age appropriately, and so on?

2. Observation of behaviors includes assessment of any unusual behaviors, agitation, or slowness.

3. Mood should be assessed as to how the adolescent reports her own mood state and also what the interviewer observes. Does the mood seem appropriate to the material discussed?

4. Assessment of thought processes include noting the manner in which the adolescent presents his thoughts. Are these thoughts coherent, or does the adolescent seem to have some difficulty staying on track? Also, what is the content of the thoughts? What are the major themes presented? Does the adolescent indicate any suicidal or homicidal thoughts? Is there any evidence of delusional thinking?

5. Finally, a brief evaluation of the adolescent's cognition would include the teenager's level of consciousness (drowsy, awake), orientation (person, place, time), attention (spell a word forward and backward), concentration (start with 100 and count backward by 7), memory (give names of three objects and ask again in five minutes), abstract thinking (describe how a pear and a banana are alike), judgment (the adolescent's understanding of her current situation).

Family Assessment

It is also helpful to address to parents the questions directed in the previous sections to the adolescent to obtain the parents' views of pertinent eating issues as these relate to their child. Often parents are quite concerned and frightened regarding the health of their child. Sometimes parents begin to question their parenting abilities and blame themselves or the adolescent for the existence of the problem. These reactions may result in feelings of anger, frustration, and helplessness. It is useful to assess how the parents have attempted to deal with the problem and what they found helpful and not helpful.

Mapping Family Interactions. During the initial interview, the therapist may begin to map out the interactions that take place in the family. For example, when one family noticed their daughter skipping meals, they began to worry and to try to force her to have meals with the family. The adolescent refused until the parents, out of frustration, refused to let her attend school unless she ate breakfast. These interactions escalated to the point that the child was staying in her room and no longer attending school.

In another family, the mother found herself feeling "blackmailed" by her son. She bought all his favorite foods and took him out to restaurants he liked to encourage him to eat. By mapping out these interactions, the therapist is then able to examine the oftentimes negative interactions that have developed.

Empirical Studies: Family Interactions. Salvador Minuchin and his colleagues base their structural therapeutic approach on the premise that family members dealing with anorexia and bulimia tend to engage in somewhat destructive interactions, leading to problems with separation and individuation. However, there is a dearth of empirical studies assessing the presence of these interactional styles and the research that has been done indicate differing results.

Lynn Humphrey analyzed videotapes of families of girls with eating disorders. Parents of girls diagnosed with Anorexia Nervosa were found to communicate nurturance but also a lack of support of their daughters' needs to express their feelings. The daughters also appeared ambivalent about disclosing their feelings. Parents of the girls diagnosed with bulimia appeared to undermine their daughters' self-assertion and attempts to "separate."

It is unclear whether dysfunctional family interactions precede onset of the disorders or whether they evolve as a response to stressors related to Anorexia Nervosa and bulimia and associated treatment. In a recent study, Danielle Galante, Hans Steiner, and I attempted to gain a further understanding of the effects of the problem on the family interactions over time. We found that family members' perceptions of their family cohesiveness and adaptability are different at various stages of their struggle with the problem. Therefore, it may be that the eating problem has an effect on the family relationships over time.

Psychometric Measures

Self-report instruments may be a useful way to gather baseline data of the adolescent's perception of eating and body issues before beginning treatment as well as during treatment in order to assess changes over time. Two popular evaluation tools include the Eating Disorder Inventory (EDI) and the Eating Attitudes Test (EAT).

The EDI has normative data for individuals age fourteen years and above. It is a sixty-four-item, eight-factor questionnaire measuring specific aspects of eating disorders. The EAT is a twenty-six-item questionnaire measuring eating patterns and symptoms of Anorexia Nervosa.

MEDICAL, NUTRITIONAL, AND PSYCHIATRIC ASSESSMENT

Following the initial assessment, the therapist in the community may find herself in the position of determining how to obtain a comprehensive evaluation of the adolescent. The serious medical nature of these problems demands that you work in tandem with a primary care physician and nutritionist for a complete evaluation and close medical and nutritional monitoring. Many of my own patients are able to attend our Eating Disorder Clinic (EDC) at Lucile Salter Packard Children's Hospital at Stanford (LPCH) on a weekly basis. However, some adolescents who live outside an easy commuting range may attend less often and be treated by a local team as well. These teams are usually formed by the community therapist who joins forces with a nurse, pediatrician or adolescent medicine physician, nutritionist, and other mental health professionals.

As a psychologist evaluating the possibility of an eating disorder, I request that the adolescent receive a medical evaluation for several reasons. First, the adolescent medicine physician will assess for any underlying organic illness that may be contributing to the present symptoms. Further reasons for a medical assessment include the need to evaluate the adolescent's current medical status for immediate treatment, evaluate chronic conditions resulting from eating disorder symptoms, and last, to begin to set up an ongoing treatment contract with a medical team.

ACUTE MEDICAL ISSUES

Adolescents may become acutely medically unstable and therefore at risk for loss of consciousness or even sudden death. The adolescent medicine physician will check the patient's heart rate, temperature, and blood pressure changes. Indicators of significant medical instability requiring hospitalization in our clinic (EDC) may be found in Table 6.1. These indicators are based on guidelines issued by the Society of Adolescent Medicine.

We have found that when adolescents remain at low weights for long periods of time, their heart rates may stabilize in response to these chronic low weights, although bone loss and delay in growth is still likely. Thus, a weight of 75 percent of ideal body weight or below is indicative of severe malnutrition and indicates medical instability.

Other life-threatening consequences of eating disorders include electrolyte imbalance that may result from purging or laxative abuse, decreased cardiac functioning as a result of declining heart mass or the use of cardiotoxins such as syrup of ipecac, and renal failures. Esophageal tears may also occur as a result of

Table 6.1
Criteria for Hospitalization of Adolescents with Eating Disorders

1. Hypothermia (temperature lower than 36.3°C)
2. Severe bradycardia (heart rate 45 beat/min. or below)
3. Orthostasis (systolic blood pressure drop of 10 points from lying [after lying for 5 minutes] to standing [after 2 minutes] or increase in pulse of 35 beat/min.)
4. Hypotension/shock
5. Severe malnutrition: less than 75 percent of ideal body weight
6. Arrested growth or development
7. Acute food refusal
8. Electrolyte disturbances
9. Uncontrollable bingeing and purging
10. Acute medical complications (such as ventricular tachycardia, Ipecac abuse, syncope, seizures)
11. Acute psychiatric emergency (such as suicidal ideation, psychosis)
12. Failure to respond to outpatient treatments

Source: Reprinted by permission of Elsevier Science Inc. from "Eating Disorders in Adolescents: A Background Paper," by Fisher, M., et al., *Journal of Adolescent Health*, *16*, 420–437. Copyright 1995 by the Society for Adolescent Medicine.

purging, leading to internal bleeding. We have had a few adolescents who have experienced such tears. One patient hung the picture of her tear in her room to remind her of the negative effect of purging on her body.

Chronic Medical Issues

Chronic conditions that may occur as a result of malnutrition should be assessed as well. Bone loss is of special concern. Adolescence is the time when most adult bone density is acquired; thus, bone loss at this time may result in permanent disability. Bone density should be assessed at intake and reevaluated annually as the patient's weight is restored. Bone density is measured on special equipment, with the individual lying on a table while a picture of his bones are taken; it is similar to magnetic resonance imaging equipment (MRI) without the noise. It is, therefore, a fairly nonintrusive test, and it gives very important information to the treatment team and to the patient.

I have found that sometimes this may be the first serious negative effect of the eating disorder that the adolescent acknowledges. Weight restoration has been associated with increase in bone density, but the longer the duration of malnutrition, the less likely it is that bone mass may be recovered.

Further long-term effects of malnutrition include stunted growth and pubertal delay. Some adolescents have not been able to regain normal hormonal functioning and they experience loss of fertility.

Weight

Obtaining the patient's weight may be important for determining whether the adolescent has fallen below 75 percent of ideal body weight (IBW) (thereby requiring hospitalization) and also for calculating body fat percentages. The body fat percentage tends to be the most important measure in regard to restoration of health, as research has indicated that approximately 17 percent body fat is necessary to maintain, and perhaps regain, bone mass. In most cases, however, weight gain is associated with a gain in body fat, and weight tends to be easier to measure on a regular basis to determine progress toward restoration of health.

In the EDC, we have adolescents first void and then remove all their clothes except the hospital gown before we weigh them. The reason for this procedure is that sometimes adolescents have been afraid of the consequences of not gaining weight (possible hospital admission) and have, therefore, hidden weights (such as batteries, rolls of quarters) in their undergarments and hair. We ask the adolescent to void first so that we can obtain a more accurate weight, and second, so that we can perform a laboratory test on the urine to determine its concentration. If the urine specific gravity is less than 1.010, it may indicate that some portion of the weight measured is actually water weight.

Sometimes adolescents will drink quite a bit of water before being weighed so they will appear to weigh more than they actually do. If the team is concerned that a portion of the weight is water, they may ask the adolescent to void again later in the afternoon and obtain another weight. One adolescent drank so much water before being weighed that once she fully voided, she had lost eight pounds.

Nutritional Assessment

The nutritionist is able to calculate the patient's percentage of body fat, a measurement that is extremely helpful in determining the amount of weight (or associated body fat) the patient needs to regain menses and perhaps to begin to regain bone mass. The nutritionist is also able to assess types of foods and amount of calories consumed on a daily basis as well as the patient's thoughts regarding eating and the amount of time she spends counting calories. Then the nutritionist is able to help the adolescent evaluate the amount of calories she needs for the level of exercise she engages in.

Psychiatric Evaluation

As a therapist in the community, you may find yourself in need of a psychiatric consultation for the adolescent patient. The psychiatrist will assess for symptoms of other psychiatric problems the adolescent may be experiencing that may contribute to the present problems. Some adolescents will have a dual diagnosis of an affective disorder, an Obsessive-Compulsive Disorder, alcohol and drug abuse, or a personality disorder. When present, comorbidity can influence treatment decisions requiring behavioral and perhaps psychopharmacological interventions.

Antidepressant and anti-anxiety medications may be useful as part of the treatment plan for some adolescents in targeting depression and anxiety. However, the decision to use medications should be made only after a very careful evaluation, as some medications may accentuate the effects of malnutrition and dehydration. In no instance is it reasonable to have medications be the sole intervention for the patient.

Treatment Settings

Following this initial assessment, the community therapist may then be in the position of determining the most appropriate treatment setting for the adolescent. This decision will be based on the medical and psychiatric acuity of the adolescent. If the adolescent is either medically unstable or psychiatrically at risk, he is admitted to the inpatient unit for refeeding, health management, and therapy. Indicators for inpatient treatment may be found in Table 6.1. The adolescent may also be hospitalized if he does not seem to be benefiting from outpatient settings, or if he is in need of psychiatric inpatient care because of danger to himself.

If the adolescent does not currently require inpatient treatment, alternative settings include partial day treatment or outpatient treatment in conjunction with medical check-ins. It is likely that the adolescent with an eating disorder may require different settings over the course of treatment.

Outpatient Treatment

Weekly individual and family therapy is usually recommended. The therapist is likely to be in the position of deciding what form of therapy may be most useful for adolescents and their families. Some therapists also find that group therapy has been helpful for these patients and their families.

Outpatient treatment may also include medical check-ins as frequently as needed to ensure safety. These check-ins are spread out as the adolescent progresses. Many of our patients dealing with anorexia are in a weight gain program. The way we generally set up these programs is to ask the adolescent how much she feels she can successfully gain weekly. We then draw a weight gain line across the time span. For example, one adolescent felt she would be able to gain .3kg weekly. If she was able to meet her goals, the adolescent was rewarded with the opportunity to reduce her medical visits.

Inpatient and Partial Hospital Setting

The treatment team in a specialized inpatient setting for the treatment of eating disorders is typically multidisciplinary, including representatives from adolescent medicine, nutrition, psychology, psychiatry, and social work. Medically, treatment may include bed rest and heart monitoring, as needed. Nutritionally, patients may need to have a liquid supplement (such as Ensure) to begin to stabilize medically and then progress to food as their vital signs are stabilized.

At first, the adolescents' calorie intake is observed until they indicate that they will take in the required calories without observation. Calories are usually begun at approximately 500 above the recent intake and raised slowly, to guard against congestive heart failure while also contributing to a slow weight gain. A nasogastric tube for refeeding is used only as a last resort if the adolescent refuses to eat. If the adolescent is at risk of purgative behaviors, she may also be watched after meals to ensure that she retains the food.

When the adolescent has become medically stable and on 100 percent food, our team at LPCH may begin what we refer to as our Phase II program. This program allows the adolescent to choose and consume his own food selections without monitoring. If the adolescent is able to gain at least .2kg daily, he may continue to eat without monitoring. However, if the adolescent falls below this goal, he is observed until reaching the goal, and then returns to eating without monitoring. This program allows the child to begin to eat on his own in preparation for discharge to either the outpatient or partial hospital program setting.

The psychological treatment involves participation in daily individual and group therapy and family therapy twice a week.

The purpose of the therapy is to explore the effects of the problem on the adolescents and their families in an attempt to help the teenagers reclaim their lives. The specifics of the treatment approach utilized in these therapies is described later in this chapter.

If the child does not require an acute inpatient setting but may benefit from more intense treatment than may be available in an outpatient setting, an alternative treatment setting may be a day treatment or partial hospitalization program (PHP). If possible, we discharge adolescents to our PHP to complete their treatment while also being able to go home in the evenings.

We recommend this transition once the adolescents have become stable and on 100 percent food. At this point, they may still need to continue weight gain and therapy within a more structured setting than an outpatient setting, but they may not require the stricter hospital setting. For adolescents to be successful in the PHP, they must have some self-motivation to take in calories and work toward health.

TREATMENT APPROACHES

Many types of therapy have demonstrated effectiveness in the treatment of eating disorders; however, no specific treatment is ideal. A number of research investigations have found the cognitive-behavioral approach to be effective in the treatment of bulimia; others have found equivocal results. Psychodynamic therapies have also shown usefulness in the treatment of eating disorders in some cases. The narrative approaches have yet to be examined in treatment outcome studies.

The family therapy approach that has perhaps been most studied in eating disorders is Minuchin's structural therapy. Within this approach, therapists attempt to help families restructure their relationships to allow adolescents to experience appropriate individuation and separation. This approach is based on the premise that family members interact in such a way as to impede adolescents' normal development, thus leading to problems for them in separation. It is unclear how these interactive styles emerge and whether they precede the onset of the eating problem or whether the eating problem invites problematic family interactions.

In the use of medications to treat Anorexia Nervosa, no studies have been conducted solely on the adolescent population. We have found medications most useful when the patients have regained at least 80 percent of their ideal body weight and medications are targeted to specific symptoms, such as anxiety or depression. For adolescents dealing with bulimia, some medications have been useful in reducing the desire to binge. However, when medications are compared to psychotherapy, they do not appear to be more effective. We have found medications helpful for some of the adolescents we work with in reducing symptoms of depression and anxiety.

A recent review of treatment outcome of eating disorders by the American Psychiatric Association reports that for patients dealing with Anorexia Nervosa four years after onset, 44 percent indicate a "good" outcome (reaching to at least 15 percent of ideal weight), 24 percent have a "poor" outcome (never reaching 15 percent of ideal body weight), and 28 percent have an "intermediate" outcome (between these two). Close to 5 percent of the patients die as a result of Anorexia Nervosa. In the treatment of bulimia, 27 percent of previously hospitalized individuals indicate a "good" outcome (binge/purge episodes fewer than 1x/month), 33 percent indicate a "poor" outcome (daily binge/purge episodes), and 40 percent fall between the two.

THE USE OF NARRATIVE

In my work, I draw quite a bit from narrative approaches described by Michael White and David Epston. I find these useful for several reasons in treating adolescents and their families with regard to the problems of eating disorders.

First, I have found the narrative approach to be respectful of the experience of adolescents and their families. The adolescent is asked to fully describe her experience of the problem, thus supporting her expertise. This strategy defies the cultural invitation to further disempower the adolescent and helps to counteract additional feelings of ineffectiveness.

Through externalization (separating self from the problem) and exploration of its effects, the adolescent is encouraged to acknowledge the problem and develop insight about it. Greenfeld and colleagues found that their patients who were able to develop greater insight into their eating problem had more positive outcomes. Externalizing the problem also allows the adolescent to explore the negative effects of the problem on her life. This invites the adolescent to "fight" the problem rather than the treatment team. Exploring the alternative story of competence and "visibility" encourages the adolescent to take back her life from the problem.

By externalizing the problem, families are also able to "blame" the problem rather than blame themselves or others, a tactic that often leads to relationship difficulties. This approach encourages the adolescents and their families to identify negative effects of the problem on their lives and thus work toward fighting these negative effects. The families identify what is negative to them and explore strategies to improve their interactions.

Consulting the Adolescent Regarding Her Story

We have found in our culture that adolescents (and women) in particular may be invited to deny their expertise and defer to others. The voice of anorexia and bulimia also asks that adolescents defer to its demands and requests the loyalty and allegiance of adolescent boys and girls. In our treatment, we want to counteract these practices of culture and of anorexia and bulimia. Rather than taking power from adolescents, we invite them to describe what they are experiencing and to take a stand on their own behalf.

I have found it to be extremely important to attempt to elicit specific information regarding the adolescents' total experience of the problem for several reasons. First, it is important for the adolescents to fully explore their own experience to assess the effects of the problem on their lives and to be able to take a stand against that problem. Second, many times adolescents report feeling "labeled" by doctors, and feel that their specific experiences are not acknowledged or understood. Finally, by exploring their own experience of the problem, the adolescents (and their families) begin to recognize that the problem is separate from the adolescent, and thus solvable.

In an attempt to explore the adolescents' experience of the eating disorder, I ask questions such as these:

How do you know when anorexia or bulimia is around?

How does it make itself known to you?

What does it say to you?

How does it make you feel?

How much of your life does it take up?

Some of the responses I have received to these questions have been (in regard to bulimia) "It is a security blanket I wish I could throw away" and "a monster on my back that is always lurking." Frequently the adolescents report that it seems to be *always* around, and they know this because it is constantly barking orders. The only time it may have something nice to say is when the numbers go down on the scale (but rarely enough with anorexia). One adolescent had difficulty articulating her experience, so she drew a picture of a dark cloud to convey it. Frequently these adolescents have difficulty self-focusing and discovering their own experience. If so, it may be helpful for the clinician to give some examples of what other adolescents have said about their experiences and to encourage the patient to compare these responses with her own perception of the problem and its effect on her life. I also sometimes use videotapes we have made of adolescents telling about their experience of the eating disorder for the purpose of providing this information to adolescents who are facing a similar problem.

Separating Self from the Problem

Differentiating the voice of anorexia from their own voice is frequently a new idea to many adolescent patients. Often they do not differentiate themselves from the anorexia and bulimia, believing the voice of anorexia to be their own voice. Sometimes the adolescents experience the problem as "totalizing" and report that they, in fact, are not separate from the problem. One adolescent incorporated her name into the word *anorexia* and stated that they were one and the same. When this identification with the problem occurs, I ask "wedge" questions. These are questions that help to put a small wedge between the adolescent and the problem. For example:

> You say anorexia takes up 90 percent of your time. Would you like it to take up less of your life?
>
> If you were to have more time, what would you like to put back in your life?

When adolescents are asked to describe their experiences and put their thoughts and feelings into words (or sometimes pictures), they begin to "objectify" the problem and to see it as separate from themselves. The adolescent who wrote the poem, "the Bad days," quoted on the opening page of this chapter, reports that putting her experience on paper helped her feel even more separate from the problem and seemed to lessen the power it had over her. Several adolescents I have worked with are putting their experiences into their writing and finding this very helpful.

Exploring the Positive and Negative Effects of the Problem

Both the positive and negative effects of the problem should be explored. Sometimes adolescents deny that there are any negative effects. They report that anorexia and bulimia promise to make them feel powerful and even "superior" because they have been able to do what they see so many people attempting: lose weight. But this is a false power as anorexia and bulimia take over their lives, take them out of their lives, and sometimes come close to taking their lives.

I have found that as adolescents begin to build trust in the therapy and to discover that you, as the therapist, are not attempting to blame or control them, they are able to begin exploring the negative effects of the eating disorder on their lives. These effects are generally the (1) amount of time the eating disorder takes, (2) isolation from peers, (3) poor self-esteem, and (4) hunger and physical discomfort.

Unique Outcomes and Alternative Stories

White and Epston describe "unique outcomes" as situations in which the individual manages to escape the dominant story. For example, the adolescent may report that she "is never able to eat dinner without purging," but then she recalls a time when she was able to do so. Similarly, in a therapy session an adolescent who does not see herself as powerful may be able to take a stand on her own behalf. These are examples of escapes from an overpowering story with an alternative and better one. One adolescent girl who had become extremely isolated over several years as a result of the anorexia was later able to call up a friend and go out with her.

The adolescent should be asked if the unique outcome represents a positive or a negative step. Many times the teenagers see these outcomes as positive, and so they should be asked how they want to expand upon these steps. As the alternative story is being examined it must be placed in context. Stories are made up of events that occur over time and are linked together by meaning to form a plot. In order for an alternative story to be powerful for the adolescent it must be grounded in the past, so past events need to be explored and linked to the current unique outcome.

For example, a young woman was able to discuss her anorexia with a friend for the first time in four years. In exploring this unique outcome, we discovered that she had been able to talk about her problem in therapy groups, with her therapist, and with her family, and so she felt she had some experience in talking with others about her problem.

This story can then be projected into the future, with the teenager envisioning possible changes that are in keeping with this alternative story. The adolescent should be cautioned, however, that the problem is tenacious and will not wish to be completely written out of existence. The adolescent should therefore prepare herself for a reappearance of the problem. One adolescent was quite thrilled when she was able to remain purge-free for two weeks, but still felt prepared when she was "home alone with a pizza" and the bulimia tried to make a comeback in her life.

Strategies for Reclaiming Lives and Becoming More Visible

When we notice these unique outcomes, I ask the adolescents how they were able to fight the effects of the eating disorder and take back more of their lives. Many times they are surprised at what they have been able to accomplish and are interested in determining what helped. Sometimes they are able to identify specific strategies that were helpful and sometimes not. When they report that they don't know what helped, we usually engage in some brainstorming about possibilities that may have contributed to their success.

Some of the strategies adolescents have identified are these: (1) keeping busy so that there was no time for bulimia to call, (2) remaining around others so that they were unable to purge, (3) posting the X-ray of their esophageal tear in the bathroom, and (4) posting on the refrigerator copies of unstable vital signs, EKG results, or bone density records to promote eating.

Through implementation of these strategies, the adolescents begin to discover their "selves" as separate from the problem and its influence, and to be able to make more of an appearance in their own lives in ways in which they would like. This is not an attempt to talk them out of the problem, but rather an invitation to them to reclaim their own voices.

Illustrating the Narrative Approach

In this section, I illustrate my use of the narrative approach with a case study, addressing the steps outlined above.

SUSAN

Susan is a seventeen-year-old who consulted me because of her problems with bulimia. She also described an assaultive experience on a date in the past, but stated a desire not to focus on this topic.

Susan reported that she has a good relationship with her friends and family, but has found that her mother especially has begun to stand outside the bathroom to see if she is purging and seems to have become more intrusive. She also has noted that she is not going out with friends at times because she does not wish to be faced with the pressure to eat and also she feels badly about her appearance.

Medically, Susan was of average weight and apparently healthy. On initial evaluation, she had been engaging in daily purging for a few months and did not appear to have suffered long-term effects, such as an esophageal tear or significant tooth enamel erosion. We scheduled weekly medical visits so that her electrolytes and potassium could be monitored as well as her weight and possible changes in vital signs.

Susan described how the bulimia would try to convince her that she was unattractive, that she needed to lose weight and so should not eat during the day. If she gave in and ate something, she would then need to purge herself of this food immediately. She felt that bulimia invited her to feel shameful and weak. It invited her to miss out on activities with friends because of her self-hate and her need to remain home in case the bulimia might show up.

SEPARATING SELF FROM THE PROBLEM AND EXPLORING ITS EFFECTS

I asked Susan to describe her experience by telling me what bulimia said to her and how it convinced her to engage in behaviors that she did not want in her life. By engaging in what White refers to as "externalizing conversations," Susan began to see bulimia as separate from herself. She described bulimia as a "security blanket I wish I could throw away" and at one point she gave it a male gender and felt it represented the pressure she feels to please boys.

As Susan examined the ways bulimia tried to take over her life and tell her what to do, she became more aware of how abusive it had been in her life and began to see the experience of bulimia as similar to her assaultive experience. She realized that both made her feel badly about her body, caused her to want to modify her body in some way, and took power from her. This discovery seemed to give her even more resolve not to allow bulimia to ruin her life.

Susan also noted the subjectively positive effects of bulimia. She described it as making her feel "safe." She felt that as she became anxious about eating too much or feeling badly about herself, she could turn to bulimia to feel better. However, she was also aware that following this initial relief, she would again feel shame regarding the bulimia, and the cycle would begin again.

UNIQUE OUTCOMES AND ALTERNATIVE STORIES

Susan was able to identify times in which she successfully avoided the invitation to feel badly about herself and times in which she felt powerful. She had been able to obtain a job and was doing quite well in a responsible position. She was beginning to turn down bulimia's invitations during the day, which helped her feel less compelled to binge/purge at the end of the day. Through exploration of the alternative story of power, Susan began to go out more with friends and to reinvolve herself in activities.

STRATEGIES FOR RECLAIMING LIVES AND BECOMING MORE VISIBLE

Susan found that the same strategies she was using to empower herself to say no to the bulimia could help her stand up to others on her own behalf. She had begun to set up her environment in such a way that bulimia was not likely to feel welcome. One creative strategy was to structure her environment so that she was never alone when bulimia was likely to show up. Similarly, she arranged to go out in groups until she built a trusting relationship with others.

Susan began to take back some of the hours she had given to bulimia. She found it helpful to stay busy during the times that bulimia was likely to arrive. In planning future events, she developed strategies for eluding the voice of bulimia and for fighting the effects of self-hate.

Bulimia had taken over approximately 90 percent of her life and she had now taken back all but about 10 percent. Susan was accepted to college. She initially had felt that she would not be able to get into a college, but through her struggle with bulimia she has become more acutely aware of her power and competence.

FAMILY TREATMENT

An integral part of adolescent therapy is working with the family. Families are deeply affected when their children are experiencing anorexia or bulimia. Parents and siblings tend to become extremely frightened and frustrated with these problems. As the family therapist, you need to bring out the family's experience as fully as possible, as well as that of the adolescent.

In my work, I use the treatment components illustrated above to understand the effects of the problem on the family and to identify the positive and negative effects of the problem. Many times, families report that a major negative effect of the problem is the struggle the parents go through in getting their child to eat. The pressure the parents feel to protect and nurture their child tends to be at odds with the pressure anorexia puts on the child not to eat or to purge. Thus, a power struggle ensues. White suggests that the child's beliefs about food and weight may even inadvertently strengthen over time in reaction to frequent challenges of these beliefs by parents and treatment teams.

Through externalization of the problem, identifying its positive and negative aspects, and recognizing alternative stories to explain it, the family may be able to begin to decrease these power struggles and work toward common goals.

Many times in family therapy with adolescents, issues of autonomy and control emerge as problematic. This is not surprising as the task of adolescence, especially in Western cultures, is negotiating an exit from the family. This requires renegotiating family relationships and working toward more separation and independence from families. If there are issues of attachment or maturational fears, the period is likely to be problematic.

Arthur Crisp has proposed that the onset of eating disorders may represent an avoidance of maturation and all that it entails. Parents find themselves in a bind when they are faced with the task of negotiating separation while adolescents are becoming physically at risk as well as appearing less able to care for themselves. Similarly, adolescents experience the bind of desiring more independence yet also being fearful of the responsibilities and challenges of maturity.

Within the narrative approach, family members explore the effects of the eating disorder on this developmental process. They identify the ways the eating disorder is impeding the adolescent's separation and work toward moving forward in this developmental process. For example, in the therapy with Susan, she identified ways she wished to continue to be nurtured and cared for by her parents as well as ways she wished to establish more independence. Her parents were able to contract with her to decrease their surveillance as she demonstrated greater self-responsibility.

THE EFFECT ON THE THERAPIST

Sometimes the tenacity, chronicity, and severe consequences of the problem on the lives of the adolescents and their families may invite the therapist also to feel hopeless and "stuck." I have felt quite angry toward anorexia and bulimia, especially in regard to how cruel they have been to the adolescents and families I see. I have also felt elated when the adolescents have been able to struggle successfully against this *extremely* difficult problem and find happiness. I have found the ideas presented in the narrative approaches to be quite useful in clarifying that the adolescent (or the family) is not the problem. If you, as a therapist, find yourself becoming frustrated with the adolescent or the family, it may be useful to remind yourself that they are all probably fighting the effects of this problem to the best of their ability.

Sometimes, despite the best efforts of the adolescent, his family, and the treatment team, the adolescent may continue to struggle with this problem for many years; some may die from the effects of anorexia, bulimia, or associated depression. I believe that any therapist who enters this work must recognize and deal with the fear of this very tragic possibility. However, I have found my work with these adolescents and their families to be extremely gratifying and exhilarating. These teenagers and their families are truly remarkable individuals who face and conquer the problems of anorexia and bulimia and often do reclaim their lives.

NOTES

P. 224, *Adolescence tends to be the prime:* Bruch, H. (1974). *Eating disorders.* New York: Basic Books.

P. 224, *School-based surveys:* Whitaker, A. H. (1992). An epidemiological study of anorectic and bulimic symptoms in adolescent girls: Implications for pediatricians. *Pediatric Annals, 21,* 752–759.

P. 224, *Growth of the weight reduction industry:* Vandereycken, W. (1984). Anorexia nervosa: Is prevention possible? *International Psychiatry in Medicine, 14*(3), 191–205.

P. 224, *increase in number of diet articles:* Pumariega, A. (1986). Acculturation and eating attitudes in adolescent girls: A comparative and correlational study. *Journal of American Academy of Child Psychiatry, 25*(2), 276–279.

P. 224, *Girls outnumber boys:* Hsu, L. G. (1989). The gender gap in eating disorders: Why are the eating disorders more common among women? *Clinical Psychology Review, 9*(3), 393–407.

P. 224, *feminine identification:* Fichter, M., Daser, C., & Postpischil, F. (1985). Anorectic syndromes in the male. *Journal of Psychiatric Research, 19*, 305–313.

P. 224, *approximately 30 percent may be homosexual:* Herzog, D. B., Bradburn, I. S., & Newman, K. (1990). Sexuality in males with eating disorders. In A. E. Anderson, (Ed.) *Males with eating disorders* (pp. 40–53). New York: Brunner/Mazel.

P. 224, *Girls are invited by Western culture:* Nylander, I. (1971). The feeling of being fat and dieting in a school population: An epidemiologic interview investigation. *Acta Sociomedica Scandinavica, 3*, 17–26.

P. 224, *When girls hit their teens:* Gilligan, C. A. (1982). *In a different voice: Psychological theory and women's development.* Cambridge, MA: Harvard University Press.

P. 225, *when hunger is the strongest:* Keys, A., Brozek, J., Henschel, A., Mickelsen, O., & Taylor, H. L. (1950). *The biology of human starvation.* Minneapolis: University of Minnesota Press.

P. 226, *certain foods may become phobic objects:* Crisp, A. H. (1967). The possible significance of some behavioural correlates of weight and carbohydrate intake. *Journal of Psychosomatic Research, 11*, 117–131.

P. 227, *core diagnostic feature:* American Psychiatric Association. (1994). *Diagnostic and statistical manual of mental disorders* (4th ed.). Washington, DC: Author.

P. 238, *structural therapeutic approach:* Minuchin, S., Rosman, B. L., & Baker, L. (1978). *Psychosomatic families.* Cambridge, MA: Harvard.

P. 238, *analyzed videotapes of families:* Humphrey, L. L. (1989). Observed family interactions among subtypes of eating disorders using structural analysis of social behavior. *Journal of Consulting and Clinical Psychology, 57*, 206–214.

P. 239, *family members' perceptions:* Galante, D., Sanders, M. J., & Steiner, H. (1994). *Characteristics of families of daughters with anorexia or bulimia: A study of treatment phases.* Paper presented at the meeting of the American Academy of Child and Adolescent Psychiatry, New York.

P. 239, *EDI:* Garner, D. M., Olmsted, M. P., & Polivy, J. (1983). Development and validation of a multidimensional eating disorder inventory for anorexia and bulimia. *International Journal of Eating Disorders, 2*, 15–34.

P. 239, *EAT:* Garner, D. M., Olmsted, M. P., Bohr, Y., & Garfinkel, P. E. (1982). The Eating Attitudes Test: Psychometric features and clinical correlates. *Psychological Medicine, 12*, 871–878.

P. 240, *guidelines issued by the Society of Adolescent Medicine:* Fisher, M., Golden, N. H., Katzman, D. K., Kreipe, R. E., Rees, J., Schenbendach, J., Sigman, G., Ammerman, S., & Hoberman, H. M. Eating disorders in adolescents: A background paper. *Journal of Adolescent Health*, 1995, *16*(6), 420–437.

P. 240, *decreased cardiac functioning:* Kreipe, R. E., & Harris J. P. (1992). Myocardial impairment resulting from eating disorders. *Pediatric Annals*, *21*, 760–768.

P. 240, *use of cardiotoxins:* Palmer, E. P., & Guay, A. T. (1986). Reversible myopathy secondary to abuse of ipecac in patients with major eating disorders. *New England Journal of Medicine*, *313*, 1457–1459.

P. 240, *renal failures:* Mitchell, J. E., Pomeroy, C., Seppala, M., & Huber, M. (1988). Pseudo-Bartter's syndrome, diuretic abuse, idiopathic edema and eating disorders. *International Journal of Eating Disorders*, *7*, 225–237.

P. 241, *Bone loss:* Bachrach, L. K., Guido, D., Katzman, D., Litt, I. F., & Marcus, R. (1990). Decreased bone density in adolescent girls with anorexia nervosa. *Pediatrics*, *86*, 440–447.

P. 242, *duration of malnutrition:* Bachrach, L. K., Guido, D., Katzman, D., Litt, I. F., & Marcus, R. (1990). Decreased bone density in adolescent girls with anorexia nervosa. *Pediatrics*, *86*, 440–447.

P. 242, *pubertal delay:* Steinhausen, H. C., Rauss-Mason, C., & Seidel, R. (1991). Follow-up studies of anorexia nervosa: A review of four decades of outcome research. *Psychological Medicine*, *21*, 447–454.

P. 243, *dual diagnosis of an affective disorder:* Halmi, K. A., Eckert, E., Marchi, P., Sampugnaro, V., Apple, R., & Cohen, J. (1991). Comorbidity of psychiatric diagnoses in anorexia nervosa. *Archives in General Psychiatry*, *48*, 712–718.

P. 243, *Obsessive-Compulsive Disorder:* Kasvikis, Y. G., Tsakiris, F. Marks, I. M., Basogul, M., & Noshirvani, H. F. (1986). Past history of nervosa in women with obsessive compulsive disorder. *International Journal of Eating Disorders*, *5*, 1969–1976.

P. 243, *alcohol and drug abuse:* Katz, J. L. (1990). Eating disorders: A primer for the substance abuse special: 1. Clinical features. *Journal of Substance Abuse Treatment*, *7*, 143–149.

P. 243, *personality disorder:* Gartner, A. F., Marcus, R. N., Halmi, K., & Loranger, A. W. (1989). DSM-III-R personality disorders in patients with eating disorders. *American Journal of Psychiatry*, *146*, 1585–1591.

P. 243, *accentuate the effects of malnutrition:* Palla, B., & Litt, I. F. (1988). Medical complications of eating disorders in adolescents. *Pediatrics*, *81*, 613–623.

P. 246, *cognitive-behavioral approach:* Agras, W. S., Schneider, J. A., Arnow, B.,

Raeburn, S. D., & Telch, C. F. (1989). Cognitive-behavioral and response-prevention treatments for bulimia nervosa. *Journal of Consulting and Clinical Psychology, 57,* 215–221.

P. 246, *equivocal results:* Channon, S., De Silva, P., Hemsley, D., & Perkins, R. (1989). A controlled trial of cognitive behavioural and behavioural treatment of anorexia nervosa. *Behaviour Research Therapy, 27,* 529–535.

P. 246, *Psychodynamic therapies:* Schwartz, H. J. (1990). *Bulimia: Psychoanalytic treatment and theory* (2nd ed.) Madison, CT: International Universities Press; Bruch, H. (1978). *The golden cage: The enigma of anorexia nervosa.* London: Open Books.

P. 247, *medications have been useful in reducing the desire to binge:* McCann, U. D., & Agras, W. S. (1990). Successful treatment of nonpurging bulimia nervosa with desipramine: A double-blind, placebo-controlled study. *American Journal of Psychiatry, 147*(11), 1509–1513.

P. 247, *when medications are compared to psychotherapy:* Agras, W. S., Rossiter, E. M., Arnow, B., Schneider, J. A., Telch, C. F., Raeburn, S. D., Bruce, B., Perl, M., & Koran, L. M. (1992). Pharmacologic and cognitive-behavioral treatment for bulimia nervosa: A controlled comparison. *American Journal of Psychiatry, 149*(1), 82–87.

P. 247, *treatment outcome:* American Psychiatric Association. (1993). Practice guideline for eating disorders. *American Journal of Psychiatry, 150*(2), 212–228.

P. 247, *narrative approaches:* White, M. & Epston, D. (1990). *Narrative means to a therapeutic end.* New York: Norton.

P. 248, *greater insight into their eating problem:* Greenfeld, G., Anyan, R., Hobart, M., Quinlan, M., & Plantes, M. (1991). Insight into illness and outcome in anorexia nervosa. *International Journal of Eating Disorders, 10*(1), 101–109.

P. 251, *"unique outcomes":* White, M. (1989). The process of questioning: A therapy of literary merit? In M. White, *The selected papers of Michael White* (pp. 8–14). Adelaide: Dulwich Centre Publications.

P. 252, *more of an appearance:* White, M. (1986). Anorexia nervosa: A cybernetic perspective. In J. Elka-Harkaway (Ed.), *Eating disorders* (pp. 117–129). New York: Aspen.

P. 255, *child's beliefs:* White, M. (1983). Anorexia nervosa: A transgenerational system perspective. *Family Process, 22*(3), 255–273.

P. 256, *avoidance of maturation:* Crisp, A. H. (1984). The psychopathology of anorexia nervosa: Getting the "heat" out of the system. In A. Stunkard & E. Stellar (Eds.), *Eating and its disorders.* New York: Raven Press.

7

CHRONIC ILLNESS AND SOMATIZATION

Julie A. Collier

"I've done a complete work-up, but I can't find anything wrong with her. I think she might be depressed." The referring pediatrician sounded frustrated. Sharon was fourteen years old and had a four-month history of abdominal pain for which no organic etiology could be found.

My evaluation of this adolescent patient revealed significant anxiety and several recent stressors, which included the loss of a favorite grandparent and a new boyfriend who was urging her to allow the relationship to become sexual. In addition, she reported that she had been molested by a neighbor as a young child. After consultation with me, the pediatrician decided to delay further invasive tests, opting instead to monitor the patient's condition closely while I initiated psychological treatment. The frequency, duration, and intensity of Sharon's pain lessened over the next three months as she began to explore issues related to emerging sexuality and loss of important relationships.

As a psychologist at Lucile Salter Packard Children's Hospital at Stanford, I encounter many patients like Sharon who present their pediatrician with diagnostic and treatment dilemmas requiring active co-management by pediatrics and mental health specialists. Common problems occurring in pediatric practice include these:

1. Difficulty adjusting to chronic illness and disabilities
2. Psychological symptoms generated by pediatric illness that complicate its diagnosis and management
3. Somatic symptoms for which no medical etiology can be identified, or medical findings that do not support the severity of symptomatology
4. Factitious illness

Any one of these issues when encountered alone can significantly complicate medical treatment and exacerbate the degree of disability. Further complicating both medical and psychological management is the frequency with which these problem areas overlap, presenting complex diagnostic dilemmas.

In this chapter, I review evaluation and treatment issues related to chronic illness, somatization, and factitious illness during adolescence, including a discussion of the frequent overlap between these processes.

Mental Health Treatment in a Medical Setting

Before exploring treatment issues that are specific to chronic illness, somatization, and factitious disorders, I address a few general issues related to treatment of adolescents in a medical setting.

Team Approach

I practice in a children's hospital and work with patients who are either hospitalized due to illness or followed as outpatients in one of the pediatric clinics. Because the presence of a chronic illness or somatic symptoms forges an ongoing relationship among the patient, family, and medical team (physicians, nurses, social workers, physical therapists, and others), psychological treatment of adolescents in a medical setting requires a multidisciplinary team approach that includes close collaboration between the mental health specialists and other members of the medical treatment team.

For mental health clinicians whose primary work setting is in the community outside a medical center, the goal of close collaboration may be more difficult to achieve because of limited access to the medical team. It is vital, however, that the community clinician attempt to establish a route for ongoing communication with the medical team to ensure that all the health care professionals involved are working toward the same goals. For example, I encountered a community clinician recently who had been treating an adolescent whom she believed to be very medically ill. The patient's physician, however, felt that the patient had only mild physical illness that was inconsistent with the severity of her somatic complaints. Had the therapist obtained a consent from the patient and her parents to speak with the physician early in therapy, her assessment of the patient's psychological problems would have been more complete.

The clinician's ability to work effectively with a particular medical team or within a particular hospital is affected by the clinician's skill in assessing the unique "culture" of that hospital or treatment team. Hospitals and individual medical services or clinics have varying degrees of psychosocial sophistication that greatly influence their ability to respond to the psychological needs of a patient in a timely and helpful way.

The level of psychosocial sophistication also affects how responsive a team is to input from a mental health professional. Understanding these dynamics and undercurrents can help a clinician to anticipate "blind spots" and tailor communication so that it has the most impact. For example, one pediatrician I work with takes an active interest in the personal lives of his patients. He wants to hear the details of my assessments and is very responsive to my suggestions. He creates an environment of psychosocial awareness on his team, making it relatively easy to work collaboratively with the other physicians and nurses on that service.

In contrast, another pediatrician with whom I work has little interest in the psychosocial details of a particular case. Merely hearing the details of the psychological assessment does not compel him to alter the way he handles a particular patient, and he has a tendency to appear irritated if too many details are provided. However, if the psychological information is presented in a way that suits his goals (that is, reducing the amount of time he must spend dealing with a difficult patient or family), and he is given very specific information about what he could do differently, he is more responsive.

The Era of Managed Care

Most psychological practice these days is influenced by the current state of our health care system. Health insurance organizations are offering increasingly limited mental health benefits and frequently "carve out" the mental health services by contracting with a separate organization whose role is to administer mental health benefits. These mental health managed care companies usually have a list of preferred providers who have agreed to provide services at a predetermined cost. Individuals must choose a preferred provider or risk out-of-pocket expenses for mental health services.

I have found that my work has been affected by these arrangements in two ways. First, mental health benefits are sometimes extremely limited, a situation that significantly restricts the type of mental health care provided. I have one patient, a sixteen-year-old girl with Crohn's Disease, whose benefits are limited to crisis intervention. This limitation means that I can see her at times of acute stress for only five sessions. Additional sessions will not be authorized unless I can document that the crisis is still exerting a substantial impact on her life.

The second way in which psychological treatment in a medical setting is impacted by current managed mental health care practices is by the administrative separation of mental health and medical benefits; this division creates a financial mind-body dualism that unfortunately parallels the split between the psyche and the soma that still characterizes much of modern medicine. Sometimes I am unable to accept referrals from pediatricians; in these cases, even though the patient's health insurance covers medical treatment at Stanford Medical Center, the mental health benefits have been assigned to an organization that does not have a contract with Stanford or any of the individual providers. This makes the goal of co-management by the psychologist and the medical team difficult to achieve.

The current system is not structured to address the vital link between mental health and physical well-being. Research has demonstrated that untreated or inappropriately treated mental health conditions can significantly increase medical care costs, and I have seen many examples of this in my own practice. The sixteen-year-old patient with Crohn's Disease, for example, has a history of noncompliance with medical treatment, which leads to exacerbations of her disease and sometimes lengthy (and expensive) hospitalizations. However, because her mental health benefits cover only a limited number of sessions under circumstances that meet the definition of a "crisis," my ability to address the longer-term issues affecting compliance with medical treatment is severely hampered.

There is hope on the horizon, however, and the potential for expanded benefits if clinicians are willing to be creative and to act as advocates for their patients. Some believe that the mental health and health care systems will become much more integrated in the push for health care reform, in part because of the growing body of research that supports the potential for offsetting medical costs by providing mental health services in general health care settings.

In the meantime, clinicians will need to be creative and sometimes persistent. The key in some situations is refusing to accept denial of an initial request for mental health services as the final answer. Pediatricians who value mental health services for their patients can sometimes be allies. I am able to see one of my patients because the pediatrician was willing to call the medical director of the health care company and insist that the patient's mental health care be provided in the same institution as his medical care because of the substantial overlap between the psychological and medical issues, warranting close co-management. The company agreed to approve my status as a preferred provider for this case rather than insisting that the patient receive psychological care outside this institution.

I have also had some success in "appealing" initial denials for services by providing additional information that substantiates the potential savings in medical costs. This is sometimes best achieved by talking with a case reviewer personally rather than communicating in writing. In many cases, helping to educate an insurance representative about the nature of the connection between the medical and psychological issues can increase the responsiveness of the system.

Assessment

The psychosocial assessment of an adolescent with chronic illness or somatization does not differ greatly from the assessment a mental health clinician would conduct in a nonmedical setting. Even so, it is helpful to highlight certain aspects of the assessment that have particular relevance in the evaluation of chronically ill adolescents or adolescents presenting with somatic complaints.

Mark Edwards and Jack Finney organized the components of a thorough psychosocial assessment along five dimensions. These provide a useful guide for conducting an assessment of an adolescent with illness or somatic symptoms (Table 7.1).

The psychosocial history (which includes family, medical, developmental, and behavioral histories) and the description of presenting complaints are standard components of any psychological evaluation. Additional areas of importance in assessing adolescents with chronic illness or somatic complaints include evidence of relationships between symptoms and psychologically meaningful events (precipitating factors) and individual and

Table 7.1
Components of a Psychosocial Assessment

PSYCHOSOCIAL HISTORY

Family

    Family demographics

    Family history of problems (medical, learning, emotional, behavioral)

Medical

    Previous symptoms and illnesses

    Previous hospitalizations

    Previous diagnostic studies performed

    Previous interventions performed

    Current interventions

    Referral questions

Developmental

    Pregnancy history

    Birth information

    Early temperament

    Growth and development (motor, speech/language, social)

Behavioral

    Preschool and school history

    Compliance rate

    Attention span

    Methods and effectiveness of discipline

PRESENTING COMPLAINTS

- Qualitative descriptions
- Onset
- Course
- Pain parameters (location, frequency, duration, intensity)

(continued)

Table 7.1 *(continued)*
Components of a Psychosocial Assessment

PRECIPITATING FACTORS
- Temporal variations
- Situational variations
- Physiological variations (specific foods, physical stressors, constipation)
- Stressful events (school, social, family, changing residence, health of family or friends)

VULNERABILITY FACTORS
- Family history of illness
- Child's psychological state
- Parental psychological state
- Coping style

MAINTENANCE FACTORS
Secondary gain
    School absences
    Avoidance of activities
    Attention
    Reaction of the family
Cognitions (distortions)

Source: Edwards, M., & Finney, J. (1994). Somatoform disorders: Psychological issues. In R. A. Olson, L. L. Mullins, J. B. Gillman, & J. M. Chaney (Eds.), *The sourcebook of pediatric psychology.* Boston: Allyn & Bacon. Copyright © 1994 by Allyn and Bacon. Reprinted by permission.

family characteristics that may make adolescents vulnerable to the development of somatic symptoms or leave them unable to cope with the demands of a chronic illness (vulnerability factors). In addition, a variety of factors may maintain maladaptive responses and behaviors (maintenance factors).

SHARON

Sharon, the fourteen-year-old adolescent with abdominal pain whom we met earlier, provides a useful illustration of these assessment points. The death of her grandmother and the start of a sexually conflicted relationship with a new boyfriend were temporally related to the onset of her symptoms and appeared to be precipitating factors. The history revealed a number of vulnerability factors including a long history of somatic complaints in her mother and evidence that Sharon had a coping style characterized by defensive denial of psychological conflict. Furthermore, it was apparent that Sharon received a great deal of attention from her parents during episodes of pain, and she was allowed to avoid unpleasant activities when she was not feeling well; both these reactions reinforced her behavior. A thorough understanding of the influence of factors in each of these areas enhanced my diagnostic and treatment efforts.

Treatment Approach

Before discussing the clinical and treatment issues associated with adolescent patients in a medical setting, I should say a few words about my approach to therapy. My preferred therapeutic approach is cognitive-behavioral. The problem-focused, skills-enhancement orientation of the cognitive-behavioral approach lends itself well to working with adolescents in a medical setting, as many of the adolescents referred for problems related to medical conditions are in a great deal of acute distress that is being compounded by their coping skills deficits. In addition, adolescent somatizers are often most responsive to a problem-focused therapy because it encourages them initially to continue their focus on their symptoms rather than suggest that they should shift focus to other "deeper" issues; this is often what they have been told, or they feel it is being implied by the referral to a psychotherapist.

Although I identify myself as a cognitive-behavioral therapist, my work is informed and enhanced by other approaches and theories such as the narrative and solution-focused therapies, and psychodynamic and existential theories. The ability of a clinician to successfully blend approaches and draw on a range of techniques is dependent on a solid case formulation.

Although the discussion of case formulation is beyond the scope of this chapter, it plays a vital role in any successful course of therapy—a point that should be noted. The case formulation is a synthesis of the factors hypothesized to underlie a patient's problem. It should reflect an understanding of the influence of multiple domains on the patient's functioning: cognitions and underlying assumptions about self and the world, family dynamics, adaptive style, stage of development, and so on. This understanding will suggest priorities for treatment and guide the timing and choice of interventions.

CHRONIC ILLNESS AND ADOLESCENCE

Chronic illness has been defined as a "physical, usually non-fatal condition which lasts longer than three months in a given year or necessitates a continuous period in hospital of more than one month." As many as 35 percent of American children have chronic conditions, according to some estimates, and a significant number of children are thought to suffer from more than one condition. One analysis of the 1988 National Health Interview Survey found that 70 percent of affected children had one condition, 21 percent had two conditions, and 9 percent had three or more chronic conditions.

The increase in prevalence of chronic illness in childhood and adolescence can be expected to continue as advances in medical treatment are made. For example, substantial improvements in the survival rates for various forms of childhood cancer have been made over the past few decades, turning some malignancies, previously thought to be acutely fatal, into chronic illnesses. Similar advances have been made in the treatment of cystic fibrosis. In 1969, the median survival age for cystic fibrosis patients was fourteen. By 1990, the median survival age had increased to twenty-eight. Advances in survival rates, however, intensify the chronic stresses and demands placed on patients and their families.

Chronic illness can result in significant stress at any age, but adolescence can intensify the demands of a serious illness. The normative tasks of adolescence, with the emphasis on physical and sexual development, intensification of peer relationships, emphasis on personal achievement, and move toward independence from parents and family, are in frequent conflict with the inevitable life disruptions imposed by chronic illness. Even patients who appeared to cope well with a chronic illness earlier in childhood may display adjustment difficulties during adolescence.

VIVIAN

Fourteen-year-old Vivian was diagnosed with Marfan syndrome when she was a young child. Marfan syndrome is a genetic disorder that has a variety of associated features including skeletal abnormalities (tall stature, long arms and legs, and long fingers), ocular problems, and potentially life-threatening cardiac abnormalities. Throughout much of her early childhood Vivian appeared relatively unconcerned about her tall stature and unique appearance. She did well in school and was popular with her peers. Approximately one year prior to her referral for mental health services, however, Vivian began to express to her parents feelings of frustration about being different from her peers. She was concerned that she would not get asked for dates because she was taller than most of the boys her age. She began to defy her parents' and doctors' directives that she not engage in strenuous physical activity, and her mother spotted her on a number of occasions playing basketball at the park.

During the initial interview, Vivian stated that she had been feeling increasingly upset about her disease and that the "straw that broke the camel's back" was being the only one in her group of friends who did not get asked by a boy to dance at a recent school party.

Although studies have suggested that adolescents with chronic illness are at increased risk for emotional problems, this knowledge does not provide practical guidance for assessing the degree of risk for an individual patient. There is tremendous variability in levels of adjustment between patients with the same disease as well as between patients with different chronic illnesses. In helping patients with this adjustment, clinicians might consider three general domains: risk—disease characteristics, family characteristics, and patient characteristics (see Table 7.2).

The particular characteristics of an individual's disease may influence his or her psychological adjustment. Important dimensions include sensory, neurologic, or cognitive impairment, visibility of the disorder (physical changes or disfigurement), and whether the illness is life threatening or involves demanding or intrusive care. Other factors that may influence adjustment include the severity of the individual's condition, and the degree of pain and discomfort associated with the condition.

A wide variety of family characteristics may influence a patient's adjustment to chronic illness. Families of low socioeconomic status are typically subjected to multiple chronic stressors and have few resources available to aid their coping efforts. The amount of social support available to a family affects the adjustment of each family member. Furthermore, the presence of individual psychopathology in a parent may lead to significant dysfunction in a family and severely affect the emotional well-being of a physically ill adolescent.

Table 7.2
Domains of Risk for Adolescents with Chronic Illness

Disease Characteristics

    Neurological/sensory impairment

    Degree of life threat

    Severity (how well managed)

    Pain

    Intrusiveness of treatment

Family Characteristics

    Socioeconomic status

    Social support

    Individual pathology in parents

Patient Characteristics

    Previous level of adaptation (such as social integration, adaptive style)

In addition to disease and family characteristics, an individual's adjustment in the face of a chronic illness will be influenced by the patient's pre-illness adaptation (if the onset of the illness occurred after birth). Evaluation of an adolescent's peer relationships, academic functioning, and coping or adaptive style as well as the teenager's degree of success in coping with past stressors provides valuable information about the patient's premorbid adaptive functioning; this information allows a clinician to make some predictions about how an adolescent is likely to manage the stress of a chronic illness.

The problems for which chronically ill adolescents are most commonly referred can be loosely divided into three general categories:

1. Adjustment difficulties that do not meet the criteria for a clinical disorder

2. Clinically significant psychiatric disorders such as anxiety and major depression

3. Management of symptoms such as pain or nausea or vomiting

Adjustment Difficulties

Most chronically ill adolescents are referred for mental health services because of difficulty adjusting or adapting to some aspect of their disease or treatment. Feelings of anger, fear, sadness, and anxiety may negatively impact their quality of life, but the symptoms do not meet the criteria for a particular psychiatric diagnosis. Early intervention for these "subthreshold" problems may prevent the development of more serious psychopathology and associated behavioral problems.

Because of the degree to which chronic illness creates life disruptions that are often in direct conflict with the demands of adolescence, emotional distress is common and may fluctuate predictably with various stages during an illness or its treatment. For example, the first two or three months following the diagnosis of cancer are extraordinarily stressful for a patient and family. Although treatment for some malignancies may take two years or more, most adolescents are able to adapt to the regimen after the initial months and settle into a routine that feels somewhat predictable, with an associated improvement in adaptive functioning.

Additional issues commonly associated with adjustment difficulties include unexpected treatment complications and a recent deterioration in functioning. Alterations in physical appearance due to treatment (hair loss from chemotherapy; steroid-related weight gain; limb amputation) can pose considerable psychological challenges for the adolescent, with adjustment difficulties frequently manifested in problems of treatment noncompliance.

Issues related to death and dying are universally stressful. Often, adolescents' concerns about their own vulnerability will be reflected in their reactions to the deaths of fellow patients.

MARTIN

This was the case with Martin, who was fifteen years old when he was diagnosed with leukemia. I had worked intensively with Martin early in his treatment when he experienced unexpected, life-threatening complications that led to significant anxiety. He had responded well to cognitive-behavioral techniques to help him manage anxiety and feelings of hopelessness. Because he had responded so well to psychological intervention and was doing better medically, we agreed that regular sessions were no longer indicated and that Martin could call me when he felt further sessions would be helpful.

I had not seen Martin for four months when I received a call from his nurse during one of his hospitalizations for chemotherapy. It was late in the day when I received the call that Martin wanted to see me. I knew that a fourteen-year-old patient named Tina had died that morning and suspected that this might have something to do with his call.

Therapist: Hi, Martin; long time no see!
Martin: [*Sits up in bed, smiles*] Hi doc! It has been a while.
Therapist: What's up? Your nurse said you wanted to see me.
Martin: Yeah, I just haven't talked to you in a while. I thought we could just talk.

For the next fifteen or twenty minutes Martin talked somewhat superficially about what he had been doing over the last few months at school and with friends. He looked somewhat anxious, and appeared to be filling time with idle conversation. I decided to help him out.

Therapist: How well did you know Tina?
Martin: [*Looking relieved*] I didn't know her very well at all, but it's seems so weird that she died because she was my age!

Martin proceeded to talk at length about his reactions to Tina's death and how her death raised significant fears about the possibility of his own.

Martin's case provides an example of how a variety of "crisis points" throughout the course of an illness can temporarily overwhelm a patient's available coping resources and result in mood or behavioral changes. Most crisis periods are effectively managed with a relatively brief course of supportive therapy aimed at enhancing coping skills. Some patients, such as Martin, benefit from intervention on an intermittent basis throughout the course of their illness.

Psychiatric Disorders

It has been estimated that close to 20 percent of adolescents are suffering from a psychiatric disorder. Although our understanding of the true prevalence of psychiatric disorders in the chronically ill adolescent population is limited, we can expect the numbers to be at least comparable, if not somewhat higher, given the extraordinary stresses and demands of chronic disease and its treatment.

Differential diagnosis of psychiatric disorders in medically ill patients can be complicated by the medical contributions of the disease or the treatment. It may be difficult to determine, for example, whether a patient is experiencing dysphoria, loss of energy and appetite, weight loss, and sleep disturbance secondary to a major depressive episode or to the effects of the disease. Many medications commonly used to treat chronic conditions can have substantial effects on mood and behavior. A seventeen-year-old patient with severe asthma told me that he would become moody and irritable when taking steroids, commonly prescribed for treatment of severe asthma attacks, and that during this time he felt like a "totally different person." Another cystic fibrosis patient reported that one of her medications frequently made her "jittery" and anxious.

The coexistence of medical disease and a psychiatric disorder may significantly complicate medical management of a patient, and may lead to excessive morbidity and even death. An adolescent boy with diabetes and a conduct disorder was noncompliant with his diabetic regimen, which resulted in multiple hospitalizations for diabetic ketoacidosis. In another case, a sixteen-year-old girl with a history of identity disorder and substance abuse, in addition to an extremely chaotic family situation, was unable to cope with the emotional demands of treatment for an ovarian tumor and failed to follow up with the recommended chemotherapy after surgery. She presented several months later stating that she was now interested in proceeding with treatment. However, her disease had become metastatic by that point, leaving her with little chance for survival.

Symptom Management

Patients are frequently referred to mental health professionals for behavioral management of symptoms such as pain and nausea or vomiting. Relaxation training, biofeedback, and hypnosis have been effective in reducing discomfort associated with many illnesses and treatment regimens. In addition to reducing discomfort, instruction in self-management of the symptoms can give an adolescent a greater sense of control and mastery, which is very important during this stage of development.

TALIA

Talia was fifteen years old when she was referred to me for behavioral management of pain associated with sickle cell disease. She described feeling that her disease had "control" of her life. At the first sign of an impending pain crisis, she was flooded with feelings of anxiety and hopelessness. She learned a variety of pain management strategies that she began to implement at the start of an episode of pain. She was eventually successful in limiting the severity and duration of the pain episodes, as well as reducing her use of narcotic pain medications. For the first time, she reported, she felt she had more control over her disease than the disease had over her.

The distinction among situational adjustment problems, psychiatric disorders, and problems of symptom management is not always clear. Patients frequently present with complex, multifaceted difficulties. For example, refractory pain problems are often associated with anxiety disorders and major depression.

TREATMENT ISSUES

Interdisciplinary collaboration and skillful attention to the development of therapeutic rapport are key elements in successful therapeutic intervention with chronically ill adolescents.

Collaboration with the Medical Team and Psychiatry

Because psychological and behavioral problems have the potential to significantly complicate treatment of a chronic condition, successful management of a chronic illness in many cases depends on a close relationship between the mental health specialists and medical team. The relationship between a chronically ill patient and his or her doctor may span many years, and this relationship often becomes a central one for a patient and family coping with chronic illness. Just as an adolescent may exhibit behavioral problems related to dysfunctional communication within a family, an adolescent patient may display psychological symptoms that are related to problematic communication among patient, family, and medical team.

JOHNNY

Twelve-year-old Johnny was referred for a psychological evaluation because his oncologist felt that his somatic complaints were in excess of what most other leukemia patients report. Johnny was an anxious boy who reported that his mood had been depressed since diagnosis three months before. His mother was also extremely anxious, and was preoccupied with her son's somatic complaints. She feared that any new complaint was a sign that he had relapsed.

The oncology team viewed this mother as extremely clinging, demanding, and overinvolved with her son. Feelings of annoyance on the part of the team led to mild to moderate avoidance of interactions with this "difficult" mother and a tendency to minimize or dismiss her reports of symptoms in her son. This dynamic, in turn, led to increased reports of somatic symptoms (both by the mother and Johnny) and complaints by the mother that the team was not "listening" to her son.

My intervention included consultation with the medical team about the dynamics in this family and the recommendation that the team make an effort to return this mother's calls in a timely fashion and spend a little extra time with Johnny and his mother when they came to the clinic. I predicted that spending additional time "up front" would result in fewer crises and potentially save them more time in the long run. This, in conjunction with individual and family therapy, resulted in improved adaptive functioning and fewer somatic complaints.

For the non-M.D. mental health professional, consultation with psychiatry is often important. Frequently, a physician's response to the apparent psychological distress of a patient is to refer the patient for psychotropic medication. We often hear, "This patient is depressed. He needs an antidepressant." Although some patients do benefit significantly from psychotropic medications, medication alone is rarely indicated. Many adolescents coping with chronic illness are experiencing reactive depression and anxiety that will be most responsive to supportive psychotherapy. Those who benefit from medication are likely to benefit most from a combination of psychopharmacology and psychotherapy.

In addition to consultation around psychotropic medications, psychiatry can be a valued resource for the non-M.D. clinician in other ways. Patients may be experiencing psychiatric symptoms that are related to their underlying disease or their medical treatment. For example, diabetic patients may report difficulty concentrating or mood swings if their blood sugars are not well controlled. Steroids, which are commonly used in the treatment of a variety of chronic disorders, are frequently associated with depressed mood and can even cause psychotic symptoms. Consultation with a psychiatrist can enhance the non-M.D. clinician's understanding of all factors potentially affecting a patient's level of functioning and expand the treatment options available to the patient.

Initiating Treatment

Despite the obvious stresses associated with having a chronic illness, adolescents are often wary (at best) of mental health providers, and sometimes they are openly oppositional to the notion of receiving mental health support. The suggestion by a physician or parent that an adolescent should talk to a "shrink" may feel like one more unwelcome intrusion at a time when the adolescent is attempting to salvage any remaining sense of control over his or her life. The first task, then, is for the therapist to develop rapport and engage the adolescent in identifying ways in which participating in therapy may be helpful.

I generally try to begin the initial session in a very nonthreatening way. When meeting with patients in the hospital, I make a quick observation of the room and look for clues about hobbies or other areas of interest that may provide a means of establishing rapport.

For example, on entering the room of a fifteen-year-old cancer patient I was greeted with, "I told my mother I didn't want to talk to anybody." She was sitting in bed, making a pair of earrings. I said to her that I could imagine that because she had told her mother she did not want to talk, it must feel frustrating to have someone come anyway. I told her I would try to keep my visit short, as she was obviously very busy with her project. I then proceeded to inquire about her earrings, commenting on her obvious talent. It was quickly apparent that she achieved a great deal of pride from her handiwork, and she began to brighten slowly as I asked questions about the materials she used and asked if she would be willing to show me some of her other creations. After about twenty minutes had passed, I commented that I had promised I would stay only a short while, and asked if she minded if I stayed a little longer. She shrugged and said, "I guess it would be all right."

It is important that the adolescent be engaged in a collaborative process of identifying goals for therapy. Many adolescents have difficulty identifying therapeutic goals, particularly if they feel that they have been coerced into seeing a therapist. For some, the difficulty in identifying goals for therapy may be related to a lack of clarity about how psychotherapy works, or how it can be helpful to people in their situation. Educating adolescents and their parents about the role of psychological intervention and the types of approaches available (behavioral therapy for anxiety or pain; family therapy for communication problems; supportive individual therapy for "venting feelings") can enhance their ability to identify ways in which therapy may be helpful to them.

It is also important to keep in mind that an adolescent may identify goals for therapy that may seem far from the "real issues." For example, I worked with a sixteen-year-old boy with a terminal diagnosis who identified his mother's intrusiveness as the only problem he had for which therapy might be helpful. Preservation of the therapeutic alliance is dependent on accepting the patient's definition of the problem.

An important element in working with chronically ill adolescents is to consider the time frame and structure for therapy. This issue is particularly relevant with patients who may be in and out of the hospital. Therapists who work primarily in a hospital setting may be faced with intermittent, time-limited therapy that occurs during hospitalizations. Ongoing outpatient therapy may be difficult to maintain for a variety of reasons. Some patients may not live close enough to the hospital for weekly therapy to be feasible. Other patients may not follow through with outpatient visits because of a desire to avoid the hospital unless they are sick. Therapists who are not affiliated with a hospital and who work in a community setting may also encounter disruptions in therapy secondary to hospitalizations. Consideration of these issues and their impact on the structure of the therapy is important in setting goals and establishing a therapeutic contract.

Cognitive-Behavioral Therapy

Reassurance, guidance, and "normalizing" feelings in a supportive, safe relationship that allows for ventilation of sometimes overwhelming emotions is often sufficient to help an adolescent cope with the stresses associated with a chronic illness. It is important to encourage the adolescent to a gradual return to prior activities, or to identify new areas of expertise or mastery when prior activities are no longer possible.

Some adolescents will require more intensive interventions to improve their adaptive functioning. Interventions should be aimed at enhancing their coping strategies and minimizing the sense of loss of control that accompanies chronic illness.

Listed in Table 7.3 are a variety of cognitive and behavioral techniques. It is important to underscore that cognitive-behavioral therapy is not merely a collection of techniques that can be applied in a "cookbook" fashion. Interventions should be chosen strategically based on the clinician's understanding of the case formulation.

Although a cognitive-behavioral approach focuses primarily on the "here and now," some patients benefit from exploratory techniques. This is particularly true when you are working to

Table 7.3
Cognitive and Behavioral Techniques

Cognitive Techniques

Daily record of dysfunctional thoughts

Identify cognitive distortions

Ask for evidence for a maladaptive thought/belief

Look for alternative explanations

Teach relationship between maladaptive thought and underlying beliefs

Behavioral Techniques

Relaxation training

Biofeedback

Guided imagery

Activity scheduling

Pleasure predicting

Modeling and role-playing

Exposure

---

challenge strongly held beliefs or assumptions that are resistant to here-and-now interventions. In these cases, exploration of the origin of the beliefs can be an effective strategy.

TERRY

The case of Terry, a nineteen-year-old cystic fibrosis (CF) patient, provides an example of the use of a cognitive-behavioral approach to facilitate improved adaptation to a chronic illness. Terry had recently given up his job because he found that he no longer had the stamina to work full time. He stated that he had always worked hard to minimize the impact of CF on his life but now felt that he was no longer able to "outrun it." This perspective had led to feelings of depression and a reduction in activity level that was more extreme than his physical status required.

With the help of a relatively brief course of therapy (ten sessions), Terry was able to adopt a new perspective on his life. He responded well to cognitive interventions aimed at helping him to identify cognitive distortions that impeded his ability to adapt to his recent physical changes. He decided that instead of trying to run from the disease (and "throwing in the towel" when it became clear that this was not possible), he would learn how to "walk with the CF." In his mind, this meant he needed to make accommodations for the illness rather than trying to deny its existence. He began to look for a part-time job that better suited his physical needs, and enrolled in computer courses to learn new skills.

DENISE

In another case, seventeen-year-old Denise was referred for a psychological evaluation by her pulmonologist who was concerned about this patient's adjustment to having a chronic illness. Denise was diagnosed with cystic fibrosis when she was an infant. Over the last three years her health had deteriorated, and she had been faced with more frequent hospitalizations. She was beginning to withdraw from her peers and was experiencing episodes of anxiety that were most severe at times when she had difficulty breathing. The anxiety would then exacerbate her breathing difficulties, which would, in turn, increase her anxiety.

Cognitive-behavioral therapy was initiated with an initial focus on anxiety management.

Denise: It happened again last night. I started to have trouble breathing and got really scared.
Therapist: What thoughts were going through your mind?
Denise: That I was going to die; that I wouldn't be able to catch my breath and that no one would be there to help me. But I tried to do what we have been talking about, and I think it helped.

Therapist: What did you do?

Denise: I told myself that I needed to calm down because the anxiety would make it harder to breathe. I tried to relax my body and put on some music to distract me from some of my thoughts. I also tried to reassure myself that there wasn't much of a chance that I would die right then, and that if I really needed someone to help me, all I needed to do was press the call button.

Therapist: Sounds like you handled things very well. What happened next?

Denise: Well, I did calm down eventually, but it was really hard. I also went ahead and called my nurse, just to talk with someone.

Therapist: Did that help?

Denise: Yeah, it was helpful to bounce some of my thoughts off someone else. I think it helped me to believe in my coping thoughts more.

Therapist: Kind of like what we were talking about yesterday . . . that you may need some practice with the coping thoughts before they start to work really well.

Denise: Yeah, exactly.

Denise was eventually able to reduce both the frequency and severity of her anxiety episodes. She reported that it helped her to feel a greater sense of control over what was happening in her body, which motivated her to pursue ways of achieving a greater sense of control in other aspects of her life.

Both Denise and Terry illustrate the challenges, frustrations, and fears of living with a chronic illness. Psychotherapy served as a vehicle for exploring the meaning of illness in their lives and provided them with opportunities to learn new coping strategies and strengthen old ones.

ADOLESCENT SOMATIZATION

Somatization has been defined as occurring when there are one or more physical complaints for which appropriate medical evaluation reveals no explanatory physical pathology or pathophysiological mechanism, or when there is related organic pathology, the somatic complaints or resulting social or occupational impairments are grossly in excess of what would be expected from the physical findings. The somatic symptoms are thought to be the product of a subconscious process involving translation of emotional distress into bodily complaints.

It is widely recognized that recurrent medically unexplained physical symptoms are common in pediatric practice. John Campo and Sandra Fritsch, in a recent review of the literature on somatization in children and adolescents, found that headaches are the most commonly reported somatic symptom, with 10 percent to 30 percent of community samples of children and adolescents reporting headaches "frequently" or on at least a weekly basis. Also common is recurrent abdominal pain, with 20 percent to 25 percent of school-age children and adolescents in available studies reporting this symptom. Other symptoms reported to occur on at least a weekly basis include limb pain and so-called growing pains (5 percent to 20 percent of children and adolescents), medically unexplained chest pain (7 percent to 15 percent), and fatigue (30 percent to 50 percent).

Note that somatization is a psychosomatic process, not a psychiatric diagnosis. DSM-IV contains a variety of diagnostic categories that involve the process of somatization in some way. These diagnoses are listed in Table 7.4.

It is unclear what percentage of somatizing children and adolescents continue to display these tendencies as adults, but studies of adult patients with somatization disorders suggest that many first became symptomatic during childhood or adolescence. One study found that 26 percent of the sample of adult persistent somatizers were under the age of twenty at the onset of their first physical symptoms. This group of patients also happened to be quite unresponsive to treatment, which underscores

Table 7.4
DSM-IV Diagnoses Potentially Related to the
Process of Somatization

Somatoform Disorders
    Somatization Disorder
    Undifferentiated Somatoform Disorder
    Conversion Disorder
    Pain Disorder
    Hypochondriasis
    Body Dysmorphic Disorder
    Somatoform Disorder Not Otherwise Specified

Psychological Factors Affecting Medical Condition
(Must Specify):
    Mental Disorder
    Psychological Symptoms
    Personality Traits or Coping Style
    Stress-Related Physiological Response

---

the importance of assessment and intervention early in life, before the disorder becomes chronic and disabling.

The Development of Somatization

A comprehensive review of the factors related to the development of somatization is beyond the scope of this chapter. In brief, however, the literature suggests a strong familial component to somatization. Numerous studies have found that somatizing children frequently have somatic complaints similar to symptoms present in family members, and there is an association between somatization and family members with antisocial personality. The degree to which these relationships represent the contribution of genetics or environment is unclear.

A variety of theories have been developed regarding somatization. Psychodynamic theorists view somatization as a psychological defense that enables a person to defend against the awareness of unpleasant emotions, conflicts, or memories by experiencing and expressing emotional distress physically. The adaptive style of "repression" (defensive denial of psychological conflict) and the construct of "alexithymia" (inability to identify or describe feelings) have been associated with somatic symptoms in the adult literature.

Learning has been identified as potentially playing a role in the development and maintenance of somatization. For example, a child's somatic complaints may be reinforced by the interest and attention displayed by a parent. School or other unpleasant activities may be avoided on the basis of somatic complaints, providing additional reinforcement for the symptoms.

Family systems theorists have viewed somatization as serving a stabilizing function within the family system. Some have viewed somatic symptoms as a form of communication and have noted the sometimes striking symbolism of the symptoms.

Finally, somatosensory amplification, a preoccupation with or heightened sensitivity to bodily states, may contribute to somatization. Somatosensory amplification is a process that involves hypervigilance to bodily sensation, a tendency to focus on weak, infrequent sensations, and a disposition to react to somatic sensations with distorted cognitions that contribute to the perception of the sensations as alarming.

Additional factors that may contribute to the development of somatization include negative life events, recent loss, and traumatic childhood experiences such as sexual abuse. Pediatric medical illness and Munchausen Syndrome by Proxy may increase a person's susceptibility to somatization later in life.

TREATMENT ISSUES IN SOMATIZATION

The nature of somatization requires active interdisciplinary collaboration; also needed is a therapeutic alliance with adolescents exhibiting somatization, and their families. This alliance must be sensitive to the barriers that commonly interfere with the somatizer's pursuit of psychological services.

Collaboration with the Medical Team

Because the differential diagnosis for recurrent somatic complaints (medical versus psychological versus both) can be very difficult to establish, often with the correct diagnosis becoming clear only over time, successful treatment requires active and ongoing collaboration with the patient's primary care physician.

One of a physician's greatest fears is misdiagnosing a problem as psychological when it has, in fact, a medical cause. The reverse can also be devastating, however, leading to unnecessary intrusive and painful diagnostic procedures, toxic treatments, and an increased risk of iatrogenic disease. Comprehensive evaluation of a patient, with a psychosocial history that is as thorough as the medical history, can guide a physician either to delay further medical intervention and refer for psychotherapy, or continue the pursuit of an organic etiology in the face of a psychosocial history that does not suggest psychological dysfunction.

A negative psychosocial history proved useful in the case of a twelve-year-old girl referred to me after her pediatrician was unable to determine the cause of her chronic diarrhea. He wondered if Factitious Disorder by Proxy might be an issue. A psychological evaluation of this patient and her family revealed none of the common markers for this disorder. Both the patient and family appeared to be functioning quite well overall. The pediatrician decided to continue with further diagnostic tests, eventually diagnosing a rare gastro-intestinal condition.

The mental health professional must be sensitive to the fact that psychopathology and medical illness frequently coexist. In some cases a patient's or family's psychopathology may be so apparent that the physician may conclude prematurely that the sole origin of the somatic symptom is psychological. This point was illustrated in a report in the literature on four cases of presumed psychogenic vomiting hospitalized on Stanford Children's Hospital's psychosomatic unit. Despite the existence of significant individual and family psychopathology, each of the four cases was eventually identified as having a medical condition that contributed to the presenting symptoms. The authors suggested that if a psychosomatic diagnosis is correct, a clinician should expect a predictable response to psychological treatment. If a patient's somatic symptoms remain unchanged after an adequate trial of psychotherapy, an organic reevaluation is indicated.

Forging an Alliance

The initial contact with an adolescent somatizer and his or her family can be a challenge. The suggestion by a pediatrician that an adolescent may benefit from mental health services is frequently met with resistance. Concerns that the physician believes the adolescent or family to be "crazy" are common, as are concerns that the physician does not "believe" the patient or thinks the discomfort is "all in his head."

In general, I utilize a coping skills approach to working with adolescent somatization. Particularly at the beginning of therapy, most adolescent somatizers (and frequently their parents) are reluctant to accept a psychological explanation for their symptoms. Consequently, they are unlikely to engage in a therapeutic process that is advertised as a vehicle for uncovering the psychological mechanisms that produce the physical symptoms. More easily tolerated, however, is a definition of therapy that highlights the need to help adolescents learn to cope with their physical symptoms so that disruptions in daily living are minimized.

WENDY

My initial meeting with fourteen-year-old Wendy and her mother illustrates these points. Wendy was referred to me by her gastroenterologist who could not find the cause of her abdominal pain. Wendy presented initially as quiet and withdrawn. Her mother presented as quite hostile. She stated repeatedly that she believed Wendy's pain to be real, and that she did not believe the pain was "all in her head like the doctors think." I explained that many of the patients who come to see me have symptoms that the doctors can't completely explain. This can be a very frustrating experience for teenagers and their families, particularly since not having a medical diagnosis means that no one can say when the symptoms will go away. When this is the case, it is extremely important that teenagers learn to cope with the symptoms so that they are able to participate as fully as possible in school, peer, and family activities. The description of my views about therapy struck a chord for this mother, as she was very concerned about the amount of school Wendy had missed. She became much less defensive and began to inquire about what techniques might be available to help her daughter become active again. Wendy became more engaged as her mother adopted a more collaborative stance with me.

No effort is made to challenge a family's belief that a symptom is "real." In fact, in the initial session adolescents and their families are encouraged to give a very detailed account of the symptomatology and its history. Often my questions require patients to provide more details of their symptoms than they provided to their physician.

The patient is immediately given the task of keeping a journal and collecting data on the intensity, duration, course, triggers, and consequences of their somatic symptoms. The journal should be maintained throughout the course of psychotherapy as it provides not only a baseline assessment of the symptoms but allows for monitoring of progress over time.

Cognitive-Behavioral Therapy

I generally incorporate behavioral techniques early in therapy to assist patients with management of their somatic symptoms. Progressive muscle relaxation, biofeedback, guided imagery, and hypnosis are useful in providing symptomatic relief, but they also begin to build a bridge between the mind and the body. Some therapists have advocated the use of psychophysiological demonstrations (such as using biofeedback) that show patients the relationship between being "rattled" mentally and becoming rattled and reactive physiologically.

Obviously, the exact approach used with a particular patient will depend on the formulation of the case. For example, when an adolescent is able to identify through the use of her journal that she tends to experience stomach pain when she is anxious about performing perfectly in a situation, she will benefit from cognitive and behavioral techniques aimed at anxiety management in stressful situations. An adolescent who has difficulty identifying and acknowledging emotional distress, and consequently has trouble relating such distress to the occurrence of somatic discomfort, may benefit from an approach that begins with increasing her awareness of psychophysiological processes through biofeedback. The case of thirteen-year-old Jena illustrates the role anxiety management techniques can play with some somatizing patients.

JENA

Jena was referred for psychological evaluation by her pediatrician following a negative medical work-up for nausea that occurred on almost a daily basis. Jena's symptom journal indicated that the nausea occurred more frequently during the week than on the weekend and was usually triggered by anxious feelings in social situations and during performances (such as piano recitals, church plays). When she became nauseated, her anxiety increased further because of fears that she might vomit. Jena responded well to cognitive and behavioral anxiety management techniques that were initially focused on limiting the vicious cycle of mutual potentiation between the anxiety and nausea.

Therapist: What happened when you went into the classroom and started to notice the anxiety?

Jena: I kept telling myself I really needed to calm down. I tried taking some deep breaths and pictured butterflies in my stomach that were starting to land on flowers to rest for a while. I also reminded myself that I have never thrown up before, so why would now be any different? That one was hard to believe, but I tried to convince myself of it anyway.

Therapist: How were you feeling at that point?

Jena: A little better. My stomach still felt jumpy, but I don't think it was as bad.

Eventually the focus of therapy shifted from managing the symptom of nausea to examining (and ultimately managing) the source of anxiety in social and performance situations.

Therapist: What thoughts were going through your head while you were waiting to go on at the recital?

Jena: I just knew I was going to mess up.

Therapist: And what would happen if you messed up?

Jena: I'd be embarrassed.

Therapist: Sure, it can feel embarrassing to make a mistake, but what would actually happen to you besides feeling bad?

Jena: I don't know. . . . I guess I think about people making fun of me because I messed up.

Therapist: Did any of the other kids at the recital make mistakes?

Jena: Oh yeah. A lot of them did. *[Smiles]* Even Sherry Wilcox—Miss Perfect.

Therapist: *[Laughing]* Even Miss Perfect? How did people react?

Jena: No one really reacted. I guess people probably feel bad when someone makes a mistake, but what else are they going to do? *[Laughs]* I know, I know . . . no big deal to make a mistake, right?

Although some patients like Jena can easily make the connection between emotional distress and somatic symptoms, others, such as fourteen-year-old Leo, cannot.

LEO

Leo was referred to me by his pulmonologist who was concerned that some of Leo's asthma "attacks" were not really asthma, but stress-related hyperventilation that produced symptoms similar to asthma (chest tightness, breathlessness, choking feeling) without the change in oxygen requirements usually associated with a true asthma attack. Leo had presented to the emergency room on several occasions with these "attacks." He was initially very resistant toward the idea that these episodes could have a psychological rather than a medical basis, but he was willing to consider exploring relaxation strategies that might help him better manage his asthma.

With the aid of biofeedback, he was taught a relaxation technique. The relationship between mental stress and physiological reactivity was demonstrated during biofeedback by having him engage in mental arithmetic that allowed him to see that something as minor as this kind of activity caused changes in his body. Although he continued to be reluctant to accept that some of the attacks were not asthma, he was able to use both cognitive and behavioral strategies to reduce the frequency and duration of the episodes.

In most cases, the initial symptom focus in therapy gives way to a more comprehensive approach to the patient's life. Fewer symptoms are presented and less time is spent directly addressing them. This was the case with Katie.

KATIE

Katie was twelve years old when she was referred by her orthopedic surgeon. Seven months prior to the referral Katie had injured her knee while jumping rope. Her recovery did not follow the expected course, and she continued to complain of severe pain in the absence of any evidence of pathology on exam or X-ray. She reported that she could not bend her knee, and she had insisted on using crutches since the injury. The only remaining medical option was exploratory surgery, which the surgeon hoped to avoid.

The surgeon had noted some interactions between Katie and her mother that raised concerns about the influence of psychological factors on her presentation of symptoms. Katie was a bright, vivacious girl who readily engaged in therapy. Her mother, who had a history of depression, was skeptical about therapy and how it could be helpful to her daughter.

Katie began keeping a pain journal and learned a variety of pain management strategies. Initially, each therapy session began with a review of how the previous week had gone, with a focus on the experience of pain and the strategies used to cope with it. Katie gradually started to appear impatient with the focus on pain during sessions, preferring instead to spend more time talking about her relationship with her mother, who she feared was very depressed and possibly suicidal. Physical therapy was initiated to help her gradually begin to bend her knee and bear weight on her leg, and the cognitive-behavioral pain management strategies helped her to cope with the inevitable discomfort of overcoming months of disuse. Her progress in physical therapy kept pace with progress in the relationship between Katie and her mother.

Hospitalization on a Comprehensive Pediatric Care Unit

Hospitalization on a specialized medical and psychiatric unit may be appropriate in cases involving complex diagnostic pictures, severe impairment in adaptive functioning (such as inability to attend school because of incapacitating headaches that are unresponsive to conventional medical therapies; being wheelchair-bound because of "paralysis" that has no medical etiology), or failed outpatient treatment. Of course, evidence that a patient is a danger to himself or someone else is always an indication for prompt hospitalization.

At Stanford, we have a ten-bed psychosomatic unit for children and adolescents that is staffed by an interdisciplinary team of physicians, psychiatrists, psychologists, milieu counselors, nurses, schoolteachers, and physical and occupational therapists. It is the ideal setting for adolescents presenting with complex medical and psychological issues because of its comprehensive interdisciplinary management of an adolescent's problems. For the somatizing adolescent, a rehabilitation approach is emphasized, focusing on restoration of function through intensive individual and family therapy, supported by physical and occupational therapies. The unit milieu reinforces activity and independent function and discourages illness behavior.

FACTITIOUS DISORDERS

A small number of adolescents who present with somatic symptoms with no clear medical etiology actually fabricate symptoms or induce illness. This syndrome is known as Factitious Disorder (FD), and is defined in DSM-IV as the intentional production or feigning of physical or psychological signs or symptoms in order to assume the sick role.

Differential diagnosis of FD can be difficult; it entails distinguishing between FD and somatization as well as establishing the role of the parent in the presentation of the symptoms (Factitious Disorder by Proxy). The key to differential diagnosis lies in determining the extent of "intentionality" in symptom production. Somatization is an "unconscious" process that transduces psychological stress and conflict into somatic symptoms. FD, on the other hand, involves "conscious" production of physical symptoms. FD differs from malingering in that the conscious production of symptoms is for unconscious reasons that relate to numerous unmet psychological needs rather than the desire to obtain external incentives.

Many adolescents and adults with FD were victims of Factitious Disorder by Proxy (FDBP), or Munchausen Syndrome by Proxy, as children. This implies that at some point during childhood or adolescence, these individuals begin to collude with the parent in symptom production and eventually assume responsibility for presentation symptoms.

We often see a continuum of collusion in FDBP/FD. Some children may have no knowledge of how their symptoms are being produced (Naive). Some children may "go along" with the parent's story without mentioning to medical personnel why they appear ill (Passive Acceptance). Other children may actively participate in the creation of illness by fabricating or exaggerating symptoms (Active Participation). At the end of the continuum are children or adolescents who may actually participate in creating their own symptoms and engage in self-harm in order to induce illness (Active Harm). It is also possible for an adolescent to develop FD without being a victim of FDBP, as in the case of a thirteen-year-old boy who produced symptoms such as lesions by scraping his skin, and weight loss by surreptitiously pouring out liquid nutritional supplement instead of drinking it. There appeared to be no parental involvement in the development and presentation of his symptoms.

The diagnosis of Factitious Disorder is difficult; it is frequently made over time after careful documentation of symptoms and responses to treatment as well as verification of all details provided by the patient. When FD is suspected and the degree of functional impairment is substantial, hospitalization on a medical/psychiatric unit is recommended to obtain closer surveillance of the patient while a thorough psychiatric evaluation is conducted. In some cases, it will not be possible to establish with certainty that a patient is, in fact, creating or fabricating his or her illness. When this is the case, the mental health professional and physician will need to work closely to minimize unnecessary medical intervention.

If it is established that a parent is playing a role in the presentation of symptoms, the issue of child abuse (related to unnecessary invasive procedures and restricted development) must be addressed and the appropriate child protection agency contacted. Enlisting the aid of child protection agencies in such cases is sometimes difficult as their workers often lack knowledge about the syndrome and are generally reluctant, as is the public, to believe that a mother would harm her child in this way. More recently, however, I have found caseworkers to be better informed about the syndrome and willing to work collaboratively to ensure the well-being of the child.

Treatment Issues in Factitious Disorders

Little is known about the psychology of adults with FD because these individuals generally lack the motivation to engage in ongoing psychotherapy. Even less is known about the syndrome in adolescents. In my experience, many of the adolescent patients identified as engaging in factitious behavior actually have some type of mild organic illness that they willfully exaggerate.

Some therapists have suggested that factitious illness may be an instance of somatization that is suggestive of an individual's unstable sense of self associated with disturbances in his or her sense of reality or in reality testing. Furthermore, it has been suggested that psychotherapeutic success may involve helping a patient to identify and articulate emotional experience, form a relationship that is no longer based on illness, and develop a more authentic and consolidated sense of self. An approach similar to that outlined for somatization may be useful to start, with a gradual shift from talking about illness and somatic symptoms to exploring and enhancing a patient's functioning in other areas of his life.

I worked with one patient who had a pattern of willfully exaggerating asthma symptoms. Early in therapy I asked her if there would be any disadvantages associated with *not* having a chronic illness. She stated that having a chronic illness was the thing that made her "special." Over the course of therapy she began to become increasingly involved in academic and social pursuits.

Illness began to interfere with attainment of her new, developmentally appropriate social and academic goals. Her identity began to shift from being an ill child to being a successful and popular teenager. This shift was accompanied by a reduction in her illness complaints, although she now reports that she wants to attend medical school and become a pulmonologist.

Diagnostic Dilemmas

The distinction between chronic illness, somatization, and factitious illness is not always easy to make. As illustrated in Figure 7.1, differential diagnosis is often complicated by the frequent overlap of these syndromes.

A patient with a chronic illness may also somatize—for example, a thirteen-year-old boy with leukemia who complained of stomachaches and headaches when he became anxious. Factitious

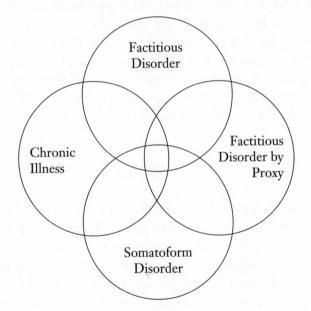

Figure 7.1
Overlap of Chronic Illness, Somatization,
and Factitious Illness

Disorder and Factitious Disorder by Proxy can coexist with true physical illness and may present as a pattern of "illness exaggeration." An example is a fourteen-year-old girl with documented mild asthma who was brought to the pediatrician's office on repeated occasions following telephone calls from her mother who reported symptoms of a severe attack. When she was examined, her symptoms rarely corresponded to her mother's phone report. Some have also suggested that children and adolescents who are victims of Factitious Disorder by Proxy may be at increased risk for the development of somatization because of the tendency of the parent to be responsive to the child primarily through bodily needs.

Unfortunately, diagnostic clarity is difficult if not impossible to achieve in some cases. I had a case of a twelve-year-old boy with a documented immunodeficiency whose mother repeatedly presented him as being more ill than diagnostic tests indicated. At times, the boy appeared to collude with his mother and would corroborate his mother's story about the illness—for example, confirming his mother's report that he was in a great deal of pain despite a complete lack of behavioral evidence that he was experiencing discomfort. In addition, however, during times of stress he also appeared to experience somatic symptoms that did not seem to be consciously produced.

FAMILIES

Although the focus of this chapter has been on individual therapy, it is important to remember that adolescents come with families. Chronic illness places extraordinary demands on the entire family. The psychological functioning of adolescents is integrally related to how their families are functioning, making family therapy at least as important as individual therapy in many cases.

I find that my role in family work with chronically ill adolescents is varied and ranges from educator ("This is normal and expected behavior for a chronically ill teenager"), to conflict resolver (either between parents and adolescents, or between parents and the medical team), to crisis counselor. Drawing on the work of Michael White, I attempt to adopt a collaborative stance with the family that is respectful of their strengths. We work together as a team to map the influence of illness in their lives and identify ways they can take a stand in opposition to the negative influence of illness and support the normal development of their adolescent.

Of course, not all families are enthusiastic participants in this process at first, particularly when the issues identified by the pediatrician as needing mental health intervention do not coincide with the parents' perceptions of the situation. As with the reluctant adolescent, the clinician will need to pay close attention to the development of a working alliance with the family that is based on the view that therapy can be a helpful process to them. Helping the family to define the problem in their own terms, and supporting the fact that their definition may be quite different from that of the referring pediatrician can lay the foundation for therapeutic success.

Adolescent somatizers often come from families with a history of somatization and other psychiatric disorders. Success in individual therapy is often in jeopardy unless the role that illness plays in the family is adequately addressed. Some have described the process of somatization as stemming from family myths that prescribe dilemmas while forbidding the kind of conversation needed to resolve them. Family therapy can be a vehicle for identifying the family myths that bind communication, allowing the adolescent and family to oppose the influence of the myths in their lives.

REACTIONS OF THE THERAPIST

Working with adolescents in a medical setting can be demanding and stressful. It is, of course, always vital that a therapist monitor her own reactions in the context of therapy. Working with somatizing patients can be long and frustrating, and the life and death issues encountered when working with chronically ill patients can exact an emotional toll on psychotherapists.

Some common indications of countertransference reactions include the following:

- Withdrawing from the patient
- Having difficulty engaging with very sick or dying patients
- Spending more time talking with nurses than with the family and patient
- Missing appointments or always passing by when a patient is getting tests or in the middle of a treatment
- Wanting to transfer the care of a patient because you feel hopeless or helpless
- Being convinced of the medical or psychological origin of the problem
- Getting drawn in by a patient
- Feeling overwhelmed by the medical problems
- Feeling bored by the endless repetition of complaints
- Referring the patient for a medication evaluation in the middle of treatment

The therapist should be alert to the signs of countertransference and consider supervision or consultation with a colleague when it is clear that her reactions are interfering with the therapeutic relationship.

Despite the demands, or perhaps because of the unique challenges, working with adolescents with medical and psychosomatic illnesses can be exciting and rewarding. To be on the front lines of the interface between mind and body is endlessly fascinating and provides rich therapeutic experiences. A statement made by J. C. Williams in 1836 captures the distinctive appeal of this type of clinical work:

No man, I am satisfied, can ever be a sound Pathologist, or judicious Practitioner, who devotes his attention to any of these systems [the mental and the organic] in preference to or [to] the exclusion of the other; through life they are perpetually acting and inseparably linked together.

NOTES

P. 265, *mental health conditions can significantly increase:* Strosahl, K. (1994). Entering the new frontier of managed mental health care: Gold mines and land mines. *Cognitive and Behavioral Practice, 1,* 5–23.

P. 265, *Some believe that the mental health:* Strosahl, K. (1994). Entering the new frontier of managed mental health care: Gold mines and land mines. *Cognitive and Behavioral Practice, 1,* 5–23.

P. 266, *components of a thorough psychosocial assessment:* Edwards, M., & Finney, J. (1994). Somatoform disorders: Psychological issues. In R. A. Olson, L. L. Mullins, J. B. Gillman, & J. M. Chaney (Eds.), *The sourcebook of pediatric psychology.* Boston: Allyn & Bacon.

P. 270, *This understanding will suggest:* Wilkes, T.C.R., & Belsher, G. (1994). The initial phase of cognitive therapy: From assessment to setting goals. In T.C.R. Wilkes, G. Belsher, A.J. Rush, & E. Frank (Eds.), *Cognitive therapy for depressed adolescents.* New York: Guilford Press.

P. 270, *Chronic illness has been defined:* Pless, I. B., Cripps, H. A., Davies, J. M., & Wadsworth, M.E.J. (1989). Chronic physical illness in childhood: Psychological and social effects in adolescence and adult life. *Developmental Medicine and Child Neurology, 31,* 746–755.

P. 270, *As many as 35 percent of American children:* Newacheck, P., & Taylor, W. (1992). Childhood chronic illness: Prevalence, severity, and impact. *American Journal of Public Health, 82,* 364–371.

P. 271, *substantial improvements in the survival rates:* Koocher, G. P. (1986). Psychosocial issues during the acute treatment of pediatric cancer. *Cancer, 58,* 468–472.

P. 271, *median survival age:* FitzSimmons, S. C. (1994). The changing epidemiology of cystic fibrosis. *Current Problems in Pediatrics, 24*(5), 171–179.

P. 271, *The normative tasks of adolescence:* Rowland, J. H. (1989). Developmental stage and adaptation: Child and adolescent model. In J. C. Holland &

J. H. Rowland (Eds.), *Handbook of psychooncology: Psychological care of the patient with cancer.* New York: Oxford University Press.

P. 272, *Important dimensions include:* Lavigne, J. V., & Faier-Routman, J. (1992). Psychological adjustment to pediatric physical disorders: A meta-analytic review. *Journal of Pediatric Psychology, 17*(2), 133–157.

P. 276, *It has been estimated that close to 20 percent:* Kashani, J. H., Beck, N. C., & Hoeper, E. W. (1987). Psychiatric disorders in a community sample of adolescents. *American Journal of Psychiatry, 144,* 584–589.

P. 282, *Reassurance, guidance, and "normalizing" feelings:* In J. C. Holland & J. H. Rowland (Eds.), *Handbook of psychooncology: Psychological care of the patient with cancer.* New York: Oxford University Press.

P. 282, *It is important to encourage:* Rowland, J. H. (1989). Developmental stage and adaptation: Child and adolescent model. In J. C. Holland & J. H. Rowland (Eds.), *Handbook of psychooncology: Psychological care of the patient with cancer.* New York: Oxford University Press.

P. 283, *exploration of the origin:* Freeman, A., Pretzer, J., Fleming, B., & Simon, K. M. (1990). *Clinical applications of cognitive therapy.* New York: Plenum Press.

P. 286, *Somatization has been defined:* Kellner, R. (1991). *Psychosomatic syndromes and somatic symptoms.* Washington, DC: American Psychiatric Press.

P. 286, *The somatic symptoms are thought:* Kellner, R. (1991). *Psychosomatic syndromes and somatic symptoms.* Washington, DC: American Psychiatric Press.

P. 286, *review of the literature on somatization:* Campo, J. V., & Fritsch, S. L. (1994). Somatization in children and adolescents. *Journal of the American Academy of Child and Adolescent Psychiatry, 33*(9), 1223–1235.

P. 286, *DSM-IV contains a variety:* American Psychiatric Association. (1994). *Diagnostic and statistical manual of mental disorders* (DSM-IV) (4th ed.). Washington, DC: Author.

P. 286, *26 percent of the sample of adult:* Shorter, E., Abbey, S. E., Gillies, L. A., Singh, M., & Lipowski, Z. J. (1992). Inpatient treatment of persistent somatization. *Psychosomatics, 33*(3), 295–301.

P. 287, *Numerous studies have found:* Edwards, P. W., Zeichner, A., Kuczmierczyk, A. R., & Boczkowski, J. (1985). Familial pain models: The relationship between family history of pain and current pain experience. *Pain, 21,* 379–384; Garber, J., Zeman, J., & Walker, L. S. (1990). Recurrent abdominal pain in children: Psychiatric diagnoses and parental psychopathology. *Journal of the American Academy of Child and Adolescent Psychiatry, 29,* 648–656; Walker, L. S., & Greene, J. W. (1989). Children with recurrent abdominal pain and their parents: More somatic complaints, anxiety, and depression than other patient families? *Journal of Pediatric Psychology, 14,* 231–243.

P. 287, *association between somatization:* Cloniger, C. R., Reich, T., & Guze, S. B. (1975). The multifactorial model of disease transmission: III. Familial relationship between sociopathy and hysteria (Briquet's syndrome). *British Journal of Psychiatry, 127,* 23–32.

P. 287, *Psychodynamic theorists view somatization:* Simmon, G. E., (1991). Somatization and psychiatric disorder. In L. J. Kirmayer & J. M. Robbins (Eds.), *Current concepts of somatization: Research and clinical perspectives.* Washington, DC: American Psychiatric Press.

P. 288, *adaptive style of "repression":* Jensen, M. R. (1987). Psychological factors predicting the course of breast cancer. *Journal of Personality, 55,* 317–342; Weinberger, D. (1990). The construct validity of the repressive coping style. In J. L. Singer (Ed.), *Repression and dissociation: Implications for personality theory, psychopathology, and health* (pp. 337–385). Chicago: University of Chicago Press.

P. 288, *construct of "alexithymia":* Lesser, I. M. (1981). A review of the alexithymia concept. *Psychosomatic Medicine, 43,* 531–543.

P. 288, *child's somatic complaints may be reinforced:* Mechanic, D. (1964). The influence of mothers on their children's health attitudes and behavior. *Pediatrics, 34,* 444–453; Lehmkuhl, G., Blanz, B., Lehmkuhl, U., & Braun-Scharm, H. (1989. Conversion disorder: Symptomatology and course in childhood and adolescence. *European Archives of Psychiatry and Clinical Neuroscience, 238,* 155–160.

P. 288, *School or other unpleasant activities:* Faull, C., & Nicol, A. R. (1986). Abdominal pain in six-year-olds: An epidemiological study in a new town. *Journal of Child Psychology and Psychiatry, 27,* 251–260; Pantell, R. H., & Goodman, B. W. (1983). Adolescent chest pain: A prospective study. *Pediatrics, 71,* 881–887.

P. 288, *Family systems theorists:* Mullins, L. I., & Olson, R. A. (1990). Familial factors in the etiology, maintenance, and treatment of somatoform disorders in children. *Family Systems Medicine, 8,* 159–175.

P. 288, *somatic symptoms as a form of communication:* Goodyer, I. M., & Taylor, D. C. (1985). Hysteria. *Archives of Disease in Childhood, 60,* 680–681; Maisami, M., & Freeman, J. M. (1987). Conversion reactions in children as body language: A combined child psychiatry/neurology team approach to the management of functional neurologic disorders in children. *Pediatrics, 80,* 46–52.

P. 288, *Somatosensory amplification:* Barsky, A. J. (1992). Amplification, somatization, and the somatoform disorders. *Psychosomatics, 33,* 28–34.

P. 288, *negative life events:* Pantell, R. H., & Goodman, B. W. (1983). Adolescent chest pain: A prospective study. *Pediatrics, 71,* 881–887.

P. 288, *recent loss:* Maloney, M. J. (1980). Diagnosing hysterical conversion reactions in children. *Journal of Pediatrics, 97,* 1016–1020.

P. 288, *traumatic childhood experiences:* Klevan, J. L., & DeJong, A. R. (1990). Urinary tract symptoms and urinary tract infection following sexual abuse. *American Journal of Diseases of Children, 144,* 242–244; Gross, M. (1979). Incestuous rape: A cause for hysterical seizures in 4 adolescent girls. *American Journal of Orthopsychiatry, 49,* 704–708; LaBarbera, J. D., & Dozier, J. E. (1980). Hysterical seizures: The role of sexual exploitation. *Psychosomatics, 21*(11), 897–903.

P. 288, *Pediatric medical illness:* Livingston, R. (1993). Children of people with somatization disorder. *Journal of the American Academy of Child and Adolescent Psychiatry, 32,* 536–544.

P. 288, *Munchausen Syndrome by Proxy:* McGuire, T. L., & Feldman, K. W. (1989). Psychologic morbidity of children subjected to Munchausen Syndrome by Proxy. *Pediatrics, 83,* 289–292.

P. 289, *four cases of presumed psychogenic vomiting:* Gonzalez-Heydrich, J., Kerner, J. A., & Steiner, H. (1991). Testing the psychogenic vomiting diagnosis: Four pediatric patients. *American Journal of Diseases of Children, 145,* 913–916.

P. 292, *psychophysiological demonstrations:* Wickramasekera, I. (1989). Enabling the somatizing patient to exit the somatic closet: A high-risk model. *Psychotherapy, 26,* 530–544.

P. 296, *ten-bed psychosomatic unit:* Steiner, H., Sanders, M., Canning, E. H., & Litt, I. (1994). A model for managing clinical and personnel issues in c-l psychiatry: The Department of Pediatric Psychiatry at Children's Hospital at Stanford. *Psychosomatics, 35*(1), 73–79.

P. 297, *continuum of collusion in FDBP/FD:* Sanders, M. J. (in press). *Clinical Psychology Review,* Special section: Input of family variables on child adjustment.

P. 298, *Some therapists have suggested that factitious illness:* Spivak, H., Rodin, G., & Sutherland, A. (1994). The psychology of factitious disorder: A reconsideration. *Psychosomatics, 35*(1), 25–34.

P. 298, *psychotherapeutic success:* Spivak, H., Rodin, G., & Sutherland, A. (1994). The psychology of factitious disorder: A reconsideration. *Psychosomatics, 35*(1), 25–34.

P. 300, *"illness exaggeration":* Masterson, J., Dunworth, R., & Williams, N. (1988). Extreme illness exaggeration in pediatric patients: A variant of

Munchausen's by Proxy? *American Journal of Orthopsychiatry, 58*(2), 188–195.

P. 300, *Some have also suggested that children:* McQuire, T. L., & Feldman, K. W. (1989). Psychologic morbidity of children subjected to Munchausen Syndrome by Proxy. *Pediatrics, 83*(2), 289–292; Barsky, A. J. (1992). Amplification, somatization, and the somatoform disorders. *Psychosomatics, 33,* 28–34; Guedeney, A. (1993). Hysterical conversion and developmental psychiatry. *British Journal of Psychiatry, 162,* 571–572.

P. 301, *the work of Michael White:* White, M. (1989). The externalizing of the problem and the re-authoring of lives and relationships. In M. White (Ed.), *Selected papers.* Adelaide, Australia: Dulwhich Centre Publications; White, M., & Epston, D. (1990). *Narrative means to therapeutic ends.* New York: Norton.

P. 301, *Some have described the process of somatization:* Griffith, J. L., & Griffith, M. E. (1994). *The body speaks: Therapeutic dialogues for mind-body problems.* New York: Basic Books.

P. 303, *No man, I am satisfied:* Williams, J. C., cited in Kellner, R. (1991). *Psychosomatic syndromes and somatic symptoms.* Washington, DC: American Psychiatric Press.

8

SCHIZOPHRENIA AND PSYCHOTIC DISORDERS

Margo Thienemann and Richard J. Shaw

The diagnosis of schizophrenia in a young adolescent is one of the most traumatic and devastating events that can happen in a family. For reasons that to a large extent still remain obscure, adolescents and young adults in the prime of their lives can develop bizarre and bewildering symptoms that in the majority of cases herald the onset of a lifelong and often quite disabling illness. Here is a classic example:

NICHOLAS

Nicholas, a healthy and happy seventeen-year-old adolescent, was raised in an affluent, middle-class suburb just south of San Francisco. His father was a partner in a successful law firm in the city, and his mother lectured in physics at a local university. After gaining admission to a prestigious Ivy League school on the east coast, Nicholas appeared destined to follow in the footsteps of his talented parents. He was an articulate and adventurous boy, who excelled academically and did reasonably well socially. It was not until a few weeks past his seventeenth birthday that Nicholas first started to develop the symptoms of an illness that would forever affect the stability and happiness of his family.

Just prior to his planned high school graduation, Nicholas became convinced that his bedroom was being bugged by the chief executive officer of a local computer software company. He believed that a control station had been set up in a neighboring house and stated that he could hear officials of the company talking about him and making derogatory remarks outside his bedroom window at night. He believed that the agents were monitoring his activities using a "heat-sensitive thermonuclear camera" that was able to videotape his activities through the walls of the house. He believed that videotapes of him using the bathroom were being shown on closed circuit television at his school. Shortly after this, he began refusing to go to school because of fears of being ridiculed by the other students. He became increasingly paranoid and suspected that agents were impersonating his parents in order to gain access to the house. At this point he was hospitalized on a psychiatric unit in a local hospital for a full diagnostic evaluation.

Nicholas never made a full recovery from this episode. He was eventually given a diagnosis of paranoid schizophrenia and started on antipsychotic medications that were somewhat effective in reducing his level of paranoia. He was able to return home but unable to graduate from high school. Six months later he was rehospitalized following a serious suicide attempt; he had tried to hang himself in his bedroom in an attempt to escape his imagined persecutors. In his more lucid moments, Nicholas was able to acknowledge that he had an illness and to speak articulately about the devastating effects of the symptoms on every aspect of his life.

Nicholas's parents are still struggling to adjust to the dramatic change this illness has brought to their lives. The much-anticipated high school graduation became for them a transition to a life of learning how to support a son who is now unlikely ever to hold a permanent job.

This is not an uncommon story for thousands of families in the United States each year. Working with the patients and their families is one of the most challenging and difficult tasks in the field of psychiatry. In this chapter, we attempt to provide some understanding regarding the nature of this illness, and a view of how therapists can intervene to bring some hope into the lives of their patients.

EARLY ONSET SCHIZOPHRENIA

Schizophrenia has been described in children as young as five years of age. The term *childhood onset schizophrenia* is generally used in children with the onset of psychotic symptoms prior to puberty, and *early onset schizophrenia* to those with onset prior to sixteen or seventeen years of age. Until relatively recently, childhood schizophrenia has often been grouped with other disorders of early childhood, which include autism, affective disorders, and mental retardation. It is now well established that schizophrenia with onset in childhood and early adolescence can be differentiated from these other disorders, based on the symptoms, chronological course, and evidence from genetic and biological studies.

Although there is considerable interest regarding the reasons that schizophrenia presents in these younger age groups, there is general consensus that schizophrenia with early onset should not be considered a discrete entity from schizophrenia in adults. In addition, first psychotic episodes in schizophrenia occur most commonly during adolescence, by which time the symptoms are indistinguishable from those in adults.

DIAGNOSTIC CRITERIA

The criteria used to diagnose schizophrenia have undergone many revisions in the past thirty years. Recent classification systems emphasize the importance of identifying both cross-sectional and longitudinal criteria. Cross-sectional criteria refer to the acute symptoms, as assessed during a mental status examination, whereas longitudinal criteria refer to the course of the symptoms over time. The chronology of the symptoms helps differentiate a number of psychiatric, medical, and substance-induced disorders that all present with psychotic symptoms.

Diagnostic criteria from the DSM-IV, include both cross-sectional and longitudinal criteria, in addition to the so-called deficit symptoms. According to DSM-IV, schizophrenia is diagnosed on the basis of characteristic positive or negative symptoms present for a significant portion of time during a one-month period; dysfunction in one or more major areas of functioning or self-care, or in the case of children and adolescents, a failure to achieve an expected level of interpersonal, academic, or occupational achievement; and continuous signs of disturbance for at least six months (Table 8.1). In addition, Schizoaffective Disorder, Mood Disorder with Psychotic Symptoms, and disorders due to the effects of a substance or general medical condition must be excluded. If there is a history of Autistic Disorder or other pervasive developmental disorder, schizophrenia is diagnosed only if psychotic symptoms are present for at least one month.

EPIDEMIOLOGY

Schizophrenia has an incidence of approximately 1 percent in the general population. Schizophrenia in early childhood is a relatively rare disorder, with an incidence estimated as fifty times less frequent than schizophrenia with onset in adulthood. Early onset schizophrenia nonetheless makes up a significant proportion of children seen in psychiatric clinics, accounting for 5 percent of referrals to outpatient clinics. The incidence rises rapidly in adolescence, accounting for 3 percent of first time hospitalizations in those age ten to fourteen years, and 21 percent in those age fifteen to nineteen years. Schizophrenia creates an enormous economic burden, both in direct costs related to psychiatric treatment, and in indirect costs related to loss of income and productivity.

The age of onset for schizophrenia appears to be somewhat younger for males than for females. The mean age for the first episode in males is twenty-one to twenty-two years, whereas in women it is twenty-six to twenty-seven years. The male to female ratio of schizophrenia is 2 to 1 in early childhood; in adults the ratio is equal.

Patients with schizophrenia are less likely to marry, and their fertility rates are lower than in the general population. The incidence of schizophrenia is higher in individuals of lower social class, which is correlated with educational level. No association has been found between race and diagnosis, and the incidence of schizophrenia appears to be very similar worldwide.

Schizophrenics have a very high rate of suicide attempts relative to the general population. Up to one-third of patients will attempt suicide, and 10 percent are successful. Those at particular risk are individuals with early age of onset, chronic relapsing course, depressive symptoms, and a higher level of education or premorbid functioning. Suicide attempts are often impulsive and lethal, making it difficult for caregivers to intervene.

SYMPTOMS OF SCHIZOPHRENIA

Schizophrenia is an illness that can present with diverse clinical symptoms. Often there is an initial prodromal period, followed by the sudden onset of psychotic or positive symptoms. These are generally easily recognizable, although not diagnostic of schizophrenia. The more pervasive, and potentially more disabling, deficit symptoms or negative symptoms develop over time. The patient may not be aware of these more subtle changes, and it is important to validate the history with information from other sources, particularly family members.

Table 8.1
DSM-IV Criteria for Schizophrenia

A. *Characteristic symptoms:* Two (or more) of the following, each present for a significant portion of a one-month period (or less if successfully treated):

1. Delusions

2. Hallucinations

3. Disorganized speech (such as frequent derailment or incoherence)

4. Grossly disorganized or catatonic behavior

5. Negative symptoms, such as affective flattening, alogia, or avolition

B. *Social/occupational dysfunction:* For a significant portion of time since the onset of the disturbance, one or more major areas of functioning (work, interpersonal relations, or self-care) are markedly below the level achieved prior to the onset. When the onset is in childhood or adolescence, there is failure to achieve expected level of interpersonal, academic, or occupational achievement.

C. *Duration:* Continuous signs of the disturbance persist for at least six months, including at least one month of symptoms (or less if successfully treated) that meet Criterion A and may include periods of prodromal or residual symptoms. During prodromal or residual periods, signs of the disturbance may manifest only in negative symptoms or in two or more symptoms listed in Criterion A in an attenuated form (such as odd beliefs, unusual perceptual experiences).

D. *Schizoaffective and Mood Disorder exclusion:* Schizoaffective Disorder and Mood Disorder with Psychotic Features have been ruled out because either (1) no major depressive, manic, or mixed episodes have occurred concurrently with the active-phase symptoms or (2)

Table 8.1 *(continued)*

mood episodes have occurred during active-phase symptoms, but their total duration has been brief relative to the duration of the active and residual periods.

E. *Substance/general medical condition exclusion:* The disturbance is not due to the direct physiological effects of a substance (such as a drug of abuse, a medication) or a general medical condition.

F. *Relationship to Pervasive Developmental Disorder:* If there is a history of Pervasive Developmental Disorder, the additional diagnosis of Schizophrenia made only if prominent delusions or hallucinations also present for at least a month (or less if successfully treated).

G. *Classification of longitudinal course* (can be applied only after at least one year has elapsed since the initial onset of active-phase symptoms):

1. Episodic with interepisode residual symptoms: When the course is characterized by episodes in which Criterion A for Schizophrenia is met and there are clinically significant residual symptoms between the episodes. Specify if with prominent negative symptoms.

2. Episodic with no interepisode residual symptoms

3. Continuous: When characteristic symptoms of Criterion A are met throughout all (or most) of the course. Specify if with prominent negative symptoms.

4. Single episode in partial remission

5. Single episode in full remission

6. Other or unspecified pattern

Note: Only one Criterion A symptom is required if delusions are bizarre or hallucinations consist of a voice keeping up a running commentary on the person's behavior or thoughts, or two or more voices conversing with each other.

Prodromal Symptoms

Up to 90 percent of adolescents diagnosed with schizophrenia have a variety of nonspecific premorbid personality traits, which include poor peer relationships, social withdrawal, lower intelligence scores compared to normals, poor school performance, and general difficulties with premorbid adjustment. Schizotypal and schizoid personality traits are reported more frequently in these individuals. Prodromal symptoms may also include delays in achieving normal developmental milestones.

Positive Symptoms

Positive symptoms refer to those symptoms seen during acute psychotic episodes, indicating that the patient has lost contact with reality. Although these symptoms are required at some point in the course of the illness for a diagnosis of schizophrenia to be made, their presence does not imply schizophrenia. Positive symptoms may be seen in any psychotic illness.

PETER

Peter was a healthy and well-adjusted fifteen-year-old boy, the son of two professional parents. He was described as an outgoing and gregarious child, well liked by his peers, and a successful and competent student.

Peter's first psychiatric difficulties appeared to start while he was on tour with his high school basketball team, his first major trip away from home. Peter's coach called his parents to report that he had been acting strangely, barricading himself in a hotel bedroom and refusing to come out despite reassurances that he was safe. He was also noted to be talking to himself in the hotel room. The coach was finally able to gain access to the room and found Peter hiding in one of the closets, with his eyes tightly closed, moaning that "they were coming to get him."

After being escorted to the local hospital, Peter was evaluated by the on-call psychiatrist, who was able to elicit from Peter the history that he believed that the "terminators" were planning to inject him with the AIDS virus. Peter reported that there were several members of this group who were tracking his movements with a radio transmitter implanted into one of his teeth and that they were able to monitor his thoughts using "mind control." Peter reported being able to hear two of the men discussing how they planned to infect him, even as he was being interviewed by the psychiatrist.

The differential diagnosis at this time was of an acute psychotic episode, of unknown etiology. He was transferred back to a hospital close to his home for further evaluation and treatment.

Delusions. Delusions are fixed, false beliefs that have no basis in reality and are not shared by members of the individual's culture. The beliefs are maintained despite compelling evidence to the contrary. They may be of a persecutory, grandiose, religious, sexual, or somatic nature. In schizophrenia, delusions are most commonly of a persecutory or somatic type, and vary according to the cultural or social background of the subject. Delusions are less frequently seen in early onset compared to adult onset schizophrenia.

Hallucinations. Hallucinations are perceptions experienced as originating from the outside world, without the presence of an external stimulus. They may be experienced as voices, visions, unpleasant tastes and odors, or tactile feelings on the skin.

Hallucinations are the most commonly reported symptoms in schizophrenia. Auditory hallucinations are present in 80 percent to 90 percent of subjects. Visual hallucinations are less common and should raise the suspicion of a medical or neurological illness. Tactile hallucinations are much less frequent and often indicate a substance-induced psychosis. Hallucinations that occur when an individual is falling asleep or waking up are termed *hypnogogic* or *hypnopompic* hallucinations, respectively, and may be a normal occurrence in individuals without any psychiatric illness.

Thought Disorder. Disorders of thought, expressed in the content of the speech are characteristic of schizophrenia. Thought Disorder may be reflected in illogical speech ("I missed school yesterday because the birds were migrating"), impoverished speech ("Well, I don't know . . . you know . . . its like . . . um, that's how it is") and loosening of associations ("I saw the man sitting on the tree branch. I bet I can take a stick and hit a rock over that fence").

Bizarre or Disorganized Behavior. Many patients with schizophrenia show bizarre patterns of behavior that may violate normal social conventions. Behaviors include wearing odd clothing, shouting obscenities, masturbating in public, or rummaging through garbage cans. Patients with catatonia by contrast may adopt bizarre, fixed postures, remaining immobile for long periods of time. Patients may also become irritable and excitable, acting impulsively in response to their delusions and hallucinations.

Negative Symptoms

Negative symptoms are more difficult to characterize than the positive symptoms as they represent a deficit in normal behavior. Their presence is associated with a general decline in the person's level of functioning, and they are often unresponsive to treatment. Although less dramatic than positive symptoms, their impact in the long term may be more profound.

VANESSA

Vanessa, an eighteen-year-old girl, was diagnosed with schizophrenia two years previously, after a six-month episode during which she expressed delusional beliefs about being the Virgin Mary and of having powers to work miracles. Following an extended hospitalization, Vanessa was able to return home, but was not able to graduate from high school. She became increasingly isolated socially and rarely left home. She stopped washing and showering, and usually slept in her clothes. At family gatherings, Vanessa remained withdrawn, failing to make eye contact, showing little facial expression and answering questions only monosyllabically.

Affect. Affect is characteristically described as *flat* or *blunted*, terms that make reference to the lack of appropriate emotional expressiveness in a person's speech and facial expression. Patients may make poor eye contact and fail to smile or laugh in response to normal social cues. These symptoms may have a profound effect on the nature of the subject's interpersonal relationships. Patients may also be described as having bizarre or inappropriate affect, such as laughing or smiling inappropriately in response to sad situations.

Asociality. Subjects with schizophrenia frequently have impoverished social relationships. They may have no close friends or contacts outside the immediate family circle and they lack the ability or motivation to initiate new friendships. Patients may also fail to maintain relationships that exist prior to the onset of their illness.

Alogia. *Alogia* is a general term to describe the impoverished thought processes seen in patients with schizophrenia. This may be reflected by a reduction in the amount of spontaneous speech, long pauses before responses to questions, or interruptions in the flow of the speech.

Avolition. *Avolition* refers to a person's lack of motivation with respect to school work or recreational interests. Subjects appear to lack the initiative and drive to succeed academically or to pursue career goals. Whereas adults characteristically show a deterioration in their level of functioning, children and adolescents additionally demonstrate a failure to achieve appropriate and expected developmental milestones. Schizophrenic patients characteristically pay little attention to their hygiene, grooming, or physical appearance.

Course of Illness

The first psychotic episode in schizophrenia occurs most commonly in late adolescence, with a peak incidence between the ages of twenty and twenty-one years. The symptoms in this age group are indistinguishable from those of adults. Schizophrenia is very rarely seen in individuals younger than five years of age. Psychotic symptoms vary little during the prepubertal years, but symptoms do become more complex with age. A majority of patients exhibit a number of nonspecific prodromal symptoms, as noted previously.

The onset of schizophrenia is often insidious, although it is not uncommon for someone to present with the sudden onset of psychotic symptoms in response to a psychosocial stressor. Approximately 24 percent of adolescents have just one episode of psychotic symptoms, but the majority experience frequent relapses and a general deterioration from their premorbid level of functioning. A residual state may develop after the initial psychotic episode, characterized by symptoms somewhat similar to those of the prodromal period, including social withdrawal, apathy, and prominent negative symptoms.

Etiology

The etiology of schizophrenia is probably multifactorial, and most models propose an interaction between an underlying genetic vulnerability and an environmental insult. Genetic studies provide strong evidence for a heritable component in adult schizophrenia. Although the incidence of schizophrenia in the general population is only 1 percent, this figure rises to 15 percent in people with one schizophrenic parent, and to 30 percent to 40 percent in individuals with two schizophrenic parents. Monozygotic twins are three to four times more likely to show concordance for schizophrenia than dizygotic twins. The risk of schizophrenia is also increased in children who have a history of complications during pregnancy, prematurity, birth trauma, and exposure to viral illnesses early in life. Infants often have lower birth weights and smaller head circumferences. They may also fail to meet normal developmental milestones during the first two years of life. It is not known whether these early insults result in changes to the brain structure, which later lead to the development of schizophrenia, or whether a genetic predisposition to schizophrenia disrupts brain development leading to the expression of symptoms in adolescence.

Neuropsychological tests in children with schizophrenia have revealed dysfunction in certain areas of the brain, including the region known as the prefrontal cortex. Studies of adult schizophrenics have revealed abnormalities in brain structure, specifically an increase in the size of the ventricles, and in some cases, a decrease in the size of the cerebral cortex.

DIFFERENTIAL DIAGNOSIS

The diagnosis of schizophrenia in adolescence should always be one of exclusion. Multiple disorders may present with psychotic symptoms, and many of them are treatable. Even in cases where substance abuse and medical disorders have been excluded, it is necessary to await confirmation from the chronological course before making a diagnosis of schizophrenia.

Pervasive Developmental Disorders

Pervasive developmental disorders (PDD), which include Childhood Disintegrative Disorder, Pervasive Developmental Disorder, and Asperger's Syndrome, generally have a distinct course and features that distinguish them from schizophrenia (Table 8.2). PDD is characterized by a person's failure to meet expected developmental milestones, and in the majority of cases is diagnosed in the first two to three years of life. Symptoms include impaired social relationships; impaired verbal and nonverbal communication, including the idiosyncratic use of words and echolalia, a tendency to repeat phrases; and stereotyped body movements. Delusions and hallucinations are rare. Schizophrenia by contrast rarely presents before the age of five years. There is often deterioration following a period of normal development, although as noted earlier, prodromal symptoms may precede the onset of psychotic symptoms.

Schizophreniform Disorder; Brief Reactive Psychosis

Children who present with symptoms of schizophrenia, but who recover without residual symptoms within six months, are classified as having Schizophreniform Disorder. Many of these individuals are later diagnosed with schizophrenia. Brief Reactive Psychosis is characterized by the onset of acute psychotic symptoms, sometimes lasting only a few hours, in response to an acute stressor. Individuals must make a full recovery to premorbid functioning within one month to qualify for this diagnosis.

Affective Disorders

Affective disorders in adolescence include Bipolar Disorder and Major Depression. In Bipolar Disorder, patients may develop both manic and depressive symptoms. Manic episodes are characterized by periods of elevated mood, grandiosity, decreased need for sleep, irritability, and pressured speech. In severe mania, patients may become acutely psychotic, with hallucinations and delusions, consistent with the themes of grandiosity, power, and special identity or relationship to a deity or famous person. Children with symptoms of depression may also report psychotic symptoms that include hallucinations, particularly voices of a derogatory nature, and less commonly, delusions.

Table 8.2
Differential Diagnosis of Schizophrenia and Pervasive
Developmental Disorder (PDD)

	Schizophrenia	*PDD*
Age of onset	Five years or older	Three years
Intelligence	Low average	Retarded range
Psychotic symptoms	Present	Absent
Social relationships	Impaired	Impaired
Language development	Normal	Delayed
Family history	Schizophrenia	PDD, Autism

It may not be possible to differentiate a child with Bipolar Disorder who is in a manic episode from one with schizophrenia who is in an acute psychotic episode. Some studies have suggested that the initial diagnoses may be inaccurate in up to 50 percent of these cases. When there is uncertainty, it is better to defer diagnosis until the different chronological courses of these two illnesses bring clarification.

Obsessive-Compulsive Disorder

Adolescents with Obsessive-Compulsive Disorder (OCD) may report intrusive obsessional thoughts as well as compulsions to act in a repetitive and stereotyped fashion to neutralize a dreaded yet improbable event. The adolescent may report fears of contamination and observe bizarre rituals in response to these concerns. There are times when these symptoms may appear to have a psychotic quality. In addition, obsessive-compulsive symptoms may be seen in prodromal schizophrenia. Generally, it will be possible to differentiate these two disorders on the basis of a careful history. Patients with OCD have intact reality testing, recognize the obsessions and compulsions as bizarre and distressing, and will often try to resist them. Rarely, individuals may be diagnosed with both schizophrenia and OCD.

Personality Disorders

Adolescents with Schizoid Personality Disorder show a pervasive pattern of detachment from social relationships and a restricted range of emotional expression, suggestive of the asociality and affective changes described as negative symptoms in schizophrenia. Schizotypal Personality Disorder is characterized by discomfort with and a reduced capacity for social relationships as well as eccentricities of behavior, odd beliefs, unusual perceptual experiences, and suspiciousness. Individuals with Paranoid Personality Disorder display a pervasive distrust and suspiciousness of others, with paranoid thoughts regarding other people's motives. Finally, individuals with Borderline Personality Disorder may have transient episodes of paranoid ideation and loss of reality testing when under stress.

Adolescents with schizophrenia can usually be differentiated from those with personality disorders based on the chronology of their symptoms. Personality disorders are diagnosed following documentation of an enduring pattern of inner experience and behavior that is pervasive and leads to significant impairment in the quality of interpersonal relationships. Acute psychotic symptoms are rare and transitory, and there is not the decline in social functioning frequently seen in schizophrenia.

DSM-IV recognizes the association between features of Schizoid, Schizotypal, and Paranoid Personality Disorders and the prodrome of schizophrenia, and allows the diagnosis of premorbid personality disorders where these syndromes precede the onset of schizophrenia.

Shared Psychotic Disorder

An unusual disorder, sometimes known as folie à deux, Shared Psychotic Disorder occurs when an individual develops a delusion in the context of a close relationship with another person who has an already established delusion. Often the parent is the person with the primary delusion and one or more children from the same family share the same beliefs. Hallucinations are rarely reported. Attempts should be made to separate the family members, by hospitalization if necessary, to assess each person independently. Those with the induced beliefs will not usually maintain them when separated from the person with the primary delusion.

Psychotic Disorders Due to a General Medical Condition

Adolescents presenting with psychotic symptoms should always be evaluated for a medical or neurological illness (Table 8.3). It is often impossible to differentiate an organic psychosis from a psychiatric illness, and a medical evaluation should never be omitted. Although these disorders may be rare, some are reversible with treatment. Every adolescent presenting with psychotic symptoms should have a comprehensive medical workup, to include a physical examination, blood tests, a urine toxicology screen, and in some cases a magnetic resonance imaging (MRI) or computerized tomography (CT) scan of the head. Treatment should not be initiated until the clinician is confident that a medical illness is not responsible for the symptoms.

Substance-Induced Psychotic Disorders

Drugs and medication, whether recreational or prescribed for a legitimate medical condition, may lead to changes in a person's mental status examination. The symptoms may depend on whether the patient is in a state of drug intoxication or drug withdrawal. Individuals may present with psychotic symptoms, periods of confusion and disorientation, and increased or decreased arousal. It is important to differentiate these states, particularly as different treatments may apply depending on the drug of abuse.

Substance Abuse. Adolescents have a high rate of recreational substance abuse. Many of the drugs used can cause psychotic symptoms, during either acute intoxication or drug withdrawal.

Table 8.3
Causes of Psychotic Disorders Due to a
General Medical Condition

CNS Disorders
    Huntington's Chorea
    Wilson's Disease
    Temporal Lobe Epilepsy
    Frontal or temporal lobe tumors
    Multiple Sclerosis

Endocrine/Metabolic Disorders
    Hyperthyroidism
    Hypothyroidism
    Cushing's Disease
    Hyper- and Hypocalcaemia
    Adrenal insufficiency
    Acute Intermittent Porphyria

Infectious Diseases
    Encephalitis
    Neurosyphilis
    HIV Infection

Connective Tissue Disorders
    Systemic Lupus Erythematosus

Nutritional Deficiencies
    Vitamin B-12
    Folic Acid

Often adolescents will admit to substance abuse during the assessment, but it is always advisable to confirm the history with a urine toxicology screen.

Cocaine and amphetamine can produce psychotic symptoms indistinguishable from those of schizophrenia, with symptoms persisting many months after cessation of drug use, particularly in individuals with chronic patterns of abuse. Cocaine intoxication is sometimes associated with the phenomenon of parasitosis, a tactile hallucination identified by the patient as a feeling that insects or parasites are crawling underneath the skin. Hallucinogens, which include LSD, mescaline, and phencyclidine (PCP) may lead to marked perceptual distortions and hallucinations, occurring while the individual retains clear consciousness. PCP in higher doses may cause agitation and symptoms of a paranoid psychosis. Cannabis may also lead to psychotic symptoms, with either hallucinations or delusions. Note also that adolescents using intravenous drugs are at risk of infection by the Human Immunodeficiency Virus (HIV), which may lead to psychotic symptoms.

Alcohol withdrawal may be associated specifically with visual hallucinations, although auditory and tactile hallucinations as well as delusions are also reported. Individuals may become combative during acute alcohol withdrawal and are at risk of alcohol withdrawal seizures.

Prescribed Medications. Many prescribed medications may lead to psychotic symptoms, even at normal therapeutic doses (Table 8.4). A full history should always include an inquiry into the patient's medication history and contact with the primary medical physician where this is possible.

INITIAL ASSESSMENT

The initial interview with a psychotic adolescent, whether in the therapist's office, at school, or in the hospital emergency room, is a crucial part of the assessment. During this time the clinician

Table 8.4
Common Medications Associated with Psychotic Symptoms

Corticosteroids
Prednisone

Amphetamines
Methylphenidate (Ritalin)
Dextroamphetamine
(Dexedrine)

Antiparkinsonian Agents
L-dopa (Sinemet)

Anticholinergic Agents
Benztropine (Cogentin)
Diphenhydramine (Benadryl)

Antihypertensive Agents
Reserpine

Antituberculosis Agents
Isoniazid (INH)

Antidepressants
Fluoxetine (Prozac)
Sertraline (Zoloft)
Paroxetine (Paxil)

Tricyclic Antidepressants
Bupropion HCl (Wellbutrin)

Anticonvulsants
Divalproex sodium (Depakote)
Carbamazepine (Tegretol)

needs to make a determination regarding the safety of the adolescent and a decision regarding whether to recommend inpatient hospitalization.

Clinical Interview

During the psychiatric interview of the psychotic patient, it is important to try to understand the experience of the adolescent. Psychosis is a mental process in which perceptions are distorted, so that even innocuous, everyday happenings may be misinterpreted. Bizarre motives may be attributed to the behavior of others. Psychosis also affects the ability of the patient to think logically and coherently. It may be difficult for the patient to organize and express thoughts clearly, a condition that may be manifested as a thought disorder.

Psychosis weakens the normal defenses that protect the adolescent from fears of persecution, humiliation, and abandonment. These fears may be reinforced by experiences of hallucinations in the form of voices commenting on the adolescent's behaviors and thoughts. These symptoms leave the teenager vulnerable to acting in irrational and often unpredictable ways, frequently in response to fears that have no basis in reality. Periods of extreme agitation, combativeness, and disinhibition may all be witnessed during the course of the interview.

For the clinician, the interview can be a difficult and unnerving experience. It is important, however, to realize that the inner experience of the clinician often mirrors what is being experienced by the patient. Anxieties in the person conducting the interview may be a clue to a state of terror or fear within in the patient. It may be helpful to the patient if the clinician is able to verbalize these feelings and in so doing convey a sense that the patient's distress is understood.

The interview should take place in a safe and nonthreatening environment, with access to ancillary staff support where this is possible. The adolescent may prefer to be interviewed in the presence of a family member. The purpose of the interview should be explained and the adolescent reassured that the primary goal is to help him or her. The interviewer should obtain the patient's past psychiatric and medical history, including the possibility of recent substance abuse. This information should be corroborated by family members and school staff. Questions regarding the presence of delusions and hallucinations need to be put tactfully. The patient should know that these symptoms occur in a variety of situations and need careful evaluation.

Inpatient Hospitalization

Evaluation of the potential for violence or self-destructive behavior is clearly of major importance, given the relatively high rate of suicide in young schizophrenic patients. Questions about this may be introduced by an inquiry into symptoms of depression or hopelessness. If the interviewer determines that the patient is at risk for suicide or violence, a decision should be made for emergency hospitalization. Generally, this will mean certification for involuntary hospitalization, even in cases where the adolescent and family agree to the decision.

At this point, the adolescent should be kept in a secure setting to prevent him or her from running away until transportation to the hospital by ambulance or police escort can be arranged. The legal responsibility for the safety of the patient remains with the therapist until the patient is hospitalized.

The therapist can continue to support the treatment by contacting a member of the hospital treatment team to provide background information, although consent should first be obtained from the patient and family. In some circumstances, it may be helpful for the therapist to maintain contact with the patient during the hospitalization to facilitate his or her transition back to outpatient treatment.

Factors influencing the decision not to hospitalize the patient include the severity of symptoms and the degree of social and family support. If the patient is at no immediate risk of suicide or violence, it may be possible to coordinate an outpatient treatment plan, which should include medical and psychiatric evaluation.

MEDICATION TREATMENT

Antipsychotic medications, sometimes referred to as neuroleptics, are the primary agents used to treat acute psychosis. The conventional antipsychotics are classified into high-potency (haloperidol; thiothixene) and low-potency (chlorpromazine, thioridazine) drugs on the basis of their side effects. They may be given by mouth or by injection; they are most effective in the treatment of acute psychotic symptoms, particularly the positive symptoms of schizophrenia. They are much less effective in the treatment of negative symptoms.

Acute symptoms should diminish significantly within one to two weeks, although nearly 30 percent of patients with schizophrenia will not respond to treatment with conventional antipsychotic agents. Patients who do respond to treatment are candidates for longer-term or maintenance therapy. Thirty to fifty percent of patients unfortunately will relapse while on maintenance medications, but this is less than the 70 percent who relapse without treatment. The goal of treatment is to maintain the patient on the lowest possible effective dose while controlling the psychotic symptoms.

Medication Noncompliance

Adolescents are notoriously poor in complying with treatment and often discontinue their medications when the acute symptoms remit, placing themselves at greater risk of relapse. The psychiatrist has the responsibility for educating the adolescent and family regarding the importance of medication treatment. The therapist plays a crucial role in supporting this work. This role should include ongoing communication between therapist and psychiatrist regarding the efficacy and side effects of prescribed medications. Tests to determine the blood levels of the medication can be useful when noncompliance is suspected but denied by the patient.

Side Effects

Antipsychotic medications have significant side effects, which are frequently cited as a reason for noncompliance with treatment. The decision to recommend medication must include a consideration of the potential benefit of treatment versus the risk of side effects. Some of the more common side effects reported are discussed below.

Acute Dystonic Reactions. Patients may exhibit the sudden onset of involuntary muscle contractions of the mouth, jaw, face, and neck. The symptoms are episodic and recurrent, lasting from minutes to hours, typically occurring in the first hours to days of treatment. In oculogyric crises, there is a dystonic reaction of the extraocular muscles of the eye, resulting in the gaze remaining fixed in one direction. Patients and family members should always be warned of this disturbing yet relatively harmless side effect; it is easily treatable using a group of medications called the antiparkinsonian agents.

Extrapyramidal Reactions. Extrapyramidal reactions generally consist of a triad of symptoms, which include tremor in the upper limbs, muscular rigidity, and slowness of movement, termed *bradykinesia*. These symptoms frequently begin in the first few weeks to months of treatment, are persistent, and may require treatment, also with antiparkinsonian agents.

Akathisia. Akathisia is characterized by an inner compulsion to be in motion. Patients are observed to pace aimlessly, fidget, and complain of an inability to sit still. Increased levels of anxiety associated with this symptom may be confused with a worsening of psychotic symptoms. Misdiagnosis may lead to a decision to increase the dose of the antipsychotic medication, which will exacerbate the akathisia. This symptom is cited as one of the commonest reasons for noncompliance with treatment.

Tardive Dyskinesia. Tardive dyskinesia is characterized by abnormal, involuntary movements termed *choreoathetoid movements*. They involve the tongue, lips, jaw, face, limbs, and occasionally the entire body. In the young, the movements sometimes begin in the limb extremities with rapid, purposeless, quick jerky movements, termed *chorea*, or as sinuous, writhing movements termed *athetosis*. The movements usually develop slowly, after continuous exposure to antipsychotic medications for a minimum period of three to six months, although some sensitive patients may develop the syndrome after a shorter period.

Up to 50 percent of children develop these movements either during treatment or in more transitory form at the time of withdrawal from medication, a condition that is termed a *withdrawal dyskinesia*. True tardive dyskinesia is generally irreversible. These movements are often embarrassing and may interfere with the patient's eating, talking, and dressing.

Neuroleptic Malignant Syndrome. Neuroleptic Malignant Syndrome is a serious, potentially life-threatening disorder characterized by muscular rigidity, sweating, confusion, and increases in the heart rate, respiratory rate, and body temperature. The symptoms develop rapidly over twenty-four to seventy-two hours and may begin at any point during treatment with antipsychotics. This syndrome requires immediate medical evaluation and hospitalization as it may be fatal if untreated. The mortality rate in adult patients developing this syndrome is 30 percent.

Atypical Antipsychotic Medications

The newer so-called atypical antipsychotic agents, in contrast to the conventional agents, are now emerging as a group of medications with both greater efficacy and in some cases fewer side effects. Several agents are currently undergoing clinical trials, and many of these will become available as treatment options within the next few years. The newer agents have generally not been tried in the child and adolescent population, but many patients who are resistant to treatment or intolerant of side effects are now being treated with atypical antipsychotics.

Clozapine. Clozapine is the prototypical atypical antipsychotic, recommended in patients who are nonresponsive to treatment. It is the medication with the greatest efficacy in treating positive symptoms. It also appears to have some efficacy in treating negative symptoms, which distinguishes it from the conventional antipsychotic agents. It is the only antipsychotic that does not cause tardive dyskinesia and may in fact lead to a remission or improvement in patients who have already developed this side effect. The major drawback is the side effect profile, which includes the possibility of bone marrow abnormalities, seizures, and excessive salivation. Treatment entails very close medical monitoring, including weekly blood tests.

Risperidone. Risperidone is a new antipsychotic with an extremely low incidence of side effects. Risperidone has virtually no extrapyramidal side effects, although it may cause akathisia. It also appears to have some efficacy in the treatment of negative symptoms. As yet, we do not know whether this medication causes tardive dyskinesia.

INDIVIDUAL THERAPY

Individual therapy has been used to promote reality testing and to facilitate the understanding of the factors that lead to relapse in patients with schizophrenia. Goals of individual psychotherapy, which should be of a supportive nature, include education, encouraging the patient's compliance with treatment, and facilitation of his or her attainment of age-appropriate developmental milestones. Adolescents with schizophrenia have particular difficulties with the issues of autonomy, identity, sexuality, and social relationships. Studies have not supported the usefulness of psychodynamic insight-oriented psychotherapy in schizophrenia.

Developmental Issues

Psychosocial development in mid to late adolescence requires the accomplishment of a number of specific tasks, which include the development of same and opposite sex relationships outside the immediate family. Adolescents with schizophrenia may not be well attuned to the subtle social cues in relationships, a deficit that can result in exclusion from their peer group. Attempts to gain social acceptance may lead these adolescents into a pattern of substance abuse, which can precipitate psychotic symptoms. In addition, the struggle for autonomy may be in direct conflict with the concerns of overprotective parents regarding their child's judgment and coping skills.

Puberty introduces the need to assimilate changes in physical appearance and may also bring up issues regarding sexual identity. The adolescent with schizophrenia who engages in premature sexual activity, either as a result of poor social judgment or in an attempt to gain social acceptance, may be at particular risk for sexually transmitted diseases and teenage pregnancy.

Social Skills Training

Social skills training is one of the most effective individual treatment interventions available for adolescents with schizophrenia. We have noted that schizophrenics misinterpret social cues and have difficulty expressing their thoughts. The goals of social skills training include improvements in the areas of social perception to compensate for perceptual and processing deficits, and attention to difficulties with verbal and nonverbal communication.

One protocol developed for social skills training is based on the algorithm Instruction, Modeling, Role Play, Feedback, Homework (IMRFH). The protocol starts with an assessment of the adolescent's behaviors that provoke criticism, hostility, and overinvolvement from family members. The algorithm is used as a guide to address specific topics. The therapist takes an active role in instructing and modeling appropriate behaviors, which the adolescent then practices in the session using role-play.

IMRFH has been used to help the schizophrenic learn how to express interest and appreciation in social situations; voice opinions and respond to criticism; and identify the content, context, and meaning of interpersonal communication. Goals of the therapy are to provide skills for use in social and vocational situations, both within and outside the family.

Cognitive Training

Cognitive training helps the schizophrenic patient learn to identify specific situations that affect his or her illness. This knowledge may help the adolescent adopt strategies to minimize his or her psychotic symptoms—for example, seeking out company at times when hallucinations are particularly intrusive, or avoiding recreational drugs that may precipitate the symptoms.

FAMILY THERAPY

Although many schizophrenics are socially isolated and lack significant peer relationships, most adolescents with schizophrenia will either be living with their families of origin or have regular contact with family members. Family interventions, particularly in combination with other treatments, have been shown effective in treating acute symptoms and in reducing the frequency of relapse. Family therapy also appears to be helpful in improving an adolescent's social adjustment and facilitating his or her return to school or work.

Education

The diagnosis of schizophrenia in an adolescent is a traumatic event for the family. For many families, this will be their first contact with psychiatric illness. Denial of illness by both patient and family members is common. Issues of blame are frequent, particularly when there is a family history of psychiatric illness.

It is essential to meet with all members of the family to explain what is known about schizophrenia and how the family can best support the treatment. Families need to be aware that this is a chronic illness but one whose outcome depends directly on their commitment to treatment.

Expressed Emotion

Follow-up studies of patients with schizophrenia discharged to live at home with their families have shown that certain patterns of communication are associated with early relapse. The major factors identified in these families include criticism, hostility, and overinvolvement on the part of family members. These factors are collectively referred to as *expressed emotion* (EE), which can be assessed in a standardized interview.

High levels of expressed emotion are associated with early relapse, independent of the severity of symptoms in the schizophrenic patient. Interventions aimed at reducing EE, such as limiting the amount of face-to-face contact between the patient and family members, have been found to reduce rates of relapse.

Julian Leff, a British psychiatrist, has described a family treatment strategy based on the four areas of intervention described as follows.

1. *Education.* Both the family and the adolescent patient are informed about the tentative diagnosis. Leff recommends education about the etiology, course, and treatment of schizophrenia. The following facts are helpful for the family:

- Families do not cause schizophrenia.
- Adolescents with schizophrenia are sensitive to stress.

- There are specific ways to reduce stress for the adolescent.
- The typical course of schizophrenia is one of relapses and remissions, but 25 percent of patients recover completely.
- Medication needs to be given even when the patient appears to be asymptomatic, to reduce the risk of relapse.
- Positive and negative symptoms respond differently to medication.

2.   *Communication skills.* Leff recommends that two therapists work together in treatment with the goal of improving communication skills in the family. The advantages of this arrangement include allowing the therapists to model effective communication and conflict resolution and to prevent either one of the therapists from being drawn into the family dynamics. Basic rules that should be established include these:

- Only one person should speak at one time.
- All family members should be given an equal opportunity to speak.
- Family members should be addressed directly and not referred to in the third person.

3.   *Problem solving.* Leff recommends that problem-solving techniques be taught by breaking down specific problems into manageable steps. One problem is selected at a time and each family member consulted to come up with possible solutions. Once a solution is agreed on, it should be framed as a trial so as not to leave the family feeling it has failed if the attempted solution is unsuccessful. Here's how it could work:

STEPHANIE

Stephanie, a sixteen-year-old girl diagnosed with schizophrenia, was consistently late for the school bus; because Stephanie's mother then had to drive Stephanie to school, the mother was often late for her own job. The problem was broken down into a number of steps for Stephanie, starting with preparing clean clothes the evening before; setting the alarm clock; getting out of bed in the morning; showering; dressing; eating breakfast; taking medications; and then being outside to wait for the bus. The therapist helped to devise creative strategies for each of these steps, leading to the successful resolution of the problem.

---

4. *Decreasing expressed emotion.* Leff recommends attempting to reduce the level of expressed emotion. Hostility and criticism expressed by family members are generally a reaction to the patient's patterns of behavior. The therapist should reiterate that these are symptoms of schizophrenia and that they require tolerance from family members. To address the issue of overinvolvement, the following recommendations may be helpful:

- Physical separation in graded increments to allow the adolescent the opportunity for greater autonomy
- Interventions, including separate collateral sessions, to strengthen the relationship between the parents
- Interventions to develop relationships between the siblings
- Interventions aimed at developing peer relationships
- Encouragement for family members to pursue independent recreational and social interests
- Development of relationships with extended family members and friends, possibly initiated by an invitation to a group educational session
- Use of brief physical separations, or time-outs, when tensions develop between family members

- Support for family members to lower their immediate expectations and to have an opportunity to grieve the lost hopes for their child

Support Groups

Families of adolescents with psychiatric illnesses are often neglected in the treatment. Parents may be reluctant to talk with extended family and friends out of concern for their child's privacy and because of the stigma of schizophrenia. The National Alliance for the Mentally Ill (NAMI) is a national group with regional and local chapters for families and patients affected by mental illness, most commonly those with schizophrenia or Bipolar Disorder. These groups are a valuable resource for family members, providing practical information about community services, up-to-date information on current treatment developments, and support from other families struggling with similar issues.

GROUP THERAPY

Adolescents with schizophrenia often have difficulties with social relationships and may benefit from inclusion in a peer group. Groups provide the opportunity for the adolescent to gain peer support, practice social skills in a controlled environment, and develop new relationships. Psychotic symptoms often diminish during participation in social activities. The group may need to be tailored to individual patients. Adolescents with active psychotic symptoms may need a group in which few demands are made on individual group members, whereas a patient with prominent negative symptoms, including social withdrawal, may benefit from a group that requires more individual participation.

Groups may focus on the implications of schizophrenia and its treatment, using a psychoeducational format. They may also focus on adolescent issues such as substance abuse and sexual practices. Groups designed to facilitate the practice of social skills will complement individual and family therapy interventions.

DAY AND RESIDENTIAL PLACEMENT

The transition from inpatient hospitalization back into the community is a difficult time for both the patient and the family. As noted earlier, a patient's risk of suicide is higher immediately after discharge. There is also the risk of early relapse. The options of both day treatment and residential treatment should be considered as part of the treatment plan.

Day Treatment

Day treatment is an important treatment option for the adolescent with schizophrenia. It may provide a transition from the intensive and supportive environment of the hospital back to placement with the family. Day treatment may also be used for adolescents initially unable to return to regular school because of their persistent psychotic symptoms or difficulties with adjustment. A good treatment program will provide a degree of structure and supervision in addition to individual and group treatment modalities that supplement the educational program. Finally, day treatment may provide an alternative to hospitalization in patients in early stages of relapse, and possibly avert the need for inpatient treatment.

Residential Treatment

Residential treatment is often thought of as a treatment of last resort for patients with persistent psychotic symptoms or behavioral difficulties. It may also be utilized in cases where the family support is inadequate to maintain the patient safely in the community. Residential treatment should generally be considered a temporary respite in these situations while intensive treatment continues with the patient and family. It is important for parents and siblings to maintain regular contact with the patient in a residential setting because in most cases the patient will be discharged back to the family. The transition from residential treatment to home is an important step that is more likely to be successful if there is careful planning and consultation with everyone involved in the treatment.

PROGNOSIS

Studies vary regarding the prognosis of early onset schizophrenia. Up to 25 percent of patients will make a complete recovery after the first psychotic episode, but 50 percent show only moderate to poor remission. Children with earlier age of onset, poor premorbid functioning, insidious onset, a family history of schizophrenia, and disorganized behavior tend to do poorly. By contrast, children with affective symptoms, above-average intelligence, higher social class, and paranoid symptoms have a better prognosis. Patients with schizophrenia have a higher risk of suicide than the general population, and 10 percent of them will successfully kill themselves. This factor should always be kept in mind when you are working with this population.

Schizophrenia is a chronic illness with profound and long-term implications. It is also an illness for which there is currently no known cure. This does not, however, imply that there is no treatment. A combination of treatment approaches can significantly improve both the individual's quality of life and the long-term prognosis. New research continues to provide reason for optimism. Recent findings in the area of drug mechanisms is leading to the development of a number of new, promising antipsychotic agents that are effective even in the treatment of the most severely disturbed patients. This optimism can make working with this population a challenging yet rewarding experience for the therapist.

NOTES

P. 311, *Schizophrenia has been described:* Black, D. W., & Andreasen, N. C. (1994). Schizophrenia, schizophreniform disorder and delusional (paranoid) disorder. In R. E. Hales, S. C. Yudofsky, & J. A. Talbott (Eds.), *American Psychiatric Press textbook of psychiatry* (2nd ed.). Washington, DC: American Psychiatric Press, p. 432.

P. 311, *The criteria used to diagnose:* Black, D. W., & Andreasen, N. C. (1994). Schizophrenia, schizophreniform disorder and delusional (paranoid) disorder. In R. E. Hales, S. C. Yudofsky, & J. A. Talbott (Eds.), *American Psychiatric Press textbook of psychiatry* (2nd ed.). Washington, DC: American Psychiatric Press, p. 415.

P. 311, *Diagnostic criteria:* American Psychiatric Association. (1994). *Diagnostic and statistical manual of mental disorders* (4th ed.). Washington, DC: American Psychiatric Press.

P. 313, *Patients with schizophrenia are:* Black, D. W., & Andreasen, N. C. (1994). Schizophrenia, schizophreniform disorder and delusional (paranoid) disorder. In R. E. Hales, S. C. Yudofsky, & J. A. Talbott (Eds.), *American Psychiatric Press textbook of psychiatry* (2nd ed.). Washington, DC: American Psychiatric Press, p. 433.

P. 313, *Schizophrenics have a very high:* Black, D. W., & Andreasen, N. C. (1994). Schizophrenia, schizophreniform disorder and delusional (paranoid) disorder. In R. E. Hales, S. C. Yudofsky, & J. A. Talbott (Eds.), *American Psychiatric Press textbook of psychiatry* (2nd ed.). Washington, DC: American Psychiatric Press, p. 434.

P. 316, *Up to 90 percent:* Campbell, M., Spencer, E. K., Kowalik S. C., & Erlenmeyer-Kimling, L. (1991). Schizophrenic and psychotic disorders. In J. M. Weiner (Ed.), *Textbook of child and adolescent psychiatry.* Washington, DC: American Psychiatric Press, p. 228.

P. 317, *Delusions are fixed:* Campbell, M., Spencer, E. K., Kowalik S. C., & Erlenmeyer-Kimling, L. (1991). Schizophrenic and psychotic disorders. In J. M. Weiner (Ed.), *Textbook of child and adolescent psychiatry.* Washington, DC: American Psychiatric Press, p. 225.

P. 318, *Thought Disorder:* Black, D. W., & Andreasen, N. C. (1994). Schizophrenia, schizophreniform disorder and delusional (paranoid) disorder. In R. E. Hales, S. C. Yudofsky, & J. A. Talbott (Eds.), *American Psychiatric Press textbook of psychiatry* (2nd ed.). Washington, DC: American Psychiatric Press, p. 419.

P. 319, *Affect is:* Black, D. W., & Andreasen, N. C. (1994). Schizophrenia, schizophreniform disorder and delusional (paranoid) disorder. In R. E. Hales, S. C. Yudofsky, & J. A. Talbott (Eds.), *American Psychiatric Press textbook of psychiatry* (2nd ed.). Washington, DC: American Psychiatric Press.

P. 320, *The first psychotic:* Campbell, M., Spencer, E. K., Kowalik S. C., & Erlenmeyer-Kimling, L. (1991). Schizophrenic and psychotic disorders. In J. M. Weiner (Ed.), *Textbook of child and adolescent psychiatry.* Washington, DC: American Psychiatric Press, p. 223.

P. 320, *The etiology:* Ninan, P. T., & Mance, R. (1994). Schizophrenia and other psychotic disorders. In A. Stoudemire (Ed.), *Clinical psychiatry for medical students* (2nd ed.). Philadelphia: J.B. Lipincott, pp. 151–162.

P. 321, *Pervasive developmental disorders:* Tsai, L. Y., & Ghaziuddin, M. (1991). Autistic disorder. In J. M. Weiner (Ed.), *Textbook of child and adolescent psychiatry.* Washington, DC: American Psychiatric Press, p. 178.

P. 322, *Children who present:* Campbell, M., Spencer, E. K., Kowalik S. C., & Erlenmeyer-Kimling, L. (1991). Schizophrenic and psychotic disorders. In J. M. Weiner (Ed.), *Textbook of child and adolescent psychiatry.* Washington, DC: American Psychiatric Press, p. 230.

P. 324, *Adolescents with Schizoid:* American Psychiatric Association. (1994). *Diagnostic and statistical manual of mental disorders* (4th ed.). Washington, DC: American Psychiatric Press.

P. 325, *Psychotic Disorders Due:* Stoudemire, A. (1994). Delirium, dementia, and other disorders associated with cognitive impairment. In A. Stoudemire (Ed.), *Clinical psychiatry for medical students* (2nd ed.). Philadelphia: J.B. Lipincott, p. 110.

P. 325, *Drugs and medication:* Tomb, D. A. (1988). *Psychiatry for the house officer* (3rd ed.). Baltimore: Williams & Wilkins, pp. 126–151.

P. 331, *Antipsychotic medications:* Gelenberg, A. J. (1991). Psychoses. In A. J. Gelenberg, E. L. Bassuk, & S. C. Schoonover (Eds.), *The practitioner's guide to psychoactive drugs* (3rd ed.). New York: Plenum, p. 135.

P. 332, *Side Effects:* Gelenberg, A. J. (1991). Psychoses. In A. J. Gelenberg, E. L. Bassuk, & S. C. Schoonover (Eds.), *The practitioner's guide to psychoactive drugs* (3rd ed.). New York: Plenum, pp. 138–155.

P. 336, *One protocol developed:* Hogarty, G. E., et al. (1986). Family psychoeducation, social skills training, and maintenance chemotherapy in the aftercare treatment of schizophrenia. *Archives of General Psychiatry, 43,* 633–642.

P. 337, *Follow-up studies:* Leff, J. 1994). Working with families of schizophrenic patients. *British Journal of Psychiatry, 164* (suppl. 23), pp. 71–76.

P. 342, *Studies vary:* Campbell, M., Spencer, E. K., Kowalik S. C., & Erlenmeyer-Kimling, L. (1991). Schizophrenic and psychotic disorders. In J. M. Weiner (Ed.), *Textbook of child and adolescent psychiatry.* Washington, DC: American Psychiatric Press, p. 236.

9

PSYCHIATRIC TRAUMA AND RELATED PSYCHOPATHOLOGIES

Hans Steiner and Zakee Matthews

Every night, my homey comes and visits me. I see the van pull up behind him, I know what they are going to do, I see the guns pointing out the window, and I am so scared I can't say a thing. I throw myself down and hope he will too, 'cause I can't say anything to warn him, but he says, what's up, man? Then he goes down, and I see the blood coming out of his mouth. Every night, for the last three years.

SIXTEEN-YEAR-OLD,

DESCRIBING A RECURRENT DREAM

OF THE DRIVE-BY SHOOTING OF HIS FRIEND

Extensive media coverage has made the general public accustomed to reports of posttraumatic stress induced by earthquakes, fires, terrorist bombings, and other types of environmental and personal tragedies. Events such as these leave indelible scars for years to come.

But this chapter is about other sources of psychiatric trauma: events in the public and private lives of teenagers who have been sexually or physically abused, often by members of their own family; who have witnessed violence both on the streets and in their homes; or who have been forced by their peers to do things they didn't want to, to have an "adventure" that turns into a nightmare. Such events create posttraumatic stress disorders. These affect not only teenagers who must survive in an urban ghetto environment combining many sources of trauma into one potent, overwhelming package, but also other adolescents who endure secret but terrifying abuse in a wide spectrum of socioeconomic settings.

Trauma-related psychopathology can sometimes appear to be the "great imposter" of psychiatry. No other diagnostic group of disorders can present with so many different symptoms. We have had patients referred to us for an inability to walk, loss of sight and voice, problems with swallowing or eating solids, pains in the abdomen and uncontrollable throwing up; we discovered that all these patients were suffering from posttraumatic pathology. We have also had Posttraumatic Stress Disorder (PTSD) patients presenting with what initially appeared to be paranoid schizophrenia, mania, depression, hyperactivity, eating disorders, and brain tumors. To deal with such adolescents means we must be prepared to confront almost anything.

Trauma-related pathology is quite common and the manifestations quite diverse among adolescents, compared to both older and younger age groups. The reasons for this are complex:

- Adolescents take many more risks than other groups. Thus they find themselves more often in situations that are potentially traumatogenic.

- Adolescents' mental structures are more fluid and flexible, so their responses to stress manifest themselves more diversely.

- Adolescents have more extensive private lives. Their age-appropriate need to create their lives separate from their parents leads them to keep traumatic events to themselves. Consequently, catharsis and abreaction are often delayed, facilitating the pathologization of stress-related reactions.

This chapter explores the lives of adolescent victims of trauma and what is currently known about their treatment.

THE HISTORICAL ROOTS OF PSYCHIATRIC TRAUMA

When Sigmund Freud began to describe psychiatric trauma at the turn of the century, he spoke mostly of events that occurred in a Victorian society: innocent children were victimized by caregivers, young women victimized by suitors.

Freud initially tied the whole notion of psychopathology to these external events, until his case material—and his own experiences in growing up—led him to think about the parent as the ultimate seducer. He then began changing his theory, focusing on the existence of internal structures that propel the growing child into sexual action, behavior, and fantasies. These, Freud held, were the more common origin of psychopathology: distortions of events in the child's life formed and maintained by her or his internal instincts.

But Freud never completely gave up the notion that traumatic events did occur and left permanent traces in children's mental health and emotional lives. One of his great discoveries is that such traces could live on unrecognized for years in certain individuals, only to erupt much later under the impact of related events into psychopathology such as dissociative episodes or conversion pain.

Although Freud's initial theorizing and preliminary clinical observations and case reports were important in directing our attention to a whole new source of psychopathology, it was not until the last ten years that child psychiatric traumatology has come into its own as a research-based science. Much more is known now about human trauma response and memory formation, and our base is expanding every day. Before we discuss what is known in this regard, let us examine a relevant case.

TIM

Tim, a fifteen-year-old young man, was examined in the California Youth Authority (CYA) where he was incarcerated for a violent crime. He had begun having major behavior problems one year after his commitment, and the staff was concerned about his safety. He reported difficulties with his peers, often culminating in violent fights. There were also verbal assaults, impulsivity, and irritability without apparent precipitants. He was reported by staff to have major problems with following directions, as though he were not aware of his own behavior. He was noted on occasion to be sad, anxious, hyperactive, and guarded. Placed in isolation several times because of his behavior, he was referred by the staff for evaluation of his impulsive and sudden mood changes, and questions were raised as to whether he should be medicated. During the psychiatric evaluation he mentioned that he had been more anxious over the past several weeks, and on occasion he had found himself fighting with other peers and not being exactly sure why.

All these behaviors could be attributed to the young man's "delinquent status" by an unsophisticated observer. After all, what do you expect from an incarcerated juvenile? But Tim later reported that in "one of my small groups, another ward talked about how his mother killed her boyfriend." A few days later, our patient began to recall a horrifying event that had occurred when he was thirteen years old. He was at home one day with his mother, stepfather, and uncle. As he sat next to his stepfather, who was eating and watching TV, his uncle suddenly entered the room, pulled out a gun, and shot his stepfather in the head, killing him instantly.

Tim had managed to forget the event until this moment. He commented that after hearing the story, he experienced vivid images of the murder: "It was like I was right there all over again." He later began to experience the intrusive images without the aid of any specific reminders. As he became more preoccupied with this vision his interactions with staff and peers reflected his mounting internal turmoil. He started missing group therapy because he was in isolation as a result of his disruptive behavior. For him, this was one way to avoid his group as well as other reminders of the event.

Tim wondered out loud "why these strange images and feelings are happening to me." He also was afraid that "people would think I am crazy if I spoke about what's going on inside my head." He told how difficult his life had been since the murder, revealing that "I just don't seem to care any more," saying that violence and delinquent behavior had become his way of life.

His developmental history revealed that he grew up in a close-knit, religious family in an inner-city ghetto. He had two brothers, and all three children were raised by a pair of conscientious grandparents with quite a bit of success. All the children did well in school. They all stayed away from drugs and alcohol, despite ample opportunity for them to indulge. They were quite active in church and the oldest had gotten a scholarship to one of California's prestigious state universities. Their father divorced their mother when they were babies and currently lived in the Midwest with his new family. There was some infrequent contact. Their mother had been struggling with a crack cocaine addiction for some years and intermittently would appear on the scene, but for the most part the boys were raised by their grandparents who were indeed their primary attachment figures. Neither of the brothers had witnessed the stepfather's murder. These boys were not as attached to the stepfather as was Tim, and neither of them had problems comparable to Tim's following the event.

Tim witnessed the murder of his stepfather while he was on a brief visit to his mother; at that time she was sober and attempting to get her life in order. The murderous uncle was high on crack at the time and acting under the paranoid delusion that the stepfather was a police informant. Soon after this incident, Tim's school performance had begun to deteriorate. He started having the symptoms of PTSD, which went unreported and unrecognized by those around him. His mother once again deteriorated in terms of her functioning and again went on drugs.

The young man became increasingly cynical about life in general and more interested in daily pursuits of pleasure than in preparing himself for the future. Stern talks from the grandparents only produced tearful promises from Tim that he would do better—promises that were fulfilled for only a short while. He began hanging out with a gang-affiliated crowd. Shortly thereafter he was arrested and sent to the California Youth Authority for participating in a robbery during which one of his new friends shot and killed the shop owner.

This case encapsulates many of the major symptoms seen in adolescents exposed to a traumatizing event. The characteristics include strongly visualized, frequent memories of the terrifying experience. There is evidence that such visual exposure is especially likely to result in traumatization, and that proximity to the traumatizing event is also very important in producing psychopathology. Other symptoms are persistent avoidance of stimuli associated with the trauma, numbing of general responsiveness, and persistent symptoms of increased arousal. For Tim, the discussion in the small group served as a reminder of the event, opening the once-closed door to images so compelling that he believed the actual trauma was recurring. Therefore, all his fears, anger, feelings of helplessness, and guilt began to surface.

While experiencing the flashback phenomena, he found himself catapulted back into the images and emotions of this horrifying event. During these episodes, he was often viewed as disorganized, suddenly angered, combative, appearing to react for no apparent reason. At times he would react as if he were threatened when in fact there was no threat at all.

All these symptoms had plagued him once before, and they were in fact the main reasons he had become increasingly delinquent. Tim had sought to control his trauma symptoms by using drugs and alcohol, but this proved to alter his sleep pattern and diminish his nightmares only temporarily. He was unable to stop his sense of a foreshortened future, his inappropriate reactions to ordinary life events, and a profound deviation from his life trajectory.

This young man fulfills the diagnostic criteria for Posttraumatic Stress Disorder (PTSD), acute and delayed onset. He had one episode of illness for a few months following the trauma. He subsequently self-medicated with drugs and alcohol. This behavior, together with his psychological suppression of events, concealed the symptoms but led to increasing delinquent acting out, which in his case can be seen as an illness equivalent. The delayed syndrome emerged after the group session in the CYA.

THE RANGE OF TRAUMA-RELATED PSYCHOPATHOLOGY

Trauma can occur throughout life, but it is more likely in adolescence, given teenagers' age-appropriate tendency toward risk-taking and experimentation. In addition, adolescents have new tools of thought, judgment, and communication available to them. Unlike children, whose response is generally to become traumatized, adolescents can better evaluate their roles and responsibilities in different circumstances, and decide that certain events are not normal, should be stopped from happening, and should be reported to others so that help can be forthcoming.

In the next sections we describe trauma-related psychopathology in detail, giving specific cases for illustration; then we discuss a theoretical model that can help us understand the development of these problems, and describe specific interventions that are the most useful in treating each of them.

An individual exposed to traumatic events outside normal human experience may develop one of the following: Acute Stress Disorder (ASD), Posttraumatic Stress Disorder (PTSD), Dissociative Disorders (DDO), and special forms of Personality Disorders (e.g., Borderline Personality Disorder [BPD] or Survivor Syndrome (see Figure 9.1). While the interconnections between all these syndromes are not completely mapped out by research, much clinical evidence suggests that they are most likely connected. Thus, if you find one, expect also to find the others. In addition, be prepared to deal with all of them in treatment, even after you have assessed the patient exhaustively at baseline and have found only one or two. Often, over time these syndromes unfold and become more distinctive under the impact of successful intervention.

Acute Stress Disorder (ASD)

The symptoms of Acute Stress Disorder following exposure to a traumatic event are characterized by all the same complaints as PTSD; however, the duration is shorter. The symptoms must

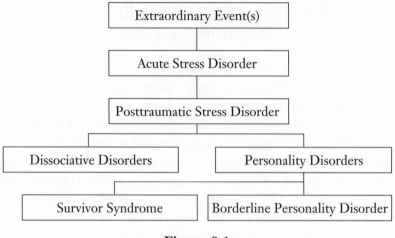

Figure 9.1
Trauma Related Psychopathology

last for at least two days but then resolve within four weeks following the event. If they persist past this time, a diagnosis of PTSD maybe given.

ASD is the mild variant of PTSD, and its distinction from PTSD in the *Diagnostic and Statistical Manual of Mental Disorders* (DSM-IV) awaits study and examination. Most clinicians, however, feel that it is a useful concept because it signals minor pathology that could put an individual at risk for major problems in the future. A diagnosis of ASD essentially allows a therapist to intervene early and quickly, thus preventing more lasting morbidity, as illustrated below:

SARA

Sara, a fourteen-year-old girl, was seen on our consultation service in Children's Hospital at Stanford following a car accident from which she had sustained significant injuries. Her prognosis for recovery from her wounds was excellent; however, the nurses noted in

Sara a profound pessimism regarding her outcome, an attitude that was simply unwarranted by the situation. They assumed she was depressed and referred her for assessment.

Clinical examination showed quickly that Sara was suffering from ASD. She had two or three nightmares each night that were exact replays of the accident, in which she had swerved into oncoming traffic to avoid a drunk bicyclist in her lane. With each dream, the oncoming vehicles—which had in reality been regular cars—grew in number and size. In the dreams Sara had just prior to her consultation, the cars had become a phalanx of Mack trucks coming toward her. She felt that there was no way to escape her certain death.

While she was in the intensive care unit (ICU), Sara's poor sleeping patterns had gone unnoticed, as disrupted sleep is not unusual for intensive care patients. In addition, many of her other symptoms from her wounds had obscured the problems with arousal from sleep, which she experienced around the clock. While she was awake, she saw flashbacks of the accident, induced by TV shows, and she despaired of ever being able to drive again given the intensity of her symptoms.

We began a series of cathartic interviews, described later in the chapter. In these interviews, themes of survivor guilt surfaced in Sara's thoughts and were quickly dealt with: at one point she began worrying and obsessing about whether she had hit a bicyclist and imagined we had kept from her the information that he was dead. Then her dream content changed: she found herself repeatedly at graveyards, looking for the appropriate funeral. At times she would see herself in the coffin as she approached the mourning parties; at other times a coffin would hold one of her parents. Although these themes clearly had dynamic significance, we did not pursue them in great detail; our questioning was limited to only those that facilitated the production of affect and material. We gave Sara much reassurance that she was the only person who had been hurt in the accident. Our words were supported with evidence from newspaper clippings and copies of the original police reports.

Within a week of our sessions, Sara began sleeping normally, her flashbacks became much less numerous and intense, she was able to watch cars and traffic reports on TV without trouble, and she freely interacted with nurses and family. The cathartic process begun in our sessions was continued by Sara spontaneously with nurses, family, and friends. We encouraged her, in the expectation that the process would be helpful to her provided everybody could stay appropriately receptive and supportive. Sara's developmental background was entirely unremarkable. Her family life was stable and there were no premorbid traumata or psychopathologic antecedents. After discharge from the hospital she proceeded in her normal adjustment without any further complications. She was symptom free after one month and began making active plans for the acquisition of a new car.

Posttraumatic Stress Disorder (PTSD)

In the case of Tim mentioned previously, we outlined the diagnostic criteria for Posttraumatic Stress Disorder (PTSD). The only additional information offered here concerns the time course of the disorder and the special diagnostic criteria for different modes of onset.

PTSD may be described as *acute, chronic,* or *with delayed onset. Acute PTSD* is indicated when duration of symptoms is less than three months. *Chronic PTSD* means that symptoms last three months or longer. *Delayed onset* indicates that at least six months have passed between the traumatic event and the onset of the symptoms.

PTSD is the most common trauma-related psychopathology, also known as the Vietnam Veteran's Syndrome. The major distinguishing feature of this syndrome in comparison to ASD is that pathology is more prolonged and intensive, causing major interference in a person's life over extended periods of time. Symptoms also do not recede as quickly, even with appropriate intervention, so that the treatment team has to be more patient in waiting for a positive response. Most likely this is due to a certain "biologization" of psychological symptoms. It seems that in PTSD, problems leave lasting biological imprints on a person's brain functioning, and these are difficult to reverse by simple psychotherapy alone.

Roger Pitman and his group at Harvard have done very innovative work in examining the influence of certain hormones on etched memory formation. Using scripted memory induction and application of memory-enhancing or re-enhancing hormones, they were able to improve PTSD in many patients. Recently, another group of researchers at University of California, Irvine, has reported success in identifying a special hormone system related to epinephrine, a main stress hormone that is responsible for memory formation under traumatic circumstances. These are promising developments that will have implications for research and treatment and should be tracked in the near future.

Patients who suffer PTSD have very often been "sensitized" to traumatization premorbidly in some form or another. Their developmental background is not as uncomplicated and unremarkable as in the case of Sara, who had ASD. Often, this sensitization involves a significant loss around the time of the traumatic event. For our patient Tim described earlier, the repeated "losses" of his mother to drug use served as such a loss. His grandparents managed to buffer him and his brothers from her tumultuous life fairly successfully, but even their love and devotion could not undo the effects of Tim's horror in witnessing the murder of his stepfather. This event induced yet another significant loss because Tim's stepfather had been helping his mother get her life together even though they had been married for only a very short while. David Brent and his group have shown in a very good prospective study that it is personally significant loss that makes a particular adolescent vulnerable to trauma.

Dissociative Disorders (DDO)

In our model (Figure 9.1), dissociative disorders are grouped under the general category of trauma-related pathologies, although other clinicians see them as separate. Our suggestion to group them together is based on our clinical experience and study of adolescents who have been exposed to severely traumatogenic environments, and yet do not manifest PTSD. By contrast, these individuals were suffering from a high degree of hypnotizability, suggestibility, and dissociative psychopathology.

There is a similarity between our subject's clinical presentation and the symptoms of individuals whom Lenore Terr has described as suffering from Trauma II response—that is, who have experienced repeated or multiple traumas. Derealization, depersonalization, amnesias, fugue states and identity disorders all can appear and combine with each other. In the most severe form the person will manifest multiple personalities, as so aptly described in *Sybil*, a story of ritualistic abuse. A series of traumatic events challenges the basic integrity of an individual's personality, causing extensive alterations in the person's sense of self regarding emotions and cognitive, volitional processes. Changes are so pervasive that these patients are unable to integrate traumatic and other experiences fully. They see themselves as fragmented by quite horrendous events that come with sickening predictability.

To add to the horror of the events, they are often perpetrated by attachment figures who are important to the adolescents. It is very difficult to maintain the illusion that mothers or fathers mean well when in fact they are the ones who are violating the child's body and soul. In these cases, the relationship to the attachment figure is quite strong and unrelenting. It keeps the child in a tight bond with no way to escape other than in a "pretend" fashion. If a child feels that he cannot absent himself from predictable and horrible events, then at least he can pretend that he is going somewhere else (fugue states); pretend that the events are not happening (depersonalization); pretend that the world in which they are occurring is not real (derealization); forget about them as soon as they have happened (amnesia); pretend that the abuser is at least two people—for example, an evil mother and a good mother (projected identity problems); or finally if all else fails, the child can pretend that he is many different people but not the one being tortured right then (identity problems or multiple personality).

This pathology occurs during normal human trauma response. Complaints of feeling numb and distant, and a sense of detachment and alienation are part of any trauma. What appears to drive these cases further into illness seems to be a clustering of traumatic events that prevents any "mental digestion" of the events and personal reintegration after fragmentation. This may happen simply because traumatic events follow one another too quickly, and dissociation in one of its forms becomes a way of life for the individual.

There is also the possibility that individuals who react to trauma in this particular fashion have some form of constitutional propensity to react dissociatively. The traumatic event in this model is a precipitant only, not a causative agent. Future longitudinal research is needed to determine which is the better way to think about the genesis of dissociative disorders. An example of the dissociative disorders is the following case of Sharon.

SHARON

A seventeen-year-old girl, Sharon, was brought to our Eating Disorders Clinic for treatment of what appeared to be Anorexia Nervosa. Although the weight criteria were met in this case, an unusual element was the relative ease with which this patient responded to weight rehabilitation; it was almost too easy, too uncomplicated. The first clue that some other problems might be involved here became apparent after Sharon was discharged from the hospital. Within twenty-four hours she took a significant overdose of Acetaminophen and had to be rehospitalized. Now the treatment team became more suspicious of the primary diagnosis because this sequence of events is quite rare in anorexics, who by and large are happy to leave the closely supervised medical environment so they can lose the weight they have gained. In this case, Sharon was happy to be back and happily complied with her weight management program. She was in no particular hurry to plan for discharge and helped out in the care of younger patients.

Sharon was the child of a professional couple: her biological father was a well-known university professor in the San Francisco Bay Area, her mother a very successful software developer with one of the local start-up companies. The mother's current husband was her third. Her first husband, Sharon's biological father, had died under mysterious circumstances in India while on business. She divorced her second husband because he had problems with drug abuse. The current marriage was about seven years in progress and was reported as satisfactory by the parents. There were no other children besides Sharon.

During her second stay, the treatment team noted new symptoms: Sharon could not recall large segments of treatment, especially family therapy. At times she wandered off the ward, aimlessly roaming the hospital. During these episodes she was always easily returned to the ward when she was found, seemingly oblivious to her current whereabouts and looking quite "spacey." During group therapy she would often stare off into space, earning herself the nickname of "the astronaut" by the other children. No predictable trigger was observed for these events, and charting did not reveal any reliable environmental precipitants. The staff even became concerned she might be having seizures, so persistent were her symptoms.

In individual treatment, Sharon had difficulty engaging with a therapist, although several tried to work with her. She had special difficulty in revealing any significant details of her past life. We asked one of our senior faculty to consult, and she was more persistent and successful than others in getting details about the patient's growing up. What emerged was a picture of an impoverished childhood, many external caretakers for Sharon from very early in her life, marital turmoil, and conflict. Still, some ingredients were missing.

The biggest clue came one day when the patient showed up for an appointment with her therapist dressed in a quite unusual outfit. Sharon's mother was raised in a strong religious tradition, always dressed modestly, and demanded the same of her daughter. That day

Sharon appeared with lots of makeup, her hair done up in a very dramatic fashion; she wore jewelry, very short shorts, and a skimpy T shirt that revealed more than it covered. There was an oriental flavor to her appearance, also an important clue. This presentation was totally out of character for her. She had never had a boyfriend and had never reported any sexual activity, yet her whole demeanor invited sexual pursuit. Waiting for her appointment, Sharon moved with a calculated seductiveness that pointed to many experiences she had never reported. So dramatic was her change that the secretary and the therapist did not recognize her at first. It was only when she began to speak with her usual voice that it became clear who she was.

More targeted exploration now revealed a very different set of facts. It turned out that the young woman had been sexually molested by the biological father from the time she was three years old. He was a professor of Asian studies, specializing in Indian mythology. He had developed a strong interest in the *Kamasutra* and justified his pedophilic incestuous behavior on the basis of a distorted interpretation of its teachings. He thought it was beneficial for children to be introduced to sexuality early so they would not develop the inhibitions he suffered in his own life. He insisted on daily touching and rubbing, which ultimately progressed to intercourse in highly intricate ways as modeled in the *Kamasutra*.

This was a secret kept in the family, of course. The mother knew about the occurrences but thought her husband, whom she adored, was well intentioned. She was grateful to him at the time for her own sexual liberation, an issue she had been working on for years in therapy prior to knowing her husband. She was greatly impressed by his academic credentials: How could she mistrust such a well-known and worldwide authority, who was popular with his students and led a highly successful professional life?

Her husband had sworn his wife and daughter to secrecy because the world was not ready for his revolutionary ideas. The couple would use their child as a demonstration object of the success of this child-rearing strategy. The mother never abandoned the child; she always remained involved and in fact was quite overinvolved and controlling at times when the girl made moves toward independence.

For personal reasons having to do with her own highly restrictive upbringing, the mother was never able to stand up to this husband who was several years her senior, despite some uneasiness about his practices. She felt uneasy about what was happening to her child, and this propelled her to compensate by being extra loving and concerned. She never protected Sharon from the daily ritualistic "preparation for a successful reproductive life" as it was planned by the father. When Sharon began complaining, her mother would rationalize the father's behavior and emphasize how much he cared for the child. Such conflicting messages inevitably resulted in pathology, for how could a preschooler make sense of any of that?

In the end, Sharon's father was killed during a fight in a brothel in India on one of his frequent trips to that continent. One can only wonder about the exact precipitant for the fight. His absence apparently ended the abuse, and evidently it did not recur with any of the other husbands. As Sharon matured, though, peculiar symptoms began to occur, which culminated in her admission to hospital as an anorexic patient.

Sharon's treatment was not nearly as uncomplicated as Tim's. Our difficulty in obtaining the details of her case history revealed many gaps, uncertainties, and inconsistencies. Her spaciness and inability to remember large chunks of time—especially conflict-laden time with her mother—represented dissociative amnesia. Her wanderings through the hospital were fugue states. During these episodes, she repeated patterns of activity from her childhood: she had often thought that her parents had built a secret maze for her in their home. She imagined that if she could figure out how to go from room to room in a secret order, she would be spared from further sexual experimentation and isolation from other children. She thought her hospitalization was yet another maze set up in a different system and if she passed, she would be allowed to go home and be happy.

A case such as this always makes a therapist feel slightly out of balance, with its many unexpected twists and turns. If you feel like a Good Samaritan with cases of ASD, then you surely feel like Sherlock Holmes in cases with DDO, especially early on. "Be prepared for the unexpected" is the general rule, both in diagnosis and in treatment. It is not uncommon to go through several false diagnoses: this girl mimicked Anorexia Nervosa quite convincingly for a while, tricking even herself into assuming this new identity. But closer scrutiny of the case shows that certain details do not fit, such as her ease in gaining weight. Cases like this one are difficult because very often the apparently appropriate family exterior cloaks the reality of the dark family secrets.

Personality Disorders Related to Trauma: Borderline Personality Disorder (BPD)

Borderline personality disorder (BPD) has long been suspected to be related to psychiatric trauma. Although few adolescents fulfill diagnostic criteria for this disorder, some do, and it is useful to discuss BPD in this context, as it represents the extreme manifestation of chronic traumatization that has led to a substantial fragmentation of the self.

Many features are common to the personality disorders: emotional instability, high reactivity to events, intense preoccupation with particular details of one's life, etched memories, and inappropriate responses to current situations. Individuals manifesting these disorders also share events suffered outside normal human experience—usually episodes of abuse and neglect in the patient's early history—and problems with irritability and impulsivity.

The main differences reside in the time course of the disorders:

1. PTSD tends to be relatively short-lived, while BPD is a personality problem, which presents with stable instability over many years.

2. Patients with PTSD have some problems in the interpersonal domain, but patients with BPD have those problems in a particularly pervasive fashion.

These problems are a part of the diagnostic criteria. The patients' relationships swing from idealization to vilification and back in the span of a few hours. This behavior points to profound attachment problems in the BPD patient, and these are not necessary ingredients for the other trauma-related pathologies. Ambivalent attachment is usually present and needs to be expected in the course of treatment of BPD. The diagnostic seesaw from overinvolvement to neglect between patient and significant others is impressive. Interpersonal crises follow imagined and real rejection as a rule, and the treatment relationship is by no means spared such fluctuations. The patient's dependency needs are sexualized and thus bound to be disappointed. Sexuality is usually experienced as highly exploitive and at times quite undifferentiated.

These cases also share many features with dissociative disorders, but the main new ingredient is the extreme ambivalence in the interpersonal climate in which these patients operate. There's no Sherlock Holmes feeling here; instead, we often feel as if we are in an emotional vice. There are constant demands that are impossible to fulfill because they require abandonment of one's professional role. Yet nonresponse leads to crises of rejection and dejection in the patients that are coercively played out: "If you do not give me an extra appointment (which I won't keep anyway), then I will kill myself (because you clearly do not understand how much I need you). If you do give me the appointment, then I will quickly show you what a loathsome creature you are for allowing me to boss you around like this: I won't show up, I won't use my therapy time well, or I'll just be bored to tears because you don't really know how to help me."

The content of the sessions is not what is primarily important. What the patient wants is this: "I will show you in the treatment process what it felt like to be a kid who was abused, neglected, and never quite sure whether I could count on anybody to do anything at all for me. I want you—complacent, happy, superior-acting therapist—to feel exactly the way I did and still do in all my important relationships. The only way to help me is to feel exactly what I felt growing up."

Here is a good example:

EMILY

A sixteen-year-old girl, Emily, came to us with a history of three suicide attempts. We were consulted after her most recent overdose, which resulted in some liver damage following her ingestion of two hundred tablets of Acetaminophen. Both Emily and her mother wanted her to be discharged to home directly from the intensive care unit because "she has her own outpatient therapist" and didn't need any further evaluation or psychiatric input. On closer inquiry, we learned that the last contact Emily had had with a therapist had actually been three months earlier.

The precipitant for the current suicide attempt was Emily's breakup with a boyfriend, Ben, ten years her senior. The breakup occurred because she was also intensively involved with another boyfriend with whom she might be pregnant. The pregnancy turned out to be a false alarm, but Ben left because he could not stand her multiple infidelities. In addition, there was considerable friction between mother and daughter regarding Ben, as he had been freeloading off the family for the past two years. Following Ben's walkout, Emily took the overdose because, in her words, "Now I was sure that Ben was the only man I could ever love." The overdose occurred after Emily had slept over at the other boy's house because she "couldn't stand the crazy jealousy of Ben" any longer and she was never going to be under the same roof with him again.

Emily's developmental background revealed that she was an only child born to a single teenage mother. Her mother had a series of live-in boyfriends who abused drugs, alcohol, and Emily at a fairly regular rate. The child was exposed to violence between adults and a series of abandonments by her mother, who would intermittently move out impulsively and leave Emily in the care of these boyfriends for several days at a time. This behavior progressed to the point that social services finally intervened and placed the child in a foster home for five years. In that home Emily, then seven, was sexually abused by another child in placement, and around age ten, she had intercourse with another foster father. She was placed back with her mother who at that time was working and off drugs and alcohol. About six months after Emily returned home, her mother's new boyfriend started a sexual relationship with the child. This lasted about one year without the mother's knowledge. When Emily was placed again and the boyfriend was charged, the mother informed the agencies that her daughter "had it coming because she acted so precociously." The whole tone of the mother's accusation was competitive and vindictive, as if she were dealing with a rival for her boyfriend's affections. However, as soon as Emily was removed from her custody again, the mother began a long series of phone calls demanding that the child be reunited with the family.

Emily's father was probably in jail for a drug-related crime and was never involved with the girl. The mother's parents were both uninvolved with the family and not prepared to help out. They cited personal illness as the main reason.

This case shows the mixture of abandonment and traumatic experiences typical for this type of patient. The tapestry of chaos and confusion persists for years, punctuated by intensive interpersonal crises. The same sequence will recur in therapy. One of our favorite images to describe treatment of patients of this kind is of a rider on a mustang without bit and saddle, going at top speed. As the physical distance between patient and attachment figures widens, the emotional positive charge becomes more evident. As the patient and attachment figures become more involved with each other, negative emotions increase. They can't live with each other and they can't live without each other.

The Survivor Syndrome

Finally, we would like to discuss a special form of adapting to trauma and problematic environments, the Survivor Syndrome: This is not a formal diagnosis in the DSM-IV—or in any nomenclature for that matter, but it is a syndrome that we think is psychopathologically quite important.

E. James Anthony first described the clinical picture of those who have survived against all the odds but who later pay a high price for their Darwinian success. Ever since, we have been captured by these patients. In the psychological literature, these individuals are usually described as resilient—as, for instance, in the landmark studies by Emily Werner and Norman Garmezy. The problem with these studies is that they tend to take too optimistic and incomplete a view of these individuals. This should be not surprising because these studies were done with measures that operate at a low level of resolution and detail. The discerning clinical eye can detect more reliably that not all is well in these survivors, despite the considerable evidence for success in their lives.

In-depth interviews over time are required to tell the whole story. A person who has managed to survive repeated trauma has done so at great cost. Survivors' ways of handling the traumatic situation are predominantly by detachment, withdrawal, and isolation. These strategies allow them to function well while the trauma occurs. Compensatory fantasies of escape, flashbacks, and emotional numbing are ubiquitous but are not experienced as problematic, mostly because the emotional coloring is blocked out. These individuals appear never to enter the phase of "mental digestion" of the event or events.

But such an adaptive stance also comes at a price: gradually these people lose all emotional responsiveness, even with events that are not reminiscent of trauma. Eventually they end up feeling empty and depleted, lacking sense and direction in life. The survivors' victory becomes increasingly hollow as their lives paradoxically improve. While survivors can function adequately in almost all aspects of their lives, they can derive little enjoyment from life.

Problems for these people eventually become apparent in two key domains: achievement and intimacy. Developmentally, these domains become most prominent in late adolescence. The literature is quite rich in descriptions of such characters. Camus's *The Stranger* is a good example. Two recent movies also deal with the same subject: *Sankofa* (directed by Haile Gerima), an underground movie, and a less realistic, Hollywood product, *The Prince of Tides*, a film version of a novel by Pat Conroy.

Here is another example:

TYLER

A fifteen-year-old young man, Tyler, was brought to us for underachievement at school. It was quite evident to his family and his teachers that he was extremely bright. His school performance, however, had been problematic: at times he would turn in outstanding work and put the class to shame; at other times he would be completely negligent and not turn in anything. This pattern had triggered an extensive investigation to determine whether he was learning disabled. The tests showed no learning deficit but pointed to a highly variable motivational state regarding learning. Nevertheless, Tyler's father placed him in a private school for children with learning disabilities to help him acquire the skills necessary for self-directed study. This strategy was only moderately successful, mainly because it was not indicated and contributed to Tyler's isolation from his old peers. He transferred back into public high school where he resumed his C+ performance.

Although he was described as a friendly youngster by his father, Tyler had remarkably few close friends. He was an attractive young man in both his appearance and general demeanor. He gave the initial impression of being sincere and honest and interested in getting help. We found it quite surprising that although he was quite handsome, he reported only fleeting and superficial relationships with girls. Many of his girlfriends were just that—friends—although on several occasions, girls had indicated interest in him. He never took the hints and invitations and instead distanced himself by becoming more involved in school work or sports.

Tyler was an extremely talented tennis player, but as with his scholastic performance, he was not able to deliver the sustained effort necessary to capitalize on his talents. Whenever he would get close to success in one domain, he would shift his attention to another, completely neglecting the former. As an illustration, when a girl became increasingly interested in him and a date was the next logical step, all of a sudden Tyler would start practicing tennis four to five hours a day. As soon as he started winning his challenge matches in the team, he would bury himself deeply in a long-neglected academic project. The net result was that when he was just about to reap the rewards for his efforts, he would turn them off by failing to pursue the finishing touches, the last steps to put closure on the project. Dates were not arranged, tennis matches with Tyler as number one or two were never played, papers were not returned with the teachers' editorial comments integrated. It was as if success was too much for him to bear. To be singled out was anxiety provoking and threatening.

Tyler's developmental background was complicated, as one might expect. His father was a highly successful trial lawyer who rose from an impoverished background in the South by hard work and dedication. He had financed his own education and was quite proud of his achievements. He had married early in college. His wife, Tyler's mother, was his high school sweetheart and homecoming queen of the small town in which they both grew up. She was a great beauty and had been brought up in a middle-class family to fulfill the traditional role of a wife and mother. She dropped out of college when she became pregnant with Tyler's oldest brother. As her husband became increasingly successful and renowned, her lack of education became more and more important and led to significant friction within the marriage. Tyler's father became critical of her and disenchanted with her Southern ways as they moved in highly sophisticated Bay area circles. Tyler's mother began to drink, secretly at first, but progressively more openly. Ugly scenes and fights ensued, and as time went on, her alcoholism became pronounced, leading to the couple's divorce. Tyler's mother remained in the family's palatial home in the Berkeley hills with the three children, while the father moved on to San Francisco.

What followed was a series of increasingly traumatic events. The mother's drinking became more and more uncontrolled. She led a promiscuous life, at times bringing dangerous men into the home. Tyler's role in the family was to cover up for his mother's behavior. He was the one who picked her up from the floor and cleaned her when she had soiled herself. In return, she showered him with affection when she was sober and heaped scorn and contempt on him for being an inadequate substitute husband when she was drunk. All this was carefully kept a secret from Tyler's father and even from his older siblings, who were involved with peers, high school, and college and could escape by staying away more easily than Tyler. Because Tyler was still of school age, he did not have such a path of external distance available to him; therefore, he had to create an inner pathway for himself.

These events coincided with Tyler's experiencing increasing trouble at school and in all domains in his life. He had always had a strong propensity to isolate his emotions, control them, and suppress them. He was much like his father in this respect. This form of emotional control allowed Tyler to tolerate the emotional roller coaster of the relationship with his mother while maintaining a reasonable outward appearance of normalcy. His avoidance of girls was understandable given his primary model of what such relationships were "really" like. His unwillingness to let others see exactly what he was capable of doing made sense, given his need to conceal his deep feelings of inadequacy, resulting from his mother's inappropriate criticisms and demands. His reluctance to stand out in any way was entirely understandable as most of his mother's attacks on him were precipitated by her rage at his appearing to be competent and therefore able to separate himself from her and function independently.

Survivors generally demonstrate two special features: they have a strong tendency to develop elaborate escapist fantasies, and they suffer from the effects of survivor guilt, like all other patients with trauma-related pathology. However, the suffering is not as immediately accessible to them early in treatment. Tyler was very preoccupied with becoming an astronaut. He had a whole collection of videos showing space flights and one of his all-time favorite movies was *2001* by Stanley Kubrick. In treatment, we could always expect a downturn of emotions and events just when he was about to get his life under control and come close to success: before graduation from high school, before graduation from college, after receiving a good job offer, or having a woman interested in him. During these times, Tyler would become intensely preoccupied with his mother's health, his brothers' lack of scholastic success, and their tendencies to drink too much. At times, he would even plead for the therapist to become involved in his siblings' lives because he could not stand the idea of being the only one in his family to derive benefit from the treatment. He would do anything to avoid drawing attention to himself, either positive or negative.

How to Differentiate

Examining an adolescent who we suspect has been traumatized is not easy. Under the best of circumstances, the general developmental stance of this age group is to avoid seeking help, and having trauma symptoms tends to strengthen this tendency. Although a variety of structured interviews and scales in the field can help us define the syndromes we have described above, the clinical interview is still the main way to diagnose this spectrum of disorders.

Special precautions must be taken, however, to obtain valid and reliable information. This is no time for strong prejudices and preconceived notions. Here are some pointers for diagnostic and therapeutic techniques that we find most useful:

1. *Be prepared to encounter trauma but do not expect or anticipate it.* There is a fine line between being appropriately watchful for hints that trauma has occurred and asking leading questions. Doing so in these cases is always problematic as many trauma victims are highly suggestible; and the more severely ill a person is, the more chronic the manifestations of trauma-related pathology seem to be. False memories are easily induced in these

patients and at times the patients find it impossible to distinguish the false memories from true events. The reasons for the confusion are complex, and there is currently a very active academic debate on how much of a memory can in fact be implanted. If anyone is vulnerable to such implantation, however, it is a traumatized patient. We encourage you to read the literature on this topic as a detailed discussion is not possible in this chapter.

2. *Use memory-augmenting techniques sparingly and carefully.* There is very little to be gained from interviews that are assisted by sodium amytal. We also believe that little information can be obtained under hypnosis that time eventually will not bring out during the normal therapeutic process. Moreover, once you have used one of these special augmenting techniques, the material that is uncovered is highly suspect in court. We suggest never using sodium amytal with adolescents, and using hypnosis only in those cases where the presenting symptom is acutely dangerous and has not responded to regular interventions in due time.

3. *Think about survivor guilt when you ask questions about the perpetuation of trauma.* Much of the patient's repetition of trauma-related symptoms and events can be understood from this perspective. Survivors always bring the concentration camp or the ghetto with them, no matter how much they have tried to leave it behind. And survivors always wonder why they escaped while others did not. They may not feel worthy to be spared and often will unconsciously seek self-destruction.

4. *Prepare yourself for your own vicarious trauma reaction.* On many occasions, after we have examined traumatized patients and have heard in detail what happened to them—and we must as part of diagnosis and treatment—we often find that we too have developed mild to moderate symptoms of Acute Stress Disorder. The most impressive case involved a young man who described to us in prison how he witnessed and participated in a ritualistic satanic slaughter of another man. The images his description invoked were with us for many weeks. Such reaction may also generate a special countertransference: that is, you may unwittingly avoid pursuing leads and fuller discussions in an

effort to protect yourself. When you work with a traumatized population, you need to make special arrangements for your own debriefing to avoid becoming cynical, distant, and unhelpful.

5. *Be patient, and allow enough time for exploration.* One of our most common mistakes in dealing with trauma issues is to rush to get all the details. Respect the defensive structures the patient has erected and be gentle in your pursuit. Once the flow of trauma-related material has started, containing it or turning it off is sometimes very difficult. This is especially true early in treatment when the problems are addressed for the first time. Extra time and extra sessions help, but you must be careful not to get into a permanent crisis arrangement with the patient. This is especially true with the more chronically traumatized patient, such as one with Borderline Personality Disorder.

6. *Be mindful that trauma can co-occur with other diagnoses, and be prepared for trauma to be misdiagnosed by others—and even by you.* The most frequently associated other syndromes are conduct disorders, depression, and other anxiety disorders (see relevant chapters in this book). But we have had adolescents referred to us for substance abuse or Attention Deficit Disorder or even psychosis and later found that they were suffering mostly from the trauma-related syndromes. Trauma is the great impostor in psychiatry, but a careful developmental history will usually be most helpful in bringing it to light.

Specific Treatment Techniques

A surprising discovery in the treatment of adolescent trauma is the small amount of good research that has been done in this area. Descriptions of this kind of pathology have been in the literature for over one hundred years, and although much is known clinically about how to approach these problems and treat them, there is very little high-quality research to guide us in choosing the best approach to treatment. This lack is understandable for new diagnoses, such as Acute Stress Disorder, which is a new-comer to the field, or for the survivor syndrome, which has not yet made it into the diagnostic nomenclature; but it is quite dis-appointing to find so little in the research literature about ado-lescent Posttraumatic Stress Disorder, dissociative disorders, and even Borderline Personality Disorder.

THE LITERATURE

A recent article by Susan Solomon and her group offers some guidance. These researchers found and reviewed twelve studies on the treatment of Posttraumatic Stress Disorder that used appropriate design and measures. None of these studies were with children or adolescents, so applying the results to our age range should be done with caution. Most of the studies dealt with Vietnam veterans or victims of rape, torture, bereavement, physical assault, and child abuse.

The general conclusion from the review is that some treat-ment was clinically meaningful. Psychosocial treatments appeared to have stronger effects than pharmacological inter-ventions. Among the most successful were behavioral techniques involving exposure. The symptoms of PTSD that were most successfully reduced were symptoms of intrusion, such as flash-backs. Exposure treatment also holds considerable risk in terms of inducing morbidity in patients; it needs to be carefully selected, applied, and monitored. Other psychosocial techniques that were successful were cognitive therapy, psychodynamic ther-apy, and hypnosis. Some medications were effective. Tricyclic antidepressants and mono-amine oxidase inhibitors showed some effect, whereas benzodiazepines did not.

Solomon and her colleagues concluded that much more research is needed before any of these interventions can be declared effective and lasting in the treatment of PTSD. In par-ticular, the group felt that studies should be directed at combined treatment approaches that used a variety of modalities, with attention paid to examining their mutually augmenting effects.

We believe that this is a wise recommendation. We agree that the most successful treatment for these patients will probably involve a variety of modalities in combination, targeting disturbances in quite different domains. We expect the findings in future studies to be akin to what we are finding in the treatment of depression about the efficacy of combined psychotherapy and pharmacotherapy.

Medications can be used to address disturbances in the basic needs domain. They can help normalize sleep and eating patterns and control emotional reactions that are far out of proportion to specific situations, cannot be worked with effectively, and create negative feedback loops in treatment itself. But, as we see below, medications are only adjuncts in the permanent treatment of these disorders. Much emphasis needs to be placed on the successful integration of traumatic material and the use of information in building new aspects of the self and strengthening areas of existing weakness. We suggest that this synergistic view of combined treatment holds the most promise.

Meanwhile, where does that leave all of us who are struggling with honest-to-goodness live patients and not just research subjects? We simply do not have the luxury to wait for research results to roll in as we face these families and their children. We have to be prepared to intervene as well as we can. The following specific interventions are based on our own lengthy experience in dealing with all aspects of trauma in many different settings with adolescents from many different backgrounds.

The Treatment of Acute Stress Disorder (ASD)

We begin with the case of Sara, described earlier in the chapter, as it is the easiest and simplest of the cases presented here. Cases such as this are apt to make you feel like Sigmund Freud himself and to endear you to family and referring physician alike, because if you intervene in a timely fashion, a good outcome is virtually guaranteed. Everybody is relieved and grateful.

According to our model, ASD represents a temporary arrest in the phase of hyperarousal of human trauma response. If such arousal can be dealt with quickly, further mending will quite likely take place with minimal guidance and intervention. The technique that is often most effective is simple catharsis.

Usually we ask the patient to describe in great detail what in fact occurred—in this case, the events leading to the accident, during the accident, and following it. The patient does not need to follow the exact time line; this is not a court report or deposition. It is important for you to follow the affective tone of the situation and stay with it, facilitating the patient's expression of emotion by appropriate remarks.

In this particular case we began the intervention by asking the patient to describe her nightmares because they were so troublesome and disruptive. She began the description haltingly, but her facial expression indicated clearly that she was extremely frightened by them. We commented on that, and this response rapidly led to Sara's describing events of the actual accident. She remembered avoiding the bicyclist and feeling tremendously relieved, but as she looked ahead again, she saw two cars aimed at her. At that moment, she was convinced she was going to die. The boom of the impact blended symbolically with the loud horns of the Mack trucks she saw in her dreams. As she described that massive phalanx coming toward her, she felt weak to the point of fainting. She remembered waking up in the ambulance, convinced again that she was dead and expecting to be taken to the morgue. Much to her surprise, she could move the fingers of her hand, a discovery that flooded her with a glorious feeling of being alive. Later, in the intensive care unit, she began to wonder whether the drivers of the other cars were alive also, and she demanded to see newspaper reports of the accident.

Sara's description began haltingly at first, punctuated by unexpectedly intense emotions. As her catharsis gained momentum, affect and cognition became more parallel and she needed fewer and fewer prompts to keep the flood coming. She confessed to being relieved after her sessions, but also commented often that she could not stop her emotions from spilling over and taking command. As staff and family helped us in further getting the patient to describe her emotions, Sara became much more calm and composed and began to put the accident in perspective on her own.

We never heard much of the relevant material directly, as Sara shared it with others—nurses, friends, parents. But catharsis does not have to be confined to one person as does truly explorative psychotherapeutic material. We take our cues from the patients, and in our experience many of them use other avenues of expression outside their consultation time. The whole intervention with Sara took about seven sessions, five closely clustered in the beginning, and two spaced apart in the month following her discharge. Some of these sessions included her parents for at least part of the time, and we used these to give the parents an appropriate update on how Sara saw her accident and what irrational issues she was struggling with unknown to them. They very quickly grasped the situation and were helpful to the point of functioning almost like a set of auxiliary therapists.

Sara's sleep normalized so quickly that we did not need to use symptomatic psychopharmacological interventions to help her regain her normal daily patterns. We did, however, ask her to keep a sleep flowsheet for about one month so we would have a record. Had her sleep patterns changed significantly in the course of intervention, we would have reconsidered our decision. We also asked for a dream diary as we wanted to track the more unavowed and inaccessible aspects of her reactions to the accident. The diary reassured us as she very quickly returned to more tranquil and soothing themes as she recovered.

Throughout her discussions, it was apparent that Sara was amnestic for parts of the events. She was very concerned about these lapses, fearing what might have happened during these times. She in fact asked to be hypnotized to be able to remember, but we suggested that time would most likely fill in all these gaps and that as far as we knew, there were no hidden secrets or surprises needing attention. As she progressed, almost all her amnesia filled in and she gained a fairly complete time line of the events, as we had predicted.

The Treatment of Posttraumatic Stress Disorder (PTSD)

Completing the treatment of a case like Tim's, described earlier in the chapter, is a much more complicated task requiring patience and skilled technique. Feeling like Sigmund Freud is simply not enough. Being able to handle patients expertly is closer to the mark.

Simple catharsis and facilitation of emotional expression will not work here. According to our model, the patient is stuck in the phase of defensive control of some of the trauma-related material. The defenses activate when the affect gets too intense and when the explorative questioning gets too close to a hidden, unavowed conflict. In comparison with Sara's treatment, the process of PTSD treatment follows a much more stop/start path, even with adequate facilitative questions. Now, proper technique also has to include special forms of reliving the events.

In our program, we use videotaped accounts of the traumatizing incident by the patient. The therapist replays these in sessions to reinduce the traumatic state. Roger Pitman at Harvard uses so-called script-driven imagery in which the patient's account of what happened is read back to him and he is asked to imagine what is being described.

Inclusion of friends and family is more problematic in this process, as some of the conflict buried in the traumatic material very often involves one of them. The interpersonal domain needs to be carefully managed and taken into account as you work with the patient, and it is definitely unwise to assume that family or friends can always be used as support.

In Tim's case, the length of his illness suggested strongly that there was more to his story than was first apparent. He in fact had two illnesses: the first one after the shooting of his stepfather, the second one while he was in the care of the California Youth Authority (CYA). As we indicated above, the thematic lead in these cases is usually survivor guilt. What keeps PTSD alive, in part, is some aspect of the trauma that is unavowed but crucial to the event, involving some imagined or real responsibility or failure. The defensive posture walls off the conflict in the situation, but it also prevents the patient from completing the processes of acknowledgment and mourning of losses.

The first clue in Tim's case was the trigger for the recurrence of the event. While they are with the CYA, residents are expected to describe a variety of offenses and assume responsibility for them. Thus, Tim had been exposed to many horrible stories in the course of his incarceration, yet none of them triggered a recurrence of his PTSD. It was another youth's story of his mother killing her boyfriend that rekindled Tim's flashbacks and intrusive symptoms. It behooved us to find out why that particular scene presented problems.

We started by having Tim discuss on videotape his version of what he'd heard in group, then what in fact had happened to him. This part of the treatment is meant to represent active exposure to the traumatic event. With each retelling and questioning, we ask for more detail and more associations to the material. We carefully monitor whether the patient is upset and to what degree within and outside the session. As a therapist gets closer to having the reconstruction complete, a massive emotional upheaval in the patient is quite common. This upheaval can result in extremely dangerous complications such as impulsive actions, suicidality, transient psychosis, careless risk-taking, and severe abuse of substances. As many of these scenarios involve the patient's guilt about having failed to act in some way, or guilt about having acted wrongly, even the most competent and self-confident adolescent can become difficult to manage to the point of having to be restrained or even hospitalized. We often warn patient and family of such complications and reassure them that we all are prepared to take over whenever the need arises. As you approach this phase of treatment, you should have a clear contingency plan as to where the patient will go if he must be hospitalized, how he will get there, and who will be involved in the transport.

We warned the staff at the CYA that we were about to explore a most significant event in Tim's history and that we wanted to be informed if his behavior outside treatment appeared to be problematic. As always, we asked the patient for a sleep flowsheet and a dream diary, but in Tim's case neither was productive before the exploration was completed.

Tim came closer to a complete description of the events surrounding his stepfather's death, and one day the floodgates opened: he confessed that he had not been open about some elements. Although he was attached to his mother, he had on many occasions been very angry with her about her reckless and irresponsible life. As his uncle entered the room, he clearly saw what was about to happen, but assumed that his uncle was about to kill his mother. At that moment, the thought flashed through his mind that this would be a possible solution to some of his family's problems. Instead of ringing out a warning, he simply sat there for what seemed like an eternity waiting for his uncle to pull the trigger. To his horror, the bullet killed the wrong person.

He was extremely despondent as he described this core event. At the time, we did not question any of his assumptions but simply let him express his extreme remorse, grief, and guilt about having had these thoughts. The session was double in length, and still the young man was quite inconsolable. We instituted some special supervision for him overnight and resumed our work the next day. That night, the youngster had a whole series of recurrent dreams that showed the incident over and over again, and sometimes the gun was in *his* hand. We witnessed the full force of emotions that previously had been controlled and pushed out of his awareness for months.

After such a crisis, much important follow-up work needs to be done. Often the patient misconstructs events and assumes too much responsibility for what has happened. In Tim's case, we went over his mother's deposition along with the police report and showed him that there were only fractions of a second involved between his uncle's entry and the firing of the pistol. What seemed like an eternity was most likely a distorted representation of time that was induced by Tim's own terror in the situation. Although justifiably angry at his mother for being neglectful and uninvolved, his fantasies about her death did not constitute murder.

After such a confession the treatment process tends to shift: the patient is now ready to rework the traumatic scene and begin to integrate information in a more realistic fashion. Because many defensive processes are at work—and at this point they yield very slowly to intervention—the faulty assumptions keep returning, sometimes in different forms. In many cases, the distorted imagery of the event fades very slowly, even with repeated realistic descriptions. As his treatment proceeded, Tim's nightmares became more intense rather than less, as in Sara's case. He did require some medication for sleep at some point, an occurrence that is not unusual in the treatment of PTSD. We gave him a sedating antidepressant for about eight weeks, with the target being improved sleep rather than mood.

In the wake of this exploration and in the process of reintegration, Tim became more depressed and tearful. He mourned the loss of both a mother who was never able to fulfill her duties and a stepfather who seemed to be such a promising substitute for his own father. His mood problems became intermittent and never quite met the criteria for major depression. In fact, the process resembled more a complicated bereavement. After eight months of fairly intensive work, Tim was mostly symptom free and again fully functional. The remainder of his therapeutic work focused on establishing a link between his trauma and his subsequent delinquent activities. For him, however, the excitement of being involved in criminal pursuits had become like a sedative that helped him avoid dealing with the losses he had now come to terms with. Now that it was no longer necessary for him to numb and divert himself from his emotions, he was much better able to return to his premorbid self; his parole for two years after this event was uneventful and successful.

The Treatment of Dissociative Disorders

The complexity of intervention with cases such as Sharon's is more difficult and challenging than either of the two preceding cases of Sara and Tim. The main new ingredient that creates major problems for the therapist is the emergence of prolonged dissociative episodes. In these, the patient forgets or avoids material, or is simply unable to stay in treatment because the emerging affective states are intolerable. Patients with dissociative disorders often present pronounced management problems and get themselves into dangerous situations without much warning. The rhythm of intervention feels much like a blindfolded treasure hunt in a labyrinth.

In Sharon's case, her suicide attempt after discharge came totally without warning. She had appeared cheerful and happy to go home. Her parents were happy to receive her. Her sleep had been excellent and she had reported no nightmares. She made plans to return to school, and she caught up with her homework in preparation for this. All was well until she entered a dissociative state while at home, in which she relived her sexual abuse. This episode was triggered when she learned that one of the boys with whom she had become acquainted in the hospital intended to call her and invite her out after his release. She began feeling inexplicably ashamed and "dirty" and took the overdose. Direct exploration of the event with her led to long silences and avoidance on her part. We had to do much defense work and gather many indirect clues to understand the episode.

Such episodes recur with a high degree of frequency throughout treatment. They do not always result in open suicidality. At times, Sharon would go into fugue states on her way to therapy if we had worked on a specially difficult topic in the session before. On many occasions she would call from other cities and apologize for being late, but say that she had lost her way and needed help to find the road to our office.

This lack of continuity in treatment is difficult to live with or plan for. The temptation for the therapist is to assume too much control and too soon. Many therapists are tempted to use hypnosis to get over this fragmented phase of treatment, which reflects the fragmentation of the self these patients are experiencing. We advocate careful and patient pursuit. In this case in particular, control was such an issue that we thought it unwise to proceed with hypnosis or rash rehospitalizations. We resigned ourselves to accepting that her treatment process would continue to leave us feeling always slightly off balance and out of sorts, uncertain of what was about to happen, and that this feeling would be an important clue to the patient's inner state.

As we expected, many important clues emerged almost coincidentally, without obvious connections. In Sharon's case, a peculiar recurrent image led to the exploration of material that ultimately led to the discovery of her ritualistic abuse. She kept seeing a light switch cover from her room in another city where the family had lived during her early childhood. The cover consisted of a clown face that always seemed menacing to her rather than funny. She would report seeing this face in some of her dissociative states or dreams but for a long time could not expand on its significance. The only further clue was that she was about five when she lived in this room.

Gradually more images returned. Sharon remembered sitting in her closet clutching stuffed animals, hearing footsteps outside as someone was looking for her, and being paralyzed with fear. She remembered angry scenes in the kitchen, with her father accusing her mother of obstructionism. She did not remember her abuse right away, but acted it out, by switching into her provocative dress and demeanor. She steadfastly denied any significance to such changes, but shortly thereafter began to date several boys at once—behavior quite out of character for her. When her abuse was brought up in treatment, the revelation did not bring any relief, but rather an intensification of her self-destructive tendencies. She felt dirty, ashamed, and unworthy of being alive.

Sharon's treatment proceeded in fits and starts for about twenty-four months. It ended when she terminated abruptly because she thought there was too much conflict between her and her mother regarding the therapist's role, and she was tired of the fighting. She did, however, accept a referral to another therapist, whom she saw for several years without her mother's knowledge. It was difficult to engage family and child together, as Sharon was simply not able at the time to confront her mother about the mother's role in the abuse, and Sharon would not allow her stepfather to be part of her treatment in any fashion.

We expect Sharon to have a difficult life, requiring many more years of intervention. On the last follow-up, her dissociative symptoms had been reduced to occasional episodes of "spaciness." Her main problems were her interpersonal relationships with men. They had always been either exploitive or insignificant and unsatisfying. She did well in the domains of work and achievement. She had no further recurrence of her eating symptoms.

The Treatment of Borderline Personality Disorder (BPD)

The treatment of this complex disorder has been extensively described elsewhere in the literature mostly dealing with adults. Here we sketch only the essentials and highlight special problems with adolescents.

The treatment of borderline patients is in many ways one of the most taxing processes in psychiatry. The combination of pervasive dysfunction in many domains and attachment problems that complicate or even bar access to a therapeutic relationship makes it very difficult for most mental health professionals to maintain a large caseload of these patients and remain effective. We all have different thresholds for how much chaos, abuse, and unpredictability we can endure. It's difficult to be alternatively idealized or devalued by the very same patient who constantly appears to be in danger of losing her tenuous grip on life. The steady stream of coercive behaviors that force involvement and assistance exclusively on the patient's terms are hard to manage for the best of us. Craig Johnson has described a clinical model to emulate when one is going to treat a number of these patients. It involves creating group supervision for all cases, with a treatment team whose members are able to help each other differentiate pure coercion from true need. This support helps the team members to prevent punitive responses fed by angry countertransference and to preserve appropriate boundaries. The last issue is particularly relevant in these cases, as there are perennial challenges to the treatment.

It is often necessary to help these patients manage their lives as well as their emotions. At times we may become too involved in their lives and bypass treatment, so safeguards need to be established to prevent this from happening. All of us recall situations in which we felt we were drowning in a BPD patient's demands as he or she was going through yet another rapprochement crisis, then felt like we were emerging from being held under water as one of our colleagues shed some new light on a particular situation that freed us from the grip of coercive behavior.

Treatment with Emily, whose case was described earlier, was no different in that regard. In the course of her hospitalization, she formed a strong attachment to one of the staff. Contrary to her initial stance, she made a rapid shift to idealizing the new therapist who could make it all better quicker, once Emily and her mother had accepted the fact that discharge was not immediately forthcoming. In three sessions, Emily told her new therapist all the traumatic material she could remember, with much graphic detail. The therapist had moved from bad to good in Emily's eyes, and predictably the patient began an intense devaluation of her outpatient therapist. When Emily was made to understand that she would have to return to her old therapist for follow-up care, there was another crisis. Her mother complained to the director of the hospital that we were unwilling to provide services to her daughter. The switch was complete and seamless, as if there had never been a negative evaluation of our efforts as little as three weeks earlier.

Emily offered material at a breathtaking rate, as if to say "See, I am an interesting patient, and I will do everything you say, just as long as you take care of me, because you are the only one who can help me." Calm insistence on the original treatment plan, along with questioning about how Emily and her mother had changed their feelings about us so quickly, produced results. The patient was transferred back to her therapist after we made sure that this arrangement was appropriate and helpful. We offered to be available as a backup system for further times of crisis, and that seemed to settle things for a while.

In the treatment pattern that developed, Emily would work on her abandonment and abuse issues quite openly and quickly as an outpatient. For the therapist, the feeling was like being Sigmund Freud all over again, but with an uneasy expectation that the other shoe was about to drop. Emily then would expect the issues that she had raised to be fixed quickly; otherwise, why had she gone through all this pain and turmoil in recalling her problems? At times, she would fabricate events to force involvement and resolution. And if she did not receive immediate gratification, she would engage in angry outbursts and denigrations.

At times, Emily would threaten to or would actually hurt herself. These episodes of self-injury were not necessarily meant to result in death, although some of them easily might have done so by sheer chance; but they often calmed her down. Paradoxically, hurting herself felt soothing to Emily at times when her anger was overwhelming and disorganizing. To see blood run down her arm after cutting herself would make her feel alive and whole.

The main problem in treating this kind of patient is the intensity of the transferential relationship, which replicates in minute detail the neglectful abandonment and abuse experienced with the primary attachment figure. Only this time, the tables are turned: the patient is in the driver's seat and the adult-mother-therapist is at the whim and fancy of this all powerful–all weak child-patient. Revenge themes appear gradually and only give way slowly to themes of abandonment-depression and terror at being left to perish. And slower yet, there is a newly developing trust that the patient will not be abandoned again and a new understanding that help comes in different shapes and forms.

At any given time, the patient's newly gained ego can crumble and give way to pronounced tantrums and acting out, especially as you work on painful material. A very common distortion of the normal explorative process in treatment is that the therapist enjoys the patient's plight and perpetuates it, similar to other adults in the patient's life. The content of the sessions very often is repetitive and not very helpful; most often, progress is evident only in the process of the sessions.

Intermittently, Emily needed to be hospitalized for suicidality, self-injury, or too much risk-taking. These episodes became farther and farther apart as her treatment progressed, and most crises could be handled by joint sessions with her mother or phone calls. At times, Emily needed to be on medication to control her rage and depression. Most of the time, though, she was not on medicine.

Patients like Emily are patients for life. After an initial treatment period of two years, her sessions were reduced to one a month at her request. She maintained progress and was able to heed the therapist's warning that she had a lifelong sensitivity to loss and abandonment and that at times of interpersonal change, she needed to come in for "prophylactic" exploration and help. This worked fine until she lost her boyfriend Ben's affections over the abortion of an unwanted pregnancy. She threatened to keep the child regardless of his wishes. He felt coerced and left the relationship. His departure precipitated another intense crisis with suicidality which was made worse by the therapist's being on vacation. The patient was hospitalized briefly and rejoined treatment after the therapist's return.

Emily's prognosis is not good for full recovery. She will need indefinite treatment, dispensed in appropriate doses, especially around critical developmental transitions. But she will be able to manage a job, and possibly a relationship or even a family.

The Treatment of the Survivor

In many ways, we have saved the best for last. Interventions with survivors of traumatic environments represent a unique challenge, but they also offer unique opportunities and rewards. These are unusual patients who have struggled against the odds and prevailed.

There are adolescents who clearly are set apart by personal characteristics that have enabled them to prevail. Michael Rutter has described them as intelligent, interpersonally attractive, and likely to approach problems in a positive fashion. They have survived because they are able to distance themselves from chaos and confusion without getting caught up in it altogether.

Initially, therapists thought these people paid no price for their success; they were often mislabeled, we believe, as invulnerable. Nothing could be further from the truth. Their success comes at a high price, although it is not always immediately obvious. Ironically, as is so often true in life, the very thing that allowed them to survive is what later gets them into trouble. Their ability to stay aloof from chaos can later become reluctance to be involved in intimate relationships; their desire not to stand out as a target turns into underachievement; their ability to stand on their own two feet in the absence of structure can become their inability to turn for help when it is clearly needed. In short, old programs that ran very successfully in a problematic environment become problems themselves in environments where there are many degrees of freedom and choice. The trick is to turn these youngsters into patients without scaring them off the difficult task of recovery.

Tyler, whose situation was described earlier, clearly fits this description. He came to treatment because his father, frustrated with Tyler's academic problems in spite of his superior intelligence, had threatened to send him to a boarding school. Tyler had friends in the area whom he did not want to lose, so he grudgingly interviewed us for the job of therapist—at least, that is what it felt like. He asked us many questions about our qualifications and theoretical outlook on life, our intellectual achievements, and our specific plan to help him. Then followed a series of sessions, when the general story of the family was discussed. Much of this account had the flavor of "well, yes, it was quite difficult, but you know it's all over now."

When we suggested that these circumstances would pose some difficulty for any young man growing up, Tyler remarked that he was quite familiar with all the problems and that he handled them fine, thank you very much. We spoke a great deal of his plans to become an astronaut. We were interested to see, however, how little he had prepared himself for such a career. His main interests in school—if any were sustained enough to be called interests—were English literature and writing. This observation was a crack in the armor: a tiny inconsistency in presentation and actual behavior. We did not make much of it, but stored it for future reference.

In fact, we think that one of the main avenues to turning these survivors into successful working patients is to attend to the subtle differences in their real and ideal self-presentations. Very often, we find that this—much more than dreams, fantasies, or similar "mushy" stuff—is the royal road to their unavowed psychology, their fears and their pain.

After one year of infrequent sessions, Tyler graduated from high school and was accepted in a well-known college. He left home after some ambivalence. He had considered abandoning school altogether to join the Air Force, but then thought better of it and started his studies. Of course, he was only thinking about his astronaut career, he said. That was why he hesitated, not because he felt any separation anxiety about leaving home. His therapy sessions dropped to zero in the next half year, as allegedly things were going well for him. Tyler had said he would contact us when appropriate. The wall had gone up again, but we thought perhaps he had what he needed to be back on track. After all, he had considerable gifts.

This was not the case. In midwinter, Tyler called. It was a desperate call, frightening in its emotional intensity, which bespoke fear and depression. He had just been informed that he was failing all his classes and he could not face telling his father. This was the first time he had actually asked for help. He wanted a joint session with his father to discuss the situation and to solicit his father's support, which Tyler was certain would not be forthcoming. As it turned out, he had left his father with the impression that he was in ongoing treatment, so it was quite clear that there were many issues to be discussed. Predictably, the father had a hard time digesting all this bad news, but with some help he offered support and financially backed his son's continued studies.

This session opened the door for many topics dealing with dependency and help seeking. Tyler was truly astonished that I was willing to write a letter to the college to state that he was in treatment and should receive some special consideration. He was even more astonished when he learned that his professors were willing to be flexible when he discussed his situation with them. And most of all, he had greatest difficulty believing that his father would be so supportive, albeit with some help from us. We should note that Tyler's father had been referred for treatment of depression in the meantime and was doing his own significant work regarding his care of his children. Tyler's mother refused to join and continued on her own downward trajectory of alcohol dependency.

The cycle described in this segment—from superficial help seeking and highly controlled independent stance to surprising and powerful emotional decompensation, to therapy aided by asking for support—repeated itself several times in the course of Tyler's treatment. During this time, his mother died from an overdose of sleeping pills; whether she intended to kill herself was unknown, but after her death Tyler's treatment cycle became very intense. Many issues of survivor guilt surfaced, paired with his rage at her blatant emotional exploitation of him when she was drunk. Her questionable sexual behavior was also discussed in relationship to Tyler's hands-off approach to women. Her death represented a true crisis; it unleashed many rageful fantasies against her and brought Tyler very close to the edge. He despaired of his own future, felt genetically doomed, and was almost longing to give up the fight.

His mother's death opened up the area of relationships with women. He actually went through an episode of PTSD followed by a prolonged phase of acute dissociative episodes. His grieving for his mother was difficult and progressed in fits and starts. But for the next two years, he cautiously and carefully became involved with several young women, after some hurtful forays in situations with a low likelihood of success. The relationships were intense and confusing, but his tenacity and his newfound ability to come for help saw him through the toughest times, and he graduated from college in five years.

On follow-up, Tyler continues to do well, with only sporadic intervention. He stopped his regular treatment at the end of college; he is now in graduate school and checks in only periodically in times of confusion. He has learned to read his emotions much better and not to be surprised by their intensity when they break through in a crisis.

In fact, Tyler has had no crises recently. He has a newfound respect for his emotions and is able to use them as guides to life, not as enemies. No longer does he lock them away in his subconscious like undesirable beasts that need to be tamed and controlled. He has no more plans to be an astronaut; instead, he is working toward a career in medicine. He has even thought of psychiatry, but is not sure about that quite yet.

He now wants to be a father, a new goal for him. He used to be afraid of raising a child, having witnessed his parents' profound difficulties with the situation. But overall, his character armor has clearly loosened; his hyper-organized, constricted, and confining personality structure has softened, and he is willing to face life with all its ambiguities and enjoy it.

༄

We have covered a wide range of problems here. In one chapter, it is possible to give only an overview of the complex issues of trauma-related psychopathology in adolescents, but we hope that we have piqued your interest. In many ways, handling these type of problems in this age group is the "calculus" of treatment because of the complex mixture of variables you must deal with. Let there be no mistake: work with victims of trauma is taxing and demanding.

But there is a unique attraction to working with this set of problems. For one, this is an area of psychopathology in which timely intervention truly produces wonderful results, especially in young people still "under construction." I hope that in this chapter we have been able to convey the levels of complexity involved in these syndromes and that we have prepared you to be realistic in your expectations for outcome.

Another attraction of dealing with these problems for many of us is the sense of satisfaction we have when we can right a wrong that was perpetrated on an adolescent, even though he or she was blameless. In doing so, you can feel that you have been able to make the world a better place.

NOTES

P. 347. *When Sigmund Freud:* Freud, S. (1978). *Werkausgabe in Zwei Banden, Elemente der Psychoanalyse,* Copyright Ltd., Mit freundlicher Genehmigung von Mrs. E. L. Freud.

P. 347, *Much more is known:* Figley. C. R. (Ed.). (1985). *Trauma and its wake,* Vols. 1 & 2, *The study and treatment of post-traumatic stress disorder.* New York: Brunner/Mazel; Spiegel, D. (Ed.). (1994). *Dissociation, culture, mind and body.* Washington, DC: American Psychiatric Press; van der Kolk, B. A. (1987). *Psychological trauma.* Washington, DC: American Psychiatric Press; Foy, D. W. (1992). *Treating PTSD: Cognitive-behavioral strategies.* New York: Guilford Press; Wolf, M. E., & Mosnaim, A. D. (1990). *Posttraumatic stress disorder: Etiology, phenomenology, and treatment.* Washington, DC: American Psychiatric Press; Wilson, J. P., & Raphael, B. (1993). *International handbook of traumatic stress syndromes.* New York: Plenum Press.

P. 350, *The characteristics include strongly visualized:* Eth, S., & Pynoos, R. S. (1985). *Posttraumatic stress disorder in children.* Washington, DC: American Psychiatric Press; Spiegel, D. (Ed.). (1994). *Dissociation, culture, mind, and body.* Washington, DC: American Psychiatric Press; Anthony, E. J., & Cohler, B. J. (Eds.). (1987). *Invulnerable child.* London: Guilford.

P. 354, *Most likely this is due to a certain "biologization":* Giller, E. L., Jr. (Ed.). (1990). *Biological assessment and treatment of posttraumatic stress disorder.* Washington, DC: American Psychiatric Press; Murburg, M. M. (Ed.). (1994). *Catecholamine, function in posttraumatic stress disorder: emerging concepts.* Washington, DC: American Psychiatric Press; Pitman, R., Orr, S. P., & Lasko, N. P. (1993). Effects of intranasal vasopressin and oxytocin on physiologic responding during personal combat imagery in Vietnam veterans with posttraumatic stress disorder. *Psychiatry Research, 48,* 107–117; Pitman, R., Altman, B., Greenwald, E., Longpre, R. E., Macklin, M. L., Poire, R. E., & Steketee, G. S. (1991). Psychiatric complications during flooding therapy for posttraumatic stress disorder. *Clinical Psychiatry, 52*(1), 17–20; Pitman, R. K., Orr, S. P., Forgue, D. F., de Jong, J. B., & Claiborn, J. M. (1987). Psychophysiologic assessment of posttraumatic stress disorder imagery in Vietnam combat veterans. *Archives of General Psychiatry, 44,* 970–976; Shalev, A. Y., Orr, S. P., & Pitman, R. K. (1992). Psychophysiologic response during script-driven imagery as an outcome measure in posttraumatic stress disorder. *Journal of Clinical Psychiatry, 54*(9), 324–326; Loftus, E., & Davies, G. M. (1984). Distortions in the memory of children. *Journal of Social Issues, 40*(2), 51–67.

P. 355, *Recently another group of researchers:* Goleman, D. (1994, October 25). New kind of memory found to preserve moments of emotion. *The New York Times,* pp. C1, C11; Cahill, L., Prins, B., Weber, M., & McGaugh, J. L. (1994, October 20). ß-adrenergic activation and memory for emotional events. *Nature, 371,* 702–704.

P. 355, *David Brent and his group*: Brent, D. A., Perper, J. A., Moritz, G., Liotus, L., Richardson, D., Canobbio, R., Schweers, J., & Roth, C. (1995, February). Posttraumatic stress disorder in peers of adolescent suicide victims: Predisposing factors and phenomenology. *Journal of the American Academy of Child & Adolescent Psychiatry, 34*(2), 209–215; Schabes, M., Matthews, Z., & Steiner, H. (1994). Predicting the prevalence of PTSD and dissociative disorders in incarcerated juvenile delinquents. *Scientific Proceedings of the Annual Meeting*, American Academy of Child & Adolescent Psychiatry, 1994, *10*(76), Poster; Terr, L. C. (1991). Childhood traumas: An outline and overview. *American Journal of Psychiatry, 148*(1), 10–20; Schreiber, F. R. (1973). *Sybil*. Chicago: Regnery Press.

P. 364, *but it is a syndrome that*: Anthony, E. J., & Cohler, B. J. (Eds.). (1987). *The invulnerable child*. New York: Guilford Press; Anthony, E. J., & Cohler, B. J. (Eds.). (1987). *Risk, vulnerability, resilience: An overview*. New York: Guilford Press; Camus, A. (1946). *The stranger* (English version). New York: Knopf; Conroy, P. (1986). *The prince of tides*. Boston: Houghton Mifflin; Gerima, Haile (Director). (1995). *Sankofa* [Film]. (Released by Mypheduh Films); Wilson, J. P., & Raphael, B. (Eds.). (1993). *International handbook of traumatic stress syndromes*. New York: Plenum Press; Garmenzy, N. (1985). Stress-resistant children: The search for protective factors. *Recent research in developmental psychopathology*, Book Supplement No. 4 to *Journal of Child Psychology & Psychiatry*. Oxford: Pergamon Press; Werner, E. E., & Smith, R. S. (1982). *Vulnerable but invincible: A study of resilient children*. New York: McGraw-Hill.

P. 368, *one of his all-time favorite movies*: Clarke, A. C. (Director), & Kubrick, S. (Writer). (1968). *2001: A space odyssey* [Film].

P. 369, *False memories are easily induced*: Loftus, E., & Davies, G. M. (1984). Distortions in the memory of children. *Journal of Social Issues, 40*(2), 51–67.

P. 376, *Roger Pitman at Harvard uses so-called*: Shaley, A. Y., Orr, S. P., & Pitman, R. K. (1992). Psychophysiologic response during script-driven imagery as an outcome measure in posttraumatic stress disorder. *Journal of Clinical Psychiatry, 53*(9), 324–326.

P. 382, *The treatment of this complex disorder*: Johnson, C. L. (Ed.). (1991). *Psychodynamic treatment of anorexia nervosa and bulimia*. New York: Guilford Press; Masterson, J. F. (1980). *From borderline adolescent to functioning adult: The test of time*. New York: Brunner/Mazel.

P. 382, *The treatment of borderline patients is in many ways*: Johnson, C. L. (Ed.). (1991). *Psychodynamic treatment of anorexia nervosa and bulimia*. New York: Guilford Press.

P. 386, *Michael Rutter has described them*: Rutter, M. (1985). Resilience in the face of adversity protective factors and resistance to psychiatric disorders. Based on Margaret Methven lecture delivered March 8, 1985, Scottish Division of the Royal College of Psychiatrists. *British Journal of Psychiatry, 147,* 598–611.

ABOUT THE AUTHORS

Julie A. Collier, Ph.D., is a staff psychologist in the Department of Psychiatry and Behavioral Sciences, Division of Child Psychiatry at Stanford University School of Medicine, and is the program director of the Pediatric Consultation-Liaison Service at Lucile Salter Packard Children's Hospital at Stanford.

S. Shirley Feldman, Ph.D., has taught at the University of Wisconsin, Monash University (Australia), and for the last twenty-three years, at Stanford University. She served as director of the Stanford Center for the Study of Families, Children, and Youth for four years (1991–1995). Her extensive research on socialization of children and adolescents is summarized in books, monographs, and more than eighty papers. In recent years, her interests have focused on adolescent development and she co-edited the influential volume *At the Threshold: The Developing Adolescence* (Harvard University Press, 1990). She has conducted longitudinal studies that span two important transitions—from childhood into early adolescence, and from late adolescence into adulthood—in which she focuses particularly on family influences on both normal and pathological development (including depression, delinquency, and promiscuity). She has been teaching in the Division of Child Psychiatry for the last eight years and serves as mentor to Child Psychiatry Fellows.

Chris Hayward, M.D., completed his residency in psychiatry in 1988 at Stanford University Medical Center and participated in research fellowships in the Laboratory for the Study of Behavioral Medicine at Stanford in 1988 and the Stanford Center for Research in Disease Prevention in 1989. In 1989, Dr. Hayward was appointed medical director of the Medical Psychiatry Inpatient Service at Stanford University Hospital and in 1992 became an assistant professor in the Department of Psychiatry at Stanford University.

Dr. Hayward's research has focused on panic disorder in adolescents and adults, the epidemiology of adolescent psychopathology in school-based studies, and the role of early puberty in determining onset of internalizing disorders in young adolescent girls. He recently completed a five-year longitudinal study of over 2,200 high school students, assessing risk factors for panic. This year he was awarded a W. T. Grant Faculty Scholar Award. Dr. Hayward is also active in medical education. In 1994, Dr. Hayward was named Teacher of the Year by graduating residents.

James Lock, M.D., Ph.D., is assistant professor in the Department of Psychiatry and Behavioral Sciences at Stanford University School of Medicine, and medical director of the Comprehensive Pediatric Care Unit at the Lucile Salter Packard Children's Hospital at Stanford. Board certified in child and adolescent psychiatry by the American Board of Psychiatry and Neurology, he has lectured widely on child inpatient psychiatry, depression, eating disorders, and behavioral problems of children. His publications are largely concerned with hospitalization for behavioral disorders.

Robert Matano, Ph.D., is assistant professor of psychiatry and behavioral sciences, and director of the Stanford Alcohol and Drug Treatment Center, Department of Psychiatry, School of Medicine, Stanford University. A licensed psychologist and marriage, family, and child counselor, Dr. Matano has nearly twenty years of experience in the field of alcohol and drug treatment. Dr. Matano has worked for a federally funded alcohol program for adolescents and their families. More recently he served as clinical coordinator for a countywide research project aimed at altering alcohol expectancies in adolescents for the Stanford Center for Disease Prevention. He is a clinician, researcher, and highly sought after consultant in the field of alcohol and drug treatment for both adults and adolescents. He has designed and implemented the Alcohol and Drug Treatment Center at Stanford, which has been rated by *Forbes* Magazine in a poll of corporate employee assistance personnel as one of the twelve best programs in the country. He has published articles and book chapters on group therapy and alcohol and drug treatment and family therapy with an emphasis on domestic violence. Dr. Matano's recent research has focused on personality character-istics and interpersonal styles in alcohol and drug treatment. He also has served as chair of the Consortium of Medical Educators in Substance Abuse since its inception in 1990.

Zakee Matthews, M.D., is a clinical instructor of psychiatry and behavioral sciences in the Division of Child Psychiatry and Child Development. He is medical director of the Comprehensive Par-tial Hospitalization Program at Lucile Salter Packard Children's Hospital, where he also directs the new Trauma Clinic. Dr. Matthews is actively involved in research aimed at understand-ing the impact on and treatment of children and adolescents exposed to trauma. He is specially trained in issues of violence presentation as a scholar at Stanford University's California Wellness Foundation, Violence Prevention Initiative Program. He received the Presidential Scholars Award in the category of public policy of the American Academy of Child and Adolescent Psychiatry in 1993. He is a consultant to the California Youth Authority.

Rebecca A. Powers, M.P.H., M.D., was Chief Fellow in Child and Adolescent Psychiatry, Division of Child Psychiatry and Child Development at the Stanford University School of Medicine. Prior to medical school she obtained her M.S. Degree in Public Health with a focus on preventive medicine. Much of her research in primary prevention involved alcohol and drug use by pregnant mothers. She has served as resident representative to the House of Delegates for the California Medical Association (CMA) and to the American Medical Association, where she is involved with grass-roots medical policy setting, including mul-tiple policies involving alcohol and drug detection, treatment, and management. Dr. Powers was recently elected by the CMA for a three-year term to serve on the Committee for the

Well-Being of Physicians. She was the 1994–1995 resident guest at the Consortium of Medical Educators in Substance Abuse for the state of California. This year she received the Presidential Scholar Award from the American Academy of Child and Adolescent Psychiatrists. This is the national award given for activities in clinical work, research, and public policy.

Dr. Powers currently serves on the clinical faculty at the Stanford University School of Medicine, where she is medical director of the Adolescent Alcohol and Drug Treatment Center. Additionally, she is in private practice in Los Gatos for children, adolescents, adults, couples, and families. She actively contributes to community awareness and education.

Mary J. Sanders, Ph.D., is director of psychological services and clinical instructor in the Division of Child Psychiatry and Development in the Department of Psychiatry at Stanford University School of Medicine and Behavioral Sciences. Dr. Sanders is also the co-director of an APA-approved predoctoral internship in child psychology. Since 1986, she has been at Lucile Salter Packard Children's Hospital at Stanford where she is a specialist in the area of eating disorders. Dr. Sanders has presented nationally in the area of eating disorders and Munchausen Syndrome by Proxy. Her other interests include child abuse and family therapy training.

Richard J. Shaw, M.D., is a clinical instructor in the Division of Child Psychiatry at the Stanford University School of Medicine. He is also a staff psychiatrist at the Stanford/VA Mental Health Clinical Research Center at the Department of Veterans Affairs Medical Center in Palo Alto, California. He is a native of Zimbabwe and a graduate of Middlesex Hospital Medical School, University of London, England. Dr. Shaw completed his residency training in adult psychiatry at the Albert Einstein College of Medicine, Bronx, New York, and a child psychiatry fellowship at Stanford University Medical Center. His major area of research interest is in the field of affect expression and recognition in schizophrenia.

Hans Steiner, M.D., is professor of psychiatry and behavioral sciences in the Division of Child Psychiatry at the Stanford University School of Medicine. He is a Fellow of the American Psychiatric Association, the American Academy of Child and Adolescent Psychiatry, and the Academy of Psychosomatic Medicine. He has received the Outstanding Mentor Award of the American Academy of Child and Adolescent Psychiatry in 1990, 1992, 1993, and 1995. He also received the Dlin/Fischer Award for significant achievement in clinical research from the Academy of Psychosomatic Medicine in 1993. In 1994, he was selected by Good Housekeeping as one of the nation's 327 best mental health care providers. He is a native of Austria and a graduate of the Vienna University Faculty of Medicine. His research and clinical work is concentrated on the adolescent age group. He is an internationally known expert in eating disorders, trauma-related psychopathology, and juvenile delinquency. He lectures widely in Europe and the United States.

Margo Thienemann, M.D., is a clinical instructor in the Division of Child Psychiatry at the Stanford University School of Medicine. She is a graduate of Duke University, where she also attended medical school. She completed her medical residency training program in internal medicine at the University of Texas at San Antonio and her residency training program in psychiatry at the University of Wisconsin at Madison. She completed her child psychiatry residency program at Stanford University Medical Center, where she also became chief resident.

Dr. Thieneman is the director of the Child and Adolescent Obsessive-Compulsive Disorder Clinic at Stanford University Medical Center and consultant to two special education programs: the Children's Health Council and the Peninsula Children's Center. She continues to divide her time between her work and her children.

INDEX